RIVERSIDE COMMUNITY COLLEGE
1916

D0154239

RN L

DATE DUE

NO 6 '92			
OC 8 '93			

Rhetoric and Irony

RHETORIC AND IRONY

Western Literacy and Western Lies

C. JAN SWEARINGEN

New York   Oxford
OXFORD UNIVERSITY PRESS
1991

Riverside Community College
Library
4800 Magnolia Avenue
Riverside, California 92506

JUN   '92

Oxford University Press

Oxford   New York   Toronto
Delhi   Bombay   Calcutta   Madras   Karachi
Petaling Jaya   Singapore   Hong Kong   Tokyo
Nairobi   Dar es Salaam   Cape Town
Melbourne   Auckland

and associated companies in
Berlin   Ibadan

Copyright © 1991 by Oxford University Press, Inc.

Published by Oxford University Press, Inc.,
200 Madison Avenue, New York, New York 10016

Oxford is a registered trademark of Oxford University Press

All rights reserved. No part of this publication may be reproduced,
stored in a retrieval system, or transmitted, in any form or by any means,
electronic, mechanical, photocopying, recording, or otherwise,
without the prior permission of Oxford University Press.

Library of Congress Cataloging-in-Publication Data
Swearingen, C. Jan.
Rhetoric and irony :
western literacy and western lies /
C. Jan Swearingen.
p.   cm.
Includes bibliographical references and index.
ISBN 0-19-506362-7
1. Rhetoric, Ancient. 2. Civilization, Occidental — Classical influences.
3. Rhetoric — Philosophy. 4. Literacy — Philosophy.
5. Dialectic. 6. Logos. 7. Irony. I. Title.
PA181.S9 1991 808'.001 — dc20 90-42930

9 8 7 6 5 4 3 2 1

Printed in the United States of America
on acid free paper

Dedicated to my parents,
Carolyn Flinn Swearingen
and Alfred Frederick Swearingen,
first voices, first teachers,
esteemed friends; and to my son,
Benjamin Jacobs-Swearingen,
that his voice and those of his generation
may thrive, and mature to nourish others.

Preface

It has once again become a commonplace that history is storytelling. The earliest rhetoricians knew this; the *epitaphia* capitalize on the invention of revisionist history, a powerful art of persuasion. The interwoven history of rhetoric and literacy constructed here, however, attempts not so much to persuade as to invite reappraisal of the complex relationships between rhetorical practice and theory in antiquity and the dissemination of literacy. As a prolegomenon for reinterpreting the histories of rhetoric and literacy, the synthesis developed here can facilitate what Priscian understood as *eidolopoieia*, permitting the dead stones, as well as the shades of the dead, to speak to the issues embedded in Western concepts of irony, rhetoric, and literacy, and illuminating the continuing centrality of those concepts to the ethics of language use and teaching today. This work joins a group of recent studies in the history and theory of rhetoric and in literacy and orality that reprises history in order to reform and broaden our understanding of literacy, literature, and language use in contemporary culture both within and outside academia. Reappraisals of the Sophists' thought and of their dual role as itinerant teachers and speechwriters for political leaders have supplemented older studies of the Presocratic philosophers, Greek poets and dramatists, and Greek rhetoric. Traditional treatments of the ancient war between philosophy and rhetoric, such as Brian Vicker's *In Defense of Rhetoric*, represent understandings of the relationship between rhetoric and philosophy that are being challenged by defenses of Gorgias, Protagoras, and Isocrates. Studies reappraising the Sophists have uncovered a richness and diversity in their thought and conceptions of language, questioning the long-standing disjunctions between the Sophists and early philosophers and between philosophy and rhetoric. My approach takes a middle ground in this revisionism, at times accepting and redefining the war between philosophy and rhetoric, at others scrutinizing the considerable unacknowledged parallels among treatments of language, thought, and rhetoric to be found in the works of classical philosophers and rhetoricians. Renewed attention to the literary and dialogical structure of Plato's dialogues, exemplified in such works as Michael Stokes' *Plato's Socratic Conversations*, and to the place of the *Rhetoric* within Aristotle's organon has led to a redirection of the preponderantly analytic and logical focus of previous studies toward an appreciation of the importance of dramatic structure to Plato's dialogues and of the philosophical substance of Aristotle's treatment of rhetoric. Plato's and Aristotle's conceptualizations of rhetoric within and in conjunction with their treatments of other issues are receiving rereadings that take more seriously their philosophies of rhetoric, as well as the rhetoric of their philosophy.

In a different arena, the past decade has produced a number of new studies of literacy in the West in different periods, as for instance: William Harris, *Ancient Literacy*; Tony Lentz, *Orality and Literacy in Hellenic Greece*; Rosalind Thomas, *Oral Tradition and Written Record in Classical Athens*; Florian Coulmas, *The Writing Systems of the World*; Harvey J. Graff, *The Legacies of Literacy*; Brian Stock, *The Implications of Literacy*; and Elizabeth Eisenstein, *The Printing Press as an Agent of Change*. Within anthropology and linguistics this inquiry has evolved into a questioning of traditional notions of oral and literate cultures as these have been applied across cultures. Jack Goody's *Literacy in Traditional Societies* and *The Domestication of the Savage Mind*, Bambi Schieffelin and Parry Gilmore's *The Acquisition of Literacy*, and Sylvia Scribner and Michael Cole's *The Psychology of Literacy* appraise the mismeasure of mind, language, and cognition that has resulted from applying overly reductive and decidedly Occidental notions of literacy and orality to cultures that possess alternative understandings of understanding. Unlike many of these studies, mine attempts a fuller and more sustained appraisal of the tandem relationship in Western culture that has long linked literacy training and uses with rhetorical theory, education, and practice from the Presocratics through Augustine's era. In broad strokes, my concluding chapter extends to the contemporary scene the appraisal of rhetoric and literacy as interdependent and mutually defining.

In developing a defense of the importance and substantiveness of Plato's critique of rhetoric, I am indebted to the welcome resuscitation of Plato's dialogics by Mikhail Bakhtin, Hans-George Gadamer, and Paul Ricoeur. I have attempted to compose an ongoing dialogue among the voices of past and present inquiries in several fields: language acquisition and cognition; the psychology of literacy; ethnographies of speaking and writing; revisionist interpretive anthropologies attending to the hermeneutic screens that shape the study of traditional and oral societies; literacy and orality studies, including ongoing appraisals of the nature of oral "literature"; genre studies of narrative and dialogue spanning the disciplines of cognitive psychology, philosophy, literary criticism and theory, and anthropology; recent feminist theories of self and voice that are illuminating significant parallels among non-Western, nonmainstream, minority, and women's rhetorics and discourses; studies of religious language and beliefs about language that continue to shape attitudes, experiences, and practices of speaking and writing, as well as reading and interpreting; and recent critical theories that alternately define or reject an ethics of criticism, attend to links between textual and social politics, and scrutinize extant concepts of the knowing and speaking subjects that meet, or seem to meet, in the acts of speaking and listening, saying and understanding, and writing and reading. Barbara Herrnstein Smith's *Contingencies of Value*, Tobin Sieber's *The Ethics of Criticism*, Paul Friedrich's *The Language Parallax: Poetic Language and Linguistic Indeterminacy*, Wayne Booth's *The Company We Keep: An Ethics of Fiction*, and Stanley Rosen's *Hermeneutics as Politics* are among the recent studies that scrutinize the overhauling of concepts of value and meaning in critical theory, literary theory, and aesthetics.

The Western aesthetic and ethical scrutiny of irony, and of related notions of linguistic deceit and lying, is as old as rhetoric and literacy; my focus on these latter can promote and facilitate closer attention to defining the aesthetic and ethical values that are implicit in models of linguistic structure and in the habits of interpretation that education imparts. The value of literacy is often unclear to precisely those students who may be most in need of the choices —

and voices — it can offer them. The voices of the past and present orchestrated here provide teachers and scholars with a group of understandings of literacy and of the ethics of language use and teaching that can be adopted in differing combinations for use in scholarship, in work with students, and in the workplace. Questions of ethics and value have laced considerations of rhetoric and irony since their first appearances in classical Greece. Dissimulation and deceit, alluring fiction, pretty lies, cunning duplicity, strategic understatement, derisive teasing, a taunting sneer: these avatars embody traits and themes that our Western literate–textual culture has traditionally viewed as being imparted by rhetoric, inherent to literature, pervasive in public discourse, and intrinsic to language itself. These preoccupations bear thoughtful scrutiny as an odd and intriguing contrast between aesthetic and ethical values. Urbanity, circumspect detachment, and ironic dissembling have been succeeded by the belief that language itself lies, a view that, as I will argue, ultimately erodes the bases for meaning and truth and consequently the phenomenon of lying as well. Differing positions on this issue are of interest and relevance, because the value and meaning assigned to literature in scholarship and teaching has long been a delicate and powerful instrument of literacy education for imparting different uses of language, assumptions about its meaning, and interpretive habits that shape understandings far beyond literary study. Celebrations of literature as clever lies bothered many in Augustine's time, much as they bother some students and parents today. Understandings of literary works, texts, and creativity in turn shape and are shaped by rhetorical concerns regarding the uses of voice, the ability and will to speak, and the construction of a shared reality within which understanding and speaking take place. My rereadings of classical and modern treatments of these issues seek to illustrate the degree of overlap, humorous recurrence, and shared concern for the human — all too human — abuses and misuses of language.

Wayne Booth's *A Rhetoric of Irony* and Walter Ong's *Ramus, Method, and the Decay of Dialogue* were important guides in my initial attempts at merging rhetoric and irony as objects of study. Along with Ong's work, Eric Havelock's approaches to early Greek orality, led me to ask why Havelock's and other classicists' treatments of orality and oral literature in ancient Greece so rarely link oralism with rhetoric. I thank Walter Ong for reading and commenting on an early synopsis of this work. In the year and a half before his death, Eric Havelock gave generous and painstaking attention to the details — and many errors — in early drafts of the Presocratic and Plato chapters. I employ his term "Preplatonic" throughout to underscore the point that Socrates did not write; his thought is represented only in the writings of others. Victor Vitanza encouraged the approach I had developed in a distant ancestor of the Plato chapter, greatly improved it through editorial suggestions, and published it in *Pre/Text* in 1982. Werner Kelber's adaptations of both deconstructionist and oralist methods to the rereading of New Testament Scripture in *The Oral and the Written Gospel: The Hermeneutics of Speaking and Writing in the Synoptic Tradition*, drawing on and integrating Derrida's and Ong's work, suggested additional nuances in the treatment of narrative, aphorism, hiding, and disclosure, and provided a model for merging and rendering harmonious the methods of different disciplines. The questions raised by religious language, and the ways in which religion redirects understandings and practices of language, are matters that link textual hermeneutics with orality–literacy studies, an intersection that has occurred in several fields. George Kennedy's *The New Testament and Rhetorical Criticism*, James Kinneavy's *Greek Rhetorical Origins of Christian Faith*, and Frank Kermode's *The Genesis of Secrecy* exemplify studies that forge integrations among hermeneutics, rhetoric, and literary studies. Roy A. Rappaport's work appraises lying as cultural pathology, particularly the diabolical lie that undermines the canons of truth and meaning. I am indebted to him as well for a generous correspondence that over several years has greatly extended my confidence in ranging between anthropological and literary appraisals of rhetoric, literacy, and lying. Richard Bauman, ethnographer and folklorist, defined in a lecture the contrast between a culture's ethical and aesthetic values as an underexplored topic in folklore studies. His way of putting the question suggested to me that irony and rhetorical dissembling, if examined from this perspective, present just such a contrast in Western culture. Of particular merit in Shirley Brice Heath's work is the attention given to the influence of religious teachings and beliefs concerning the status and authority of scripture upon entry-level schoolchildren's literacy acquisition.

Literary theorists' renewed appraisal of cultural and ethical value is moving in directions that can be companionably merged with ethnographies and psychologies of literacy. My concluding chapter proposes that, albeit in reductive versions that belie the original theories, many recent applications of postmodernism and deconstruction to literary study and literacy training have once again promoted conceptions of language, self, and meaning as fictive: an aestheticization of *ethos* that is shared by many rhetoric and composition pedagogies. Yet the creating of self, meaning, and culture through the insights provided by critical theory can guide reconstruction, and, in conjunction with newly forged definitions of the value of literacy, literature, and rhetoric, take us beyond writing zero degree in ways that Heath, Bruner, and others have proposed for reanimating the language and culture of the classroom. Louise Wetherbee Phelps' *Composition as a Human Science*, Henry Sussman's *High Resolution: Critical Theory and the Problem of Literacy*, and David Bleich's *The Double Perspective: Language, Literacy, and Social Relations* define welcome directions for critical theory as a handmaid to improved literacy instruction. As a teacher, a teacher of teachers, and a historian of that way of teaching language use that has long been called rhetoric, I am indebted to Peter Elbow and Ann Berthoff for their contributions to an understanding of the ethical and political nuances entailed in any pedagogy. Their concern for preserving dialogical interactions in the classroom has been an important stimulus for a closer attention to the dialogues of antiquity than I had initially intended, and to considerations of the roles that can be played by dialogue in both literacy and rhetorical education.

George Kennedy's work as a historian and analyst of the many schools of rhetoric in antiquity has informed and corrected this study at many points. His earliest as well as his most recent work provide a bedrock for studies in ancient rhetoric, models for extending the scope of its study, and the good example of a constantly evolving understanding of the field of rhetoric as a whole. I am deeply indebted to him for reading the manuscript in its entirety twice; he provided diligent corrections and generous suggestions, particularly on Cicero and Aristotle. The initial draft of the entire manuscript would not have been possible without the generosity of a year's leave of absence from my duties at the University of Arizona granted by Edgar Dryden and Charles Davis. Curtis Church, former associate editor at Oxford University Press, read the initial prospectus, provided informed direction and encouragement, and saw the manuscript through the early stages of review. Louis Mackey, longtime mentor and able scholar in Kierkegaard and medieval and classical philosophy, helped chasten several impertinences in my treatment of Aristotle's four causes. I thank my colleagues Charles Chiasson and Richard Bett for their help with double-checking the Greek citations and classical philosophical references. In concert with graduate students in two seminars on feminist theory, my colleague Susan Hekman, along with Kathleen Welch, Susan Jarratt, and Barbara Biesecker, have been beloved adversaries in the enterprise of working out the alliances between feminist theory, postmodernism, and rhetoric suggested in the concluding chapter. The penultimate draft of the last chapter received a much needed haircut in the able hands of Michelle Ballif. On the eve of going to press, the manuscript benefited from my participation during June and July 1989 as a Princeton Fellow in an NEH Summer Institute for College Teachers, "Approaches to Language in the Greek Enlightenment: Ethics, Rhetoric, and Poetics." My department chair, Judith McDowell, and Dean Thomas Porter provided encouragement and substantial support for my participation. Warm thanks to Elaine Fantham of the classics department at Princeton for convening the institute and for ensuring that we directed our attention at least once each week to questions of *la pédagogie*. The month at Princeton permitted me to attend to numerous small points in the early chapters, and reminded me of the continuing resistance to Havelock's work, and more broadly to oralist approaches, within classical philology. Also imparted was the daunting realization that classical philosophy and philology have ground rules for textual analysis and interpretation that are on some points quite inconsonant with those regularly employed by scholars in English and speech communication. On these matters the twenty-five participants from four different disciplines chastised and edified one another as we inaugurated attempts to define a more integrated approach to ethics, poetics, and rhetoric. In its final stages the entire manuscript was pruned and polished with the aid of patient and unstinting labor by Laurie Jacobs and Cindy Williams. Clifford Browder, diligent and undaunting copyeditor, detected numerous errors and improprieties throughout the manuscript; his knowledge of Greek and Latin enhanced already astute and helpful comments.

Henry Krawitz, associate editor at Oxford, provided additional careful comments and corrections with admirable promptness and courtesy. For any remaining errors and oddities of translation or transliteration—always the peril of the generalist—I assume full responsibility. To William P. Sisler, former vice president and executive editor of Oxford University Press, I am indebted for encouragement, persistence, and a sustained patience that has long since surpassed my understanding. He has counseled me through a series of revisions and decisions with wise perspectives on the disciplinary boundaries I so brazenly dissolve. I count myself fortunate to have worked with an editor who is an exemplar to his profession and a guide for the perplexed.

The rhetoric of the family, its discourses and dialogues, is often more crucial than any schooling in shaping self and voice. To the many voices of my family I am indebted for a legacy of dialogue, an ongoing conversation about values and issues, the fluent and ready responses of Southern orality, the eloquent and articulate cadences of the Sunday sermon, the deconstruction of same over Sunday lunch in the Presbyterian manse. I learned from my father a love of literature and history, and a fascination with the duets of philosophy and theology that continue to shape our culture's ways of thinking, speaking, writing, reading, knowing, and believing. I received from my mother an estimable eloquence and wisdom. Always well-read and well-spoken, she has a conscientious and resolute attention to moral discourse and reasoning on a daily basis that is free of the axiomatic or doctrinal rigidities usually associated with religion and ethical rules. She taught me to yoke feeling and reason in the careful and sustained appraisal of alternatives, values, choices, and consequences, in finding my way among those probabilities that have always been among the *capitae* of rhetoric. To David Jacobs I credit a preoccupation with both irony and rhetoric that rivals and sometimes surpasses my own. Our son Benjamin speaks in both our voices, finding his own ways with words, providing the corrective therapy of an echo, and the phenomenon of the unprecedented as well. Thanks to David and Benjamin for strategically well-placed absences to shore and grove; in several of those June spaces, hopes of completion began to flourish.

Arlington, Tex.   C. J. S.
July 1990

Contents

Rhetoric and Irony

Introduction

In the case of Socrates this self-knowledge was scarcely so full of content, for it properly contained no more than the separation and differentiation of that which only subsequently became the object of knowledge. The expression "know thyself" means: separate yourself from the other.

SØREN KIERKEGAARD, *The Concept of Irony*

For in old days at all events the system of instruction seems to have imparted education both in right conduct and in good speech; nor were the professors in two separate groups, but the same masters gave instruction both in ethics and in rhetoric. . . .

Socrates robbed [the liberal sciences] of this general designation, and in his discussions separated the science of wise thinking from that of elegant speaking, though in reality they are closely linked together. . . . This is the source from which has sprung the undoubtedly absurd and unprofitable and reprehensible severance between the tongue and brain, leading to our having one set of professors to teach us to think and another to teach us to speak.

CICERO, *De Oratore* III, xvi, 57–61

Irony has penetrated all languages of modern times. . . . It has penetrated into all words and forms. . . .

. . . In rhetoric there is the unconditionally innocent and the unconditionally guilty; there is complete victory and destruction of the opponent. In dialogue the destruction of the opponent also destroys that very dialogic sphere where the word lives. In classical antiquity this sphere did not yet exist.

MIKHAIL BAKHTIN, *Speech Genres and Other Late Essays*

Literacy and lies, rhetoric and irony; though these pairs may seem like mismatched socks, their juxtaposition herein is far from an arbitrary alliance. The attention given to these phenomena, and increasingly to the spectrum of terms by which they were known, is intriguingly prominent during the earliest centuries of literacy in the West. Their ancestors recur and converge in the language of the Preplatonic philosophers, and are given new shadings among the many voices depicted by Plato. They are regularized by formal definition in Aristotle's systematizing work, and reappraised in the ethical critique of Greek rhetoric that is advanced by Cicero and extended by Augustine. Each of these comfortably respectable figures is approached here as performing a role that has been defined in modern anthropology, that of the participant–observer. Though often depicted as exponents of the patterns of thought and of the literary humanism that shaped early Western literacy, these figures are also critical observers of the advent of philosophic thought and literary humanism, appraisers of its merits and pitfalls, and critics of both the progress and the limitations that were being inculcated by literacy and particularly by its emergent subdivisions: rhetoric, literature, and philosophy. They witness what has often been taken for granted in modern times: that a powerful template was struck when the practice and teaching of a conventionalized, standardized, public, political, and literary language called rhetoric coincided with the convergence of education and literacy. With widespread use of writing came conventions, standardizations, and competing orthodoxies in orthography, grammar, genre definitions, and aesthetic criteria.

Philosophical schools evolved in erratic tandem with rhetoric and literature, sometimes disavowing writing entirely, as did Socrates and many Stoics. Many philosophers denounced rhetoric and literature alike as weak, as illusory and uncritical thinking prepared for public consumption; their scorn was matched in the popular mind by the dismissal of philosophy as technical quibbling and semantic hairsplitting that bore no relevance to common life. Classical understandings remain familiar and remarkably consistent, further evidence that the template struck in that era continues to shape our conceptions of knowledge, thought, eloquence, formal discourse, literary practice, literacy, and self. One particularly curious element in the template functions as a leitmotif throughout this examination. Western subdivisions and criteria of formal language and thought, of educated thinking and discourse, have recurrently linked both literary and rhetorical discourse with deception and fiction. Associations that linger in today's critical and aesthetic lexica were already old when Cicero wrote. Rhetoric is an art of lying, most readily found in the politician. Irony is a dry, understated, and dissembling manner of speaking typical of the educated and the upper classes. Literary fictions are lies, beguiling in direct ratio to their illusoriness. Writing and rhetoric encourage deceptiveness. Language lies. Truth is an illusion. A flawless eloquence is not to be trusted. Political speakers are suspect because they rely on speechwriters.

Studying the emergence of the earliest identities and intersections among irony and rhetoric, literacy and lying, can illuminate the present "crisis" of literacy: the debates about content and canon, the redefinitions of critical thinking and its value, the concerns about cultural pluralism and its limits, and the reappraisals of Western conceptualizations of self, voice, autonomy, individualism—of the knowing and speaking subject. The earliest surviving texts of literate educated Greeks record dissent about parallel issues: the locus and meaning of truth, cultural values and their proper repositories, and the essential elements and most effective media of education. There is speculation about the effects of various forms of language on thought and cognition. *Krisis*—the term itself dates to the period under examination—denotes a turning point, an event requiring or provoking judgment, and the act itself of judging. As it was at the point of onset, and now too in a state of alleged decline, literacy is in a state of crisis; it both attracts and demands our judgment, decision, choice, and action. To that end, this study revisits the judgments and proposals that directed literacy in its earliest centuries, and proposes that our "crisis" may be viewed as a portentous turning point rather than as the latest downfall of Western civilization.

Plato, Cicero, and Augustine develop strenuous warnings against the disciplinary boundaries and reductive schematizations within those divisions that were emerging in their own times. Plato warns that if writing rather than philosophical discussion becomes the medium of instruction in the schools, students' minds will be weakened; they will come to confuse memory and knowledge with mere recall, memorization, and copying. Techniques of memorization, the *memoria technia* taught by the earlier poets and rhetoricians, are widely mocked as lessons for the feebleminded. "As for me," Themistocles is reported to have said of them, "I'd rather learn how to forget."[1] Cicero laments the "severance of tongue and brain" that is being brought about by the divergence of philosophy and rhetoric. The philosophers, he charges, cannot speak to the world any longer, while the common fare provided by the rhetorical curriculum teaches outlines and forms but no content or thought. His concerns parallel contemporary attitudes toward and thinking about literacy, education, disciplinary divisions, and pluralism. Observing the numerous parallels between commentaries on the transitional literacies of the past and those of the present can only improve our understanding of transitional literacy as a recurring phenomenon. The periods of transitional literacy addressed here might be envisioned as two ends of a parenthesis: the period during which logical and literate forms of discourse assumed paradigmatic status in Western culture, and the current period that has been characterized as a postliterate era moving toward secondary orality.[2] Within this parenthesis has evolved a markedly stable but also complex group of thought processes, language patterns, and metalanguages that continue to be constitutive of what we call literacy.[3]

Claiming to retell the stories of early logic, rhetoric, and literature from the integrating perspective of early literacy necessarily runs the risk of what rhetoric has long termed the genetic fallacy, and deconstructionism, more recently, the myth of origins. This revisionist history of early literacy proceeds from the premise that there are specific and identifiable classical sources for modern concepts of linguistic relativism and indeterminacy, concepts that are essential elements in the logocentric ontology that has shaped Western philosophy and poetics for so long.[4] At these headwaters of Western literacy—rhetoric, logic, literature—are to be observed myriad sources of the distinctively Western association of literature and rhetoric with lying, the paradoxical pairing of persistent mistrust of and respect for the powers of rhetoric, scorn toward academic philosophy, and the simultaneous if contradictory placement of these disciplines at the center of the forms and methods of education for more than two millennia. Changes in the use of the term "irony" provide a particularly provocative trace of the unsettling swiftness with which beliefs and attitudes concerning reliability were changing at the onset of Western literacy. Plato likens the *eiron* to the rhetor in the *Sophist*, where the Eleatic Stranger asserts an identity between Sophist and philosopher as "dissembling imitators" (*eironikoi mimetai*) of truth. Though primarily a paradox and riddle of definition, this assertion is a reminder that Plato and others of his era were among the last to use *eiron* exclusively as a term of rebuke. Aristotle's *Poetics* and *Ethics* particularly recommend "the ironic manner of Gorgias" as depicted by Plato for its wit and intelligence,[5] and provide some of the first prescriptions of irony as an attractively gentlemanly understatement, an admirable inscrutability which he particularly recommends "in speaking to the vulgar."[6]

Understatement, inscrutability, and dissembling have remained familiar attributes of "the educated" in the West, reinforced by caste and class, and conducive to the gap that has come to divide public from private ethics. In some cultures women are veiled in public. In the West, among the educated and privileged, public words are customarily regarded as veiled, assumed to be disingenuous posturing, "mere" rhetoric. Similarly, Western literary aesthetics have incrementally promoted indirection, elusiveness, ambiguity, and fictionalizations of voice and self. Candor, trust, and canons of truth are teased and undermined by literary irony and political rhetoric, yet our tastes and practice reveal an enjoyment of this semantic and ethical *frisson*; our literary aesthetics persist in advancing the belief that to produce and apprehend irony or, most recently, an authorless illusoriness, is a mark of intelligence. Detachment, objectivity, a certain amount of skepticism, a willingness to question received opinion, command over abstractions, generalizations, and logic, and analytical probity—all these hallmarks of Western thought are so highly valued that they are now conceived of as universals or at least as inevitabilities of human thought. Many cultures, in sharp contrast, place high value upon collective, cooperative, and reciprocal concepts of truth, meaning, reality, and language.[7] Western educated culture has instead taught—and presumably valued—divergent, agonistic, individualistic, and pluralistic models of thought and language. The interrogative, analytic bent has advanced increasingly skeptical and pluralistic understandings of reality as well. How early did detachment, the object language of propositional logic, and the willing suspension of belief come to be equated with intelligence? Why are writing, literature, and literacy itself still so regularly associated with the production of lies in Western tradition? These genealogies can be traced not only within the classical period, but in a longer span that links Plato's banishment of the poets with Derrida's ubiquitous announcements of the illusoriness of textual meaning.

Unraveling and reweaving the histories of rhetoric, literacy, logic, and literature disrupt the historiography that has guided work in each of these sometimes stolidly separate disciplines. The paucity of studies linking early rhetoric, early philosophy, and early literacy results from a prejudice that deserves some comment. The low regard in which scholars of classical literature and philosophy have long held rhetoric exemplifies one subject of this study: the paradoxical disdain for rhetoric, the language model so singularly central to the classical and modern curriculum. Kirk and Raven's otherwise outstanding treatment of the Preplatonic philosophers includes no rhetoricians and few Sophists. Just as Plato denounced the Sophists and banished the poets from his republic, philosophers' and classicists' scorn toward rhetoric has left a distorted picture of its relationship to philosophy in virtually every period. A similar distortion has prejudiced an understanding of the mercurial relationships among literature, history, and rhetoric, as witnessed by one particularly telling annotation in the Loeb translation of Cicero's *Orator*: "History was regularly regarded in antiquity as a branch of rhetoric, much to the disadvantage of history."[8]

Rather than looking at Plato, or Augustine, or Cicero as exemplars of what we now hold to be a unified literary humanism and literate standard, I focus instead on their differences from the modern conceptualization of a univocal classicism and, for the same reasons, on their differences from one another. Their critiques of canon and curriculum were addressed to very different eras; each defined different questions and answered with different objectives. Their appraisals tell us that, as rhetoric and literacy became more widespread in Greek and Roman culture, their modes, uses, abuses, and effects varied greatly. These figures were in their own times friends of innovation and reform, and opponents of earlier "classical" canons that in each era had already begun to ossify. However, they also provide a record of consistency in certain areas, and of continuities within the debates about a core rhetorical curriculum that remained remarkably stable inside the confines of school and academy. Then, as now, proposals for reform in curricular and extracurricular uses of reading and writing influenced tastes and practices in rhetoric, philosophy, and literature. Classroom practices and texts changed more slowly, became more codified, and finally assumed the status of residual, prescribed logics, grammars, and methods of interpretation.[9] Several parallels between the transitional literacies of then and now emerge out of an emphasis on differences among classical periods and figures comprised therein. *What* is read and known, tolerated and valued — the canon — undergoes changes from period to period, but what is *done* with what is read and known in the schools follow an increasingly abstracted and codified congregation of methods: definition, narration, description, analysis, predication, linear exposition, and logico–argumentative proof. Accompanying these methods were the modes of rhetorical presentation that became precursors not only to many literary genres, but in subsequent periods to habits of literary interpretation as well.

When Alexander Luria studied cognition among nonliterate Afghans, his subjects chuckled in sympathy for the odd stranger who asked them to define a circle, thinking he did not know what one was. Primary schoolchildren express similar confusion when the kindergarten teacher during their first show-and-tell session asks inexplicably, indicating a teddy bear, "What is that, Jenny?" The how and why, the value, of defining a circle or a teddy bear are not self-evident. Seriousness and jest alike are brought to the examination of similar scenes of language learning and rhetorical education in antiquity by their indigenous observers. Contemporary research in several fields is of help in establishing links between classical rhetoric and early literacy, and in examining the persistent association of literacy with skills, specifically with the skills now familiarly taught in English literature, rhetoric, and composition classes.[10] Rhetoric and literacy have always been so thoroughly intertwined that the story of how they shaped each other has yet to be told in detail. The lenses of our scholarly spectacles have fostered myopia; "rigor" has obscured simultaneities by insisting on focus — on one subject or issue — as subjects are divided into fields and subdivisions. The scholarly habituation to specificity and thoroughness, itself one of the subjects of this study, has made it difficult to devise a sound methodology for coordinating an investigation into the multiple points of intersection and mutual influence shared by rhetoric and literacy. Establishing these connections in the classical world requires the integration of histories of writing, computations of circulating manuscripts in various periods, and estimations of the frequency of their uses in schooling and in leisure reading.

Among the many meanings accrued by literacy in the West has been access to knowledge defined as textual content—literary, philosophical, theological, and scientific. Studies of circulating manuscripts in different periods provide a record of what and how much people read outside of school that is essential to understanding the value placed on literacy and on literature. Comparisons of literate and oral cultures conducted within cognitive psychology, anthropology, and ethnography supplement historical studies of rhetoric and literacy in the West and further clarify the intersections among culture, literacy, literature, and, particularly in the West, rhetoric. Drawing on these perspectives at different points, I reappraise rhetoric as prototypically literate and textual, reversing the traditional emphasis on rhetoric as primarily a practical oral *techne*. What was the relationship between rhetoric and emergent uses of writing? What were the local—Attic and Ionic—oral habits of mind and language that shaped early literacy and early rhetoric alike? Conversely, how did the largely oral practice of early rhetoric shape subsequent rhetorical training as it adopted a written medium, became embedded in educational curricula, and directed the conventions of literate discourse patterns? Provisional answers are developed here; more await articulation.

The complex understandings and definitions of literacy today comprise patterns in cognition, lexicon, and discourse use that have been, in the West, markedly metalinguistic and recursive. Early logic and rhetoric alike provide evidence of an emerging conceptual self-reference in standardized forms. Many of these continue to typify formal and particularly academic discourse. "In the following discussion I will argue that" is arguably the lineal descendant of forms of metalinguistic self-reference forged by Preplatonic philosophers and rhetors. Parmenides distinguishes his "correct theory" (*logos*) from his report of erroneous opinion (*doxa*): "At this point I cease my reliable theory and thought concerning Truth. From here onwards you must learn the opinions of mortals, listening to the deceptive order of my words."[11] Heraclitus comments metalinguistically on the semantic motives of the Delphic oracle when he says that she "neither speaks, nor conceals, but only gives signs." He defines paradoxes of knowledge and its presentation; his invective hints that his discourse was part of a bitter battle then being waged over language and truth. "The wise-seeming man preserves, [that is], knows, only what seems; furthermore, retribution will seize the fabricators of lies and the [false] witnesses."[12] Once the parallel between rhetoric and the Preplatonic notion of *doxa* is illuminated, Plato's attack on rhetoric can be re-viewed as of a piece with his banishment of the poets. Precisely because rhetoric was *doxa*— mere opinion—it was the object, along with "the poets," of Plato's attack. Aristotle extends the attack of philosophy on poetry when he memorializes the quip that "Homer taught the poets to lie." In addition to philosophical metalinguistics, an important classical source for the beliefs in linguistic contingency and unreliability can be found in early conceptualizations of "poetry" as a made thing. Plato characterizes both literature and rhetoric as "making," as artifice, as *poiesis*, a crafted thing, as "contrivances" when the meaning is pejorative—equivocal meanings that persist among modern uses of the term "fiction." Before and following Plato, the family of *poie*-terms are widely distributed and denote verbal phenomena now commonly treated as distinct from one another: poetry, drama, narrative, the argument following the narrative or statement of thesis in a formal rhetorical exposition, and dialectical proofs. In classical antiquity, it was when literature was first conceptualized as literature—as, in the modern sense, *poiesis*, a made thing—that it came to be associated with lying or, more neutrally, with fabulation. The same process, I propose, occurred in the case of rhetoric.[13]

The theme of making things, making them up, contriving them, parallels quite suggestively the discussions of being, not-being, and coming-into-being that were going on among the philosophers during the fifth and fourth centuries B.C. For this reason, I compare the early discussion of *apate, pseudos*, and *poiesis* that link lying with making verbal artifacts—whether poetic, literary, or philosophical—with what I argue are cognate philosophical discussions of being and not-being. This conjectural rereading of the Preplatonics along with the rhetors and poets focuses on parallels among what at first seem to be unrelated discussions of rhetoric, poetics, logic, and writing. It bothers some of the Preplatonic philosophers, Parmenides foremost among them, that "what is not" or "not being" is discussed at all. Yet they exhibit a dawning awareness that referring to "what is not," even if to proscribe inquiry therein, conjures up and delves into the forbidden territory simply by naming it. Alternately, refusal to look into "what is not" is regarded as willful ignorance on the grounds that it is impossible to know what something is without inquiring into what it is not, a procedure Plato terms *diaeresis*, a synergistic movement of "mixing and separating" that was superseded by Aristotle's definition of definition *per genus et differentiam*.

"Saying that which is not," "the pursuit of not-Being," and "this true statement that I speak" are examples of language used to define a particular kind, use, or status of language itself. It refers to itself before it speaks, and in constituting itself for the first time as a kind of statement, "refers" to what had been a tacit, unexpressed, unsystematic linguistic ontology. My concern is to trace how the ontology and epistemology implicit in the early metalinguistic uses became an explicit and finally a systematic ontology centered in language and logic, an onto-logic. Being was captured and partitioned, colonized as it were, by increasingly grammatical architectonics of meaning, a process that is traced with illuminating delicacy in Heidegger's meditations on early Greek thinking. My readings of the Preplatonics and Plato ask how and why this onto-logic so persistently devalued rhetoric and literature, and pursue the reasons why it did so, reasons that I propose are far less random than they initially appear to be. Rhetoric and poetry are persistently denounced, though not always jointly, because they are orally performed or delivered, because they are arts of opinion and "mere" probability, and because they are "made," fiction, crafted. We can now, perhaps, understand these "oral" media as competing "literacies" of sorts during a time when there was a battle for the control of Being, Truth, Language, and Reality. The arena became the struggle to control education, curriculum, and political discourse. Grammar, now a homely staple of literacy education, is not a self-evident way of understanding or teaching language. It is the product of a specific kind of logocentric—and specifically sentence-centered — application of philosophical analysis that was not programmatically defined until Aristotle's period, and that has undergone a multitude of reconceptualizations since.

A grammar of language is a philosophy of language, and a philosophy of language is an ontology, hence Derrida's "grammatology." Put another way, a philosophy of language and a philosophy centered in language are two different things. The West in most periods has been dominated by the latter philosophy. With a grammar based on terms, the abstract, classifiable — and classifying — terms that had been evolving between the Preplatonics and Aristotle, a parts-of-speech syntactic model joined the conventions of metacognitive and metalinguistic self-reference and reached critical mass. Joined together, these have given Western literacy features that, though by no means universal, have remained surprisingly constant. A grammar may never fully control what is written, but in the West a logocentric conception of grammar has controlled beliefs about the meaning of written and oral discourse alike, and, through genre distinctions made possible in part by grammatical analysis, has driven wedges between kinds and uses of language. These kinds and uses impose another level of metalinguistic consciousness, embodied in terms for kinds and uses of language: "rhetoric," "poetic," "expressive," "imaginative," "logical," "story," "narrative," "argument," "illocutionary," "constative," "expository," "fiction," and a host of others. The earliest exponents of metalinguistic consciousness and an attendant ontology expressed in abstractions also inaugurated distinctions among various kinds of truth and falsehood. From these emerged the familiar distinctions among rhetorical dissembling, literary fiction, and probabilistic logic that, perhaps because they were based on mode, obscured significant parallels in substance.

It would be absurd to suggest that literary fiction and probabilistic logic, and the related associations between lying and writing or lying and political discourse, are uniquely Western or even exclusively post-Homeric within Western tradition. However, these elements of Western literacy, even if they are not unique to the West, have received extensive emphasis in all periods and have become canonical in Western aesthetics and language theory. Political discourse and politicians are enthusiastically suspected in many cultures. What is unusual and possibly unique about the evolution of

Western rhetoric and literacy is the placement of an already controversial formula for political discourse—rhetoric—in the role of arbiter of discourse aesthetics and at the center of the educational curriculum that disseminated literacy. Among other contradictions, this placement in antiquity ran counter to a philosophical tradition that explicitly denied rhetoric truth and falsehood and presented itself as sole arbiter of truth. In a direct parallel with Plato's banishment of the poets, Aristotle classifies "rhetoric, poetry, and prayer" as modes of discourse that, while they have meaning, are neither true nor false.[14] Yet these modes, much more than philosophical discourse, remained the lingua franca of the large majority, even among the educated literate, and coexisted with successive philosophical mandarinates who continued to dub these modes devoid of truth or falsehood and to characterize them, somewhat paradoxically, as "lies." So it was, my story goes, that early on in Western literate tradition dissembling and rhetoric, fabulation and literature, literacy and lies came to be recurrently attached to one another both by blame and by praise. Despite its self-appointed sinecure as guardian of truth, philosophy also came to be associated, particularly outside the academies, with certain kinds of verbal trickery, semantic dodges, quibbling, and hairsplitting. Foreshadowed by Homer's cunning Odysseus and by the blindness and insight memorialized in Sophocles' Oedipus, the specific kinds of literary artifice, rhetorical dissembling, and philosophical quibbling that came to be associated with lying and deception have also in the West been persistently associated with intelligence. An incremental series of equations, enhanced and extended by theoretical elaboration, forged the links among the concepts of *poiesis*, mimesis, figurative language, probability, rhetoric, apparent versus real truth, and irony.

Plato's characterizations of Socrates in dialogue illustrate alternatives to the ethical dangers he finds lurking in poetry, rhetoric, and certain uses of writing. Through his characterizations, Plato argues that an inequality of knowledge or power or both between speaker and hearer, however temporary, is essential to both irony and rhetoric. Similar separation, distance, and concomitant control, he proposes, occur in the case of writing a "treatise," that is, a monologue text; the resulting compendium claims or gives the illusion of totality and finality. Poetic illusion and imitation depend on a similar impermeability and require a willing suspension of disbelief. "Poetry," according to this view, is like a monologue text or a rhetorical speech regardless of whether its medium is written or oral. Like a text, the rhetorical speech has no interlocutor. The rhetorical audience, like the reader of a text, cannot talk back. For these reasons, I propose, Plato judges rhetoric, poetry, and written treatises alike to be ethically and epistemologically corrupt uses of language, and writes the dialogues as dramatizations of, and antidotes to, the seductive powers of *monologos*. The pedagogical and ethical concerns central to Plato's and Augustine's treatments of language are particularly well-suited models for contemporary realignments of the relationship between the teaching of literacy and scholarly treatments of literature, irony, and rhetoric. Reprising classical articulations of the ethical issues inherent in language teaching, theory, and practice requires dusting off a vocabulary that is virtually nonexistent today, a vocabulary that defines an ethics of language teaching and use. Why has this vocabulary gathered dust? The reactionary tendencies of "literature and morality" discussions during the 1930s, paralleled by recent jeremiads concerning canon and cultural literacy, should not avert the discussion entirely. Though purportedly aristocratic, and therefore presumably conservative, classical thinkers are surprisingly comfortable guides for addressing literacy within contemporary ethical and cultural contexts. Political analyses of modern literacy such as those by Oxenham, Cressy, Habermas, Freire, and Raymond Williams are consonant on many points with themes in Plato's and Augustine's treatments, a compatibility that encourages further study of the relationships among ethical norms, academic scholarship and theory, and linguistic behavior.

Excepting the Preplatonics and Aristotle, the figures approached in this study articulate what may be styled a minority position critical of mainstream Western metalinguistics and of some of the uses of literacy that it promotes. I argue that, though its proponents have never long remained in the ascendant, the minority position has functioned as an antistrophe to the more dominant linear-monological–grammatical–logical systems imparted by those conceptualizations of logic and rhetoric that have come to be known as Aristotelian. The pervasive academic and literary convention of a single author and a single subject work has been shaped by the dominant system, as were the literary habits of mainstream literacy.

Plato, I argue, is among the first to practice and promote an alternative metalinguistics, and to insist that language theory and practice sustain an integration with ethical values and truth criteria, an enterprise that was continued by Cicero, the Stoics, and Augustine. It is in this endeavor that Plato assigns to dialogical dialectic alone the capacity for "true" philosophy and simultaneously for "true" rhetoric." For those who love wisdom, he asserts, dialogical dialectic can be conducted only in a series of discussions among interlocutors possessing knowledge, candor, and good will. In contrast to the numerous modern views of Plato as the first abstract idealist, or as the first fully literate and literary philosophical writer, I emphasize his ties to and defense of elements in the traditional oral *paideia*, and his exposition of the merits of avoiding and suspecting closure, conclusion, and monologue textuality.

The influence of Aristotle's highly schematic and analytic logic, of formulaic rhetorics derived from his work, and of his compartmentalization of subjects was formidable, even within classical antiquity. Cicero's treatments of the Middle and New Academy record this influence and challenge it in an alternate integrated metalinguistic theory and practice developed in his dialogue treatises on rhetoric. His retraction of *De Inventione* in the frame dialogue introducing *De Oratore* inaugurates a discussion of antidotes to the technical and reductive schemes then taught in rhetoric. Cicero's success in these efforts was ironically reversed when *De Inventione*, his student notes outlining the kind of rhetoric to which he later objected, became the only one of his rhetorical works widely known in the Middle Ages and the Renaissance. To temper the prominence accorded *De Inventione* in studies of Cicero's rhetoric, I emphasize that, like Plato's, many of Cicero's treatises are dialogues, a form that allows him to replicate the fluidity of oral discussion, holding several voices and points of view in suspension in order to stimulate thought and understanding of a subject. Another aim of his markedly polyvocal and polystylistic work is defined in his view that Latin prose style lacks a standard; most philosophical treatises and rhetorical models were then written in Greek. He sets out to achieve and provide this standard in his own work, an effort that I approach as an attempt to alter the paradigm for literacy that was then being transmitted from Greek into Latin culture. The truth or falsehood of rhetorical discourse is a prominent concern in Cicero's treatises; interlocutors in his dialogues express the suspicions Romans felt toward their Greek teachers of rhetoric because of the Greeks' alleged indifference to and mockery of notions of truth.

Augustine's most memorable contribution to the minority position may be his characterization of his conversion as an "escape from rhetoric." Though this can be interpreted as a blanket dismissal of rhetoric, it also invites close attention to the details of Augustine's objections to rhetoric. My examination of these objections draws on several of his works and finds that they address broad concerns, forming an anatomy of what Augustine found wrong not simply with rhetoric, but with much language teaching, use, and theory in his time. Though Book IV of *De Doctrina Christiana* begins with the announcement that "this is not a treatise on rhetoric," it reconstitutes elements in classical rhetoric and philosophical semantics, and constructs with them an unprecedentedly hermeneutic doctrine of *logos*, accompanied by recommendations for its effective dissemination through the spoken word. *De Doctrina* turns rhetoric and logic to the tasks of textual interpretation. Like Plato, Augustine depicts semantic as well as epistemological contingency as arising out of the limitations of the human mind and will, not out of any inherent characteristics of language. According to this view, it is because of the limitations of the human mind and spirit, some of them chosen and thereby open to ethical evaluation, that conventional language is incapable of representing truth and reality with any finality or completeness. Augustine's *logos* represents an internalization and hypostatization of the Greek philosophic *logos*, whose ultimate authority had remained elusive, though both Heraclitus and Theophrastus had earlier linked it suggestively with one great *theos*, "above gods and men the greatest." Augustine's *logos* also marks an interiorization of dialogue; the dialogical model that informs Augustine's epistemology, semantic theory, hermeneutics, and use of *sermo* (conversation) in defining the role of homiletics draws on rhetorical antecedents. The doctrine of *logos* as both interpretation and understanding and of its dissemination through homiletics arms a criticism of much rhetoric and literature as malpractices. In this, Augustine both exemplifies and accelerates an internalization of logocentric categories that are in some respects independent of theology. The Augustinian dialogue between self and soul, like Plato's dialogue dialectic between interlocutors, emphasizes participatory constructions of reality and meaning whose ground is the collective process of seeking and affirming, and whose goal—understanding—is a guide rather than an object, product, or possession. The involvement of the inner self in this process is a psychologizing move expressed by Augustine's extra-theological conceptualization of the mind as essentially, though not exclusively, conceptual and linguistic—as of, for, and through the word. The persistence of this view, and further evidence of its independence of an explicit theology, is exemplified by a modern commonplace often invoked in Freshman Composition: how do I know what I think, until I see what I say?

The minority position that is here defined and represented by Plato, Cicero, and Augustine has advocated shared, interlocutionary, and dialogical modes of thought and language. Other proponents of such views have recurrently sought ethically consistent and epistemologically sound alternatives to eristic dialectic, rhetoric, and logic, and in particular to the formalized thesis-defense or thesis-proof mode that ensures separation and division not only of subject from subject but of person from person as well. Monological, linear discourse modes have controlled Western textual conventions more often than not, but in becoming overly abstract or restrictive, have prompted revolt. German and English Romanticism, as well as the more recent oralist revival of nonabstract modes of thought and language—folklore, myth, verbal art, poetry, performative verbal art—can be understood as reactions against excessive linearity and textualism. Dialogue has never remained in the ascendant for long in the official history and understanding of our literate–textual culture, where linear and monological forces foster its decay. Perhaps it is because dialogue has never remained very long at the center of formal discourse structures in the West that several of its inversions and alter egos have been prominent: a host of conceptualizations of rhetorical dissembling and irony, a fascination with literature as lying. In our unease about these modes, perhaps we acknowledge the perennial ghosts of ourselves as always speaking to or being spoken to. If it is true that we are now moving outside of the long parenthesis that has enclosed literacy in the West, albeit for the few who have known or been shaped by it, and that we are moving into a postliterate culture marked by a diversity of secondary oralities, perhaps we can resuscitate some of the dialogical voices that have been there all along in defining new literacies. Literacy as we have known it may be passing; the literacies of the future await our definition. It is to the labor of that definition that this study directs itself.

Proem

I Strophe

The first Greek inscriptions (c.450 B.C.) inscribe a very different content from that which we normally associate with literate texts. It is something that is being said aloud rather than silently stated or recorded. It has the quality of an oral announcement addressed to a particular occasion or a particular person. In several early examples the statement is framed as the utterance of the object which speaks to the observer: "I am Nestor's cup" or "Mantiklos dedicated me." In some cases the statement is even placed inside a balloon issuing from the figure's mouth, as in modern comic strip illustration.

ERIC HAVELOCK, *The Literate Revolution*

II Antistrophe

On a winter day in a preschool, Benjamin sits in a chair, his legs dangling off the end and swinging. He has been waiting for his turn to read a storybook to the others. The teacher places a record on the nearby phonograph. Benjamin sits, holding the book in his lap, ready to turn the pages. He holds the book so that it will face the children sitting on the floor in front of him. As the record plays, a "beep" indicates when he should turn the page. Intently, he listens for the beep, and turns each page as it comes. The children lose interest, and walk over to the teacher, asking when it will be their turn to "read."

III Strophe

Children have to learn at a very early age to perceive situations, determine how units of these situations are related to each other, recognize these relations in other situations, and reason through what it will take to show their correlation of one situation with another. The familiar routines described in the research literature on mainstream school-oriented parents are not heard in Trackton. They do not ask or tell their children: What is that? What color is that? Is that the way to listen? Turn the book this way. Let's listen and find out. They do not simplify their talk about the world for the benefit of their young. Preschoolers do not learn to name or list the features of items in either the daily environment or as depicted through illustration in printed materials.

SHIRLY BRICE HEATH, *Ways with Words*

IV Antistrophe

Seven four-year-old children are gathered around a table with their preschool teacher. They are learning about opposites. The teacher takes out a stack of cards with pictures. The children say, "Hooray, we're going to play same and different." The teacher holds up two cards, one with a picture of an ice cube, and one with a picture of a steaming teakettle. "Are these the same, or different?" "Different," the children answer, sitting up very straight and proud to be getting the answer right. "What is the difference?" "Hot and cold." Two more cards are chosen. One shows an old man with a long white beard and a walking cane. The other shows a small boy with black hair. "Are these the same, or different?" With more hesitation, the children look at one another. Finally, one says, tentatively, "different." "What is different?" "Black and white—the man has white hair and the boy has black hair." "No," the teacher says. Another child says, "tall and short." "No," the teacher says, "this is a hard one." "The man is OLD, and the boy is YOUNG; YOUNG and OLD."

1

Before Being or Not-Being Was: Logos and Logic Among the Preplatonics

When neither Being nor Not-being was
Nor atmosphere, nor firmament, nor what is beyond.
What did it encompass? Where? In whose protection?
What was water, the deep, unfathomable?
   Neither death nor immortality was there then.
No sign of night or day.
That One breathed, windless, by its own energy:
Nought else existed then.
   In the beginning was darkness swathed in darkness;
All this was but unmanifested water.
Whatever was, the One, coming into being,
Hidden by the Void,
Was generated by the power of heat.
   In the beginning this [One] evolved,
Became desire, first seed of mind.
Wise seers, searching within their hearts.

RIG-VEDA 129

And the goddess received me kindly and took my right hand in hers, and thus she spoke and addressed me:

   . . . Thou shalt inquire into everything: both the motionless heart of well-rounded Truth, and also the opinions of mortals, in which there is no true reliability. But nevertheless thou shalt learn these things (*opinions*) also — how one should go through

all the things-that-seem, without exception, and test them.
. . .

For this (*view*) can never predominate, that That Which Is
Not exists. You must debar your thought from this way of
search, nor let ordinary experience in its variety force you
along this way, (*namely, that of allowing*) the eye, sightless as it
is, and the ear, full of sound, and the tongue, to rule; but (*you
must*) judge by means of Reason (*Logos*) the much-contested
proof which is expounded by me.

PARMENIDES, Fragments 1, 8

> For nothing can be sole or whole
> That has not been rent.
> WILLIAM BUTLER YEATS

Their entire purpose is to accelerate the intellectual awaken-
ing which "converts" the psyche from the many to the one, and
from "becomingness" to "beingness"; this, if our thesis is correct, is equivalent to a conversion of the image world of the
epic to the abstract world of scientific description, and from
the syntax and vocabulary of narrativised events in time to-
wards the syntax and vocabulary of equations and laws and
formulas and topics which lie outside of time.

ERIC HAVELOCK, *Preface to Plato*

> Logos and logic, crystal hypothesis
> Incipit and a form to speak the word
> And every latent double in the word.
> WALLACE STEVENS, "Notes Toward a
> Supreme Fiction"

The Preplatonic thinkers remain ciphers, tantalizing and ultimately
irretrievable. They sought words that could express the "motionless
heart of well-rounded Truth": *aletheia* — the unconcealed — in assertions of hidden unity, harmony, and of truth. Their efforts at defining relationships between thought and language gave birth to a
metalanguage, a vocabulary of ideas, concepts, and terms defining
the nature of their own statements. Only enigmatic fragments of

their original texts survive, alluringly protean tracings of mental spaces and shapes. A new reality of thought was being brought into being through the banishment of opinion and beliefs and through attacks on the reliability of perception. Newly plowed cognitive and linguistic furrows yielded conceptions of thought and language that now seems unquestionable: logic is a universal of thought and cognition; grammar is intrinsic to language; opinion and traditional wisdom are of less truth and less value than the knowledge that reflection and careful study can achieve.

The fragmentary condition of their original writings complicates the retrieval and understanding of the Preplatonics. Many Preplatonic "texts" survive only in quotations by later philosophers. Their words filter through a selectively transcribed oral tradition. Further complicating efforts at understanding the Preplatonics in their cultural milieu, reappraisals of the primary texts in this century under the auspices of oral literature scholarship suggest that many of the Preplatonics were not primarily prose writers; they were poets and speakers.[1] The writing that preserves their discourse retains verse schemes that would have been familiar to audiences whose ears have been trained by Homeric epic narrative.[2] Yet unlike the epic and lyric poets, they are unraveling narrative epic schema, disrupting the lulling familiarity of oral poetry's rhythmically transmitted word pictures. Instead of painting word pictures, they speak of "being" and "the one," of "the unmoving" and "motion," of the unchanging and change, of coming-into-being and passing-away, of mixing and separating and blending — concepts that they increasingly apply not only to the physical world, but to the worlds of language and thought as well. Their poetic idioms challenge the content of epic poetry; mingling new and old, they unravel and reweave.

Parmenides frames his discourse on the Way of Truth and the Way of Opinion with a narrated quest, a vision in which he visits the goddess:

> The mares which carry me conveyed me as far as my desire reached, when the goddesses who were driving had set me on the famous highway which bears a man who has knowledge through all the cities. Along this way I was carried; for by this way the exceedingly intelligent mares bore me. . . . And the goddess received me kindly, and took my right hand in hers, and thus she spoke and addressed me.[3]

In more aphoristic Preplatonics abrupt transitions from the prophetic to the bathetic abound. Heraclitus and Gorgias in particular seem fond of teasing shifts from serious to banal, abstract to concrete, as if to subject their listeners to linguistic vertigo. The subject seems to be a proverbial solution to drunkenness, but in a flash Heraclitus shifts to metaphysics: "All men have the capacity of knowing themselves and acting with moderation. A man, when he gets drunk, is led stumbling along by an immature boy, not knowing where he is going, having his soul wet. A dry soul is the wisest and best."[4] The careening alternation between mundane and metaphysical may be as much the product of stretching extant terms to their limits as it is a carefully crafted philosophical analogy,[5] but "metaphor" and "analogy" are unavoidably anachronisms when applied to the Preplatonics; similarly, only in modern terms can they be said to mix genres or shift levels. The wet soul of the drunk led by a young boy mingles with generalization and proverb — all men can act with moderation. Conclusion (or is it simply an appositive?): a dry soul is the wisest and best. Sequences like these record a gradual disruption of oral epic "poetry," of the rhythmic cadences and familiar scenes that preserved the Homeric message intact, of the characters, events, and divine agents which were its primary substance. Heraclitus' metaphor — proverb? epigram? aphorism? axiom? — of the drunk is syllogistic in contour; it moves from general to specific to conclusion. It is self-contained, an integrity of "account" that is but one among the many meanings of *logos*. Unlike later formal logic, Heraclitus' discourse is more than a well-formed sequence of logical statements. He propounds, teaches, and exhorts through proverbially expressed moral axioms. The middle premise — there is no middle "term" — is more cleverly, and poetically, crafted than the spare propositions of later syllogisms. The conclusion is a joke as much as a recently derived truth: philosophers should have minds as dry as bones, and live apart from the life of pleasurable excess that drunkenness represents.

There is another kind of metamorphosis intimated by this particular passage, an alchemical transformation of metaphors for wisdom. Earlier images for wisdom, insight, and divination emphasized sweetness, plentitude, ceremonial libation. A Hymn to Hermes (c. 676 B.C.) tells of the Thriae, who by eating of the honeycomb "brings all things to pass":

There are certain holy ones, sisters born—three maidens gifted with wings: their heads are to be sprinkled with white meal, and they dwell under a ridge of Parnassus. These are teachers of divination apart from me, the art which I practiced while yet a boy following herds, though my father paid no heed of it. From their home they fly, now here, now there, feeding on honey-comb and bringing all things to pass. And when they are inspired by eating yellow honey, they are willing to speak truth; but if they be deprived of the gods' sweet food, then they speak falsely, as they swarm in and out together.[6]

In stark contrast, Heraclitus' boy leads a staggering drunk who, because his soul is "all wet," is incapable of moderation and thereby also of knowing all things. In the new philosophy, knowledge is a product of control and is represented by dryness.

The Preplatonic *Logos*

> You must listen to the undeceitful progress of my argument. At this point I cease my reliable theory and thought concerning Truth.
>
> PARMENIDES, Fragment 8

> The Law [*Logos*] of the universe is as here explained.
>
> HERACLITUS, Fragment 1

A reliable order of words *about* the order of things the Preplatonics came to call *logos*. *Logos* stands alone, intact, its integrity as a statement defined as always true, "reliable," outside of time and place. It was this "timeless," "always" quality that arguably made *logos* statements, as well as statements about *logos*, fertile ground for the development of predicational copula, the timeless "is" that emerged out of Preplatonic uses of "being" and "isness." Heraclitus' *logos* about the drunk and the boy forms an argument of sorts, but is not yet as dry as argument would become when desiccated by the strict rules of formal logic. Nonetheless, Heraclitus' sequence of statements makes a point in itself, free of the contexts of narrative or ritual repetition. Though no longer epic or ritual song, the Preplatonics' *logos* is more poetic in most cases than the rhetoric that would be practiced only a short time later by the Sophists. The

Preplatonic voice, as often as not, is a forceful polemic, simultaneously didactic and iconoclastic. Though only fragments remain of the earliest pavement of their new "way," the novel *hodos*, these are enough to distinguish it from the narrative event and speech sequences of rhythmic epic strophes. Is it the older road of the *rhapsodoi*, which Parmenides alludes to, a specifically linguistic "way along which wander mortals knowing nothing, two-headed, . . . deaf as they are blind, amazed, uncritical hordes, by whom To Be and Not To Be are regarded as the same and not the same"?[7] The world of *doxa* (opinion, belief) is also under attack, the ancient way of received wisdom, unquestioned belief and doctrine. Those who walk this "way" Heraclitus characterizes as drunks, and Parmenides as sleepwalkers; these are the "sightseers" memorialized in Plato's myth of the cave.[8] For their challenges to traditional custom and belief, countless Preplatonic philosophers and Sophists were exiled; many were executed, like Socrates, for blasphemy or atheism. Aristotle too died in exile, charged with blasphemy.[9]

The Preplatonic *logos* and lexicon changed shape, form, and meaning with chimerical speed during precisely the period when literacy began to spread. Indeed, the conceptual requirements of philosophizing may have provided one of the incentives for an increased dissemination of literacy. Alternately, it is plausible that the changing contours and vocabulary of Preplatonic philosophy were shaped in part by the growing use of writing in schools and in preparing speeches for the political arenas of court and assembly. The specific mechanisms of this reciprocal relationship continue to provoke debate.[10] Was literacy a prerequisite for abstract thought and for skepticism, or did abstract thinkers adopt writing after they had begun to shape the methods and objectives of their inquiry? Heraclitus' and other aphoristic Preplatonic fragments seem much like traditional oral proverbs with their vividly memorable images and narrative elements, those mainstays of oral literature that intimate a preliterate milieu.[11] Yet in stark contrast to oral epic's characteristic repetition of familiar stories, Preplatonic discourse is explicitly iconoclastic, irreverent, radically different in language and content from anything that had preceded it. Despite the necessarily oral "publication" of their "texts," and the fact that they composed for oral delivery, many Preplatonics were writers as well; their writings, sold and circulated, threatened established belief, custom, and hierarchy and were cited in hearings deciding on their punishment. The civic piety they challenged was centered not in any timeless ancient tradition, however, but rather in the much newer democratic order instigated by Solon's reforms.[12] The protoliterate *nomos* embodied in the rhetoric of the assembly and in the dramatic performance of the epic cycle was to be succeeded by the codification of laws and culture through inscription. It was this newer *nomos*, now conscious of itself as "convention" and given mythic exposition by the dramatists, that, much more than any ancient tradition, was vying with the Preplatonic conceptualizations of *logos* for control over Athenian education and politics.[13] Sophocles' *Antigone* provides a particularly intriguing trace of a parallel struggle between the old and the new ethics. The earlier *nomos* of tribe and family was supplanted by fiat in the new *poleis* by a hierarchical public assembly elect, represented in Creon, restricted to and controlled by soldier–landholders, and implemented by public political rhetoric. In Euripides' *Hippolytus* Phaedra expresses her horror at the disruption instituted by the new order and its language: "This is the deadly thing which devastates well-ordered cities and the homes of men—that's it, this art of oversubtle words. It's not the words ringing delight in the ear, that one should speak, but those that have the power to save their hearers' honorable name" (486–89).

Heraclitus' *Logos* is translated alternately, according to context and conjecture, as "law," "order," "argument," "discourse," "words," and "saying." Like those of Empedocles, Heraclitus' conceptual worlds—of words and things alike—are made up of harmonic opposites, tensions, cycles, and complements—Fire and Water, Earth and Air—but they also function at a second level of opposition, that between the world of ever-changing opposites and a conceptual world that never changes, that "is one." Thus *logos* denotes simultaneously the reality of unity in the physical world, and the reliability—the "truth"—of its expression in well-ordered words: "When you have listened, not to me but to the Law [*Logos*], it is wise to agree that all things are one."[14] Only *logos* statements can represent what Heraclitus calls the *palintropos harmonia*—the always turning harmony—of the universe, the order, law, principle, or thought that rests "at the still point of the turning world."[15]

Empedocles' depiction of the creation of all things through the conflict of opposites differs from Heraclitus' on several points.

Empedocles uses *neikos*, connoting verbal wrangling, rather than *polemos*, denoting warfare, terms whose different nuances are obscured by divergent, inconsistent translations of both terms as "warfare," "opposition," "argument," "discord," and "strife." The hypostatization of the key terms "being" and "[what] is," or "[that which] is," ancestors of the philosophical conception of "substance" as well as of the predicative copula, present some of the thorniest problems of translation and interpretation. Heraclitus uses *to pan*, "the all," as an alternate for "what is" and "the one." Parmenides uses *einai*, "to be," and *esti*, "[it] is," "[that which] is," an infinitive with an implied but unstated subject, an ambiguous neologism which continues to stimulate debate.[16] Empedocles recurrently uses *esti genesthai*, "is becoming" or "is coming into being," another conceptual neologism that has provoked controversial discussions of relative degrees of being and of reciprocal relations among "opposites" that had become abstracted, plausibly, from the study of elements in the physical and notional worlds. *Esti genesthai* hovers on the line dividing theology and cosmogony from science and ontology, precisely the boundary whose crossing led to the charges of blasphemy and atheism brought against the Sophists.

Because it denotes a hidden unity and harmony "out there," Heraclitus' "the all" (*to pan*) is arguably a usage on its way to transformation from ontological claim to grammatical subject. It can be viewed as a precursor to the syntax of class nouns deployed in the logic of terms — "All men are rational beings" — developed by Aristotle. Parmenides' "isness" or "being," for which we feel compelled to supply a pronoun subject: "that which is," carries intimations of a conceptual ontology and syntax. In Plato's discourse these begin to form statements of definitions: What is an *x*? Is *x* of this or that sort? Sometimes with regard to *phusis*, the nature of things, and sometimes with regard to *logos*, the order of language and reason, *esti genesthai* defines the means by which things and thoughts come into being and pass out of being exclusive of any divine or human agency.

Empedocles and Heraclitus exemplify a programmatic use of opposites and concepts of flux to define a whole, an underlying order. Their uses of opposites, tensions, and complementarities seem at odds with Parmenides' dictum that Being and Truth have no coming-into-being, and with his proscription of inquiry into what is not.[17] Yet amid all his opposites and flux Heraclitus also asserts "that which alone is wise is one" and proclaims that this hidden order, itself an aspect of *logos*, "is willing and unwilling to be called by the name of Zeus."[18] Empedocles and Heraclitus posit a whole underlying or beneath or invisible to empirical scrutiny, a whole that parallels the promise given by Parmenides' goddess, to reveal the still heart of well-rounded truth. One among the Preplatonic pairs of oppositions concerns *logos* itself, and distinguishes it from received opinion, law, custom, and traditional religious belief, *nomos* and *doxa*. The postulating of characteristics and capacities for all, including characterizations of the discourse in which such postulates are expressed, arguably prompted the analytical and sub-sequent logical use of generic abstract class terms as the subjects of "true" *or* "not true" propositions. Within the perspective of this gradual development, the apparently divergent thought of Heracli-tus and Empedocles on the one hand, and of Parmenides on the other, can be seen as complementary. They share the notion of complementary opposites in their emphasis on one true way as the *statement* of and about those opposites—the ordering, unifying *logos* statement. In the conceptualization and practice of this kind of statement hovers an emergent consciousness of thought and lan-guage as directed, chosen, and constructed "ways," replacing the well-worn and well-known paths of epic narrative, ode, and rhap-sode.

Those who do not inquire into "nature/substance" (*phusis*) or the "universe" (*kosmos*) are called sleepwalkers. Followers of the new way are enjoined by Heraclitus and Parmenides alike to remain awake, to deliberately reverse experiential or received knowledge. "Nor let ordinary experience in its variety force you along this way, the eye, sightless as it is. The hidden harmony is stronger than the visible."[19] Parmenides denounces the combination of opposites it-self as "that way along which wander mortals knowing nothing, two-headed, . . . by whom To Be and Not To Be are regarded as the same and not the same."[20] The Ionian Anaxagoras condemns the Greeks' belief on "Coming into Being and Passing Away." "No Thing comes into being or passes away, but it is mixed together or separated from existing Things. Thus they would be correct if they called coming into being 'mixing' and passing away 'separation off.'"[21] Which "Greeks" does he refer to? The "relativists"—Heraclitus and Empedocles — or the ordinary mortals, the blind, unhearing hordes condemned by Parmenides? Then, as now, one thinker's "truth" was called by others "false opinion" and "lie."

Parmenides implicitly condemns received accounts of how things come into being by locating traditional accounts in his treatment of the world of opinion, the conventional and, in his view, spurious domain of the sleepwalkers. "Thus therefore, according to opinion, were these things created, and are now, and shall hereafter from henceforth grow and then come to an end. And for these things men have established a name as a distinguishing mark for each."[22] Here is suggested an equation of common belief with both *doxa* and *nomos* — the words, customs, and laws of human making. The displacement of *nomos* by *logos* seems to have had the additional effect of rendering religion myth; the Homeric canon as well as the dramas came to be regarded as man-made *poiesis*, as deceptive "fiction" wrought of lies, custom, and experience *and thereby* not reliable. With this displacement, the gods are overthrown; *logos* is hypostatized, made both the means and the object of knowledge, and finally apotheosized: "that which alone is wise is one; it is willing and unwilling to be called by the name of Zeus."[23] Belief in degrees of being and not-being is located in the "false" realm of opinion, as is the belief that being and not-being are the same. A generation before Heraclitus, and two before Parmenides, Xenophanes (c. 530 B.C.) provides an earlier cosmogonical trace of the metamorphosis that realigned the ratio between philosophy and religion. "There is one god [*theos*] among gods and men the greatest, not at all like mortals in body or in mind. He sees as a whole, and hears as a whole. Without toil he sets everything in motion, by the thought of his mind. He always remains in the same place, not moving at all, nor is it fitting for him to change his position at different times. For everything comes from earth and everything goes back to earth at last."[24]

Parmenides warns against conscious, philosophical inquiry into not-being, and banishes coming-into-being as mere name and opinion. The mantic and hortatory contours of his proscriptions hint at doctrinal disputes: hear my reliable words; now listen to the deceptive words. His polemic defends the independence and superiority of reason and *logos* over perception and opinion; his definitions of *logos* record some of the earliest conceptions of truth, being, language, and thought as interpenetrating: "For it is the same to think and to be."[25] "Being has no coming-into-being and no destruction, for it is whole of limb, without motion, and without end. And it never Was, nor Will Be, because it Is now, a Whole all together, One, continuous."[26] In contrast, "All things that mortals have established, believing in their truth, are just a name: Becoming and Perishing, Being and Not-Being, and Change of position, and alteration of bright color."[27] Language (*to legein*) and thought (*to noein*), jointly constitutive of being and reality, come to be named as the only true belief (*pistis alethes*); they "quench" and vanquish into "the unseen" both "Coming-into-Being and Destruction."[28] Henceforth, truth and knowledge will be of what always is and of what is one. All else by decree merely seems, and is to be shunned by the averted, inward-looking gaze of the new mind's eye. It is only in the world of "common opinion," of "lies," that things come into being and pass away. It is in that world that "men have given specific names to all things."[29] The fictive and deceptive nature of convention, appearance, and opinion are given among their first expositions in Heraclitus' and Empedocles' scrutiny of the world of phenomena, perceived reality, and opinion, the world of flux and change, coming into being and going out of being, the "birth and perishing." It is this world—this way of seeing and being in the world—that, Parmenides repeatedly emphasizes, is extinguished by the Way of Truth.

Though many interpretations construe Parmenides' idealism as opposed to Heraclitus' and Empedocles' relativism, the two schools can be also been seen as complements to each other. Heraclitus and Empedocles focus on and use the language of cosmogony made up of cycles and moving and combining elements: Fire and Water, Air and Earth. "This ordered universe [*kosmos*] . . . was ever and is and shall be ever-living Fire, kindled in measure and quenched in measure."[30] Their report of this eternal cycling seems very like the belief system of the "way" Parmenides proscribes because it "steers intelligence astray," the way ordinary mortals wander, "deaf as they are blind, amazed, uncritical hordes, by whom To Be and Not To Be are regarded as the same and not the same, and (*for whom*) in everything there is a way of opposing stress."[31] When examined carefully, however, Heraclitus' polemic in favor of perception and seeming can be seen as itself ordering and law-giving, establishing a new ratio between the worlds of change and the world of the One. He equates change and an eternal "struggle of opposites" or cycling of opposites not only with an "order" in the cosmos, but also with the moral and ethical dimensions of lies and truth and intellection. The world in which humans perceive and decide and act is the deceptive world of *doxa* (opinion), and also of *nomos* — the received or constructed laws by which decisions are made. To contrast this world with the underlying unity and order of *logos*, Heraclitus serves up pithy aphorisms in a lexical tossed salad, mixing the terms of his new cosmology with sardonic characterizations of the world of ordinary mortals and opinions. The results are witty, ambiguous as an oracle, and surely woke up a few sleepwalkers. "One should quench arrogance rather than a conflagration." "That which is wise is one: to understand the purpose which steers all things through all things."[32]

Flux and contingencies in the worlds of appearance, human opinion, perception, values, choice, and politics are paralleled here aligned to the "opposites" and constant change in the natural world. The statement of these constant changes is a *logos* statement of what always is; thus *logos* carries the sense of "law" in some passages. "The Law ([*Logos*] *of the universe*) is here explained; but men are always incapable of understanding it, both before they hear it and when they have heard it for the first time. . . . Therefore one must follow (*the universal Law, namely*) that which is common [*xunon*] (*to all*). But although the Law [*Logos*] is universal, the majority live as if they had understanding peculiar to themselves."[33] The many — ordinary people — fail to comprehend the One: the order and nature of things defined in the Preplatonic cosmo-logos. The universal law which Heraclitus propounds is hard for most to understand, yet he asserts it *is* universal and *must* be followed. It is also common to all — that is, a "common bond" [*xunon*] — the unity binding the harmonious universe and the principle of coherence of statements about that unity. Heraclitus' One and the Many are of words and of realities at the same time. Plato expresses the same relationship in a way that is plausibly the descendant of Heraclitus in that it sustains the coextensive emphasis on words and things, and the *dunamis* linking definition of terms and the conjuring of essences. Many, Plato contends, comprehend this or that beautiful thing, but few seek an understanding or reach an apprehension of Beauty.[34]

The first definitions of the "all" the "one," and "that which is common to all" emphasize that it is invisible to the ordinary eye and beyond the immediate. Heraclitus' *logos* both is and is about independent statements expressing something which is "common to all," links all, and should thereby be "followed." *Logos* is order and orders things; it is binding and binds. "For though all things come into being in accordance with this Law [*Logos*], men seem as if they had never met with it, when they meet with words and actions such as I expound, separating each thing according to its nature and explaining how it is made."[35] A master of ambiguity and double meaning, Heraclitus propounds the *logos* in vivid terms of what it is not, and leads to new intuitions and understandings through inference and indirection, a method that is notably consistent with his cosmology. "The hidden harmony is stronger than the visible."[36] Like truth, he announces, "Nature likes to hide."[37] Where Parmenides attempts a programmatic definition of the Way of Truth, Heraclitus dramatizes that "way." Yet like those of Parmenides, his expositions have a double signification: any statement about the world of flux and change, including the human contingencies of opinion and traditional belief, is "about" that world and way of being which most in it are not aware of. From the perspective of "ordinary mortals," the philosphers' teachings would be either unintelligible or false. As "reliable statements" (*logoi*) about that world and way of being as analyzed and known, the Preplatonics exemplify and bring into being the *logos* which *is* conscious, "awake." The double signification of Preplatonic discourse, exemplifying and enacting the *logos* that is being talked about, further amends the reductive equation of Heraclitus with a relativist position, and that of Parmenides with an idealist position. Diogenes Laertius records that Heraclitus "used also to call opinion the sacred disease: and to say that eyesight was often deceived. That the whole world in its turn again is consumed by fire at certain periods and that all this happens according to fate. That of the contraries, that which leads to production is called war and contest, and that which leads to the conflagration is called harmony and peace; that change is a road leading upward, and the road leading downward; and that the whole world exists according to it."[38] Heraclitus has traditionally been remembered for such "relativist" epigrams. "Those who step into the same river have different waters flowing ever upon them."[39] "The lord whose oracle is at Delphi neither speaks nor conceals but only gives signs."[40] These take on a different meaning if the first is seen as a denunciation of the common-sense perception that the river is always the same, and the second is seen as criticism, rather than clever appreciation of, traditional religion.

The range of views within and across the Preplatonics' work seems disorganized, deliberately vague, even contradictory by modern disciplinary standards. The force and seriousness of any individual fragment is difficult to determine until read in the context of the others, and even then interpreters resort to the anachronism of reconciling apparent contradictions in modern literary or logical terms. Although designated a relativist within doxographical tradition, it is clear enough that Heraclitus means his definitions of the relativity of perceptions and experiences to propound the unreliability of the senses. Heraclitus says, "The hidden harmony is stronger than the visible," but he also asserts, "Those things of which there is sight, hearing, knowledge: these are what I honor most."[41] We honor, respond to, are affected most by those things which we experience directly. Paradoxically, the hidden, the concealed becomes a truth (*aletheia*, the unconcealed) stronger than mere appearance, a whole, an order, timeless, accessible to thought and *logos* alone. The familiar modern classifications of idealist and relativist are risky at best when applied to the Preplatonics; too often such modern polarizing distinctions have distorted by resolving the incontrovertible complexity and oracular opacity of their interstitial language.

Parmenides has been viewed as the grandfather of Plato, as the quintessential "idealist" who dogmatically rejects all relativisms in warnings that sound as doctrinal and oracular as the traditional religion he opposes. He frames his warnings within a vision and expresses them in incantatory poetry. The *Logos* and Being he defines are teachings of "the goddess," a Homeric or possibly Eleusinian frame that would have been familiar to his listeners. But what the goddess tells him would not have been. "Thou shalt inquire into everything: both the motionless heart of well-rounded Truth, and also the opinions of mortals, in which there is not true reliability.

But nevertheless thou shalt learn these things (*opinions*) also — how one should go through the things-that-seem, without exception, and test them."[42] Parmenides' use of poetic and oracular language may be a bow to convention or a conscious utilization of the only formula then in existence for talking about the sources and nature of knowledge. An alternate way of understanding Parmenides' use of this formula is as a consciously transitional use of the authority of "myth" as a vehicle for a new order of knowledge. The hybrid medium of the text prefigures an alteration in the relationship between epic, poetic shamanistic, and conceptual philosophical expressions of being and not-being. It is only when "story," "plot," "tale" (*muthos*) come to be seen as unreliable, as contrived accounts, as fictive, that space is created for some other order of truth. "Listen to the reliable order of my words," proclaims Parmenides, reliable because, he asserts, "I speak truth; I have been spoken to by and of 'well-rounded Truth.'" A more explicitly defined use of this literary–theological "mythic" frame occurs in Plato's presentations of Socrates recounting myths. In the *Gorgias*, Socrates mock-apologizes for telling the story of Zeus' assigning three judges of the dead as they pass into the afterworld. Explaining his seemingly inconsistent behavior, Socrates says that "this is what I have heard and believe to be true; from these stories on my reckoning we must draw some moral."[43] The stories are "true," or rather, they become so when from them a conceptualized truth is drawn.

Parmenides anticipates many of the paradoxes of predicative, referential, ontological, and literary truth criteria that continue to entertain philosophers today. If one is to establish a linguistic and noetic *Logos* as reality, if being and truth are to be promoted as of the mind and contained by philosophic language, one must have rules for defining the false. In order to define positive knowledge and its proper media of expression, one must delineate rules for what is and what is not a proper or attainable "object" of knowledge. Explicit and implicit definitions of this kind still guide inquiry and expression. But to denote "what is not," as Parmenides calls it, is to speak of, and therefore bring into being, the very entity — not-being — whose pursuit has been forbidden. Plato's *Sophist*, with an explicit nod to "Father Parmenides'" proscription, tackles the complexity of stating being and not-being through an analysis of the syntax of "is" and "is not." Unlike Plato's resolution, neither of

Parmenides' two ways around this problem is syntactical, perhaps because the logic of sentences now known as grammar had yet to be defined. The first of Parmenides' solutions resides in the goddess's proclamation of the unshaken heart of well-rounded Truth, in which she links Truth and its pursuit to a self-conscious soul/intellect monitoring itself, steering itself in the right direction. Parmenides' second solution occurs in the proviso by which he clearly marks the beginning of his discussion of the way of seeming. "Here I end my trustworthy discourse and thought concerning truth; henceforth learn the beliefs of mortal men, listening to the deceitful ordering of my words."[44] Parmenides enacts Heraclitus' dictum "that which is wise is set apart from all things," in a very literal sense. In both their discourses truth is coming to be defined as an object pursued through detachment, as apprehension of a hidden and intangible One, as a timeless and eternal Law, as Unity, as Xenophanes' *Theos*, wholly other. As the groundwork is being laid for the conceptualization and authorization of Truth as knowledge, the Truth and Being of the oracular world retreat; Being is replaced by beings.[45] Parmenides and Heraclitus, though different in many ways, still draw on the language of that oracular world. Perched at the edge of the cave that would later be condemned by Plato, the Preplatonics define a boundary—*horizomenos*—the frontier at which the goddess's *sophia* is being exchanged for the philosopher's *logos*.

The objectification of truth and knowledge effected through the Preplatonic *logos* marks a deliberate severance of knower from known and constitutes the known as object.[46] The movement toward conceptualizing the known as an object is evident in the Preplatonic syntax that makes modern interpreters want to supply subjects where there are none in the Greek. The "is" and "all" and "one" impart ontological unity to statement and reality at one and the same time. Even in Plato's discourse, "to be" verbs are not consistently independent, and alternate with strangely tangible verbs in sentences such as "Motion blends with Being" and "Can Change mix with Rest?"—allusions perhaps to the alternate phrasings of Anaxagoras and others that had been adopted by the Sophists of Socrates' generation. Classicists trained in modern analytic philosophy have been somewhat imprecise in translating such passages, and have imported pronoun subjects as well as "is" syntax where there is none in the original.[47] The dry matter-of-factness of these modern translations has obscured both the complexity and the importance of the emergence of the copula as a "timeless is,"[48] as a grammatical technology, and as the syntactic and lexical counterpart of the more numinous Being. Once established, the propositional "is" eroded and fractured the poetic verse, rhythms, and narrative that had stitched discourse together, and replaced them with a logosophical discourse directed at finding, defining, testing, and proving concepts rather than at representing events. The transition to this language is a gradual metamorphosis. Like that of Heraclitus, Gorgias' discourse draws — quite plausibly by design — on the incantatory powers of the Eleatic *epicheirema*, "the idiom of the oracle, the riddle, the double entendre, the 'unrealistic,'"[49] but through this elliptical form and mantic delivery propounds completely novel conceptualizations of knowledge.

The conceptualization of *logos* both as the principle by which independently true statements or statements about Being could be made, and as the making of such statements, stimulated a line of analysis that led eventually — but not, I propose, until Aristotle — to the definition of syntax in terms of units, with the concept of terms as units. It was a grammar of terms, linked with the philosophical concept of Being as "isness," that provided the syntactic materials for isolating a free-floating copula that could link subject and object.[50] "You know what you can recall" is true of the oral noetic economy; Preplatonic discourse demonstrates that, even within the oral noetic, the structure and content of that which is remembered, once it is defined as knowledge, shift vastly.[51] Oral noetic economy is held in place by mnemonic devices such as rhythm, song, and narrative formulae, and relies heavily on repetition, emulation, and collaborative, shared thought, language, and knowledge. In contrast, the philosophical traditions represented among the Preplatonics begin to shape what can be thought of as an alternate noetic economy, one that places a high premium on innovation, interrogation, skepticism, analysis, debate, authority, and proof, and that comes to both rely on and be shaped by new uses of writing. These contours and terms, protean as they are among the Preplatonics, are haunting shades of a poetic past and portents of the philosophical–rhetorical future. Received opinion, traditional religious practices, and ultimately the Homeric canon are rejected as repositories of wisdom and knowledge. Knower is separated from known by the act of *skepsis*—by standing back and looking *at*—and by the tow-headed epistemology of being and not-being, true and false, a binarism that is brought into being, ironically, by Parmenides' and his contemporaries' proliferating denunciations of the pursuit of not-being.

The Poets' Deceptions: *Poiesis*, *Pseudos*, and *Apate*

> Since from the beginning all have learnt in accordance with Homer. . . . Both Homer and Hesiod have attributed to the gods all things that are shameful and a reproach among mankind: theft, adultery, and mutual deception. They have narrated every possible wicked story.
>
> XENOPHANES, Fragments 10–12

> Pythagoras, son of Mnesarchus, practised research most of all men, and making extracts from these treatises he compiled a wisdom of his own, an accumulation of learning, a harmful craft.
>
> HERACLITUS, Fragment 129

> Therefore all things that mortals have established, believing in their truth, are just a name: Becoming and Perishing, Being and Not-Being, and Change of position, and alteration of bright color.
>
> PARMENIDES, Fragments 7–8

The quality of unreliability so consistently attributed to *doxa* is elaborated with equal fury in Preplatonic polemics against "the poets." It is not wholly implausible to imagine that the poets' performances of epic and cosmogonomic *muthoi*—with their narrative "motion" of ever becoming and ever perishing "bright changing hues"—are among the *doxai* of "Not-Being" denounced by Parmenides. This view of the poets' word pictures conjures one import of the Homeric Eris, who travels on the many-colored rainbow to sow dispute by telling different stories. Like the epic "lies," she would be supplanted—by eristic debate—among the Preplatonics' and Sophists' polemical attacks upon tradition and one another.

The unthinking opinions of ordinary mortals are not the only sources of "seeming," of deceptive perceptions and misleading words. These "blind" opinions are alleged to be aided and abetted by the poets and their lies.

True and not-true, reliable and unreliable, are principal dichotomies shaping and shaped by the conceptualization of *logos*. "It has been said, but I say unto you" is a distinction widely used by prophets and teachers. Parmenides uses it to distinguish "my trustworthy discourse and thought concerning truth" (*piston logon ede noema amphis aletheies*) from common opinions (*doxai*) framed as "the deceitful ordering of my words" (*kosmos emon epeon apatelos*).[52] Why does the Preplatonic polemic so persistently emphasize the deceitful and the false? Why was it necessary for the Preplatonics to purchase their truth with the considerable energy they expend denouncing the beliefs, opinions, and perceptions of ordinary mortals as false, and defending the dangerous contention that traditional religious beliefs are deliberate deceptions perpetrated by liars? For *logos* to become the basis of *and* vehicle for inquiry (for reasons that merit more scrutiny than they have received), "ordinary" conceptions of reality and language as well as traditional religion and literature had to be discredited. An almost inordinate amount of attention is directed at defining the nature of the falseness (*pseudos*) and deception (*apate*) in the worlds of opinion and perception inhabited by ordinary mortals, a falseness that is attributed to the poets' words as well.

Heraclitus warns, "The most wise-seeming man knows, preserves only what seems; furthermore, retribution will seize the fabricators of lies and the false witnesses." Not only the form of such *logos* statements but also their eristic iconoclasm link the Preplatonics to one another. It initially appears contradictory that they denounce the constantly shifting stresses and eristics in the world of opinion only to enter the contests themselves. Mockery of Homer, Hesiod, and other revered writers recurs in epithets that are memorialized in Aristotle's rebuke — or is it literary praise? — that "Homer taught the poets to lie." Heraclitus asserts: "Much learning does not teach one to have intelligence, for it would have taught Hesiod"; "Homer deserves to be thrown out of the contests and given a beating."[53] Xenophanes blames the poets for "narrating civil war, every possible wicked story of the gods: theft, adultery, and mutual deception." As an alternative he proposes, as Plato does in the *Republic*, that there should be "decent stories, pure words, noble thoughts and endeavors."[54]

No longer firmly moored by the lulling rhythmic verse and scenic familiarity of epic storytelling, the philosophic discourses of ideas are shaped by another kind of visualization, of words as objects, a possible influence of the reader's eye on the ear that may have functioned as a propaedeutic for the emergence of abstract concepts. At least some forms of visualization and conceptualization would seem to be reliant on writing. Yet Heraclitus denounces Pythagoras' "research," his compiling of wisdom, as a harmful craft. Yielding a similar conundrum, Parmenides employs familiar epic cadences to exhort his audiences to abandon traditional received opinion, including the epic cosmogonies of "the poets." Hesiod, Pythagoras, and Homer himself are denounced by the Preplatonics as fabricators of lies, a battle that bears reexamination as something other than simply a war between writers and nonwriters, between oral poets and literate philosophers. Nor is it simply a war between the poets and the philosophers per se. Parmenides and Empedocles use poetic idioms. But these polemics, and their peculiar focus on lies, and on *poiesis*—understood as fabrication—as lying, can be understood as a war for control over reality and language housed within the disputes over "what is," "being," and "the reliable word." It is this element of the war more than any other that may explain the impassioned denunciations of traditional religion and epic alike as "the poets' lies." The Sophists, conscious perhaps that they were *constructing* their *logos* statements, might have hurled "poet" at the rhapsodists and at other Sophists to impute that "you made it up." Classical philology in this century supports this interpretation with evidence that it was a relatively narrow period—of two to three hundred years—during which a "Homeric tradition" defined religion, cosmogony, and custom through the newly inscribed, performed canon of the *Iliad*, the Homeric Hymns, and the dramas. The philosophers were waging war with other "makers."[55] The poets' "what is" the philosophers defined as "is not," as "not being," as false (*pseudos*), as deception and lying (*apate*). Epistemology, ontology, and veracity are being reassembled in all this, and reconstituted through a pointedly linguistic alchemy.

Concern with veracity and lying as intrinsic to certain kinds and uses of language surfaces early in Greek writing. The Homeric depiction of "cunning" Odysseus portrays a kind of cunning whose suspiciousness and dangerous impiety are also emphasized in the subsequent dramatic portrayal of Oedipus. Both characters are depicted as able to shape reality through denouncing an old way or by luring listeners into a new one. Far from representing a tradition diametrically opposed to that of the philosophers, these poetic depictions and others work in concert with the logocentric philosophers, to the extent that they define a preoccupation with and suspicion of the cunning, blasphemous, or deceitful word. The Preplatonic vocabulary displays several groups of terms that are key players in reshaping this algebra of word and intellect: "reliable" and "dependable" versus "false" and "deceptive" words; the timelessness, motionlessness, and hidden unity of truth and its statement in *logos* versus the always shifting and changing, the ever coming into being and passing away "bright hued" shapes and appearances—that is, the deceptive appearances—of perceived reality and of poetic imitations of that reality. Yet it is the analysis and reflection permitted by the *visual* perception of written words, that may have been an essential condition for the emergence of formal abstract thought. This apparent irony diminishes somewhat with the distinction between perceived words and perceived phenomena and events, when the perceived word—reading—is taken up with a conceptual sequence directed at seeing concepts, as well as words, with "the mind's eye." Metaphoric visual analogies between reading and thought, and emphasis on "seeing" the hidden truth and unity propounded by the philosophers, have left many traces in Western understandings of thought and language. The word "idea" (*idea, eidos*) has etymological roots in visualization, as does the pejorative *eidolon*—"shade" or "idol"—the "mere semblance" that Plato adapts from the term for the ghosts of the dead and uses for poetry and rhetoric alike. With *idea* and *noein* both, the objects and the processes of thought are conceived of as "mental realities," as thoughts that can be thought about, as "insights." The "visualizable thoughts" that were the words, terms, and "forms" of the early Greek philosophers have become permanent lexical fixtures in the grammar of logic and in the syntax of "mature" Western literacy as well.

The formulation of logic and the shape of Attic literacy may well have affected each other synergetically in a reciprocal relationship, unique to that time and place, that entailed the devaluation of older religious and cultural beliefs. With *logos* the Preplatonics banish the scenes and persons, gods and punishments of the epic narrative world. In a remarkably short time, that world has been acclaimed no longer real; it has become "myth," entertaining literature, illusion, a lie. Along with the conceptualization of *logos* as the *one reliable* statement of true realities comes an emancipation of sorts, epic and myth become "poetry," make-believe, fiction; they are forced to relinquish their prior roles as quasi-historical chronicle, religious doctrine, and repositories of wisdom, but are thereby freed of representational and truth-bearing tasks to become play, art, mimesis, and "pleasant illusion."[56] The spread of literacy during this crucial period is of heightened interest in the context of today's transitional literacies, because it is increasingly clear that in any transition from story to statement, from story to argument, there are several modes of literacy vying with one another. Like the Preplatonic philosophers, many of "the poets" composed in writing, as did the dramatists, but their compositions were written for oral performance. They were retelling earlier stories in different ways. Not only as writers but also as speakers, the philosophers increasingly broke with narrative paradigms, verse forms, and oracular ellipses to originate discourse forms that we now associate with literacy: abstract, logically subordinated, self-reflexive, and "fully iterated" exposition.

Havelock's appraisal of sixth- and fifth-century vase paintings points out a "calligraphic" shape in the inscriptions of names and labels adjacent to the scenes depicted on many vases. One example is the François vase of 570 B.C. He suggests that most of its viewers would have recognized the letters as shapes but not much more, and that most of those viewers were probably not readers.[57] The calligraphic aesthetics of early Attic alphabetic literacy suggests what he terms as "craft literacy" in which the shapes and arrangements of the letters and words are widely varied, and guided by the eye. Shape and arrangement as much as acoustic value and meaning seem to prevail. In contrast, the standardized orthography that marks the wider spread of writing and reading promotes social learning: sharing of read texts and shared memory of what has been read, promoting different ways of managing what is available to be read. Over this management, I propose, the philosophers, poets, and dramatists were at war.

Like the "functionally illiterate" of today, most viewers of *stoichedon* inscriptions in the fifth century "were not primarily interested in a quick reading of an important statement, because (so I infer) they could still rely on hearing it uttered in order to be informed."[58] Readers, in short, did not flourish during the Preplatonic era. The alphabetic technology that had evolved in the centuries just before the Preplatonics was brought about not only by the addition of symbols for vowels, but also by the addition of new consonants that permitted the accurate representation of individual, "pure" sounds.[59] Following the line of analysis that has been advanced by Ong and Havelock, among others, this characteristic gave alphabetic transcription of spoken language an independence from syllabic units that assumed a prior familiarity with textual and semantic content. With the alphabet, entirely new statements could be *made*, hence perhaps the use of *poiein* — to make — for "the poets," and protestations of the reliability of "my statements," "my ordering of words," on the part of the philosophers. *Mousike*, the old *paideia* of sung verse and dance, was dying, being slowly superseded by the visual patterns of letters and words, by the "dissecting eye" and analytic spirit that these seem to encourage.[60] Ways of knowing as well as the content of knowledge can only have shifted accordingly, transmitted by seeing the sounds of words rather than by visualizing what was heard. "Writing restructures consciousness."[61] The thought world of the Preplatonics indelibly but ambiguously shaped both writing and literacy as they emerged in the West. Yet it must not be forgotten that for many centuries the majority, even of the educated, did not write copiously as much as they used writing as practice and mnemonics for specialized kinds of oral discourse — public speaking and literary performance. The first "books" — the "writings" of philosophers, speechwriters, and rhetoric instructors — may initially have been not much longer than the Sophists' *schemata* — lists of arguments or phrases.[62]

It may have been in part the phonetic accuracy of the Greek alphabet that made language, once it was written, "an object available for inspection, reflection, analysis." A reader can "look back," quite literally, at what "his oral counterpart could not and never wanted to." Writ large, this alphabetic technology, quite possibly *because* it was conceived of as a *techne*, inaugurated the practice of written literature and history in their modern senses and fostered explicit distinctions between them and oral epic "myth." In this relabeling of genre was also a reconfiguration of the past as linear, of "a past that could separate itself from the present, and from the present consciousness."[63] Is historical fact truth, or record, or both, or neither? Is Homer history? Is Hesiod cosmogony or myth? Are contingently expressed and carefully qualified statements more true than categorical statements? Myriad modern conceptions of truth, fact, and myth underlie these questions. The Preplatonic Sophists' expositions of rhetoric develop cognate questions and insights about how "speech" works. Gorgias' "Encomium on Helen" provides an irreverent but at the same time sobering pronouncement: "When men can neither remember the past nor observe the present nor prophesy the future, deception is easy." It was during this period, when the authority of the orally transmitted memory of the past had been challenged, and the new patterns not yet fixed, that rhetoric came of age.

Preplatonic Rhetoric: Sophists or Statesmen?

> Their persuasions by means of fictions are innumerable; for if everyone had recollection of the past, knowledge of the present, and foreknowledge of the future, the power of speech would not be so great.
>
> GORGIAS, Fragment 11

> Poetry had now become *logos*, which for Gorgias is human communication, but also by definition persuasive communication, for the preserved word had always been so. It could win preservation for itself only as it cast that total spell which the sophists (mistakenly?) sought to retain for oratory.
>
> ERIC HAVELOCK, *Preface to Plato*

> Hippias: What ignominy it is, then, that we should know the nature of things and yet, when we assemble together, we the leading experts [*sophotatoi*] of Hellas, in this sacred hearth of

Hellenic knowledge [*sophia*], and in that very city's greatest
and most magnificent household, in pursuit of that very
knowledge—that we should have nothing to show worthy of
this noble renown but fall to bickering among ourselves like the
most vulgar of mankind.

PLATO, *Protagoras*

At what point, exactly, did the famous *eikos*, the argument from
probability attributed to Corax and Tisias as well as to Protagoras,
begin to be associated with sorcery, deceit, or more mildly, an awe-
some power of the new rhetoric? Aristotle asserts, "The 'Art' of
Corax is composed of this topic."[64] Plato condemns the fact that
Gorgias and Tisias esteemed probability over truth.[65] That the *eikos*
was associated with Sophists of ill repute is suggested by the fact
that even Aristotle—no enemy of arguments of probability—cautiously places the *eikos*, the "Art of Corax," under the heading of
fallacious proofs, and feels called upon to define it at length, providing a careful distinction between proper and improper uses of
probabilistic logic. "Wherefore men were justly disgusted with the
promise of Protagoras, who said he could show them how to make
the worse appear the better argument, for it is a lie, not a real but
an apparent probability, not found in any art except Rhetoric and
Sophistic."[66]

The *eikos* is nonetheless central to Aristotle's systematic divisions
between philosophical and rhetorical modes of logic and argumentation. Even within the *Rhetoric* he divides sophistical from proper
arguments, and Rhetoric from Sophistic as disciplines. Close scrutiny of any one Preplatonic rhetor, Sophist, or philosopher suggests
that the divisions between rhetoric, sophistic, and philosophy that
after Aristotle came to be taken for granted, were far from complete. The early Sophists were also among the earliest rhetors; the line
dividing Preplatonic philosopher and Sophist is less clear when the
forms and terms of their arguments are compared. In this context,
Parmenides' warnings against the Way of Opinion can be viewed as
founding articles of linguistic and logical doctrine. By denouncing
ordinary speech and opinion, Parmenides and subsequent philosophers instigated a fissure between everyday, common opinion and
belief, and the specialized technical rules that came to define and
protect the truths expressed in philosophical language: *logos*. Hence-

forth truth would be restricted to logical validity, a move that shaped the conceptualization and practice of rhetoric as well.

The earliest rhetorical formulas (*schemata*) for legal argumentation were contemporaneous with the Preplatonic philosophers' disputes over being and not-being, sameness and difference, necessity and choice, permanence and change. Though the story of early technical rhetoric has been told many times, an extended account of its links with Preplatonic philosophy awaits further exposition. The relationship between the teaching and theory of early rhetoric and its actual practice remains ambiguous. Were the early rhetors great lawyers, great statesmen, or great speechwriters?[67] Was formal rhetorical training mandatory or elective in the Greek schools of the fifth and fourth centuries B.C.? Did this training primarily prepare students to give speeches, to write speeches for others, or to teach rhetoric?[68] Did the influence of rhetoric spread because it was required training for most, or because it was widely practiced by those who controlled public discourse structures and writing? That there was some association made between various kinds of sorcery and rhetoric is clear enough from the dubiously sincere aphorisms Gorgias embeds in the "Encomium on Helen." "The inspired incantations of words can induce pleasure and avert grief; for the power of the incantations, uniting with the feeling in the soul, soothes and persuades and transports by means of its wizardry. Two types of wizardry and magic have been invented, which are errors in the soul and deceptions in the mind."[69] Parmenides' warnings against the pursuit of not-being parallel these depictions of word sorcery. Parmenides' warnings and Gorgias' ambiguous acclaim share a mantic contour.

Yet the early technical rhetoric of both Sicily and Athens has often been characterized in more homely terms, as a sturdy practical invention born of political necessity, and as comprising a group of technical forensic formulae stimulated by land reforms and democratization. Empedocles, Protagoras, and Gorgias were among the first recognized teachers of rhetoric, and were widely recognized as wordsmiths as well, because they were acclaimed speakers of incantatory power. Gorgias was among the first to play on — and to explicitly refer to — the power and potential of language once it is regarded as a manipulable power. Redefined as "speech" (*logos*), this kind of language comes to be understood as everyday, ordinary opinion (*doxa*), and as common (*koine*). As it becomes known as rhetoric, speech (*rhetorike*) comes to be seen as initiated and controlled by humans, rather than by an inspiring muse or goddess. No longer fixed by necessity, as it presumably had been in a canonical oral tradition, public "speech" was not in the end displaced by *logos* as Parmenides defines it, by an equally fixed body of true statement, though logic did assume the character of an integrated and finite whole without movement or change. "Speech" flourished as rhetoric. Among Sophists and Preplatonic philosophers alike, it came to be officially defined as part of the chimerical, always changing world of appearances.

Why, then, does Gorgias, presumably a promoter of rhetoric, repeat the view of "speech" (*logos*) as deception and lying held by those philosophers who rebuked it? "Their persuasions by means of fictions are innumerable. . . . As it is, when men can neither remember the past nor observe the present nor prophesy the future, deception is easy; so that most men offer opinion as advice to the soul. But opinion, being unreliable, involves those who accept it in equally uncertain fortunes."[70] The opponents of living speech — the *logos*-centered philosophers — from their very beginnings seemingly remained a small, widely scorned minority. If so, Gorgias may here express, with ambiguous force, the views of the multitude. Alternately, he may express but also neutralize the fear and contempt many felt toward the new rhetoric by depicting the powers of speech in language evocative of the Eleatic *epicheirema*, the form Parmenides employs. Gorgias' views parallel the Way of Opinion defined by Parmenides and Heraclitus, and are expressed in a diction that bears stylistic continuities with Empedocles' poetic mode of discourse as well. If Gorgias' is a parodic rendering of the views he propounds, it is much more subtle and philosophical than we would expect of this ostensibly "practical" Sophist in a legation to Athens from Sicily. Gorgias' subtlety may convey mockery of Parmenides' denunciations of any and all opinion in favor of the timeless and unified *logos*. The ironic "manner of Gorgias" referred to by Aristotle is often interpreted as an allusion to the ornate use of "figures" — of antithesis, matching clause and syllable length, and parallel endings. Just as plausibly, the "manner" to which Aristotle alludes is Gorgias' irony, his "dissembling," to make a subtle or ambiguous point by indirection and understatement. This would constitute a double mockery of Parmenides, for not only does Gorgias parody Parmenides' use of incantatory style and terminology, but he further snubs him by "stating that which is not." He deliberately makes a statement that he does not — or cannot — mean. This apparently perverse ambiguity and facility with paradox is further exemplified in Gorgias' proof that nothing exists.

As with many of his speeches, Gorgias' "On Being" became a familiar exercise piece in argumentation. It is recorded in the report of Sextus Empiricus and others. Sextus outlines the argument:

   I. Nothing exists.
      a. Not-Being does not exist.
      b. Being does not exist.
         i. as everlasting.
         ii. as created.
         iii. as both.
         iv. as One.
         v. as Many.
      c. A mixture of Being and Not-Being does not exist.
  II. If anything exists, it is incomprehensible.
 III. If it is comprehensible, it is incommunicable.

The conclusion to "On Being" is a veritable index of Preplatonic themes, now turned on their heads by the kind of tour-de-force reductio that Gorgias and other Sophists — along with Socrates — were famous and disliked for. "Further, speech can never represent perceptibles, since it is different from them, and perceptibles are apprehended each by the one kind of organ, speech by another. Hence, since the objects of sight cannot be presented to any other organ but sight, and the different sense-organs cannot give their information to one another, similarly speech cannot give any information about perceptibles. Therefore, if anything exists and is comprehended, it is incommunicable."[71] Through parodic hyperbole, Gorgias proves the Heraclitan postulate, itself of dubious sincerity, that only a dessicated *logos* can represent truth, and extends it to its logical corollary: that the truth it can represent must be totally imperceptible. Speech, then, cannot say or communicate anything. Yet it is the only vehicle we have for communicating. Opinion, necessarily expressed in speech, is simultaneously false and inevitable.

In the "Encomium on Helaen" Gorgias defines two kinds of "word wizardry": "errors in the soul" and "deceptions in the mind." Parmenides forbade the way of "the opinions of mortals," where "by custom they name two forms"—opposites—"one of which ought not to be."[72] If Parmenides' proscription is applied to early rhetorical practice, we can detect in it a warning against arbitrarily chosen, forced dichotomies, the *dissoi logoi* that provided training in eristic moots and influenced the development of formal dialectic. Is Helen innocent or guilty? Is my client a thief, or a long wronged and loyal husbandman? The client may be neither; but in the then new rhetorical *agon*, jury, judge, claimant, and lawyer must have initially been at a loss as to how to frame the question. The Protagoran *eikos*—resembling truth, likely—came to be recognized, and scorned, as equally a "fiction"—an approximation used to distort questions and manipulate cases. How would the lines be drawn among truth, probabilistic hypothesis, conjecture, and outright but persuasive deception? Like its rhetorical descendants—the topics and commonplaces defined by Aristotle—the *eikos* was, it seems, both entering common usage and in Parmenidean terms an instance of not-being. Even the first of Aristotle's *Categories* might be reviewed as an ontological *eikos* of sorts: does it or does it not exist? Yet once ontology is tied to articulation and demonstration, it enters the world of human control and initiative. Do not bring these word-forged opposites into being, Parmenides warns. If you do, you will be lost forever on that road of the wayward, splay-brained masses, for whom to be and not to be are one and the same.

Gorgias can be understood as defining an alternate way out of this conundrum through the "two types of wizardry and magic" he defines in the "Encomium on Helen." Is it not possible that seeking, cultivating, or propounding timeless essences is what he terms the "deception in the mind"?[73] If so, the "error in the soul" is like unto it. If one knows of, but refuses to participate in, the world of mortals and their opinion—if one classifies opinion, and indeed all human speech, as by its very nature corrupt, deceptive, fragmenting—then one has little imperative for action, decision, effecting change. Is not change one of the forbidden *docta* of Parmenides, for whom that which is, and is real and true, does not change? "Ignore the one way [opinion] as unthinkable and inexpressible (for it is no true way) and take the other as the way of Being and Reality.

How could Being perish? How could it come into being? If it came into being, it Is Not."[74] Perhaps because this attitude can produce a contemplative passivity, Gorgias denounces it as an "error in the soul."[75]

Parmenides seems to be engaged in the this-not-that dividing game himself, when he claims *logos* for himself and leaves all oppositions, comparisons, and degrees—the rhetorical modes, in short—to the sleepwalkers who wander two-headed, always backward turning. This shadow world of mere opinion and half truth, from Parmenides' point of view, is part of the flawed world of an anthrocentristic cosmology.[76] Empedocles, Gorgias' teacher and a student of Parmenides, seems to disobey Parmenidean doctrine when, in some of his antithetical pronouncements, he defends the human mind, language, and senses. The physical world in all its multiplicity and in the ongoing recombination of its elements is a burgeoning plenitude, an ever-changing world of life. It is a "double process" that interests Empedocles: "at one time it increased so as to be a single One out of Many; at another time again it grew apart so as to be Many out of One." Nonetheless, these elements have their own characters and, "besides these, nothing else comes into being, nor does anything cease," otherwise "what could increase the Whole?"[77]

Gorgias' irreverent commentary on the One and the Many draws attention to an implicit logic underlying, and defying, the philosophers' cosmogony. "It [Being] cannot be Many, because the Many is made up of an addition of Ones, so that since the One does not exist, the Many do not exist either."[78] Gorgias calls attention to the systematizing thought that is defining these Ones and Manys in their eternal alternating increase and reassimilation. His logical reductio exposes these "truths" as physical as well as notional, as establishing principles of both physical and conceptual reality—*kosmos, phusis*, and *logos*—principles that are irrevocably other than the worlds they capture in a conceptual language. The One and the Many, paradigms for Aristotle's definition by genus and species, emerged directly out of this cosmology.

The forensic and dicastic necessities imposed by democratization—among a soldier–citizen elite, that is—were not the only sources of early rhetorical theory and practice. Gorgias' surviving texts suggest that, in some cases at least, rhetorical theory and practice were both more theoretical and more directly integrated with the philosophy of the period than has traditionally been acknowledged. Observe the parallelism between Parmenides' list of things that mortals wrongly believe are true and the subsequent rhetorical *topoi*: "To think is the same as the thought that It Is; for you will not find thinking without Being, in [regard to] which there is an expression. For nothing else either is or shall be except Being, for Fate has tied it down to be a whole and motionless; therefore all things that mortals have established, believing in their truth, are just a name; Becoming and Perishing, Being and Not-Being, and Change of position, and alteration of bright color."[79] A similar list is defined in Empedocles' list of "female figures": "Growth and Decay, Rest and Waking, Movement and Immobility, much crowned Majesty, and Defilement, Silence and Voice."[80] These opposites, developed in both Eleatic and Ionian philosophies, and listed as a table of Protagoran opposites by Aristotle, deserve further examination as direct ancestors of subsequent rhetorical *topoi*.

Tisias, Corax, and Gorgias are credited with inaugurating rhetoric as a distinct *techne*. Lists of arguments outlined and then exemplified effective speeches. The terms employed in the early outlines suggest poetic, dramatic, and philosophic precedents; *prooimion*, *agon*, and *epilogos* expanded into the five-part outline reported in the *Phaedrus: prooimion, diegesis, pistis, epipistis, epilogos*. To us these parts may seem obvious parts or modes of all discourse, and so general as to be empty categories. Yet they remain the backbone of both legal discourse and expository writing: an introduction (*prooimion*); a narration of the facts (*diegesis*) or statement of the issue, subject, or thesis; arguments for (*pistis*) and against (*epipistis*) the case as presented; and a conclusion reiterating the point or overall case (*epilogos*). To this outline of the parts of a speech was added a catalogue of "figures" of speech, the "poetic" devices which Gorgias became known for in subsequent rhetorical histories. Yet even these figures and devices seem not to have been thought of as exclusively poetic in any modern sense of that term; they were defined as well by patterns of antitheses that provided logical and syntactic companions to rhetoric, and formal grammar, as well.

Patterns shaped and were shaped by the dramatists' reforms: the addition of a second actor by Aeschylus provided for the dramatic representation of dialogue as well as of agonistic argument. Imported into the Academy, dramatic dialogue, rhetoric, and philosophic *logos* provided Plato with both the media and the objects of his literary representations. In the earliest practice of rhetoric emerges another group of elements, enumerations of arguments and kinds of argument that were understood at first as subdivisions within each part of a speech. Translation presents problems on this point; *logos* is used in varying degrees of specificity to denote "argument," but also "speech," throughout the works of Parmenides, Heraclitus, Empedocles, and Gorgias. *Logos* can mean a hypostatized "law" or "order" or "word-reason," but it is also used to denote a "discourse," "that which I am saying which is true," an "expressed thought," an "argument," or even a "proposition." It denotes at once the general principle through which scattered particulars are gathered, and the principle by which they are arranged. Its etymology implies that *logos* is on one level a *ratio*, a verbal discourse "logarithm." It is both the principle of discourse, hence the translation of *logos* as "discourse" or "power of discourse" in some settings, and the substance or content of discourse thus composed, distinguishing it from *muthos, epos, nomos*, and *doxa*. It is both the principle by which individuals construct true or valid statements, with emphasis on the constructedness of those statements, and the content of such statements once constructed. As prerequisite and precursor to definition (*horizomenos*), it is the process allowing for the establishment of a subject area from which a given discourse proceeds. As organic order or arrangement, it directs the sensible and valid iteration of relevant parts of that subject. Nonetheless, at some point during the first generations of rhetorical practice and theory, the term *rhetorike* comes to define speech making and speeches as a distinct class of *logos*.[81] Subsequently, the relationship between *rhetorike* and *logike*, rhetoric and *logos*-logic, became a perennial bone of contention and source of confusion. Even so, within rhetoric, *logos* continued to denote certain kinds of arguments as well as certain kinds of stories.

During the period 420 to 350 B.C. there emerged a practice and theory of rhetoric that was distinct unto itself. Its elements included the following: (1) a list of the parts of a speech and, in that list, an as yet only implicit paradigm for invention and arrangement; (2) a conception of persuasion based on an observation of audience psychology that would become schematized in Aristotle's notions of *ethos*, *pathos*, and *logos*; (3) a growing list of "figures," the Gorgianic *schemata* of both logical syntactic structures and "poetic" embellishments — ancestors of the schemes, tropes, and figures — which aided the articulation of distinct sections of argument and expression; and (4) a list of topics of argument or kinds of arguments: stasis and change, sameness and difference, is and is not, physical qualities and attributes which Parmenides very briefly emblematizes as "alteration of bright color." Within the next generation, in Aristotle's *Categories* and *Topics* these would become ten kinds of "terms," distinctions among kinds of questions, and statements; in the *Analytics*, rules for predication; and in the *Rhetoric*, heuristics for rhetorical invention and logical analysis.[82] This genealogy was interrupted with memorable force but little practical effect by Plato's treatments of rhetoric and *logos*. I approach his dialogues not only as fluid in genre and philosophical allegiance, but also as standing at midpoint between the taxonomies of rhetoric and logic developed through the end of the fifth century and Socrates' death, and the incrementally more rapid fixation of most forms of speech and reason that had occurred by the mid-fourth century, exemplified not only by Aristotle's teaching but by the shape of his discourse as well.

2

Rhetor and Eiron: *Plato's Defense of Dialogue*

> Philosophy is the true home of irony, which might be de-
> fined as logical beauty, for wherever men are philosophizing in
> spoken or written dialogues, and providing they are not entire-
> ly systematical, irony ought to be produced and postulated.
>
> FRIEDRICH SCHLEGEL, *Lyceum Fragments*

> At the base of the genre lies the Socratic notion of the
> dialogic nature of truth, and the dialogic nature of human
> thinking about truth. The dialogic means of seeking truth is
> counterposed to official monologism, which pretends to pos-
> sess a ready-made truth. Truth is not born nor is it to be found
> inside the head of an individual person, it is born between
> people collectively searching for truth, in the process of their
> dialogic interaction.
>
> MIKHAIL BAKHTIN, *Dostoevsky's Poetics*

> In rhetoric there are the unconditionally right and the un-
> conditionally guilty; there is total victory, and annihilation of
> the opponent. In dialogue, annihilation of the opponent also
> annihilates the very dialogic sphere in which discourse lives.
>
> MIKHAIL BAKHTIN, *Estetika*

In Plato's era a growing lexicon of technical terms and distinctions
abound. Form and content, language and reality, sign and signified

are wedged apart, opening a philosophical and linguistic rift, and precipitating an increasingly diverse array of terms for these relationships.[1] Throughout the dialogues multifaceted examinations of these terms and of the realities to which they refer give voice to numerous concerns about the increasingly conscious and deliberate wedging apart that is often called "separating."[2] Pejorative terms incrementally indict what Plato deems negative elements in rhetoric and writing.[3] The language taught and produced by Sophist, rhetor, and writer alike he terms an *eidolon*, the old word for the shade of the dead, also used of statues, suggesting perhaps that Plato viewed some of the new conceptual languages as ghosts, representations without substance, and chimerical semblances — as "traces" in the Derridean lexicon. Like Parmenides, Plato pointedly attacks those words and uses that are drawn from the lexicon established by always changing custom (*nomos*). The language thus constructed becomes, in his analysis, a travesty of truth, rendering thought and communication unstable. Language user, language itself, he asserts in the *Sophist*, are becoming *eironikoi mimetai* — literally, "dissembling imitators." Plato is no reactionary traditionalist. His attacks on the Sophists and on rhetoric are not designed to promote a return to any traditional values. Like the Sophists, he promotes novel forms of thought and language, and inquiry into those forms. He is among the first to call such inquirers *philosophoi*, a term he uses to distinguish his practices from those of the Sophists.[4] Yet in the *Sophist* the critique of rhetoric and the Sophists is extended to the philosopher; the dialogue concludes with the observation that there are two kinds of Sophists, each a dissembling imitator of truth: "One who can dissemble in long speeches in public before a multitude, and the other who does it in private in short speeches and forces the person who converses with him to contradict himself."[5] The first type of Sophist is the more familiar target of Plato's critique: the sophistic rhetor who cleverly twists his words and dissembles knowledge he does not possess in order to sway public opinion. The second type of Sophist bears a suspicious resemblance to Socrates, whose short speeches and questions in private dialogue often force an interlocutor to contradict himself.

Plato and perhaps even more so Socrates, as depicted in the dialogues, were Sophists themselves in the sense that they contributed to an expanded conception of wisdom, encouraged the development of abstract terms, and provided formal definitions of the

most expeditious settings, goals, and internal structures for philosophizing. In the formulations of Plato's interlocutors can be detected lineal descendants of Preplatonic debates as well as ancestors
of Aristotle's *Categories* — in particular, the five "great kinds" or
"forms" (*megista gene, eide*): being, sameness, difference, change,
and rest. Of these, all but the first had been described by Parmenides as parts of the way of opinion. What, then, distinguishes
Plato, and the "true philosophy" dramatized in dialectical dialogues, from the sophistic abuses which he depicts as a constant
threat to proper philosophizing? I approach Plato's attack on the
Sophists, articulated in part through explicit juxtapositions of dialogue and rhetoric, as being also an analysis of the nature and
effects of literacy. When in the *Sophist* Plato hypothetically extends
the critique of rhetoric, in the guise of "the Sophist," to include the
philosopher as well, he may be viewed as integrating earlier extensive attempts to grapple with the epistemological, ontological, and
cultural consequences of pluralistic linguistic models and assumptions. The pluralism he addresses I appraise as resulting from what
he perceived as a de facto conspiracy among literacy, rhetoric, and
philosophy. If Plato's wide-ranging inquiries are examined from this
vantage point, then rhetoric per se, which is often regarded as the
primary target of Plato's critique, can be seen as but part of a larger
whole. An equally important element in Plato's criticism of the
Sophists, I propose, is his defense of dialogue as an alternative and
antidote to both writing and sophistic rhetoric. The linguistic assumptions which a "dissembling imitation of truth" disseminates
are of as much concern to Plato as the interpersonal ethical abuses
he finds within the rhetor–audience situation. The dialogues suggest that some Preplatonics and some Sophists, Gorgias among
them, provided bases for later theories of linguistic relativism and
indeterminacy when they posited that language and knowledge itself are by their nature fragmentary, incomplete, constantly shifting, fraught with not-being, illusion, and absences.

When Plato analyzes rhetoric and irony, he often depicts them as
dangerous concomitants of the uses of writing and of the formulaic
language models which some Sophists used in their teaching and
practice of rhetoric. The cumulative force of Plato's analysis is to
assert that outlines, building-block names for parts of speech and
speeches, and the agonistic structure that was one legacy of dicastic
rhetoric were fostering linguistic, aesthetic, and ethical instrumen-

talism. An instrumentalist view of language and linguistic interactions is one which posits that language is used primarily to do or make something, to bring into being a new reality, and thereby to effect a change in thinking. In such an ideology of language, wisdom tends to get supplanted by knowledge and knowledge by information.[6] It is the sophistic emphasis on *techne*, one which Plato denounces but thereby sustains in his emphasis on its differences from *episteme*, that is singled out most often as inaugurating such an instrumentalist conception. Through numerous appraisals of the neutral craft concept of *techne*, intentional dissembling — "those slight hypocrisies without which our civilization does not seem to work" — is represented as both rhetorical technique and a consequence of linguistic contingency.[7] The dialogues are both the locus for discussing these issues and exempla of alternatives to linear, monologue, and written discourse paradigms. The defense of dialogue and the critique of sophistic rhetoric are related to each other not only by the structural examples provided in the form of the dialogues, but also through the metaphors of writings and speeches as lost, abandoned children and of speech writers and makers of laws as pasters-together and demolishers of words.[8] *Letter VII* helps resolve the apparent contradiction between Plato's criticism of writing and the fact that the dialogues are written, and facilitates distinctions between writing as a medium and the substance of different fields as well. "Whether it be on law by a legislator or on any other subject, one can be sure, if the writer is a serious man, that his book does not represent his most serious thoughts."[9] He reiterates in *Letter VII* the equation drawn in the *Phaedrus* between writing and abandoned children, and the proscription on putting into writing matters of greatest substance and import.[10] Dionysus of Syracuse is roundly censured for putting an account of Plato's teaching in the form of a treatise, "putting it together as if it were a treatise of his own, quite different from what I taught him."[11]

Writer, Rhetor, *Eiron*: The Sophistic Teachings

Despite the negative connotations given "Sophist" by Plato and Aristotle alike, *sophistes* bore no strongly negative connotations prior to Socrates' era. Instead, "Sophist" and its variants in Greek denoted teachers of philosophy, rhetoric, practical knowledge, and verbal skill who were gradually supplanting the poets at the center of the Greek *paideia*.[12] The dichotomy Plato expands to contrast "true" *philosophoi* with "false" *sophistai* is part of his polemic, though it is not hard to hear in this contrast echoes of Parmenides' Way of Truth and Way of Opinion. When Plato, Aristophanes, and Xenophon speak of the "Sophists," they use the term hyperbolically and with pejorative connotations to refer to all the proponents of the "new education." Aristophanes includes Socrates in the group.[13] Plato's remedies and antidotes to the sophistic teachings can then be understood as improvements from within, generated in and through dialogues that place Socrates among the Sophists. Uses of writing, the nature of memory and knowledge, the paradigms for oral and written discourse, the epistemology and ontology implicit in specific terms and discourse structures, the relationships among an individual, what he says, where he says it, and to whom—these are the subjects of dialogue after dialogue with the Sophists, as the titles of many dialogues indicate: *Gorgias, Hippias, Protagoras, Cratylus, Theaetetus.*

Writing and Literacy

Aristophanes' and Plato's parodies of writing imply that writing was gaining in popularity and was being utilized in several ways, some of which disturbed traditionalists and permitted Plato to appeal to select views held by cultural traditionalists, even though the kind of philosophizing he promoted was largely without precedent. In accounts of how writing should be used, Plato recounts the shame and fear public speakers have if they are seen with a written text.[14] They may be thought "Sophists," a term which in the *Phaedrus* seems to be used as an equivalent to logographer—a wordsmith or "speech writer." Across the dialogues, speech writers, Sophists, poets, and drafters of laws are equated with one another because they use writing; what they write is viewed as bogus, fake, at third remove from reality. Like rhetoric, writing is depicted by Plato and other detractors as an illusory mode of representation, as "mere" technique.[15] In the school curriculum of this period writing was beginning to replace acoustics and repetition, both as a mnemonic and as a medium of instruction. In combination with reading, memorization, and recitation, students other than those specializing in speech or other professional writing were learning to compose in writing, and presumably therefore to produce writings. Yet throughout the previous century and a half—the era of the Preplatonics—interdependent proscriptions of writing, rhetoric, and public debate had been articulated pointedly. Earlier, seventh-century Spartan law explicitly forbade inscribing laws, teaching or practicing rhetoric, or allowing criticism of laws.

If the contention that full or widespread literacy was achieved only during Plato's generation can be provisionally accepted, his objections to writing become much less curious and inconsistent than they at first seem.[16] Revisionist histories of literacy in this period can clarify the place of writing as an object of Plato's attack by putting it alongside his seemingly unrelated critique of the Sophists. Although the poets had been composing in writing beginning in the eighth century, writing skill was arguably not widespread until the fifth. Even by the fifth century there was as yet no "corresponding increase in fluent reading." It may not have been until the middle of the fourth century that the transition to full literacy had been accomplished. Thus the fifth century, the era of both the Preplatonics and of Socrates, constitutes a period of craft literacy, or semiliteracy in which writing was taught at the elementary level, but reading skill was rarely taught, and then only in adolescence.[17] The fifth-century evidence also permits the conclusion that in that era the term *biblion* denoted not books but single sheets, or notes, tabular manuals which were little more than lists, texts of speeches that, much like scripts for drama, were written as scripts for a discourse that would be delivered orally.[18] Most "literary" rhetorical works—as we know from fifth-century rhetors and later from Plutarch's report—were initially "published" orally. Public inscriptions were virtually the only form of widely available, readable text; the spelling and orthography of the inscriptions are erratic and, as often as not, more calligraphic than reliably phonetic. Inscriptions on vases are similarly idiosyncratic by our standards; it is unclear whether the letters were decorative or communicative or perhaps a bit of both.[19]

The Kulix of Douris (c. 480 B.C.) portrays a "writing" lesson[20] where three students stand, each facing a seated teacher. One teacher holds a scroll up so that it faces the viewer of the vase, not the student. Another holds tablets and a stylus and looks at a tablet, while the student stands in front of him. The scroll facing the viewer of the vase contains two fragments: Homeric hexameter opening lines, but with faulty spelling and transitions. The position of the teacher's stylus in the second case indicates he is writing something, not correcting with the flat ("eraser") end. Reinterpreted in this way, the scroll held up to the viewer arguably represents a schoolroom situation in which the student is given the first three words of a longer passage which he is supposed to have memorized. The erratic spelling may suggest that he has garbled the recitation. In the second case, contrary to traditional interpretations, which see in it a depiction of the teacher correcting a student's written composition, it is plausible that the teacher is depicted writing a theme or free composition which he will then ask the student to memorize and recite.[21] Though writing figures prominently in this writing lesson, it may be the means and not the end of the lesson. Until Socrates' era, records of classroom practice as well as jokes linking writing with childish exercises indicate that writing was still regarded primarily as a child's exercise used in memorization and recitation. The primary pedagogical medium seems still to have been predominantly acoustic and oral. Plato alleges dangerous links between writing and Sophists: the Sophists not only teach the speechmaking *techne* using writing as a mnemonic; they compose and write speeches for others.

References to manuals for rhetorical composition in the *Phaedrus* and to "compendia" of selections from the poets in book 7 of the *Laws* hint that the traditional oral *paideia* that imparted the ability to memorize whole pieces by heart was being impaired or superseded by the spread of writing and reading habits.[22] Though reading was still less common than writing, it was nonetheless beginning to shape the composition of rhetorically structured discourse invented on the spot by public speakers who were using the models provided in written manuals, outlines, and later, as Lysias' speech in the *Phaedrus* suggests, full texts of speeches. Reading, writing, and rhetoric converged in many different ratios to supplant the cycles of speaking and hearing that had been shaped by earlier oral learning and its memorization patterns. The speaker in the assembly had to come up with something on the spot, and was trained for this in the eristic moots exemplified by the *dissoi logoi*, formulaic statements of contrary propositions.[23] Writing was used in this training in outlines which were filled in extempore; in composing an entire speech, which was then memorized verbatim; and in compendia of quotations which were memorized like maxims and could be inserted at appropriate points in a speech composed in the heat of debate.

If we examine Plato's critique of writing against these uses, it appears much less inconsistent with his own practice of writing than at first glance, where Plato seems to overemphasize the mnemonic and composition-drill exercise aspects of writing over its more substantial capabilities for preserving and transmitting culture. The warnings Plato articulates, particularly in the *Phaedrus*, are directed primarily at the introduction of writing instruction at the elementary level in the late fifth century, and at the practice of delivering a prepared, written speech in the assembly, particularly when the speaker was not its author. Plato's polemic implies that, for all but professional writers, the classroom use of writing would be shed with maturity and with a concomitant "internalization" of the material and stylistic patterns it had imparted, and that mastery and performance of an oral, acoustic milieu were still the objectives of education. The attack on writing in the *Phaedrus* also suggests how the content of rhetoric was increasingly guided by writing. Phaedrus remarks that the great public speakers are afraid to leave written speeches behind them lest they be called Sophists.[24] This can only mean that writings were ridiculed, and that those who produced them were suspected of ambition or pretense. Knowing how to write—that is, perhaps, having gone to school—was prestigious, but distributing writings or speaking from a written text were regarded as bad form. Plato's remarks may be intended to appeal to cultural resistance to the fact that reading and memorization of written texts were replacing the older aural mnemonics of a curriculum that remained centered in *mousike* as late as the 480s.[25] Phaedrus' remark also suggests that not all practicing rhetors were Sophists; that many had come up through the ranks as practicing statesmen; and that few, perhaps, wanted to admit that they had paid a ghostwriter, or even to give that appearance by being seen with a written text.

The myth of the invention of writing told by Socrates in the *Phaedrus* addresses an entirely different and perhaps more complex phenomenon—the possible psychological and cognitive effects of using writing as a mnemonic in the classroom and elsewhere. Socrates says that students who use writing in this way receive "a quantity of information without proper instruction," and that, paradoxically, they become "forgetful."[26] They "know" many things, but without any guidance (*soi genomenoi aneu didaxes*), therefore they "know" less. They recall, but cannot remember. He charges that, by depending on "external signs" rather than on their own "internal resources," students come to confuse recollection with memory, and information with knowledge. These "confusions" had perhaps always been present in the oral *paideia* through which students learned to recite epic poetry to music, but the fixed form and content of epic poetry were neither "information" nor "knowledge." Socrates' objections to the Sophists' use of writing, then, parallel his objections to the uncritical absorption of the epic encyclopedia that had been the rule during the poets' *paideia*. The parallel is only partial, however, for the content of Attic rhetoric was distinctly different from the content of the Homeric canon in several ways. The Sophist taught speakers how to arrange and articulate "matters," views, and arguments, using exempla from reality, the poets, or other speeches. Plato's lengthy analyses of sayings (*rhema*), everyday talk (*lege*), sounds (*phonai*), and true meaning-bearing discourse (*logos*) are more than records of the grammatical and semantic quibbles which divided one group of Sophists from another. His interlocutors define and sort out the proliferation of kinds of discourse which were being generated helter-skelter—in Plato's view—and clarify the substance of these distinctions in relationship to memory, recollection, information, knowledge, and opinion. Both writing and compositions memorized from written texts foster, in Plato's judgment, confusions among the distinct discourse modes which the *philosophoi*—the producers of "true rhetoric"—are just beginning to comprehend and deploy.

Even discounting a certain degree of polémical venom directed at the Sophists and at sophistry, the distrust of writing and writers expressed in Plato's era contrasts sharply with the view of early Greek literacy developed by nineteenth-century philologists. In trying to account for the anomalous rise of abstract, scientific philosophy in Greece between the seventh and fifth centuries B.C.—the "genius" of Greek thought—historians posited an early, widespread, and sudden emergence of a comparatively sophisticated literature, the Homeric canon. Out of this, the nineteenth-century story goes, an inexplicably precocious Greece evolved historical, cosmological, and then scientific–logical texts that were presumed to be written for mass — albeit educated and aristocratic — consumption. Recent studies of circulating manuscripts and reading habits make this hypothesis next to impossible to defend.[27] Reports indigenous to the era further erode the plausibility of an early, widespread reading literacy. If literature, literacy, and writing were firmly entrenched and highly valued by the fifth century B.C., why the scorn and ridicule of writing and its teaching in such great "writers" as Aristophanes and Plato? Throughout the period bounded by Aeschylus' *Suppliants* and Plato's *Letter VII*, numerous passages express a mistrust of the written word, and particularly of the document detached from the writer.[28] It remains an enigma that Attic Greece was alone among the cultures of the ancient Near East in never developing a scribe culture of the kind that had the effect of dividing power between the warrior caste and the "men of skill, trained to use the clumsy elaborate script system."[29] Unlike the scriptural religions that prevailed in the kingdoms of Judea, Egypt, and Asia Minor during the same period, Attica had no heavily centralized king–priest–scribe hierarchy. Solon's reforms, and the imposition of a limited democracy during the same period, seem only to have intensified earlier Hellene resistance to centralized and hierarchical authority.[30] Viewed in all these contexts, Plato's objections to writing, though expressed in writing, are no more inconsistent than Aristophanes'. Aristophanes is not writing books to be bought in the marketplace, but plays to be performed; he writes scripts. Similarly, Plato is not writing a treatise, but a dramatized dialogue that represents Socrates engaged in a discussion during which he objects to monologue treatises and enacts an alternative to them. Reports of reading habits and philosophical schools in second-century B.C. Alexandria as well as in Cicero's era indicate that the Platonic or Aristotelian dialogue remained a preferred genre for philosophical writing, and that the philosophical schools remained centered oral discussion as a medium. As with Plato's, philosophical dialogues were often read aloud or performed at evening symposia, after which they would be discussed.[31]

Comparing Plato's analysis of the technology and psychology of writing with his critique of rhetorical discourse and dissembling, as parts of a defense of philosophical dialogue, illuminates parallels which are otherwise far less clear. The content of received, canonical Homeric literature, hypostatized as "the poets," is attacked as *doxa*, unexamined opinion, and as an "imitation" or "idol" of reality. Both rhetorical and written discourse, or at least the kinds of rhetorical and written discourse to which Plato objects, are said to be—wrongly—produced according to outlines and rules. For this reason they too are "semblances" (*eidolai*). They are shells, as it were, with specious, if any, content. Each of these formulaic discourse types was objectionable to Plato *because* it was formulaic, or in the process of being formulized, as much as because it was written. Not only writing and rhetoric, but also deceptive or at best deliberately manipulative forms of probabilistic reasoning—the *eikos* in particular—were being taught in the Sophists' schools. In Plato's analysis, writing lends itself to giving the appearance of knowledge in two ways. First, two of its physical qualities, that it can be memorized and also circulated, make it a powerful mnemonic as well as an ostensibly complete representation or "container" of knowledge and truth. These uses of writing and of writings, Plato argues, foster confusions among memory, recollection, information, and knowledge. Second, since writing can appear to "say" things on its own, it encourages the production of deliberate misrepresentations. Moreover, he charges, writing does nothing to foster thought; it induces repetition and intellectual laziness, traits that link it explicitly to Parmenides' Way of Opinion and Plato's own renunciation of the poets elsewhere. Writing, as then deployed, is judged by Plato to be an enemy to the development of philosophy and intellection. These elements in the critique of writing developed in the *Phaedrus* run against modern claims that literacy brought about or facilitated Greek philosophy and science.[32] Instead, Plato's account depicts writing as analogous to rhetoric and poetry: it is less open to question or challenge than the viva voce exchange of philosophic dialogue. Far from stimulating inquiry, writing forestalls it.[33]

Rhetoric

Fifth-century attitudes toward writing, including those articulated by Plato, suggest some of the reasons why Greece provided so propitious a setting for the emergence of rhetoric. Greek epic and rhetoric embody the primacy Greeks had long given to the spoken word, verbal cunning and craft, the poet's song, and finally the suasive powers of the rhetor.[34] Sicilian rhetoricians allegedly imported rhetorical "manuals," the *schematai* and the *eikos*, to Attica. Solon, Pericles, and other military leaders, together with dramatic depictions of Homeric characters, were Attica's first indigenous "teachers" of rhetoric.[35] Until the Sophists formulized specifically forensic patterns and gave these patterns technical labels, there was a looser terminology for suasive speaking which bore traces of its epic and dramatic origins well into Plato's usage.[36] The poets' performance of Homeric epic had been one channel through which cultural wisdom and quasi-religious values were transmitted in a performance that represented, modeled, and preserved specific forms of discourse. Thus the orators stepped into a performative, acoustically sensitive, audience-oriented situation. It was precisely this readiness on the part of the audience to be lulled by acoustically hypnotic cadences and familiar, visually vivid phrases that Plato objected to. Yet like the Preplatonics, he had to adopt or adapt some of these familiar discourse patterns, if he was to communicate at all, and he did.

Plato borrowed the dramatists' dialogue form to represent the philosophical discourse process used by Socrates. Like the script to a drama, Plato's dialogues represent exchange, interaction, response; the give-and-take of philosophical process cannot be captured by expository or narrative form. Unlike these genres, Plato's dialogue is bereft of sustained monovocal sequences or of narrative details describing facial expressions, inner feelings, or motives.[37] Through this spare medium, shorn of the familiar *epos* and *muthos*, Plato presents and examines the Sophists' rhetorical teaching. He charges sophistic rhetoric with giving an appearance (*phainesthai*) of knowledge without its substance, and with using probabilities (*eikos*) and semblances (*eidolai*) to persuade an audience. Tisias' alleged teaching on probability is parodied in the *Phaedrus*: "There are even some occasions when both prosecution and defense should positively suppress the facts in favor of probability, if the facts are improbable. Never mind the truth—pursue probability through thick and thin in every kind of speech; the whole secret of the art of speaking lies in consistent adherence to this principle."[38]

The Sophists, according to Plato, were teaching rhetoric as an art of persuasion (*peitho*) that would allow the rhetor to dispense with knowledge of any other art. "Socrates: There is no need to know the truth of the actual matters, but one merely needs to have discovered some device of persuasion which will make one appear to those who do not know to know better than those who know. Gorgias: Well, and is it not a great convenience, Socrates, to make oneself a match for the professionals by learning just this single art and omitting all the others?"[39] This definition leads Socrates to term rhetoric a "semblance [*eidola*] of a branch of politics."[40] If the rhetor's material is apparent and not true knowledge, and if he is trained to prefer probability to truth if it will be more persuasive, he becomes a "dissembling imitator" (*eironikos mimeta*) of truth.[41] Plato's condemnation of writing as the empty physical representation of what is already a representation of thought—speech—parallels this attack on rhetoric as an illusory semblance (*eidola*). Rhetoric and writing are then in this view alike, thrice removed from what they represent. Plato asserts that rhetorical speeches are semblances of genuine political exchange because, when Sophists represent or write speeches for others, they are producing substitutions, "stand-ins" for knowledgeable political discourse. Rhetoric's double jeopardy is not only that it is thrice removed as a representation. Its equally serious flaw is its deliberate incompleteness. It is a partial, "slanted" representation of an issue; its power depends on a probabilistic logic, the *eikos* (apparently or seemingly true, having the marks of truth). Its final damnation is rendered by Plato's judgment in simultaneously ethical and epistemological terms. Rhetoric can succeed only for as long as the audience is less knowledgeable than the speaker. In this, he charges, rhetoric purposefully perpetuates mass ignorance.

In the literature stretching from the Preplatonics through Plato, *doxa* is used to denote this "ignorance," the content of the minds of the many, the masses, those who prefer belief and received opinion, received "doctrine," to knowledge. Parmenides equates them with "sleepwalkers." Heraclitus speaks of those who cannot distinguish waking from sleeping, and compares them with those who hear but do not understand. Yet Parmenides and Heraclitus are themselves somewhat doctrinaire didactic orators, engaging in prophetic lience even as they denounce other word weavers for creating pretty lies. Much like Plato's Socrates, they rebuke and abuse their listeners at times in order to wake them up. A generation later, Plato attacks any and all public speakers for abusing their audiences in much more insidious ways, abuses that are central objects of his attack on rhetoric. It is the manipulation and thereby perpetuation of traditional, received, "conventional" beliefs that Plato opposes in the rhetors. Objections to the poets' uses of *doxa* are extended to the new generation of wordsmiths, the rhetors and Sophists who were Socrates' contemporaries.

"*Doxa* is therefore well chosen as a label not only of the poet's image of reality but of that general image of reality which constituted the content of the Greek mind before Plato. Its general significance prevailed in the end over its poetic one. If it originally united the two, this is precisely because in the long centuries of oral culture and oral communication it was the poet and his narrative that bore the responsibility for creating the general vision and preserving it and fastening it upon the minds of succeeding generations of the Hellenes."[42] *Doxa* denoted not only "opinion" or "belief" but also the explicit decisions made in the assembly meeting, a meaning that persists in "doctrine," denoting a collectively acceded to and thereby warranted belief. *Doxa* may be understood as the content not simply of traditional poetry or religion but of rhetorical speech as well. The "material" of rhetoric, once conceived of as such, was a storehouse of the incremental, traditional, and always changing beliefs of the culture—the *koinoi topoi*. This storehouse, once formulized, began to function as a preserver, arranger, and transmitter of cultural knowledge—as a noetic economy[43] unto itself. Though it functioned, much like epic before it, as a storehouse, its design and structure were quite different from the orally transmitted, acoustically fixed poetic canon. Rhetoric was not a repository of fixed canonical, "classic" epic narratives. It was shaped instead by a period when malleable, adaptable, "component" discourse patterns were needed.

Viewed as itself a form of *doxa*, rhetoric can be understood as a replacement of one kind of opinion with another, in a context of new discourse structures and new modes of authority where there was as yet no weight of tradition to ground or check its substance, forms, and suasiveness. It was the apparent truth—historical and philosophical—of the new argumentative structures, alluringly laced with quotations from traditional poets, which formed a particularly insidious combination, in Plato's view, and prompted no doubt the long list of pejorative terms and phrases he uses in his attacks on "the poets" and rhetoric alike: idol, semblance, imitation, information without knowledge, dissembling, deception. Was the activity of manipulating opinion with opinion possibly more powerful in Plato's context than in our own? Today opinion no longer carries authority; instead of defining a ruling, albeit unexamined, paradigm, opinion functions more often as a qualifier: "it's just my opinion"; or it denotes a group of widely held but debased views, as in public opinion polls. Plato's account and others describe the perception that just when some of the Sophists were beginning to get a grasp on knowledge, other Sophists subverted that effort by selling a watered-down version of it. Plato depicts the rhetoric practiced in the public square and courts as nothing more than the substitution of one order of *doxa* for another. The "error" of poetic semblance, which he disparagingly terms *mimesis*,[44] is only reduplicated and multiplied in rhetorical commonplaces, probabilities, and structural outlines for persuasive speeches on any subject.

Plato's critical account of the rhetorical manuals of his period provides a list of structures and strategies that have remained remarkably constant for two millennia, paradigms that can still be found in the table of contents of many writing textbooks. Through several exaggerations and outright errors in his review of the "composition manuals" of his day, Plato alleges that the Sophists' teaching of rhetoric was far from standardized or consistent, and that it was not yet fully distinguished from the diverging philosophical schools which would coalesce and promote alternative technical logical formulae for definition, dialectic, induction, and syllogistic proof. Prototypes of these logical and rhetorical processes appear in Plato's tabular outline summarizing "the technical manuals":

1. an introduction (*prooimion*)
2. a statement of the facts supported by the evidence, testimony, or witnesses (*diegesis, marturia*)
3. positive proofs (*tekmeria*)
4. arguments from probability (*eikoi*)
5. proof and supplementary proof (*pistosin, epipistosin*)
6. refutation and further refutation (*elenchon, epexelenchon*)
7. insinuation (*hypodelosin*)
8. indirect compliments and indirect blame (*parepainos, parapsogos*)[45]

In the discussion that follows this list, Gorgias and Tisias are cited as originators of the teaching that "probabilities are more to be esteemed than truth." They "make small things seem great and great things small by the power of their words, and new things old and old things the reverse."[46] Protagoras is cited as a proponent of "correctness of diction, . . . tearful speeches, . . . rousing large companies to wrath, and soothing them again by his charms when they are angry, and most powerful in devising and abolishing calumnies on any grounds whatsoever." Finally, in a baldly contradictory assertion, Socrates remarks that "all seem to be in agreement concerning the conclusion of discourses, which some call recapitulation [*epanodos*], while others give it some other name." Phaedrus says; "You mean making a summary [*kephalaioun*] of the points of a speech at the end of it?"[47] An indirect import of all this is that neither the process nor the name for the "recapitulation" or "summary" are the least bit agreed upon. Other contradictions and errors lurk as well. Aristotle and subsequent classical sources permit the conclusion that Plato here reverses important elements in his portrayal of Protagoras and Gorgias. It was Gorgias who was known for his florid language and "emotional" appeals, and Protagoras who endured long-standing rebuke as the originator of the claim he could make 'the greater appear the lesser cause' [*logos*]." To complicate matters further, Aristophanes makes the *eikos* an invention of Socrates, and it appears in the list of charges against Socrates in the *Apology*.[48]

In the *Phaedrus* Socrates juxtaposes two serious countersuggestions to the sophistic methodologies he has irreverently summarized. First, he recommends "taking a synoptic view [*sunaoreon*]," bringing together in one idea the "scattered particulars," "to make clear by definition [*horizomenos*]" the particular thing which will be discussed.[49] Then, he proposes, one must go back and divide the general idea into its natural subdivisions (*to palin kat'eide dunasthai temnein*), taking care to follow its inherent order.[50] These two processes together form *diaeresis*: mixing and separating, going back and forth between definitions of the general idea and testing it against its particulars until an improved understanding has been reached. Testing by question and answer extends this procedure further, clarifying the issue and generating further statements for discussion. This larger sequence Plato terms dialectic. "Is there anything worth having that can be systematically acquired if it is divorced from dialectic?"[51] For "dialogue," "dialectic," and "inquiry" the terms *dialektike* and *dialegesthai* alternate most frequently, with an occasional *koine skepsis* that emphasizes not only the structure but also the communality of such inquiry. Yet throughout the dialogues there emerges no single consistent or coherent account of an entire process, start to finish, of dialectic, dialogue, or philosophizing. Indeed, the *Sophist* concludes with the somewhat ominous conjecture that the Sophist and the philosopher are one and the same.[52] A rationale for the absence of a systematic characterization of dialectic is expressed in the enigmatic comment in *Letter VII*, to the effect that the most serious thoughts cannot and should not be put into writing. The account of *diaeresis* given in the *Phaedrus* provides only a faint outline, a trace of the full procedure being recommended. Why? Very possibly because to formulize dialogue or dialectic — "true rhetoric" — would be to render it a rule-governed *techne* and thereby to open it to the very charges Plato brings against writing and rhetoric as *technai*.

Plato contends that terms and statements cannot be manipulated in meaning or used to manipulate others if they are persistently submitted to the scrutiny of dialectic, because dialectic requires the active involvement of both speaker and listener. The speaker must listen, the listener must speak. In contrast the rhetorical arts, as he represents them in the discussion of manuals in the *Phaedrus*, depend on creating discourse structures and techniques that deliberately avoid defining terms, and comprise monologue discourse modes designed for use in situations where the testing of dialogue dialectic does not and cannot take place. It is unlikely that the terms Plato lists are a completely fair representation of the technical rhetorical terms and practices of that period. Yet they cannot be totally inaccurate; Plato's rendering heavily emphasizes manipulating indirectness, incompleteness, and informal modes of proof. The *tekmeria* that follow the narrative of the facts are "proofs" by sign or probability. They join the witnesses (*marturia*) in support of the narrative "testimony" or "report" that defines the issues of the case. These converge with the *eikos*, the Protagoran argument of probability, as direct predecessors to the rhetorical enthymeme as it would come to be defined by Aristotle: "rhetorical argument" which begins with "either a probability or a sign."[53] Plato's summary of the rhetorical manuals also provides traces of Preplatonic disagreements over logic. Among the rhetoricians, the many understandings of *logos*, its nature, and its uses were merging with the Sophists' rhetorical *technai* and manuals. Alternately, the *technai* of logic and those of suasive rhetoric had not yet been divorced from each other, as they were to be in Aristotle's definition of the science of logic as an analytic method, a distinction that placed logic in sharp contrast to the practical *technai* of rhetoric.

Plato's appraisals of rhetoric anticipate many of the lines of this immanent divorce: for the practical and strategic reasons iterated in Aristotle's *Rhetoric*, the suasive orator should not define his terms too exhaustively. To such strategic ambiguity Plato strenuously objects. The testing of terms and propositions in a dialectical dialogue, which Socrates offers as a replacement for monologue rhetoric, was also practiced as eristic by Sophists and rhetors, but often — and this is arguably Plato's point — in a deliberately obfuscating manner: the techniques of gerrymandered definition, refutation and supplementary refutation, insinuation, and indirect praise and blame are joined with existing rhetorical applications of ever more elaborate and indirect refutative arguments (*elenchus*). The Megarians in particular were known for practicing forms of dialectical debate structured as question and answer. Zeno and Euclides, among others, developed a more radical strategy, a monologue dialectics in which the argument itself was posed in interrogative form. The Cretan Liar paradox attributed to Zeno, the Megarian reductio ad absurdum, and the elenchic rebuttal of inferences which could be derived from premises rather than of the premises themselves, provide further evidence of the burgeoning interpenetration of rhetorical with logical paradigms.[54]

Plato's criticism of rhetorical formulae and strategies is consistently epistemological and ethical in emphasis; he proposes that rhetorical purpose, broadly understood as discourse context, is as much a determinant of meaning and acceptability as logical validity. His defense of dialogue dialectics should be reappraised in this context as something more than a defense of a logical, truth-seeking, question-answer structure centered in definition and *diaeresis*; it is directed with equal force at making a case for the necessity of interpersonal good will and collaborative purpose. These latter, and not logical truth alone, distinguish dialogue from public assembly speechmaking. In the *Gorgias*, Socrates' exchange with Gorgias emphasizes Plato's concern with the ethical, interpersonal context that he defends as a necessary condition for philosophizing. Gorgias persistently maintains that rhetoric is by definition for use "before a crowd"; he refuses to define it outside that context.[55] Socrates retorts that the rhetor's knowledge is always specious because "in a crowd" means "among the ignorant," a point that Gorgias readily concedes. Socrates argues that in speaking before crowds the rhetor uses techniques that Gorgias says are neutral, neither good nor bad, in ways that deliberately mislead the audience, because that audience, by definition ignorant, will not be able to distinguish between what appears to be true and what really is.

Plato further charges that many Sophists instruct the rhetor to deal in persuasion with no reference to truth, and in situations where that omission will go unnoticed by the audience. In these objections to the public setting of rhetoric, Plato characterizes rhetoric as a culturally sanctioned species of dissembling. One of numerous examples of this emerging view occurs in his considerations of the eristic moots. Among the philosophers the *dissoi logoi* — proofs of opposite propositions — might be a useful propadeutic for inquiry and a mind-sharpening, if agonistic, exercise. Plato presents Socrates using precisely this technique on many occasions, particularly with a villainous Callicles or Thrasymachus. But "among the ignorant" and "before a crowd" the same argumentative and logical structures become ethically and philosophically questionable. It is the dual — epistemological and ethical — problem of dissembling or imitating truth which impels Plato's "hunt" for the Sophist that is taken up in the dialogue that bears that name, and leads to its concluding conflation of rhetor, philosopher, and *eiron*.

Irony

In Plato's time, *eiron* was a term of rebuke, meaning "you dissembling scoundrel"; *eironeia* denoted deceptiveness through guileful understatement or masking of self. It was not until Aristotle that irony denoted anything other than despicable, mocking pretense.[56] Thrasymachus hurls *eiron* at Socrates in the *Republic*, and there it is clearly meant abusively. In the *Sophist* it means "dissembler, pretender," with strong negative connotations. That "Socratic irony," as early as Aristotle, came to denote a philosophically subtle and aesthetically sophisticated manner of articulation should not keep us from observing that Socrates and Plato use it to denote dissembling and deceit. Interestingly, it is Gorgias as often as Socrates whom Aristotle uses to illustrate an exemplary ironic manner.

The multiple meanings and values which irony has accumulated in Western literary aesthetics make it difficult to defend the contention that Plato's equation of rhetor, philosopher, and *eiron* is damning. Yet it is impossible to ignore the prominence of Plato's emphasis in the *Sophist* and *Gorgias* on rhetoric as dissembling toward and thereby manipulating "the ignorant." Irony and rhetoric continue to depend on a guileful wordsmith duping, however temporarily or clearly, of a guileless audience. The very patterns which Plato warns against have become habitual; both rhetoric and irony are viewed as tolerable, inevitable, and even attractive instances of guile. Yet before these attitudes became entrenched by precisely the practices Plato tries to avert, neither irony nor rhetoric could have meant what they have since come to mean. In composing his objections to writing and rhetoric, Plato emphasizes the availability and accountability of the speaker or writer to the audience. He prefers viva voce discourse to written discourse because in dialogue any speaker's meaning can be immediately confirmed by a question from a listener. Dialogue discourse is preferable to textual or rhetorical monologue discourse because there is less likelihood of misunderstanding and, concomitantly, more likelihood of a productive process of inquiry. Plato develops the position that deceptiveness is an inherent and sometimes deliberate function of monologue discourse, whether written treatise or rhetorical speech. The metaphors of abandonment, idolatry, and phantasms help deploy an ethical–epistemological critique of the layers of misrepresentation and the degrees of distanciation introduced by monologic discourses.[57] Plato likens writings to abandoned children, and to orphans who die or live homeless without a parent to tend them; they circulate without "protection" among those who can and those who cannot understand them. Rhetorical speeches and texts alike are depicted as phantasms and chimeras, as illusory semblances of meaning, truth, or knowledge, engaging those who create them and those who accept them in a kind of idolatry, mistaking the image for the reality.

Gorgias, like subsequent defenders of both irony and rhetoric, argues that linguistic idolatry and semblance making are inevitable or, at the very least, already in practice, and furthermore that language itself is an inherently neutral *techne*, consisting of always changing conventions (*nomoi*). Plato objects to the establishment, by fiat and practice, of the view of language that Gorgias represents, a view that persists in contemporary linguistic science as exemplified by Saussure: "The word 'arbitrary' calls for comment. The term should not imply that the choice of the signifier is left entirely to the speaker (we shall see below that the individual does not have the power to change a sign in any way once it has become established in the linguistic community); I mean that it is unmotivated, i.e. arbitrary in that it actually has no natural connection with the signified."[58]

From this viewpoint rhetoric, grammar, genre, and mode are regarded as neither good nor bad in and of themselves. Gorgias asks, does the wrestling teacher go to trial for murder if one of his students kills someone in a wrestling match? Extending the example to rhetoric, he proposes that there are no inherent or predictable consequences of a given discourse structure. Aristotle replicates Gorgias' defense of rhetoric as morally neutral: "What makes the sophist is not the faculty [of rhetoric] but the moral purpose."[59] These defenses beg the question that Plato poses — a more difficult, fundamental question concerning an emergent epistemology spawned by the conceptualization of linguistic indeterminacy. Plato asks, if people are taught, explicitly or implicitly, that speech in both an everyday and a technical sense deals with the construction of apparent, probable, or contingent truth, and that its effect is to "influence opinion," won't they be increasingly likely to use it in just that way? The ultimate triumph of the Sophists will then be their absorption into consciousness and the assimilation of their views into cultural practice. Once rendered invisible in this way, they will become assumptions about the nature of language, and concomitantly about human nature as well.[60] Plato's depictions develop this line of argument with concerns that are broadly cultural and ethical, comprising questions of semantics and epistemology as well as of the relationships between language and truth, and of the beliefs that determine the nature and uses of knowledge.

The Gorgianic and Aristotelian defenses of rhetoric as a neutral *techne* rest on the belief that public or political discourse is already of a certain kind or nature, in place and contingent, inevitably changing in meaning because of the nature of *nomos*, and incapable because of its "common" contexts of approaching any philosophic or scientific truth. Paradoxically, the notion of linguistic contingency developed in these views is paired with the notion of semantic autonomy: Gorgias' statement "If it is comprehensible, it is incommunicable," and Aristotle's tabular conceptualization of syllogisms. The notion of discursive or conceptual autonomy anticipates subsequent characterizations of textual meaning centered in the view that a discourse or text, once "completed," is to some extent independent of its originator and its original audience alike, intact in meaning, and no longer seen as determined by their place in any sequence or context, or as determined by the accessibility of the intended meaning of the speaker. Instead, discourse becomes interpretable in a way epitomized by Ricoeur: "Hermeneutics begins where dialogue ends."[61] Interpretation assumes a situation in which several different, sometimes equally defensible meanings can be ascribed to the same "text." The Sophists who were contemporaries of Socrates and who provided students with model speeches for memorization enacted this principle, and were expanding a component-parts approach to rhetorical composition. The rhetor of Plato's era was, in short, being taught to exploit the linguistic indeterminacy which results from semantic autonomy, a paradox that occupies many of Plato's efforts at averting the burgeoning pluralism of beliefs and practices in his era. Classical models for rhetorical speeches, the rules of predicate logic, and many subsequent methods of textual interpretation have maintained that what a written discourse means, once it is articulated, is "fixed" by writing in varying degrees and becomes independent of the contexts of intention and understanding that shaped its original expression. Plato's position is noteworthy in its unwillingness to impose this independence or to restrict the conceptualization to the notion of semantic autonomy enclosing truth. Two bases can be defended as underlying his refusal. In the *Sophist*, Plato's examinations of true and false statement and of discourse as a "class of being" establish that an utterance is not capable of being fully detached from the ongoing context of discourse and that it is always either true or false. For Plato, setting, sequence and context are not only necessary compo-

nents of meaning, but also indispensable criteria for epistemological and ethical evaluation. In contrast, Aristotle divorces "rhetoric,
poetry, and prayer" from "true and false discourse," a category he
reserves exclusively for logic.[62] Emphasizing a different basis for
discourse and truth, Plato posits that each speaker's good will and
candor must be simultaneously semantic and ethical, so that with
and through interlocutors there can be a common inquiry into
the meaning of terms and propositions.

In examining false statement, Plato presents arguments which
sustain an interpenetration of ethical with semantic categories.
How does he get from "false" to "deceitful" to "ironic"? Through
addressing a certain kind of self-awareness and intention—though
not intention in all the senses it has today. For Plato, if an individual says something which is factually true in order to deceive the
listener, the meaning or comprehensibility of the statement is for-
feited, and it constitutes a far greater crime than inadvertently saying something which is not true, or, as with the unregenerate rhetor,
conflating knowledge and opinion. "For some of these imitators are
simpleminded and think they know that about which they have only
opinion, but the other kind because of their experience in the rough
and tumble of arguments, strongly suspect and fear that they are
ignorant of the things which they pretend before the public to know.
. . . Then shall we call one the simple imitator [*haplon mimetes*]
and the other the dissembling imitator [*eironikos mimetes*]?"[63]
Only the latter receives full moral censure on the grounds that the
knowing dissembler undermines the very canons of truth. This segment of the discussion in the *Sophist* also considers whether discourse is a "class of being." Through the existence of discourse our
ability to discourse exists. "If we were deprived of discourse we
should be deprived of philosophy . . . ; we must come to an agreement about the nature of discourse, and if we were robbed of it by
its absolute non-existence, we could no longer discourse."[64] The
discussion has also established that "not-being" exists as one of the
"classes of being permeating all being," but only insofar as understanding something entails knowing the "other," that is, what something is not.[65] This premise is extended to discourse as a whole, so
that the question becomes, does not-being mingle with opinion
(*doxa*), speech (*lege*), and discourse (*logos*)? If not-being does mingle with these, then both false opinion and false discourse come

into being: "To think or say what is not—that is, I suppose, false-hood arising in thought [*dianoia*] or in words [*logos gignomenos*]."[66] This portion of the discussion concludes with "if *falsehood* exists, then *deceit* exists" (my emphasis), a conclusion which jars the modern reader in part because of predicationalist biases that have dictated an axiomatic distinction between reference mistakes and deceit.

The terminology Plato uses persistently links saying something which is not with falsehood—the Parmenidean concern. So far so good. A corollary is then drawn that links falsehood (*pseudos*) with deceit (*eironeia*). False discourse is defined as any discourse which states nonentities in any context other than the clearly labeled dialectical discovery of what is, which must be pursued at times by separating what is from what is not. Herein lurks Plato's way around "Father Parmenides'" proscription of inquiry into what is not. The statement of nonentities outside the context of dialectical heuristics understood as such by all participants constitutes, Plato charges, a "production" of falsehood. The production of such false-hoods is then paralleled to the production of illusory images and to mimesis. "Since the existence of false speech and false opinion has been proved, it is possible for imitations of realities to exist and for an art of deception to arise from *this condition of mind*."[67] This art of deception (*apatetike*) is held to be destructive of discourse itself. Here again can be noted an interpenetration of moral and semantic flaws that defines subtle differences between self-destructive lying and irony on the one hand, and Socratic dialectic on the other: "To take pleasure in thus always bringing forward opposites in the argu-ment—all that is no true refutation, but is plainly the offspring of some brain that has just begun to lay hold upon the problem of realities. For certainly, my friend, the attempt to separate everything from everything else is not only not in good taste but also shows that a man is utterly uncultivated and unphilosophical. . . . The complete separation of each thing from all is the utterly final oblit-eration of all discourse. For our power of discourse is derived from the interweaving of the classes or ideas with one another."[68] If com-pared with the tabular summary of rhetorical manuals in the *Phae-drus*, this catalogue can be seen as defining, with very different purposes, what is being learned between the lines of the "neutral" rhetorical *techne*. The logical, analytical procedures of *dissoi logoi* proofs pro and con the same thesis, the elenchic questions challenging explicit or implicit premises of an opponent, the breaking down of a statement into its parts — these are linked not only with an unproductive argumentative procedure but with conditions of mind, as it were, that permit immature contentiousness, destructiveness, and finally an abandonment of discourse altogether. Further, Plato proposes, if separating everything from everything else and bringing forth opposites in argument are not directed at subsequent synthesis, integration, and understanding, then the agent of those separations is guilty of a simultaneously epistemological and moral crime.

The Elean Stranger proposes that dialectic should not be taught to anyone other than those who "pursue philosophy in purity and righteousness."[69] The sophistic dialectician "runs away into the darkness of not-being," like the Sophists who "strongly fear and suspect that they are ignorant of the things which they pretend before the public to know."[70] This parallel links the rhetor's pretense and irony, understood in its pejorative Platonic sense, as deceit or dissembling. Even if they deny the existence or accessibility of truth, the Sophist-trained rhetors work in a situation where the audience lacks the sophistication that permits a distinction between truth and opinion and thus will be deceived. One quality that reveals this trait of the sophistic rhetor in public argument is his fear of being discovered as a pretender — a fear that Plato links to his aggressiveness in debate, as well as to his "running away into not-being." Perhaps for these reasons, in the *Sophist* the motive of the speaker, the nature of what is said, and the exploitation of an audience's ignorance merge in Plato's critique to condemn sophistic rhetor and sophistic dialectician alike.

Plato's "True Rhetoric": Dialogue

The *Theaetetus* opens with a short dialogue between Euclides and Terpison recounting how it was that Euclides brought the transcription from Megara and why he chose to write it as he did. Like the frame in some of the other dialogues, this proemic narrative provides evidence of the dialogue's origin and functions as an authenticating pedigree. The *prooimion* also offers an explanation of how and why the text has been adapted "for convenience" into a particular kind of dialogue form. Euclides explains that he has omitted some of what Socrates "actually said": the interlocutionary narrative phrases such as "and then I said," "and then he agreed, saying. . . . " Terpison concurs that this is a more accurate and direct account of the exchange.[71] We might suspect Plato of a subtle joke in providing this frame. He does not, after all, include a dialogue explaining how Plato acquired Euclides' text. The frame could be dismissed as good fun, as a simple allusion to narrative economy or dramatic craft. However, Plato's denunciations of drama and poetry should warn us against assuming that he is exercising playful poetic license. While he does analyze the forms of discourse, he does not normally play with them in the modern aesthetic sense. To do so would constitute what he has defined as false rhetoric: deliberate misrepresentation, guile, and the manipulation of forms as art for art's sake. Given these concerns, it is hard to defend the view that one aim of the dialogues is to encourage a willing suspension of disbelief or, conversely, a belief in the illusion that a dialogue is "really" taking place. The sequence of dialogues that begins with the *Theaetetus* focuses relentlessly on the formal conventions of written, spoken, rhetorical, and philosophical language as vehicles of thought, communication, law, and knowledge. Recurrent queries entrench the view that the forms of language should neither be confused with nor regarded as constituting realities in the physical and conceptual worlds.[72]

Instead, Socrates and, in the *Sophist*, the Elean Stranger, lead their interlocutors in an "escape" begun in the *Phaedrus*—the "divine madness" through which philosophers transcend the restrictions of opinion (*doxa*) and convention (*nomos*). Only by transcending *nomos*—custom, tradition, and conventional linguistic usage—can the mind apprehend concepts in and of themselves without mediation by physical phenomena or by conventional linguistic representations. The process depicted in the dialogues is one of always approaching but never achieving full apprehension of *eidos* and *idea*. The deliberately revolutionary epistemology and lexicon Plato is in the process of evolving seems to be moving toward a conceptualization of knowledge not as content per se but as sight understood as insight. When the *eides* or *ideai* are appre-

hended through discourse with others with the mind's eye of comprehension, they supplant both the old gods and conventional opinion, both *doxa* and *nomos.*[73] An orchestration of old and new
forms of discourse permeates the dialogues, alternating with each
other in surprising and instructive ways. In the *Phaedrus* Socrates
defines as a god-given "madness" the escape from human convention, only to then employ a poetic convention—the metaphor of a
prisonhouse—to characterize human convention. Plato adapts an
extant dramatic convention—a dialogue "script"—as the best medium for presenting Socratic philosophizing. "True rhetoric" can be
transcribed as dialogue and elude the pitfalls of monologue treatises
because, Euclides claims in the frame of the *Theaetetus*, it most
cleanly and without intrusion presents the interpenetration of subject, persons, and structure. The *Theaetetus* and *Sophist* focus persistently on how syntax affects understanding; the form, as well as
the give-and-take of the discussion, become an epistemological and
ontological paradigm for discourse as one of the "classes of being."[74]

Plato's promotion of dialogue as "true rhetoric" emerges slowly,
and among other themes, in the *Phaedrus, Gorgias, Theaetetus,*
and *Sophist*. The metaphorical equation of rhetoric with love is a
well-known and stirring theme of the *Phaedrus*, and one which
complements Plato's other metaphors of communal enterprise and
mutual care.[75] These are more than, because prior to, metaphors in
the sense of "mere" literary devices, since they also figure as ontological enterprises, simultaneously depicting and "bringing into being" dialogue as "true rhetoric" and as the "true home" of knowledge. In portraying love and escape, which figure so prominently in
the *Phaedrus*, metaphors of family relationships, procreation,
birth, and other combining, generative processes recur in the depictions of dialogue. Verbs denoting blending, mixing, mingling, sharing in, and weaving are used to characterize the relationship among
words in a sentence, as well as the relationship among sentences in a
discourse. The metaphor of maieutics—midwifery—figures in the
examination of knowledge and philosophical inquiry in the *Theaetetus*. The compatible metaphor of parents and offspring is introduced with similar import in the *Phaedrus*, to depict the relationship which should exist between individuals and their thoughts and
utterances.

The metaphors of mixing, blending, and weaving not only define relationships among ideas (*eide*) and classes (*gene*) of being, but also characterize the processes of stating and discoursing. It is the act of collaborative synthesis, more than any other single process, which Plato emphasizes with the terms "mixing," "weaving," "blending," and "sharing in." These terms characterize the sentence, the smallest unit of *logos* (discourse), as a web (*sumploke*), and the objective of discoursing as putting together (*sunaoreo*). The *diaeresis* of definition and analysis are preliminary steps in a process which leads toward understanding, portrayed as weaving and blending ideas and classes of things in sentences which are then tested. Statement making does more than just name something. It gets us somewhere by interweaving verbs and nouns.[76] The characterizing of statement making as simultaneously grammatical and epistemological mental activity aligns the logic of statement making with an account of the spirit in which statements should be made. "Those names [*onomata*] which are spoken in order and mean something do unite, but those that mean nothing in their sequence do not unite."[77] While apparently tautological, this depiction of grammatical entities with a sense-making utilizer of those entities keeps the collaborative context of discourse strategically visible.

Modern logic and grammar typically treat words as minimal units of referential meaning. Plato's characterization emphasizes that nouns alone do not have meaning; as in Parmenides' characterization, they are "merely" names (*onomata*). Those that are woven together in order *and* mean something do not simply mean, but unite. "Our power of discourse is derived from the interweaving together of the classes or ideas with one another."[78] The modern academic ear prefers, perhaps, the terms "if–then," "since," and "therefore," which occur in parts of the *Sophist* and persistently in the *Parmenides*. They are more familiar logical connectors and seem clearer, evidence that philosophy has come to be associated with abstraction, with progressions "from the opaque to the clear" and from the vestigally metaphorical to the purely logical.[79] But in a sense the "mixing together," "blending," "weaving," and "mingling" verbs are clearer. Could Plato have indicated by this alternation among terms that he is not attempting an independent logical lexicon which will stand on its own, independent of the mixer, blender, or weaver?

The metaphor of maieutics appears in the *Theaetetus*, where it is used to characterize the relationship among the individuals engaged in a dialogue, their mutual enterprise of helping one another give birth to ideas. Socrates likens himself to a midwife in an extended analogy which begins with the announcement that his mother was a "brave and burly" midwife.[80] The midwife, he asserts diaeretically, is also the true and only matchmaker, a facility which he parallels with the philosopher's ability to put classes of things together in order to produce the best offspring: truth. "I tell you this long story, friend Theaetetus, because I suspect, as indeed you seem to think yourself, that you are in labor, great with some conception. Come then to me, who am a midwife's son and myself a midwife, and do your best to answer the questions which I will ask you."[81] The sequence of this discussion not only illustrates *diaeresis* leading up to dialectical question and answer; perhaps more important, it also emphasizes and necessarily defines the purposes and nature of such inquiry.

Maieutics is used throughout the dialogues to represent the kind of relationship that should exist among interlocutors in a dialogue. Their good will and trust of one another are as essential as their candor in saying what is true, hard as that may be. This is far from easy or "natural." Plato intimates that it is a labor as hard and painful as that of physical birth. In dialogical exchange the *dianoia*, or inner dialogue of thought, is brought into the world of interlocution only with the help of each interlocutor's maieutic relationship to the others. Each guides the others' attempts to say what they are trying to say by candidly responding when they find error, ambiguity, or wrong intent. Dialogue, particularly when defined as a heuristic and epistemological enterprise, is reconstituted by Plato as far more than a random exchange of opinions, or just "talk." Less formal and less purposive ordinary conversation generates a mutually constructed reality. When interlocutors have the sense of helping each other find words to talk about a subject—when they both have an interest in and wish to know about or seek understanding of that subject—there is a maieutic exchange going on. As a more formal, directed procedure, dialogue brings into being mutually constructed terms and statements, and culminates in mutually "constructed" understanding. In this it is diametrically opposed to the asymmetrical, adversarial, and agonistic imposition of one view or argument (*logos*) on another, the pattern that Plato censures in both rhetoric and writing. In contrast, maieutics characterizes the attitudes which the participants in philosophical dialogue should have toward one another, and extends the verbs — the blending, mixing, mingling of terms and propositions — to include a larger set of attitudes and purposes among interlocutors. The participants in dialogue should be trying to give birth to meaningful and productive discourse, jointly "authored" — parented, nurtured, and nourished — by the blending voices of the dialogue. The interlocutors "plant seeds" in one another, and are "parents" of truth and understanding in one another.[82]

The metaphor of parents and offspring is employed in the *Phaedrus* and *Letter VII* to define the responsibility of individuals for the discourse they produce. Whether a statement has meaning — its semantic substance — and what a statement refers to — its semiotic or referential viability — are tied through this metaphor to a parental relationship between individuals and their utterances or writings. By equating what an individual expresses with offspring, Plato emphasizes an inviolable connection between genesis, context, and meaning, a pointed rejoinder, perhaps, to Parmenides' banishment of coming-into-being and passing away. The meaning of a statement comprises its authors' avowal of what they say; their good will and care for those they speak with, as well as for the discourse they produce; and their willing placement of their own discourse in dialogue with that of others. It is for this reason that "true rhetoric" cannot be stated in a monologue, in a "treatise," or implicitly, in a written dialogue. "Even the best of such compositions can do no more than help the memory of those who already know; whereas lucidity and finality and serious importance are to be found only in words spoken by way of instruction, or, to use a truer phrase, written on the soul of the hearer to enable him to learn about the right, the beautiful, and the good; . . . such spoken truths are to be reckoned a man's legitimate sons, primarily if they originate within himself but to a secondary degree if what we may call their children and kindred come to birth, as they should, in the minds of others."[83]

Both meaning and instructiveness — *apodeixis* — are grounded equally in the forms of the dialogue process and in the speaker's attitude and manner; they are not measured solely by the "content" of the discourse. Plato's analogy between written treatises and abandoned children implies insurmountable limitations in written texts. "Once a thing is committed to writing it circulates equally among those who understand the subject and those who have no business with it; a writing cannot distinguish between suitable and unsuitable readers. And if it is ill-treated or unfairly abused, it always needs its parent to come to its rescue."[84] The correct treatment of any subject is to be found only "when a man employs the art of dialectic, and, fastening upon a suitable soul, plants and sows in it truths accompanied by knowledge. Such truths can defend themselves as well as the man who planted them."[85] These comments immediately precede a recapitulation of the subject which began the *Phaedrus*: Lysias' speech writing and, more generally, the speech writing and discourse patterns which shape rhetoric. Drawing on the Preplatonic metaphor of sightseers and sleepwalkers, Plato presents the view that the use of a written, prefabricated speech, whether in private or public, marks its user as "unable to distinguish between dream and waking reality," and that what is written is a phantasm—a ghost, a shade of the living.[86]

In *Letter VII* the parallel denunciation of Dionysus of Syracuse for writing a treatise focuses on the impossibility of formulating a discursive summary of the products, the "offspring," and "fruits" of dialogue and dialectic. If Dionysus "has written anything on the first and highest principles of nature, he cannot to my way of thinking have had any sound knowledge of the subject on which he writes; if he had, he would feel the same reverence for truth as I, and would not have dared to expose it to discredit in a world with which it is out of tune."[87] Dionysus, it is charged, has failed to understand that neither the process nor the content of dialogical inquiry can be stated discursively, because "content," understanding, and truth reside in the participants' ongoing pursuit of truth attended by knowledge amid a common life. "It is not something that can be put into words like other branches of learning; only after long partnership in a common life devoted to this very thing does truth flash upon the soul, like a flame kindled by a leaping spark. . . . If I thought that any adequate spoken or written account could be given to the world at large, what more glorious life work could I have undertaken than to put into writing what would be a great benefit to mankind and to bring the nature of reality to light for all to see?"[88] Here it is alleged that the partitioning of discourse, and its removal from its "true home" — dialogue — will inaugurate a succession of semblances, phantasms, misunderstandings, and abuses, all occasioned by what in the *Sophist* is termed the detachment, separation, "cutting into bits" of parts of discourse. Whether analyzing a sentence or depicting the entire enterprise of discoursing and understanding, Plato consistently uses "detachment" and "abandonment" to emphasize that method alone cannot produce or contain truth. "It is only when all these things, names and definitions, visual and other sensations, are rubbed together and subjected to tests in which questions and answers are exchanged in good faith and without malice that finally, when human capacity is stretched to its limit, a spark of understanding and intelligence flashes out and illuminates the subject at issue. That is why any serious student of serious realities will shrink from making truth the helpless object of men's ill will by submitting it to writing."[89] "True rhetoric" is one among several phrases Plato employs to characterize dialogue discourse, and to contrast dialogical philosophizing with the kind of philosophy that some, he charges, seek as a superficial veneer, "like the tan some get by exposing themselves to the sun."[90] Practitioners of monologue discourse and treatise writing are not the only Sophists charged with flaws in form as well as substance. Those who take discourse apart without reassembling it, or who discourse solely to take apart, violate the Parmenidean dictum quoted by the Elean Stranger in the *Sophist*:

> Never let this thought prevail, saith he, that not-being is.
> But keep your mind from this way of investigation.[91]

To separate each part of discourse from every other is destructive; to say that which is not is falsehood; if falsehood exists, deceit exists. To pursue the question of whether what is not has existence is to run the risk of bringing into being what is not, falsehood, and the machinery for manifold strategized deceits. Among its many other themes, the *Sophist* etches the very fine ethical and epistemological lines that distinguish the evil destructive negator from the good philosopher who uses analysis to test, refine, and reformulate ideas. Yet the *Sophist* concludes, disturbingly, with a conflation of philosopher and Sophist that is dubious in its sincerity.

Dialogue and Dialectic: The Philosopher as Sophist

Despite his recurring definitions of proper philosophizing and true rhetoric as both dialectical and dialogical, Plato gives no little attention to the contingencies of meaning and intent which result from even a properly dialogical exercise of dialectic. His depictions of dialectic as the Socratic method of seeking truth through asking questions, and as testing by question and answer, are superseded in the *Sophist* by the notion and practice of dialectic as a more technical procedure: as the logical technique of arguing opposing propositions. The *Sophist* revives the *dissoi logoi*, and forges through their structure of opposition and exclusion an expressly parodic commentary on them. Yet the technical—though not particularly eristic—depiction of opposing propositions shifts the balance of the conceptualization of philosophy and logic ever so slightly toward the detached self-containment accomplished in Aristotelian dialectic. Incremental arguments and examples drive toward the conclusion that a wholly analytic and negative dialectic will result in the destruction of discourse: opposing propositions, rather than interlocutors' different statements in dialogical settings, become the "materials" of dialectic, so that the attempt to sustain an integration between dialogue and dialectic is seriously undermined. "Is it [the statement] opposite?" is a very different question from "Do we disagree?" or "Are we saying the same thing?" or "Is this true?"

In the *Sophist*, organized as a diaeretical "hunt" for the elusive Sophist and his true nature, there is much scrupulous exercise of definition, *diaeresis*, and dialectic as question-answer-question. Since one goal of the discussion is to isolate what it is that the Sophist does that is sophistic, there is a maddening doubling up of terms. Like other dialogues, the *Sophist* draws its structure and form in part from what it is about. The processes and terms of the discussion find their alter egos not only among the interlocutors but also in the elusive subjects of the discussion. The diaeretical procedure works heuristically to bring about a sometimes painful epistemological and linguistic self-consciousness. The initial analysis of nouns and verbs and their combination leads into an examination of sophistic or improper forms of their combination. In the case of the Sophist, that which "is not" is carved away, leaving hopefully "what is." This in turn produces a conundrum. If the Sophist *is not* the true philosopher and if he *is* the perpetrator of falsehood and deceit, there next emerges the question of whether defining his being is itself an instance of the forbidden: bringing not-being into being. The quest is an amusing and — dare it be said? — sophistic exercise in the chimerical qualities of definition. At another level, and in connection with a different issue entirely, the *Sophist* embodies a seemingly unavoidable result of linguistic self-consciousness. The analysis of nouns and verbs and propositions, especially when cut off from the larger enterprise of philosophizing with others on a subject, seems to engender a proliferation of notions of linguistic arbitrariness and contingency, a momentum that is increasingly palpable as the *Sophist* progresses.

In other dialogues Plato alleges that the Sophists exploit the fact that audiences prefer to be delighted and flattered in their unexamined opinions rather than be challenged with an unfamiliar truth, so that the Sophists become peddlers of a dissembling imitation (*eironikos mimetes*) of truth. Paradoxically, the relationship between Socrates and his interlocutors in the dialogues, and more subtly, the character of the Elean Stranger in the *Sophist*, has struck many as paradigmatically ironic. Socrates seems to be pretending ignorance only to outstrip his opponents in a display of seemingly eristic debate. For the purposes of argument, he seems to state positions which he doesn't really hold, only to show how flawed those positions are once his listeners have agreed to them. He asks his interlocutors in seeming good faith to define "justice" or "truth," only to proceed by a series of questions to refute their definitions. In all this, Socrates seems to be the skilled practitioner of the very rhetorical tactics which Plato denounces, and concomitantly to be a master ironist. However, a close examination of what it is that Socrates *does* leads to the realization that he doesn't really fit the role of *eiron*, despite the fact that he later came to serve as its exemplum.

Socrates' motive is not what it seems. It appears to be aggressively interrogative, but it is didactic and maieutic as well. The truth of his individual statements is dubious, in the sense that he says things he doesn't mean, says the opposite of what he means, or gives answers which he rapidly converts into questions. He seems, in short, to use all the tricks Plato condemns the Sophists for. Close scrutiny of Socrates' logic chopping and manipulative dissembling illuminates a composite portrait of Socrates in dialogical exchanges that conveys a subtle lesson, just as Plato says dialogue should. Socrates pretends ignorance, not knowledge, a distinction which immediately separates him from the Sophists but also seems to place him in the camp of the *eiron*. However, it is his conclusions, and not his questions, that are fictions, and they recur in dialogues which never conclude. Still, Socrates' motive seems to be to frustrate and tease his audience as much as to engage in helpful, benign maieutics, a quality in Socrates that Kierkegaard characterizes as a negative ironic attitude far deeper than mere dissembling. "He brought the individual under the force of his dialectical vacuum pump, deprived him of the atmospheric air in which he was accustomed to breathe, and abandoned him. The expression 'know thyself' means: separate yourself from the 'other.'"[92] Socrates' questions and testing of his interlocutors' thoughts deprive them not only of received opinion and common knowledge, *doxa* and *nomos*, but also of the more recent *doxai* and *nomoi* embedded in and being disseminated by the rhetorical *technai*. The complementary element missing from Kierkegaard's portrait of Socrates is the theme of freedom from convention amid a maieutic and lifelong common life. It was a much later tradition, I propose, the Cartesian setting of self-imposed epistemological isolation, programmatic doubt, and the experience of thinking in isolation, that sharpened the instruments of alienation and abandonment to which Kierkegaard objects. Though the notions of social and spiritual isolation implicit in Kierkegaard's portrait had gradually come to characterize the isolated "scholar" above and apart from the common world, and the ironic detachment which such isolation sometimes brings with it, these notions of alienation and of irony were born in a much later period, and ignore the communal enterprise so central to both the conceptualization and the practice of Plato's dialogues. The recurrent criticism of eristic debate, negation, and monologue discourse, the objection to one individual's treatise or speech or point of view as always inadequate, should serve as warnings against any easy reduction of Plato's Socrates to the Cartesian and Faustian contours he was given in subsequent philosophical and aesthetic traditions. Nonetheless, as Kierkegaard's vignette so brutally asserts, Socrates and the Sophists, as depicted by Plato's Socrates, are of a kind.

Knowledge and understanding, as they were being constituted by

Socrates and the Sophists alike, are marked by the ability to see distinctions and to define opposites. The nature of the truth is said to be clearer, and capable of being clarified, only with some understanding of the false. Even at the levels of syntax (literally, "putting units together") and grammar ("writing") — subjects which are given one of their first systematic examinations in the *Sophist* — the view is developed that statements can be *made* only by separating, by knowing the difference between, one part of speech and another. But the "weaving together" of these forms also implicitly relies on an ability to make distinctions. Collaborative thinkers can separate and divide in order simply to separate and divide, or can separate and divide in order to know better and to understand not only "things," but ultimately, and only through and with each other, truths and meanings.

Socrates' refusal of his interlocutors' yearning for conclusions may seem teasing, but is crucially different from the sophistic rhetor's or *eiron*'s pretended omniscience. The Socrates given us by Plato doesn't teach conclusions. Nor does he give the impression that he really knows. Instead, he gives the impression — sometimes playfully, often irritatingly — that he does not know, as he teaches the processes of dialectical inquiry through dialogues that are presented as evolving among colleagues. Segments within each dialogue exemplify the failing of this ideal, as assorted tough guys refuse to accept the rules and indeed attempt to refute the rules in word and deed alike. Emphasis on the interlocutory context of dialectic is also embodied in the characterization of dialectic as the art of "true opinion," and by its juxtaposition with rhetoric as the art of false opinion. The dialogical dialectic presented by Plato may be viewed as an improved version of the rhetoric as then practiced, and Socrates the "true philosopher" as an improved version of the eristic and sophistic dialectician. Aristotle's depiction of rhetoric and dialectic as methodological counterparts (*antistrophai*) attempted silence on the issue of rhetoric's truth, and became the authoritative, definitive alignment for several subsequent traditions. Plato's solution to the dichotomy between dialogue dialectic and rhetoric — to unify both under dialogue — nonetheless continued to influence conceptualizations of philosophical rhetoric, and preserved an awareness of the rhetoric of philosophy.

I have re-viewed Plato as attempting to temper the contingencies

he saw being disseminated by Sophists and rhetors alike. By inventing and promoting the dialogue form, he created an alternate and
an antidote to what he judged to be ethically dubious and epistemologically corrosive practices. The conclusion to the *Sophist* seems to
subvert his enterprise by collapsing the distinction between Sophist
and true philosopher. In this, however, lurks a subtle irony. "Objec-
tively," that is, through a technical exercise of definition, *diaeresis*,
and dialectic, a definition of the Sophist has been constructed.
"The imitative kind of the dissembling part of the art of opinion
which is part of the art of contradiction and belongs to the fantasy
class of the image-making art, and is not divine but human, and has
been defined in arguments as the juggling part of productive activity—he who says that the sophist is of this descent and blood will, in
my opinion, speak the exact truth."[93] This deliberately technical
exercise of dialectic has produced a definition which stands in ironic
relationship to the truth: that there *is* a difference, and a very
substantial one, yet the form of the concluding statement intimates
that the difference cannot be technically defined. The conclusion
can be read as itself a dissembling imitation of truth, by way of
implying that all definitions, if technical, are also imitations. The
techne of rhetoric, and now the *techne* of dialectic as well, if we take
the portrait in the *Sophist* at face value, are components of an
increasing formulization and institutionalization of rhetoric to
which Plato objects. One way of exemplifying the inadequacy of
both these *technai*, indeed of any *techne* per se, is to enact the abuse
being described. The result is irony, but an irony which points a
finger at the more clear-cut irony of imitating truth and may thereby
be the first instance of the maieutic therapeutic irony characterized
as a possibility in Kierkegaard's magisterial appraisal of irony: *The
Concept of Irony, with Constant Reference to Socrates*. "When irony has been mastered in this way, when the wild infinity within
which it storms consumingly forth has been restrained, it does not
follow that it should then lose its significance or be wholly abandoned. As philosophers claim that no true philosophy is possible
without doubt, so by the same token one may claim that no authentic human life is possible without irony. . . . Irony is an excellent
surgeon. For when irony has been mastered, as previously re-
marked, its function is then of the utmost importance for the personal life to acquire health and truth."[94] From this perspective

emerges the possibility that it is a parody of sophistic definition which concludes the *Sophist*, as a means of emphasizing by example the excesses in overly technical definition and logic chopping which the Elean Stranger has expressed throughout the dialogue. Yet it is the Stranger who articulates the concluding definition. Both the arguably parodic quality and the suspiciously conclusive substance of this passage hint that it is not to be taken seriously. The phrase "in my opinion" evokes the opinion-mongering Sophists and at the same time conveys the Socratic message that philosophizing is the art of true opinion. If this is a practice of true opinion, the Socratic crime of dissembling by claiming to speak "the exact truth" has been committed. Anyone trying to get at the exact truth will necessarily utter opinion. But to say that "this, in my opinion, is the exact truth," is a deftly crafted self-contradiction on one level, and a dissembling assertion on the other. The true philosopher says, "in my opinion" to denote that what he says may or may not be the exact truth. The Sophist, on the other hand, would never actually say "in my opinion," because to do so would subvert his apparent authority.

Those of us who are proper Socratic dialecticians should be suspicious of these combinations. If we detect that this passage violates both the letter and the spirit of earlier dialogues, we have learned something; a paradoxically maieutic relationship emerges among reader, the Elean Stranger, Theaetetus, and the Platonic voice constructing the dialogue. If we assume the context of maieutic dialogue, the motive behind the seeming conclusion becomes apodeictic — a test that can ultimately further our understanding. In the double and triple entendre there is much teasing and much irony, as those terms are now understood. Today's critical and interpretive machinery encourages us to define and appreciate such irony in ways that Plato would probably disapprove of and that are out of keeping with his definitions of dialogue. It is of course impossible to know his intent conclusively or to know what he meant, in writing the conclusion to the *Sophist*; like all writings, this one wanders helpless without its parent to come to its rescue. Yet the blatant self-contradiction of concluding a dialogue on the dangers and impossibility of comprehensive final definitions with an "exact" definition forces us to become interlocutors, and not merely interpreters, and thereby participants in the possibility of a textually deployed dialogical discourse.

While he was not successful in replacing rhetoric with a merger of dialogue and dialectic, if indeed that was his attempt, Plato successfully articulated the importance of the interdependent relationship between understanding a speaker's motives and understanding what is said. If regarded as a record of sorts, Plato's account traces how pervasively rhetoric, as a hierarchical discourse system, was effecting changes in assumptions about the nature and functions of language. In linking rhetoric with the *eiron*, Plato effectively describes how both rhetoric and irony parallel each other as linguistic sensibilities shaped by asymmetrical, dominant–subordinate interactions that require all participants to allow for the possibility of pretense and dissembling. To allow for that possibility, Plato shows, is a fundamental assumption implicit in rhetoric and in irony, an assumption about language that undermines alternate criteria of truth, knowledge, and meaning. Irony can be seen as a belief about human nature as well. It has come to function as a perceptual context, a stance by which we apprehend utterances and texts with an awareness of the possibility of duplicity. One of Wallace Stevens' supreme fictions captures this delicate equipoise of linguistic self-awareness and nascent duplicity:

> Logos and logic, crystal hypothesis,
> Incipit, and a form to speak the word
> And every latent double in the word.[95]

In the span of the century separating Parmenides from Plato, philosophical discourse had outgrown its epic and poetic forbears, had been adapted in various forms to the requirements of rhetoric, and had generated a lexicon which would permanently alter the contours of formal thought in the West. Many, including Plato's Socrates, disobeyed Parmenides' proscription of inquiry into what is not, and their disobedience took many forms. "Is it, or is it not?" became the first of Aristotle's Categories. Definition was dependent on the same distinction: "Is it?" "Of what sort is it?" Both these procedures require the establishment of a boundary between "is" and "is not." Aristotle locates every latent double in the word solidly in words and in the machinery of logic. Dialectic contracts in Aristotelian usage and comes to denote "two words" representing synecdochically two *logoi* understood as "propositions," and matures quickly as an instrument for testing the strength of "opposite" propositions. The notion that there are at least two sides to every story shaped, and was extended amid, the interpenetration of rhetoric and probabilistic logic, and furthered the notion that nonlogical matters are always debatable because our knowledge of them and our beliefs about them are necessarily and always incomplete, ungrounded, or constantly shifting. Though this notion is strikingly similar to Plato's vision of dialogue as an ongoing evolving discourse of understandings, it lacks the positive emphases on understanding and on an ongoing maieutic that brings forth and is directed toward truth. Aristotle records and thereby preserves the Sophists' deliberate exploitations of probabilistic and semantic ambiguity in the *Sophistical Refutations*, but also inaugurates accolades directed at irony as an admirable mark of the well-educated gentleman. Plato leaves us with a deceptively simple alternative to this *dialectica epidemica*: the notion that every latent double in the word can be restored to its human—all too human—originators, and that its more negative latent tendencies can be neutralized amid benign maieutic dialogues.

3

Aristotle: A Logic of Terms, a Rhetoric of Motives

> He imposes orders as he thinks of them
> As the fox and snake do. It is a brave affair.
> But to impose is not
> To discover.
> WALLACE STEVENS, "Notes Toward a
Supreme Fiction"

> To make a proposition is to turn many things into one (for the end to which the whole argument is directed must be included in a single whole), while to make an objection is to turn one thing into many; for the objector distinguishes or demolishes, conceding one proposition and refusing to concede another.
> ARISTOTLE, *Topica*

Aristotle's treatises on logic and rhetoric have had profound and indelible effects on Western language models, teaching, and use. I do not propose that Aristotle himself initiated or secured these effects. What was transmitted through the Aristotelian corpus synthesized and codified extant notions of language, arranged them into practical "arts" (*technai*) and theoretical "sciences" (*epistemai*), and proved particularly powerful in shaping those Western assumptions and theories regarding language that have come to be embodied in curricula. What was by Aristotle's own definition a codification of extant linguistic conventions and logical rules has gradually assumed the status of linguistic and logical fact. Consciously learning a set of conventions is quite different from absorbing the tacit, implicit conventions and beliefs of one's culture.[1] This is as true for ethics as it is for grammar. The strongest taboos are rarely stated and remain unwritten. Three-year-olds master verb tenses and noun cases without a grammar book. They do not learn to produce or state definitions, groupings by abstract genus ("tools," "fruit"), comparisons of same and different, bigger and smaller, or any other logical operations, unless asked or encouraged to do so.[2] At Piaget-inspired preschools, children are taught to identify "same" and "different." "Hot" and "cold" do not readily come to their minds when they are given a picture of an ice cube alongside a steaming tea-kettle. Most children are unable to use abstract time terms until they reach age six or seven; even some adults live their lives quite successfully without any firm sense of how long ten minutes or an hour is. To the perpetual astonishment of their elders, children learn to talk without being formally taught, to make sense without "knowing" logic. All these examples suggest the difficulty of determining or defining any innate characteristics of thought and language. As with the slave who is shown to have "recollected" mathematical knowledge in Plato's *Meno*, the child of today "knows" very ambiguously, in part because cultural conceptualizations of knowledge shape how the child experiences and names knowing. Are children fulfilling a mental destiny, activating universal mental capacities, when they distinguish "same" and "different," or are they learning to answer in terms of the categories provided and hence learning those categories for the first time?

To study grammar is to learn grammar, not language. The grammar, rules for predication, and conventions of expository argumentation by which most language instruction is still conducted are descendants of Aristotelian terms and methods. In contrast with Plato's warning that to divide discourse is to risk doing away with its powers, Aristotle erects a massive system built upon divisions. Logic and rhetoric, ethics and politics, physics and metaphysics are separated from one another, and their relationships to one another are defined. Rhetoric is placed in two locations, as a subdivision of the art of politics, and as the branch of the science of logic which deals with persuasive rather than true discourse.[3] The *Categories* and *On Interpretation* lay the foundation for many subsequent grammars, semantics, and predicational logics by defining discrete parts of speech and rules for their combination with one another within sequences of propositions. The *Categories* focuses on different kinds of single words—the parts of speech—particularly on generic versus proper nouns, and delineates what we have come to term subject and predicate roles. Aristotle's definitions of the relationships between a word and that to which it refers, and of the meaning of sentences, construe both as "conventional" (*nomos*), building on earlier Sophists' analyses of reference and semantics as conventional, and sustaining the conventionalist line of the discussion represented in the *Cratylus*. Truth, as distinct from meaning, is domiciled within the constraints of predication. "Combination and division are essential before you can have truth and falsity."[4] *On Interpretation* delineates kinds of meaning, and the means by which meaning and truth can be assessed. Only logical discourse, that which is produced by the explicit and conscious "combination and division" of *diaeresis* and dialectic, is capable of truth or falsity. "But while every sentence has meaning [*semantikos*], though not as an instrument of nature but, as we observed, by convention, not all can be called propositions [*apophantikos*]. We call propositions those only that have truth or falsity in them. A prayer is, for instance, a sentence [*euche logos*] but neither has truth nor has falsity. Let us pass over all such, as their study belongs to the province of rhetoric or poetry. We have in our present inquiry propositions [*apophantikos*] alone for our theme."[5]

Several themes in Aristotle's thought mark a fissure between previous and subsequent conceptions of language forms, meanings, and uses. Truth and falsity are rendered formal characteristics of propositions; formal logical procedures—combination and division—are established as the necessary but not sufficient causes of truth. Discourse types are partitioned according to the nature of their meaning and the means of their production, dual criteria according to which rhetoric, poetry, and prayer are said to have meaning but are denied truth and falsity. Not only discourse types but also their study is partitioned. The study of conventional meaning and persuasiveness, but not truth, is deemed the province of rhetoric, a restriction that separates rhetoric, so central to subsequent formal language instruction, from the study of truth and falsity. Henceforth, to study rhetoric would be to study conventional meanings and to use the understanding of those meanings to effect persuasion and decision.

Thinking of language as a group of conventions alters linguistic behavior in unpredictable and often inscrutable ways. A similar objectification of ethical conventions through analysis transforms ethics from a set of culturally transmitted beliefs and values that have the spontaneous directive force of reflex and are experienced as instinctual most of the time, to the study of exemplary types, so that ethics becomes a body of knowledge of rules for behavior, and finally an object of anthropological study.[6] Among the educated, the experience of language as a spontaneous and transparent medium of thought and expression came to be replaced by the study and consciousness of language as an object of knowledge; Aristotle's emendations of earlier attempts at naming language assign categories to language, thought, and discourse through which they can be "taught" and "learned." Gregory Bateson has deemed linguistic self-consciousness a propadeutic for lying unless careful proscriptions limit the uses of such self-consciousness. I extend his comments on kinesics to the case of verbal language. "If you are going to have self-consciousness about your kinesics, then you have to have very careful devices for preventing people from using their kinesics for lying. You see, that's the point about not knowing. If people don't know what the signals are for love and hate, they can't lie about love and hate. If they know the signals, then they can lie. Human beings are sort of on the edge of being human in this respect. They partly know and partly don't know."[7] The word "know" here is crucially ambiguous. On one level we do "know" the signals for love and hate, just as three-year-olds "know" nouns and verbs. However, it is far from inevitable or universal to know these things *as signals*. To know through naming what we know or that we know relies on an epistemology deploying metacognitive terms and, in the case of language, a metalinguistic grammatical vocabulary.[8]

A double issue—whether to teach conventions, and whether to teach them *as* conventions—sharply distinguishes Aristotle from Plato. Should people be explicitly taught names for words and kinds of language and their uses? What rules can be built into such descriptions and their teaching that will prevent their abuse? Plato's answer is that such descriptions and rules alone should never be taught, that they must always be part of a truth-seeking enterprise, and that they should be evolved and perpetually amended within a community in an atmosphere of mutual trust, good will, and candor. Plato and Aristotle alike observe a proliferating plurality of rhetorical and philosophical vocabularies already in circulation and use. Plato in effect tries to stop this circulation and to eliminate some of the vocabularies. Aristotle takes a different route, attempts to organize the existing descriptions and rules for use, and posits that a separate "discipline," ethics, will take care of abuses. His rhetoric provides a system of language use and a conception of practical logic configured in terms of pigeonholes and rules: concepts and names for language that have had the effect of institutionalizing a conventionalist, instrumentalist linguistic self-consciousness and of increasing the ethical as well as epistemological distance between language and its users. In the *Phaedrus* Plato applauds a similar kind of self-consciousness and distance as a "divine madness" which comes when convention (*nomos*) is recognized and transcended. Promoting escape from the prisonhouse of language leads him to denounce rhetoric as mere technique, a how-to, a set of rules, a new set of linguistic conventions that will be learned *as conventions*; "true rhetoric" can and should be an escape from conventions.

Once understood as such, once named as convention rather than reality or truth, should convention be taught? Aristotle says yes and proceeds to define, or rather to invent, a multitude of taxonomies of conventional, standard uses: grammatical rules, logical forms, rhetorical and stylistic devices. He assigns to convention and opinion—*nomoi* and *doxai*—the roles of the definitive materials of rhetoric. The word for "word" that predominates in Aristotle's treatment of rhetoric is not *logos* but *onoma*, or "name," another index of the emphasis on commonly understood, conventional, and therefore successful communication. The concepts of the sign (*semeion*) and the common (*koine*) also figure prominently in the *Rhetoric*. "Signs and probabilities" are defined as *the* principal materials of rhetorical enthymemes. Where Plato resists an exclusively semiotic or conventionalist approach to language, and rejects the linguistic materialism implicit in systematic "grammatical analysis," Aristotle builds an entire logic and rhetoric on them.

Three corollaries to these differences are developed in each of the following sections. First, I propose that while Plato tried to integrate and standardize education and language use under the guidance of a truth-seeking philosophy, Aristotle accepted and indeed promoted a "departmentalization" of the arts and sciences that had the effect, albeit an effect beyond his control, of institutionalizing technical rhetoric. Plato said, in effect, "the whole system is wrong; we must change it before it gains any more momentum." Aristotle begins with the implicit assumption that the system is already firmly established, and that what must be done is to organize and improve upon it. Aristotle's rationale seems to have been "divide and preserve." He divorces rhetoric from logic but leaves several channels wide open between them — the topics, the notion of dialectic as a counterpart (*antistrophe*) of rhetoric, and the notion of the enthymeme as a rhetorical syllogism.

Second, Aristotle's terminology for arguments, argumentation, the parts of speech and their relationship to one another, and the substance and purposes of rhetorical versus logical argument, are significantly different from Plato's. Plato's *logos* is quite different from Aristotle's *logos* and *logike*. Aristotle's *logos* often means simply, but also technically and conventionally, "sentence" and "proposition." In this sense *logos* as it had existed from the Preplatonics through Plato's usage, broadly denoting truth-bearing philosophical discourse, is replaced by a series of more precise, tagmemic technical terms defining relationships within and among sentences. Axioms, theses, premises, and propositions stating general truths head the logical schemata. Topics, commonplaces, examples, signs, and probabilities head the forms of rhetorical argument that Aristotle defines. *Logos* is replaced by logic on the one hand, and on the other by a contingent rhetorical semantics determined by motive and effect. *Logos* is rendered architectonic, and is partitioned into the logical instrument of scientific inquiry and the rhetorical art of persuasive technique.

Third, because of its function as a paradigm for subsequent rhetorical treatises and manuals, Aristotle's *Rhetoric* had the effect of institutionalizing a rhetoric that was divorced from logic and thereby from any criteria of truth. Aristotle's descriptive and analytical precision did indeed improve upon and consolidate extant rhetorical theory directed at *koine*, the common argot of both public discourse and practical teaching in the language arts. For all but the few who studied logic, the *koinoi topoi* became the paradigm for formal, learned language use and teaching. Aristotelian rhetoric was institutionalized as the paradigm for formal public discourse, "literate" discourse and, concomitantly, literacy. In this emphasis I may seem to discount Isocrates' profound influence on the literary texture of rhetorical discourse, and upon the conception of rhetoric as a substantive philosophical discipline among the liberal arts. However, I sustain full emphasis upon the architectonics of taxonomy that the Aristotelian approach invested in subsequent curricula in order to illuminate the degree of its divergence from Plato's vision of rhetoric as dialogue.

Aristotle's divisions are so firmly and clearly defined that they seem a delineation of natural boundaries. He believed — as did Plato, for that matter — that a subject must be defined before it can be known, and that definition depends on *diaeresis*. Yet defining and classifying the media of definition present special problems. The nature of language and thought, unlike that of many other objects of study, had by the fourth century B.C. come to be discussed only by observing their "representations, likenesses, images, and copies."[9] Spoken words (*phonai*) were conceptualized as "signs" for thoughts, and written words (*grammata*) as signs for spoken words. The use of the term "sign" for these relationships may be one index of an internalization of writing as a metaphor for thought and language in this era.[10] In the *Cratylus* and the *Sophist* Plato warns, in effect, "Beware of teaching people to think of language as signs, or as names, or as any one thing. If they begin to take any one of these metaphors too literally, they will begin to use language as a system of signs. If they begin to think of language as rhetorical, they will begin to use it more consciously in rhetorical ways." Though Aristotle did not heed Plato's warnings, he specifically addresses them, possibly in an attempt to refute and discount them.[11] More practical, perhaps, or impatient with the idea that only a few should pursue finer demarcations while the many contin-

ued to fall victim to the powers of unscrupulous Sophists and dema-
gogues, he attempted one whole, readily accessible, and systematically organized account of thought and language—a plausibly benign motive that deserves mention before turning to an examination
that will focus primarily on the divisive and disjunctive effects of
Aristotle's system.

The Rationale: Divide and Preserve

> Two Horn'd Reasoning, Cloven fiction,
> In Doubt, which is Self contradiction.
> WILLIAM BLAKE, "The Gates of Paradise"

It is not so surprising that Aristotle should seek to defend, preserve,
and protect the arts and sciences by dividing them. They were already becoming partitioned among the philosophical schools and
within the Sophists' rhetorical teachings. Plato's dialogues provide
a running account of the many terms and issues generated by this
burgeoning pluralism. The *Cratylus* and the *Sophist* are direct precursors in Plato's dialogues to the issues treated in the *Categories*;
Plato examines three different concepts of words then circulating.
Are words signs (*semeia*) for thoughts—simple referents which
point to and stand for? Are they names (*onomata*), assigned to
things by custom and usage, as suggested by *o-nomos* (the custom,
the law)? Or are they representations (*eikones*) which call to mind a
mental image, an understanding, a concept? At the end of the
Cratylus the question remains undecided, with Socrates characteris-
tically saying that it depends on how you look at it: "Surely no man
of sense can put himself and his soul under the control of names,
and trust in names and their makers to the point of affirming that
he knows anything. . . . Perhaps, Cratylus, this theory is true, but
perhaps it is not."[12] This conclusion to the *Cratylus* provides yet
another instance of Plato's programmatic inconclusiveness, for it
embodies the principle that no one single discussion can state or
resolve a question of complexity. Instead, current theories of words
are presented, much like the modern wave and corpuscular models
of light, as theories which depict some of the characteristics of

words while necessarily excluding others. Diaeretical definition, for Plato, is never final. Each definition excludes as much as it includes, by definition; knowledge is an incremental, changing, contextual, lifelong process, not the product of any one discussion. It cannot be contained, fixed, concluded, or stated. Thus, while he presents proliferating theories of words, language, truth, and rhetoric, Plato does not line them up, compare them, and pick a winner; instead, he dramatizes their discussion as means of improved and ongoing understanding.

However, in the world outside the ongoing Socratic dialogue, "the many" were arguing about which one model was right. In the polis and the classroom many were teaching and practicing philosophy and rhetoric with varying degrees of allegiance to the true and the good. The Socrates depicted by Plato readily admits that "the many" are not particularly responsive to the most subtle or sound of philosophical questions and methods. They had begun to adopt the formalized disjunctive category structure characterized by Parmenides as the Way of Opinion, with its focus on sameness and difference, lesser and greater, information-dense iterations of a subject's nature, characteristics, and physical attributes. Antiphon, Socrates' contemporary, articulates one of the effects of such classifications in the social sphere following Solon's reforms. "We revere and honor those born of noble fathers, but those who are not born of noble houses we neither revere nor honor. In this we are, in our relations with one another, like barbarians, since we are all by nature born the same in every way, both barbarians and Hellenes." Such classifications, he contends, promote discord and will continue to do so, unless the notion of a human nature "common" to all is promoted. Human implementations of justice in the new courts, he asserts, often ring contrary to nature; for this reason, law should be minimal. He intimates disapproval of legal rhetoric for similar reasons; "human nature" will win out over the weaker justice proceeding from the law. "He himself is wronged by the man against whom he gave evidence; for he is hated by him for having given truthful evidence. And [*he is wronged*] not only by this hatred, but also because he must for the whole of his life be on his guard against the man against whom he gave evidence."[13] Despite Antiphon's pointed and poignant warnings, adversarial argument had already become entrenched as a lingua franca in forensic debate and assembly speeches among the newly enfranchised landholding soldier citizenry.

Though not adversarial in tone, Aristotle's *Organon* follows a relentlessly systematic procedure of division, definition, and hierarchical subordination beginning with his treatment of single words, and extending into his delineations of logic, rhetoric, and poetics. His discourse itself replicates these patterns: it is strongly taxonomical and subordinative, referring to, naming, and constituting classes and kinds of speech, soul, and knowledge. What are the parts of speech, and how are they related to one another? His answers define them as instruments. What are the parts of an argument, of reasoning? His answers establish names for those parts and define rules for their combination, procedures that further extend the object language implicit in the notion of genus. Predicational grammar and logic, each defining the other to a certain extent, have come of age. Though he, like Plato, wrote philosophical dialogues, Aristotle's subsequent influence as a philosopher and a rhetorical theorist has been as a writer of systematizing treatises, a legacy that has further entrenched logical expository prose as the norm for formal truth-bearing discourse. The treatises compiled as the *Organon*, or "Instrument," proceed incrementally and cumulatively, each part dependent on and extending its predecessors. Yet these treatises had no "typical" order prior to 200 A.D. Single units — nouns — are treated first, then groups of kinds of nouns leading to subject and predicate distinctions (*Categories*). The elements and kinds of sentences, along with rules for determining their meaning, truth, and falsity, are examined next, together with rules for combining and arranging groups of sentences (*On Interpretation*). The *Prior Analytics* extends these rules further into a technical syllogistic system, Aristotle's deductive logic for reasoning from premises. The *Posterior Analytics* provides heuristics of discovery and demonstration, rules for inductive logic and for testing the conclusions thus derived. The *Topics* overlaps, extends, and repeats portions of *On Interpretation*, the *Posterior Analytics*, and the *Rhetoric* that deal with kinds and arrangements of arguments.

Particular sorts of elements are divided in Aristotle's system, highlighted and hypostatized by the taxonomical nomenclature. It is quite different to represent justice as the goddess Themis or Dike, to discuss justice as an adjective which may or may not be correctly attributed of something, and to discuss whether or not there is justice.[14] In Aristotle's treatments, an explicit divergence among these related modes of discourse and representation is given extended exposition. With similarly transitional explicitness at the level of words within sentences, Aristotle treats the "verb" (*rhema*) as an "odd kind of noun" and distinguishes it as a word which has a time reference but also "indicates that something is said or asserted *of* something." He verges on a definition of the copula: "verbs by themselves, then, are nouns; . . . they indicate nothing themselves but imply a copulation or synthesis *which we can hardly conceive of apart from the things thus combined*."[15]

Aristotle occasionally alludes to the neologistic elements in his enterprise, as when he says, "let us call them (for want of a better term) 'indefinite verbs' those which are used indiscriminately of all things." Even at the level of discriminating single parts of speech, one can see the novelty of all this for Aristotle, who is discovering and naming, but also bringing into being, language as an instrumental system with parts and rules for combination. Many other possible treatments of language excluded by his system recurrently surface as minority positions in subsequent eras, but it is Aristotle's work that first preserved names for the parts of speech and the procedures of logic that have subsequently been taken as innate characteristics of language, thought, and even the mind itself.

The *Categories* examines "names" with a systematic and analytical detail that warrants the use of the abstract terms "noun," "subject," and "predicate" in translations. Ten categories of nouns are defined, each of them necessary to the distinctions Aristotle draws among subjects, predicates, and predication. The *Categories* is not only the ancestor of many formal grammars, but parallels the rhetorical topics as configured by Aristotle. This parallel is particularly clear in *topoi* designated by a single noun in which the noun subject is presented as having a nature that can determine how it should be approached. The *Categories, On Interpretation*, and *Topics* share the definition of words as "symbols or signs of affections or impressions of the soul; written words are the signs of words spoken. There are thoughts in our minds [*en te psuche noema*] unaccompanied by truth or falsity, and others that have necessarily one or the other."[16] With this characterization of language as an object of study,

Aristotle begins his classification of the kinds, meanings, forms, and uses of both language and thought. The opening passages of the *Categories* and *On Interpretation* assume, in a sense, what they then seek to define and provide rules for. Once beyond the general characterization of language as semiotic, that is, as first and foremost referential, Aristotle addresses the instruments and rules of reasoning (*sullogismos*) in the *Categories* and *On Interpretation*. His distinctions and divisions draw together but also rearrange themes treated by the Preplatonics, the Sophists, and Plato.

Aristotle uses *diaeresis* both as the instrument of his study of subjects and as itself a subject. "Let us first of all define noun and verb, then explain what is meant by denial, affirmation, proposition and sentence."[17] The entire discussion is necessarily conducted in and through the elements which are themselves the objects of the study. Preplatonic usage focused on mounting a *logos* which, while clearly distinguished from mere opinion (*doxa*) was not distinguished or conceived of as divided from other kinds of philosophical discourse such as propositions and axioms, kinds of sentences that begin to be given names in Aristotle's characterizations. Virtually every sentence and section of Aristotle's discourse is peppered with *or*s dividing series of names for things, distinctions among entities, and a progression of disjunctions. This procedure generates long lists whose items must then be subdivided into classes. The classes are put into groups, the relationship of the groups to one another is defined, and finally rules are given for using, combining, and separating each of a multitude of classes, each of which contains a multitude of individual items. An iterative, taxonomical pattern extends the notion of family groups (*gene*) and categories (*kategoriai*) into syntax itself and from there into entire sections of treatises, each of which deals with a category or subcategory of the "subject." The *diaeresis* which Aristotle recommends is exemplified by his discourse, structuring its parts and generating the next series of topics, a procedure that is not only impressively systematic but may well be the origin of the idea that something so architectonically systematic and focused on formal relationships among words and ideas is compelling.

The nature of words, sentences, meaning, and truth defined in Aristotle's work coalesces finally as syntax, the necessary precursor to the formalization of a systematic, teachable, and reproducible grammar. While it may not be arguable that the conceptualization of language as *made* from signs was "caused" by writing, it is at least arguable that the self-consciousness of signs imparted by Aristotle's descriptive taxonomies conduces to an awareness of language as crafted, as a made thing, a focus that imparts a pointedly material and mechanical extension to earlier notions of *poiesis*. Aristotle's grammatology is a production model that provides architectural plans for the construction of propositions out of subjects and predicates. General versus proper nouns are defined in partial and full extension: some men, all Athenians, every horse. Rules for combinations of these phrases in subject and predicate positions take up a good portion of *On Interpretation*, laying the groundwork for the distribution of terms among propositions which is developed in his syllogistic. An explicit distinction is drawn between incidental and substantive senses of the copula: "Homer is," for example, cannot be inferred from "Homer is a poet," because the latter does not predicate being of Homer.[18] This designation of an "incidental" use of the copula resolves by fiat the Parmenidean problem of being and not-being which takes up a good part of the *Sophist* by reducing not-being to a matter of opinion (*doxa*) on the one hand and of logico-grammatical negation on the other. "As, however, for that which is *not*, it is not true to say that it "is" somewhat, because it is a matter of opinion. The opinion about it is not that it is; it is that it is not."[19] The distinctions, reductions, and component parts layed out in the *Categories* and *On Interpretation* are a necessary accompaniment to the redefinitions of linguistic genres, their meanings, and use which take up the logical treatises and the *Rhetoric*.

From Categories to *Koinoi Topoi*:
Of Words, Sentences, Proofs, and Arguments

An initial purpose of the *Categories* is to define the nature of meaning as the relationship between words and their referents by classifying terms as of three kinds: equivocal, univocal, and derivative. Aristotle focuses on these "names" (*onomata*) as subjects (*hu-*

pokeimena: that which underlies; that which is laid down or assumed). He then distinguishes the essential from the inessential
status of all qualities and terms that may be predicated of the ten
kategoriai. He tries, with some success, to limit himself to verbal
rather than ontological questions. When he speaks of the "essence"
(*ousia*) of the term "man," he refers to its definitive and unvarying
use, its "isness" as a word. The fine line implicit in this solidifies the
distinction between ontology and the logic of syntax, between existential and predicative deployments of grammar, but the line erodes
occasionally. *Ousia* is used consistently instead of *einai* (being);
"predicates" are said to be present or absent *in* subjects.[20] The
"meaning" (*semantikos*) of a single term in Aristotle's system depends on whether what it denotes is irrevocable or arbitrary in
status. This in turn requires the distinction between "substantives,"
such as "man," and qualities or traits. Only *ousia*, the first of the
kategoriai, denotes essences. "Man is an animal which reasons."
"Callias is beside the house." Securing the differences among these
terms would seem to require an ontological or, at the very least,
conceptual grounding, yet Aristotle resolutely talks about them as
kinds of *terms*. The list of categories provides a listing of types of
words based on an essential or "always there" referentiality of the
term, or alternatively on the kind of nonessential quality the term
names.[21] Aristotle asserts the rule that one may not predicate *of* a
subject what is "in" or "essentially of" the subject. This requires a
strong division between "parts" of speech or what Aristotle in other
places terms *stoicheia*. In the *Categories*, however, "subjects" are
defined *in terms of* "predicates." The first of the ten categories,
ousia ("isness, is it?") defines primary referential nouns such as
"man" as first substances because they refer to an "it is." "Secondary substances" are defined as nouns denoting a class (*genus*) such
as "man." Sentence meaning is thus restricted to predication. We
may predicate "man" of *a* man, but not a man of "man." Extending
this subordination, Aristotle postulates that all predicates of the
predicates of a given subject are also true of the subject. Somewhat
problematically, the word translated by the English "predicate" is
the title of the entire treatise: *kategoriai* (categories, headings, master terms). Veritable phalanxes of predicates are assembling in the
wings, with one subject's predicate defined as another predicate's
subject.

The extended classification of *onomata* provided in the *Categories* lays the foundation for a parts-of-speech grammar, a topical schema of arguments based on verbal "elements" (*stoicheia*), and a logic of "terms"—subjects and predicates. The pride of place given the ten categories ensures that it is the kind of term, more than any other single factor, which will determine the classification of propositions and arguments throughout the *Topics, Analytics*, and *Rhetoric*. The concept and use of the term *topoi* are distributed among meanings whose diversity is sustained in English translation as "subject" (the kind of term or topic which begins an argument, understood as the smallest unit of meaning, whether expressed in a sentence or in a single word)—a distributive group of meanings for *topoi* that is in Aristotle's usage equivalent to *stoicheia* in many but not all instances. But the term also denotes a commonly held belief or expression, the *koinoi topoi* (literally, commonplaces) deployed by the rhetoricians. These overlapping uses are reflected in the variant translations of the term that names the first category, *ousia*; "isness," "substance," "primary substance" versus "secondary substance," or "essence."[22] The central rhetorical term *koine* means "common," "universal," "colloquial," "familiar," or "shared," yet denotes quite different things in the phrases *koinoi topoi* and *onoma monon koinon*: the "common topics," or arguments recommended to the speaker, and "having only a name in common." These alternations among terms are reminders that, despite the apparent magisterial authority of Aristotle's lists and procedures for dividing, defining, and further subdividing, these terms and procedures were in what could be thought of as a quasi-experimental state, being tried out and isolated in several particular ways, and systematized in alternate ratios across Aristotle's work. The procedure deployed in the *Categories* is to select out nouns which are names for "it is" as *the* primary subjects; focusing first on single-term reference rather than on sentence meaning inaugurates a complex set of rules for predicational correctness vis-a-vis certain kinds of subjects. The adaptability of the unit "predicates" established in the *Categories* is further enhanced by their parallelism with the component parts Aristotle establishes in cognate systems. When examined collaterally with the *Topics'* four "general bases of argument" and twenty-eight topics, and with the cognate list of *koinoi topoi* in the *Rhetoric*, the *kategoriai* can be seen as a master list of terms and subjects that not only systematized predicational syntax and logic, but also drew from and were bequeathed by rhetorical argumentation, the modes, and the *staseis*.

The ten categories are classified according to meaning.

1. what	*ousia*	"isness," essence "is it?"
2. how large	*poson*	size, quantity, dimension
3. what sort	*poion*	made of what, material
4. related to what	*pros*	toward what
5. where	*pou*	place, location
6. when	*pote*	time
7. in what attitude	*keisthai*	position, posture
8. how circumstanced	*echein*	state or condition
9. what doing	*poiein*	what making, makes what
10. what having done to	*paschein*	what suffering, affected by

Of this list, Augustine would remark that "it made difficulties for me, because I thought that everything that existed could be reduced to these ten categories."[23] Aristotle himself readily concedes that defining kinds of nouns, the existence of the things to which they refer, and their meanings in combination with one another is tricky business. A word of the first category may be either a subject or a predicate; a word of the seventh category may be a subject but will more often be an adjectival predicate. Here are among the earliest articulations of what are now thought of as differences among prepositional, adjectival, and predicational relationships in a rule-governed, "logical" syntax. Similarly, the four subjects of reasoning/bases of arguments defined in the *Topics* provide general approaches for any discourse:

1. definition	*horos*
2. property	*idion*
3. genus	*genos*
4. accident	*sumbebekos*

Just as the *Categories* extends the extant conceptualization of words, definition in the *Topics* is said to be a very specific kind of *sentence*, and can be seen as answering the first category *ousia*, "what is it?" The four "general lines of argument" defined in Book II of the *Rhetoric*, and the more specific "lines of argument upon which genuine enthymemes may be based," increase the number of alternative characterizations, protocols, and choices. The "general lines of argument" in the *Rhetoric* comprise and expand on existing forensic and deliberative taxonomies; among the twenty-eight accompanying rhetorical "lines of argument on which genuine enthymemes are based" appear terms and types of statements which also appear in the *Categories*, some paralleling the list of bases of argument/subjects of reasoning defined in the *Topics*.[25]

general lines of argument; the *koinoi topoi*:	twenty-eight lines of enthymematic argument:
1. possible and impossible	1. opposites
2. fact past	2. modification of key word
3. fact future	3. correlative ideas and relative terms
4. degree	4. the stronger, greater degree or size
	5. considerations of time
	6. turning an opponent's words against him
	7. definition of terms
	8. use of ambiguous terms
	9. logical division
	10. induction
	11. previous decision or general consent
	12. dividing a subject, enumeration of parts
	13. consequences

14. inference from contrasting opposites

15. inference from inconsistency of expressed and truly held views

16. rational correspondence, analogy

17. from results to antecedents

18. inconsistencies of choice in similar circumstances

19. establishing the possible as the real motive

20. inducements and deterrents

21. things which are supposed to have happened but seem incredible

22. examining contradictions in report and fact

23. stating reasons for prejudice or slander

24. making the cause the effect

25. neglect of a better plan

26. defending choice of action inconsistent with precedent

27. previous mistakes

28. meanings from proper names

The parallels among this list and the taxonomies defined in the *Categories* and *Topics*, though erratic, suggest the viability of approaching the ten categories as a master list for taxonomies developed in other works, despite the fact that not all the lists, when observed collaterally, are grammatically, ontologically, or logically consistent by modern standards.

The purpose Aristotle defines for the *Topics* is to lay down principles for reasoning from generally accepted opinions (*endoxai*) about any problem in a way "which will avoid contradiction." This method of reasoning, logical syllogism (*sullogismos logos*), is further characterized as one through which, certain things having been laid down, certain other things will *necessarily* follow. The value he defines for this method is "mental training" (*gumnasia*) that will take place through conversation (*enteuxeis*—his version of Plato's dialogue?) and philosophic inquiry (*philosophia episteme*). He distinguishes four kinds of such reasoning: demonstrative (apodeictic), dialectical, contentious (eristic), and false (sophistic). In the *Topics*, the bases of all arguments are said to be equal in number and identical with these subjects of reasonings. Arguments (*logoi*) begin with propositions (*protaseis*); the subjects of reasonings (*sullogismoi*) are problems (*problemata*). In both cases there are "four bases and objects": definition, property, genus, and accident.[26] The four shared bases of argumentation (*logos*) and subjects of reasoning (*sullogismos*) defined in the *Topics* have subsequently been termed the four "predicables," a misleading label because they spell out procedures not for constructing but for analyzing a proposition or problem, in order to discover whether it "has arisen" from a definition of something, or from a property, a genus, or an accident. While the label "predicable" conforms to Aristotelian and subsequent depictions of predicative term logic, it obscures the equally important characterization of the predicables as both topical and procedural *heuristics* for argumentation, an important point of overlap linking the topics, the categories, and the list of rhetorical *topoi*. A significant index of the explicitness of this orchestration is to be found in the *Topics*; when the predicables are introduced, Aristotle alludes to their listing in the *Categories* as well.[27] Definition, property, genus, and accident permit the location of the origin, object, subject, or base of either a "proposition" or "problem." Once this is determined—that is, once a sentence has been classified and reduced to its key term or primary subject—that term or subject can be located in the list of ten categories. "Such then is the nature and such is the number of the subjects about which arguments take place and the materials on which they are based."[28]

This concludes the logical and procedural section of book 1 of the *Topics*. Next, and somewhat abruptly, follows a consideration of a very different kind of analysis of propositions and problems. A proposition, the starting point of an argument, should be judged by its conformity to opinions (*endoxai*) held by "everyone or by the majority or by the wise — either all of the wise or the majority or the most famous of them — and which is not paradoxical. . . . Views which are similar to received opinions are also dialectic propositions, and so also are propositions made by way of contradicting the contrary of received opinions."[29] Syllogistic reasoning, as defined here, aims at "choice and avoidance or truth and knowledge" and states something "about which either men have no opinion either way, or most people hold an opinion contrary to that of the wise, or the wise contrary to that of most people, or about which members of each of these classes disagree among themselves."[30] The divisions under the definition of syllogistic reasoning provide the rule that statements be assessed in terms of their conformity with generally held opinions in the case of propositions, and with "general truths" in the case of problems.

Are the procedures laid out in the *Topics* "earlier" versions, or alternately, condensed versions of the division of logic from rhetoric asserted in *On Interpretation*, and of the definition of rhetoric as a "counterpart" of dialectic in the *Rhetoric*?[31] The similarity among these procedures, though erratic, is instructive. The material of all beginning statements of both reasoning and argumentation are designated as commonly held opinions (*endoxai*). Investigation is defined as the aim of reasoning (*sullogismos*), whose starting points are designated as *problemata*; a more ambiguous aim is defined for arguments (*logoi*), whose starting points are designated as propositions (*protaseis*). The accord of propositions with commonly held opinions, and the lack of that accord in the case of problems, would seem to support the view that the *Topics* provides a condensed version of the divisions which are developed more fully in the *Analytics* and *Rhetoric*, with the *Analytics* elaborating the subjects of reasoning, and the *Rhetoric* the bases of arguments. In these more elaborated distinctions, propositions stating "general truths" become the starting points of dialectical syllogisms, and statements of "commonly held opinions" become the starting points for rhetorical enthymemes. In the *Topics*, however, the distinction is more simply between "reasonings" and "arguments."

The distinctions configured among these conceptual and procedural divisions are difficult to comprehend at first, because the lack of a firmly established vocabulary is quite evident, and manifests itself in ambiguous or equivocal uses of terms that can be understood as strategic, or bungling, or both. Attempts to clarify the terminology through alignment with later predicational logical terminology pervade the footnotes of many translations.[32] While well intended, such glosses obscure both the sometimes stumbling originality and the boldly systematizing pattern of Aristotle's work. It is somewhat misleading to present him as "finally getting right" what others had only dimly perceived. His treatments could more plausibly be viewed as selecting from, reorchestrating, and extending a discrete set of logical–grammatical taxonomies already in existence. Had these characterizations been different, or had they been selected and arranged in different ways, the development of subsequent Western concepts of mind and language would have been strikingly different. To give only one example, Stoic logic is a logic of sentences rather than of terms. The differences between Stoic and Aristotelian models are instructive. In Stoic logic, as in contemporary speech-act theory and sentential calculus, nothing smaller than the sentence is examined, with the goal of providing elaborate logical rules for the combination of different kinds of sentences. In contrast, Aristotle focuses on the combination of different kinds of terms; term and predicate distinctions provide the rules for combinations of sentences.[33]

In his treatments of the *koinoi topoi* and categories, Aristotle's distillation of previous models—his own unique contributions notwithstanding—inaugurates a residual logic of sorts, a "selection of items from an earlier, more complex and sensitive science."[34] Hegel defined this kind of ongoing assimilation of past discoveries as, at worst, a reduction of knowledge to mere information:

> What in former days occupied the energies of men of mature mental abilities sinks to the level of information, exercises, and even pastimes, for children. . . . This bygone mode of existence has already become an acquired possession of the general mind, which constitutes the substance of the individual, and, by thus appearing externally to him, furnishes his inorganic nature.
>
> What results from the use of this method of sticking on to everything in heaven and earth, to every kind of shape and form, natural and

spiritual, the pair of determinations from the general schema, is . . . a synoptic index, like a skeleton with tickets stuck all over it, or like the rows of boxes kept shut and labelled in a grocer's stall. . . .

A table of contents is all that understanding gives, the content itself it does not furnish at all.[35]

While perhaps unfair as a characterization of Aristotle's work as a whole, this is a useful characterization of the divisions and tabular taxonomies Aristotle constructs in the *Categories, On Interpretation, Topics*, and *Rhetoric*. What had been a discovery, hard won and debated, still undergoing investigation and change, becomes listed in tabular form, is defined as *methodos*, and comes to be understood and used as an instrument, and to be regarded as a linguistic fact. It is as "information" that Aristotle in the *Organon* provides a series of ways of approaching objects with "isness" to be defined, and defines a process in which kinds of words come to be listed among other kinds of objects. Listing in outline fashion the parts of a speech occurs in the rhetoric manuals parodied by Plato and indeed is one of the prime objects of his parody. Yet it is precisely the pattern of listing and classifying that permits Aristotle's alignment of rhetoric and dialectic as "counterparts" (*antistrophai*).

The Institutionalization of Rhetoric

It is tempting to criticize Aristotle for not examining the possible consequences of rhetorical classifications and nomenclature, especially since Plato correctly anticipated some of those consequences. A probabilistic conception of argumentative logic and a semantic theory based preponderantly upon conventional meaning were transmitted to later eras and into the canons of formal written and spoken discourse. The lines dividing truth, fact, and probability, as well as the appropriate forms of statement for each, were blurred by divergent proliferating taxonomies. The interdependence between language use, concept formation, and discourse in contexts of human relationships were displaced, at the official philosophical and curricular level, by rule-governed logic, by convention-based semantics, and by referential depictions of both words and sentences.

A practical and adversarial model of rhetoric, whose proper subject matter and material were understood to be opinion, became the central curricular medium of instruction in the language arts. Regardless of whether emphasis was placed more on propositions opposed to one another through the instrument of dialectic, or upon opponents' arguments in an agonistic relationship imposed by the conventions of viva voce debate, the logico-rhetorical system defined by Aristotle emphasized manipulation — using and making language artifacts through an infinite number of possible recombinations and divisions of words, sentences, propositions, and arguments.

The *Rhetoric* also embodies an attempt to reform and improve Greek language education and use, and specifically the rhetorical curriculum which Aristotle, like Plato, believed was in serious trouble. Just as Plato made some accurate predictions about how certain deployments of technical rhetoric, if allowed to persist, would permanently alter the understanding and uses of language, so Aristotle foresaw perhaps that Plato's uncompromising position could lead to a dangerous split between the two educational aristocracies of the time: the philosophical schools and the public academies that trained young men for public and political life. If an absolute division between rhetoric, an instrument of practical education for public oratory, and dialectic, training in speculative and investigative logic with no practical end, became institutionalized, the worst kind of demagoguery would take over in the public domain, while the philosophical schools would continue to fragment into warring epistemologies, logical systems, and world views. By Cicero's era these developments had occurred, though perhaps with less destructiveness than might have been the case, because of the sometimes confusing, divided but corresponding, and incomplete severance of logic from rhetoric in Aristotle's system. Though he divided the practical language arts and the theoretical logical sciences, he built into their primary definitions conceptual overlaps that preserved the explicitness of their parallels with one another. Rhetorical argument retains its status as the counterpart of dialectical syllogistic reasoning; the rhetorical example is presented as a form of rhetorical argument which is the counterpart of logical induction. The *topoi* parallel the axioms, premises, and general truths which stand at the head of the logical chains of reasoning. In both logic and rhetoric, division and combination—whether of subject or of *to-poi*—are presented as the fundamental prerequisites to any knowledge, including knowledge of the forms of language and thought.

Aristotle's Lyceum claimed to be an improvement over some of the Sophists' schools because, like Plato's Academy, it was a permanent community where all members took part in the teaching, and where the favored mode of inquiry was dialogue, hence the name "peripatetic" for those who discoursed while walking. Despite Aristotle's later influence as a composer of monologue treatises and of subordinated, linear–discursive formulae, the relationships and teaching within the Lyceum were conceived of as dialogical, much along the lines of Plato's ideal.[36] Plato's integration of "true rhetoric" with dialogical philosophic inquiry failed to address the problematics of public political discourse, particularly the processes of decision and persuasion. Aristotle's *Rhetoric*, while it treats these problematics, is articulated as philosophic inquiry, perhaps in agreement with Plato's criticism of rhetoric manuals as tabular and formulaic presentations of models for composing speeches. Yet unlike Plato's interlocutors, the author of the first complex, systematic rhetoric is not visibly rhetorical himself. In contrast to Plato's explicit reference to the frame and conventions employed in writing the dialogues, in the *Rhetoric* Aristotle adopts a written convention that is never alluded to, one which is neither dialogical nor explicitly rhetorical. The *Rhetoric* is presented as a *study* of those things which effect persuasion. The subject of the relationship between speaker and audience takes up much of the *Rhetoric*; yet the relationship between Aristotle and his audience is rendered virtually invisible by his reportorial exposition. Where he might appropriately have discussed his own technique, *per exemplum*, in a treatise on techniques of effectiveness, the *Rhetoric* employs the pattern of monologue treatises, and makes autonomous referential statements which locate "these matters" in categories that already exist, presumably with no need for confirmation by an audience's assent. In this the *Rhetoric*, along with Aristotle's other work, is a foundational enactment of the rhetorical authority of linear and monologue discourse. This discourse, whether practiced in speeches or in chains of written discursive reasoning, rhetoric as a discipline has undertaken to both define and improve.

The implicit relationship between Aristotle and his audience is inherently rhetorical, an element in the teaching situation that Plato addresses in the *Gorgias* and in the Protagoras section of the *Theaetetus*. When one teaches, Socrates asks Gorgias, is one not being persuasive?[37] Socrates' point is that one "finds" or "learns" knowledge and truth; it makes no sense to talk of being persuaded of true versus false knowledge, only of true and false opinion and belief. Even Gorgias concedes that it makes no sense to speak of being persuaded in the case of mathematics and many other forms of knowledge. Aristotle extends this stock topic in an allusion to the teaching of geometry as a subject in which rhetorical language and arguments would be ludicrous.[38] In a counterpoint to Socrates' quip on teaching, Aristotle defines a firm disjunction between persuasion and instruction: "Before some audiences not even the possession of the exactest knowledge will make it easy for what we say to produce conviction. For argument based on knowledge implies instruction, and there are people who one cannot instruct. There, then, we must use, as our modes of persuasion and argument, notions possessed by everybody, as we observed in the *Topics*, when dealing with the way to handle a popular audience."[39] In drawing distinctions between teaching and persuasion, knowledge and belief, Aristotle talks *about* rhetoric in a way that presents it as an object of knowledge. Once known as an object of knowledge, and designed to affect opinion and belief, rhetoric can be used more efficaciously to do just that, particularly among those "whom one cannot instruct." This stance invites an examination of the *Rhetoric* as itself an excellent example of persuasion; seldom has what Aristotle says *about* debate been analyzed either as debatable or as an attempt at persuasion. Though the uses of what he recommends are debatable, and have remained perennial objects of invective or acclaim, *what* he describes is generally regarded as being the way that he presents it, as accurate factual description arranged in efficient taxonomical pigeonholes. One unfortunate but amusing consequence of taking too literally Aristotle's statement that rhetorical persuasion is in the domain solely of rhetoric is that it obscures the persuasive force of Aristotle's "scientific treatise."

To construct a truly comprehensive descriptive treatment of rhetoric would entail describing and even recommending some of the practices to which he and Plato alike object. As with the interlocutors in Plato's dialogues, the different points of view comprised in the *Categories, On Interpretation*, the *Analytics, Topics*, and *Rhetoric* provide ample means for understanding epistemological and logical limitations in rhetorical argument, resources that coexist somewhat uneasily with the "how to" passages of the *Rhetoric*. In many of these, Aristotle directly recommends strategies for deceiving, outwitting, misrepresenting, distorting, and dissembling before opponent and audience. That the *Rhetoric* is infrequently regarded as itself a piece of rhetoric suggests the extent to which Aristotle may be deemed a rhetorician *per exemplum*. It is precisely the invisibility of his rhetoric that makes the *Rhetoric* powerfully persuasive. One of the most recurrent bits of advice in the *Rhetoric* is that the most successful rhetoric doesn't appear to be rhetorical. Aristotle's manner of presentation says, "Is not this analysis of persuasion instructive?" The form of the *Rhetoric* silently and persuasively reinforces *what* is said, not only of rhetoric proper but of language arts in all the disciplines. "The arts of language cannot help having a small but real importance, whatever it is we have to expound to others; the way in which a thing is said does affect its intelligibility. Not, however, so much importance as people think. All such arts are fanciful and meant to charm the hearers. Nobody uses fine language when teaching geometry."[40] Nor should they, when expounding the nature of rhetoric. A serious treatise, the *Rhetoric* both follows its own rules and further entrenches the expository, monologue analytical treatise as the norm for serious, "scientific" writing. "Wherefore those who practise this artifice must conceal it and avoid the appearance of speaking artificially instead of naturally; for that which is natural persuades, but the artificial does not."[41]

In talking about "what is" within a logical discourse that is conceptualized as fully autonomous, self-contained, and true — as had been the Preplatonic *Logos* — Aristotle hypostatizes his own lexicon and logical formulae. This hypostatization of logical discourse in the manner of the *Rhetoric*'s expression marks an official merger of methods which, though they originated within oral philosophical discourse, further cemented the relationships among philosophy, rhetoric, and literacy.[42] Paradoxically, Aristotelian and post-Aristotelian divisions of subjects, along with the nature of the rules defined in the *Rhetoric*, ensured that the complex of logico-discursive paradigms defined and exemplified in the logical treatises would not

be taught in the one "course" which disseminated literacy throughout the classical world: rhetoric. What came to be thought of as
"fanciful" language arts, the arts of "appearance" (*phainesthai*),
defined stylistic norms for rhetorical speeches and for poetry
alike — as first witnessed by the companionable relationship between the *Rhetoric* and *Poetics*. It is unfortunate that Aristotle's
dialogues are lost, the popular "literary" enterprises which, along
with Plato's and others', influenced literary writers and philosophers for the next four centuries. These would have given us a
useful sample of Aristotle's role as exemplar to literary–philosophical as distinct from scientific treatise writers. The exempla provided
by the literary–philosophical dialogue form coexisted with the descriptive taxonomies of stylistic forms which are provided and repeated in the *Rhetoric* and *Poetics*, and influenced poetics and
rhetorical style for fifteen hundred years, contributing to the contours assumed by literacy and to the *letteraturizzazione* of rhetoric
in several periods.[43]

The habit of equating both rhetoric and poetics with frivolous or
ornamental stylistics is amply exemplified in Book III of the *Rhetoric*. Its separate treatment of style as diction has repeatedly deferred
serious attention to the logical and epistemological nuances of "poetic" or "metaphorical" language. By Aristotle's time, Gorgias was
well known for his often humorous treatments of these issues, and
for his belief in the magic of such language.[44] Gorgias' style is
roundly denounced by Aristotle as an example of an ineffectively
florid, contrived, poetic, "merely" ornamental style which in Aristotle's view is outworn and no longer taken seriously.[45] Yet Aristotle
also praises, somewhat paradoxically, the ironic manner of Gorgias
as depicted by Plato. The *Rhetoric* can be seen as crafted in part
according to the rules of style defined in Book III, where Aristotle
distinguishes poetic from prose diction; ornamentation from clear,
current, and ordinary words; and artificiality from naturalness.
"We can now see that a writer must disguise his art and give the
impression of speaking naturally and not artificially. Naturalness is
persuasive, artificiality is the contrary; for our hearers are prejudiced and think we have some design against them."[46] In this, Aristotle implies that, because the audience in a rhetorical situation
already suspects that the speaker has a "design" on them, the speaker must appear natural, spontaneous, and without craft. Rhetoric is

most successful when not obviously rhetorical; naturalness is a carefully contrived appearance. If this rule is applied to the *Rhetoric* itself, we can see that the most effective rhetoric for a writer of a treatise on rhetoric is one which affects nonrhetoric by using plain language, by being precise, by producing a treatise rather than by delivering a speech, and by stating what appears to be true. Pervasively, in Aristotle's descriptions, good rhetoric is *apparent* truth, fact, or knowledge.

How far does this rule of controlling appearance extend into the subdivisions of rhetoric? Does it extend to the treatment of *ethos, pathos*, and even *logos*?[47] Is the character a speaker presents, as Aristotle suggests, as contrived as the actor's role? Should it be? "When delivery comes into fashion, it will have the same effect as acting (*hupokritike*). . . . A gift for acting is a natural talent and depends less upon art, but in regard to style it is artificial. . . . The style of written compositions is most precise, that of debate is most suitable for delivery. Of the latter there are two kinds, ethical and emotional; this is why actors are always running after plays of this character, and poets after suitable actors."[48] Though in book 1 Aristotle links *ethos* with conveying an impression of good will, knowledge, or virtue, it is the appearance of good will on the part of the speaker which stimulates the good will of the audience, and encourages "those feelings that so change men as to affect their judgments."[49] Here are expressed two different points of view on the same subject. Under the heading of "style," *ethos* is likened to the actor's art and linked with an emergent art of delivery. Under the heading of the three modes of persuasion in rhetoric, *ethos* is defined as character communicated through the appearance of certain emotions and behavior. In this guise *ethos* is linked directly if not inevitably with *pathos*, insofar as the audience's feelings are roused, countered, or matched by the speaker's apparent character.

Tantalizingly cryptic remarks about kinds of writing occur in the midst of Aristotle's discussions of style, character, and delivery. They are reminders that genre boundaries constraining writing conventions were not yet discrete, and that the *Poetics* is one of the first extensive expositions of formal definitions of genre, plot, and literary style. Full emphasis must be placed on definition in this assertion, because it would of course be ludicrous to claim that there were no epics, plays, poems, elegies, hexameters, or Gorgianic figures in earlier practice. However, Aristotle's comments intimate that explicit genre distinctions, particularly with regard to writing, were just then emergent. He articulates a consciousness of classifications among what to him are still closely related: drama, actors, rhetoric, delivery, speeches written for delivery, and writing as a more "precise" medium than debate. Though Aristotle draws on dramatic analogues in portions of his treatment of style and delivery, he says nothing about the formal conventions of dramatic scripts as themselves a kind of writing, when he distinguishes "precise" writing from less precise rhetoric. Given Plato's insistence on the dialogue form for both spoken and written discourse, it is noteworthy that Aristotle never comments on Plato's adaptation of the dialogue, *as a form*, to the objectives of both writing and "true rhetoric." The writing Aristotle recommends, by assertion and by example, is the treatise, the form to which Plato explicitly objects in *Letter VII*, because of its pretense of comprehensiveness and conclusiveness.

Does Aristotle express an indirect criticism of Plato's theory and practice alike, when he criticizes those who, in not availing themselves of writing, "are silent" when they have something to communicate? He not only defends the study of both writing and speaking as branches of rhetoric, but characterizes their role as complementary and definitive of "the educated." "The one requires a knowledge of good Greek, while the other prevents the necessity of keeping silent when we wish to communicate something to others which happens to those who do not know how to write."[50] There could be no more explicit a definition of the interdependence of rhetoric and writing with the clearly desirable condition of being educated, a condition which with the same direct allusions to writing and voice are today termed literacy. Is the logic of probability that Aristotle presents as the definitive mode of argumentation in rhetoric defended as one which gives the appearance of truth with none of its substance? This had been Plato's objection to rhetorical speeches and writings alike. In the case of Aristotle, I think the answer must be both yes and no. He does present and directly recommend probabilistic argument as effective in direct proportion to its resemblance to or imitation of truth. But in so presenting it he gives any subsequent educated audience of such argumentation the information which will render this particular kind of dissimulation less effective. He gives but also takes away, leaving his own view about the wisdom of such practices a highly circumspect neutrality on the matter. "But since the whole business of Rhetoric is to influence opinion, we must pay attention to it, not as being right, but necessary."[51] Equivocations like these continue to prompt attacks on Aristotle's rhetoric as the ancestor of Machiavelli and manipulative advertising on the one hand, and defenses which present it as soberly philosophical and high-minded on the other. The more malign view sees Aristotle as shrewd, practical, and even cynical about human nature, as a trickster who helped perpetuate technical rhetoric as a bag of tricks, as gamesmanship in agonistic debate, and as a compulsively taxonomical series of pigeonholes. In the more high-minded view, Aristotle's statements about contriving appearances in order to deceive, trick, win, or defeat are excused as descriptions of what is done, not of what should be done, while the many intersections of the *Rhetoric* with the logical system are strongly emphasized.[52] So various is the *Rhetoric* in its topics and treatments that it cannot ultimately be reduced to either an instrument of evil or a prolegomenon for more dignified understandings of persuasion, communication, and careful reasoning.

Because the contours given rhetoric in Aristotelian tradition became so central to subsequent education in language, logic, and literature — to "literacy" broadly understood — it is useful to review its contents in a highly condensed form to facilitate a comparison with "literacy" or "being educated" as these have subsequently come to be defined. The *Rhetoric* presents accessible, simplified versions of the taxonomies and lists of logical structures developed in the *Categories* and *Topics* adapted for ready use. Aristotle adds a list of modes of persuasion (*pisteis*) which help direct the choice of subjects and arguments: in some situations, the most forceful means of persuasion may be the speaker's apparent character (*ethos*); in others, effectively moving or changing the audience's mental attitudes (*psuche pathemata; pathos*); in still others, the logical or apparently logical (*logos*) treatment of the subject. Within the treatment of *logos* are listed the four general, twenty-eight specific, and eight specious ("sohistical") lines of reasoning. It is as *logos*, apparently rational argument, that rhetoric is defined as a counterpart (*antistrophe*) of dialectic. Political, forensic, and ceremonial oratory are distinguished as the three kinds of rhetoric. A treatment of style and delivery provides guidelines for choosing kinds of words and phrases and for controlling the appearance of character through delivery, which is likened to the actor's art (*hupokritike*).

I have argued that Aristotle's treatments of language and logic constitute a preponderantly instrumentalist, semiotic, referential, predicational, and rule-governed conceptualization of language and its use. If the nature of the linguistic sign is arbitrary, and logical rules are the necessary instruments for constructing truth, then it would seem that rules must be provided for all language use, logical and otherwise. While Aristotle may have conceived of his descriptions as neutral definitions of methods, they have subsequently functioned normatively, as rules. The logical treatises develop systems for constructing and assessing logical validity; the *Rhetoric* provides instruments for choosing subjects and arranging their articulation to the end of effectiveness, defined as suasiveness. The division of logic from rhetoric relegates the study of words to the domain of rhetoric — a system defining the manipulation of words. The manipulation of the meaning of things by rearranging words is articulated in the *Rhetoric* as a series of tropes which are most successful when used in speaking to the ignorant. The educated purportedly know the self-evident meaning of things by the careful application of broad, general principles. Plato's understanding of the relationships among words, referents, and concepts is quite different from Aristotle's, yet both of them present arguments that distinguish the powers and culpability of the rhetor from any intrinsic characteristics of language, and record the view that rhetorical discourse works most effectively with audiences ignorant of its devices. What distinguishes Aristotle from Plato perhaps most sharply on this issue is Aristotle's acceptance and promotion of "giving the appearance of" (*phainesthai*) and "dissimulation" (*eironeia*) by rhetor and "gentleman" alike.

The Aestheticization of Irony

Modern discussions of both irony and illusion have capitalized on the idea of the lie of language. It is said that in the very nature of words and language lies the seed of double, overdetermined, and manipulable meanings. But to what extent do beliefs about the nature of language shape how language is used — uses which in turn recursively affect changes in beliefs about its nature? Regardless of his neutrality in dealing with the speaker — audience relationships institutionalized by rhetoric, Aristotle joins Plato in asserting that the rhetorician, not rhetoric, manipulates language. Rhetoric is an inevitable outgrowth not of the nature of language but of human nature; individuals, not language, lie. Yet fictions, invalid arguments, and rhetoric are all, in their own way, lies. Aristotle's successful rhetorician is able to persuade an audience that things are the way he says they are. And the way he says they are is very often not so. Two different senses of "lie" are important here. First, there is referential error with the intent of deceiving. Error alone is not a lie; it is simply a mistake, or what the Preplatonics called *pseudos*. But to say of a rhinestone "this is a diamond," whether to make someone happy or to realize a huge profit, is to be deceitful, to willingly, knowingly, and deliberately mislead another person. The Preplatonics' *apate* and Plato's *eironikos mimetes* denote this more reprehensible kind of lying. Fiction and rhetoric alike have been classified as benign lies, acceptable to the extent that they don't hurt anyone, and insofar as the fabulator is not perverse. Self-expressive misrepresentation, however, is a different kind of lie, often less benign than fiction, which announces itself as such. Self-deception and other-deception as often as not involve matters of feeling, knowledge, and belief, internal mental states which are said to be other than what they really are. A seducer says, "I love you, I want to marry you," to a woman he has every intention of leaving the next morning. A woman says, "I am very happy," to herself and to her family every day for years, until one day her suppressed misery surfaces and she abruptly leaves. Even though the terms "lie," "rationalization," "fiction," and "rhetoric" are employed with some degree of interchangeability, in instances like these the common factor which has long rendered such phenomena targets of ethical evaluation is the presence of conscious deceit vis-à-vis a trusting audience — the factor that led Plato to equate rhetoric, because it requires a "trusting" audience, with irony, defined as conscious intent to deceive. Rhetoric and irony, for Plato, are morally wrong because they are deliberate, knowing lies.

In contrast, Aristotle firmly separates the moral status of rhetoric from the rules governing its practice by providing a separate discussion of ethics, including an ethics of discourse. When he considers rhetoric from an ethical point of view, Aristotle, like Plato, links it directly with irony. Unlike Plato, he qualifies his condemnation by saying that the gentleman must sometimes use this kind of speech when talking to the ignorant. "The proud man . . . must be open in his hate and in his love (for to conceal one's feelings, i.e., to care less for truth than for what people think, is a coward's part), and he must speak and act openly; for he is free of speech because he is contemptuous, and he is given to telling the truth except when he speaks in irony to the vulgar."[53] The proud man, and the good man, are "free of speech" in that they don't use rhetoric; they are contemptuous of rhetoric. As was true for Plato, the good man — at least among his peers — is open, candid, and concerned with the truth. Irony here is construed as a kind of necessary evil, as an inevitable mark of the contempt felt for audiences so ignorant that they will not understand what you are saying. From a moral point of view, irony is in one sense as much the "fault" of the audience as of the speaker. In the *Ethics* Aristotle addresses the question of truth telling as a moral category. "The truthful person is an intermediate between the pretense which exaggerates, or boastfulness [*hyperbole*], and the pretense of understatement, or mock modesty [*eironeia*]"[54] — a distinction that parallels the distinction made in the *Poetics* between the *alazon* or buffoon in drama, and the *eiron* or sly dissembler who strategically and skillfully understates. As an extreme, and as a form of dissembling, irony is condemned because it is not accurate truth telling. In the moral realm rhetoric, irony, and an ignorant audience constitute one another.

Examined collaterally, the *Poetics* and the *Rhetoric* confirm parallels not only between rhetoric and irony, but between the rhetorician and the poet as well. Both are presented as fabulists; only their purposes differ. Whether the fabulist regards his audience as ignorant or not, the success of his words relies on the extent to which they are taken to be reality. It is in this context that Aristotle warns the rhetorician against trying to use historical examples. If one's purpose is persuasion, he argues, a scrupulous adherence to factual reality is much less effective than the invention of probable accounts. Though the successful manipulation of erroneous popular preconceptions is best effected by the enthymeme, Aristotle advises the rhetor, if he must use examples rather than arguments, to invent a repertoire of illustrative anecdotes rather than depend on examples from history, which he proposes do not serve rhetorical purposes very well; he distinguishes two kinds of inventions: parallels in actual fact, and fables.[55] These "events, real or imaginary," are said to be most useful as openers for eulogies and polemics. The skillful use of real and imaginary examples was later to become a major criterion for judging the skill of both rhetor and poet. As Aristotle codifies these techniques he distinguishes historical from fictional invention only to class them together, and to promote fictive exempla as the more dignified materials of rhetoric and poetry alike: "Hence poetry is something more philosophic and of graver import than history, since its statements are of the nature rather of universals whereas those of history are singulars."[56]

Socrates, too, rather liberally mixes historical examples with fables as illustrations in his discussions, yet without defining the distinction that Aristotle develops between factual and fictional example. Plato's depiction of Socrates' practice emphasizes instead that the excerpting of real events from their contexts is equivalent to creating a fiction through rearrangement; the status of specifics used to exemplify an issue (such as "what is justice?") resides not in their factual reality but in their thematic philosophical truth and thereby their instructive forcefulness. Aristotle divides his assessment of exempla into two categories. In the domain of logical reasoning, an example is true to the extent that it accurately summarizes an inductive inference. In the domain of rhetoric, an example is appropriate to the extent that it persuades. Despite his repetition of the quip that "Homer taught the poets to lie," the association of any and all fabulation with lying, central to later aesthetics, is foreign to Aristotle. Fabulation is either well done or poorly done. Lying is an ethical matter for Aristotle, as nicely witnessed by his reputed answer to the question, "What do people gain by telling lies?" — "That when they speak the truth they are not believed." This view is illustrated within the list of enthymematic *topoi*: "Since men do not praise the same things in public and in secret, but in public chiefly praise what is just and beautiful, and in secret rather wish for what is expedient, another topic consists in endeavoring to infer its opposite from one or the other of these statements."[57]

Though there is no direct association drawn between *heuresis* (discovery, invention) and irony in the *Rhetoric*, the parallel between *ethos* and dissembling lurks close to the surface. In the *Rhetoric*, as in the *Ethics*, irony is directly mentioned as a kind of wit and dissembling appropriate to the gentleman. "Irony better befits the gentleman than buffoonery. The ironical man jokes to amuse himself, the buffoon to amuse others."[58] The rhetorician is advised to use an ironic tone of understatement and deference when debating an opponent: "a modest irony, 'He certainly said so-and-so, but I said so-and-so,' may be used to defend one's speech against one's opponent."[59] One of the most direct prescriptions for verbal irony appears, oddly enough, in the *Ethics*, where irony is specifically equated with understatement and verbal dissembling — that is, with saying or expressing a veiled or guarded version of what one means. In the *Rhetoric* the emphasis is more on irony as a trait of character, a manner appropriate to the gentleman, in contrast to the earlier colloquial use of *eiron* as a term of abuse and condemnation, implying not only "scoundrel" but "low-born."[60] Aristotle explicitly equates *eironeia* and *litotes* — the exclusively verbal and interpersonal irony of understatement — with an admirable character trait: restraint, deference, and sometimes condescension toward a low-born or ignorant audience.[61] It is tempting to speculate that this revised sense of irony is not unrelated to Aristotle's articulation of rhetorical dissimulation more broadly — *ethos* — as a necessary and admirable craft. In the *Poetics* Aristotle classes irony as a species of comedic humor. The *eiron* is juxtaposed with the *alazon* as a dramatic type, and is said to be either the dissembler or the "comic ridiculous." He is one who puts on a mask which is "ugly and distorted without causing pain."[62] The *eiron*'s ugliness, according to Aristotle, lies in his *pretense* of ignorance and condescension; he is an inverted buffoon. Or he may be distorted in other directions, such as pretended knowledge, or pretended aristocracy which is later revealed to be a sham. This cluster of definitions conforms more closely to the colloquial sense of irony then current: ugly and scurrilous because dissembling. In discussing dramatic form, Aristotle defines what we now call tragic irony, or an ironic sequence of events, when he describes *peripeteia*: "In the finest form of Tragedy, the Plot must be not simple but complex and involves a change or reversal of fortune."[63] Complexity and reversals of "fate" remain modern connotations of event irony; it is worth noting that Aristotle, in the *Poetics*, which grounds subsequent discussions of literary form, listed these elements as major criteria to be used in assessing drama but does not link these event sequences to irony. The first English appearance of "irony" was an application to dramatic plot in Bishop Connop Thirwall's "On the Irony of Sophocles" in 1833.[64] The prototype for an irony of fate in events is defined in Aristotle's conceptualization of *muthos* and strongly influenced subsequent poetics, yet it is not linked with the concept of irony until the nineteenth century.

For Plato, irony is intrinsic to rhetoric and renders it a deceitful act because it entails a willful, programmatic separation of what one knows to be true from what one says. The dissembling imitator is held by Plato to be morally and intellectually corrupt because of this infidelity to truth. Unlike one who is mistaken and innocently believes he knows, the *eironikos* intentionally dissembles knowledge in order to deceive an audience. The classification system used by Aristotle strikingly alters irony as Plato defines it. In the division of the language "arts" into separate categories, each with its own matter, method, and purpose, Aristotle separates questions of intent from questions of meaning and method. Irony is no longer an important cognate to all rhetoric; as *ethos* it becomes instead a rhetorical tool, a mask which may be effective in certain situations. The adversarial situations of logical disputation and rhetoric demand techniques, not virtue. Ethical situations demand fidelity to truth and virtue, not technique. Fabulation is a matter of felicitous arrangement that has no necessary ties to intent. By discussing irony in three different places—the *Poetics*, the *Rhetoric*, and the *Nichomachean Ethics*—Aristotle adopts a way of dealing with the issues surrounding irony which now, perhaps, seems obvious and appropriate. Irony is sometimes a verbal technique, sometimes an act of deceit, sometimes an effective strategy, sometimes a situation in which an unnamed "fate" is the agent of reversal. Contemporary scholarship continues to employ this Aristotelian arrangement, in that deception, double meaning, and strategic understatement are examined by widely divergent disciplines under a number of headings. The double bind; the confidence game; the ironic narrator; the schizophrenic personality; the deceptive relationship between the conscious and the subconscious mind; the notions that "God," the author, or the subject are dead, that "the human condition" is an ironic deceit or tragic joke; literary and religious attempts to go beyond words into silence because words are inevitably "inadequate"—each of these modern *koinoi topoi* borders directly on issues and phenomena that were examined in classical treatments of both *ethos* and irony. In part because of the methodological divisions originated by Aristotle, questions surrounding irony and its more recent derivatives—linguistic contingency, illusoriness, and unreliability—tend to be discussed separately, sometimes under epistemology, sometimes under ethics, psychology, linguistics, or literary criticism. Paradoxically, however, consciously deceptive uses of double meaning as well as their apprehension are possible only within the context of the rhetorical tradition as conceptualized and developed by Aristotle. It is often an invisible backdrop; but without it there would be no terms and categories for talking about all the speaker–audience, speaker–text, text–world, word–world contingencies imposed by an aesthetics of irony and its subsequent derivatives.[65]

4

Cicero: Defining the Value of Literacy

> In despising rhetoric, philosophy atoned for a guilt incurred ever since Antiquity by its detachment from things, a guilt already pointed out by Plato. But the persecutors of the rhetorical element that saved expression for thought did just as much for the technification of thought, for its potential abolition, as did those who cultivated rhetoric and ignored the object.
>
> THEODOR ADORNO, *Negative Dialectics*

> Hence it is that, in the case of various kinds of knowledge, we find that what in former days occupied the energies of men of mature mental ability sinks to the level of information, exercises, and even pastimes, for children; and in this educational progress we can see the history of the world's culture delineated in faint outline. . . . It is, that is to say, a synoptic index, like a skeleton with tickets stuck all over it, or like the rows of boxes kept shut and labelled in a grocer's stall; and is as intelligible as either the one or the other.
>
> FRIEDRICH HEGEL, *The Phenomenology of Mind*

Cicero has received so much attention in the history of Western humanism, rhetoric, and belles lettres that any further analysis of his work might seem either redundant or contrived. Yet the very diversity of his influence invites reviewing. The breadth and divergence of views comprised in his work have often been obscured by the selective approaches of single disciplines. Because they have not focused on the relationships among the many themes he takes up, specialized, single-topic approaches to Cicero have distorted the complex networks of subjects and genres he addresses: histories of rhetoric, law, philosophy, and religion; technical treatises on rhetoric; letters and speeches; and "literary" dialogues after the fashion of Plato and Aristotle.[1] Most studies of Cicero and his precursors in substance, style, and genre have been produced within select, modern disciplinary boundaries, and consequently leave unresolved some fundamental questions while simultaneously obscuring the answers to others. As a literary figure, Cicero is known for his stylistic theory and exemplary practice in abundant letters, speeches, and dialogues. Cicero remains one of the few extensive primary sources on ancient and classical philosophy, and is generally regarded as an eclectic disciple of the Middle Academy.[2] In rhetorical history and theory Cicero has been known as the decisively influential translator of Greek technical rhetoric into an expanded and Romanized Latin form which he also practiced, though not always in strict conformity to his own rules. These separate definitions inevitably obscure the interdependence, even integration, of Cicero's treatments of rhetoric, philosophy, and literature. My rereading of Cicero's handbooks, dialogues, and letters on rhetoric suggests directions for supplementing our approaches to Cicero's rhetorical theory, and for understanding that theory as far more than a composite of technical, literary–philosophical, or forensic approaches to rhetoric. Correcting distortions, to be sure, introduces alternate distortions. These rereadings selectively emphasize elements in Cicero's theory and practice which are explicit rejections and reformations of extant rhetorical traditions, and assemble the scattered particulars in which Cicero presents himself, variously, as restoring the curriculum of Plato's Academy, as correcting the relativisms introduced by Aristotelian and Stoic logic, and as promoting and producing a stylistically mature, substantive Latin literature which did not yet exist.

De Oratore, Orator, and *Brutus* depict a wide range of views concerning the state of Latin learning in the first century B.C. Many

voices relay a host of appraisals whose relationship to Cicero's purposes and positions remains intriguingly ironic and debatable. The
voices who speak in his rhetorical works convey a burgeoning pluralism of views. Greek literature, we are told, was known to the
majority of the educated primarily through compendia of apt quotations which had been selected from the poets and were used in
rhetorical stylistics exercises. Aside from Epicurean and Stoic ethics, which in some ways functioned as secular religions, "philosophy," variously defined, was regarded by many Romans as an im-
practical, dilletantish Greek import. Philosophers were seen as
scornful of public life, and were ignored or ridiculed. Rhetoric had
suffered similar deterioration since its ideal setting amid the liberal
sciences in Plato's Academy, for it had become a dreary course of
rote drill and maxims which, according to Cicero, even its teachers
barely understood. Antonius, his childhood tutor depicted as an
interlocutor in *De Oratore*, is made to assert, with dubious sincerity,
the stock view that rhetoric is and always will be an art of willful
ignorance: "The activity of the orator has to do with opinion, not
knowledge. For we both address ourselves to the ignorant and speak
of matters unknown to ourselves."[3] The belief in a degenerate state
of learning was perhaps both the challenge and the pretext propel-
ling Cicero into the roles of reformer and revisionist. He has often
been viewed quite differently. There are ample examinations of Cicero's continuity with other elements in Graeco-Roman culture, and
of his deserved status since the Renaissance as the exemplary literary–rhetorical humanist. This emphasis has been fueled, perhaps,
by an often nostalgic classicism of modern liberal arts disciplines
that has perpetuated the image of Cicero as a protector of Roman
aristocratic and republican values—a profile that has obscured what
I find to be an equally important role as a reformer and as a serious,
substantive philosopher of language and culture. Hence the focus
on the revisionist elements across his work as a whole, and particularly on radically reformist elements in his treatment of rhetoric.
The writings of his exiled years were no idle entertainment. Among
other aims, Cicero's transformations have the explicit purpose of
reuniting two disciplines—rhetoric and philosophy, "tongue and
brain"—which he alleges had increasingly diverged during the period from 300 to 100 B.C.

Examined collaterally, Cicero's works coordinate views that integrate critiques of Stoic dialectic as excessively eristic; of Academic skepticism as dogmatically probabilistic; and of technical rhetoric as a rote and puerile reduction of the philosophical rhetoric espoused by Plato and Isocrates. Cicero's critiques of various depictions of these decays not only integrate one "subject" with another within each discussion, but also contend, with an explicit nod to Plato as a precursor in this enterprise, that any division of subjects marks an artificial and harmful partitioning of a whole, "the liberal sciences."[4] The long-standing influence of *De Inventione* has distracted attention to Cicero's reformulation of rhetoric as much more than a simple translation of Greek technical rhetoric into Latin. His "rhetorical" treatises provide for a redefinition of philosophy, located within a broad integrated field, the *artes liberales*, that he defends as a resuscitation of the curriculum of Plato's Academy.[5] Many of the views given prominence in the speeches of Cicero's interlocutors are explicitly counter-Aristotelian and recommend an abandonment of technical rhetoric, "the rhetoricians' workshops." Aristotle is charged with being "the first to undermine the Forms."[6] Yet Cicero's identification with Plato and the curriculum of the Academy is dependent on opposing Plato to Socrates, whose relationship is seldom seen as antithetical today.

Many elements in the conceptions of Socrates, Plato, and Aristotle that are given voice by Cicero's interlocutors substantially diverge from the traditional concepts of Cicero as either a technical rhetorician in the tradition of Aristotle's *Rhetoric*, or a literary humanist like Isocrates propounding an idealized model of eloquence. Cicero's dialogues on rhetoric persistently focus on the history and effects of the partitioning of the liberal arts as well. He presents the judgement that this partitioning began with Socrates, was extended by Aristotle, and has been damaging at both theoretical and practical levels.[7] Among the charges brought against separatism are several incipient contingencies introduced by separating speech and thought, tongue and brain. Neither philosophy nor rhetoric any longer provides viable instruments of thought, language, education, or knowledge. The quality of writings has been affected as well. In *De Oratore*, Antonius accuses the philosophers of false advertising in using titles such as *On Justice*. The book on such a simple, seemingly clear subject is mangled, "incomprehensible, . . . so inextricably are they entangled in closely reasoned and condensed dialectic."[8] In a contention that obliquely echoes Gorgias' statement "if anything is comprehensible, it is incommunicable," Cicero proposes that it is the philosophers' precision, paradoxically, that makes their discourse incomprehensible. "As a result, the learned lacked eloquence which appealed to the people, and the fluent speakers lacked the refinement of sound learning."[9] The divergence of philosophy and rhetoric is traced back through the fragmentation of the liberal sciences and the "plurality of schools that virtually sprang from Socrates."[10] Those who, "following Socrates, affirm nothing but refute others" are singled out for rejecting positive philosophy and rhetoric alike.[11] The philosophers, it is said, scorn rhetoric and shun writing; thus anyone who is not a formal student of philosophy must rely on "vulgar" hearsay, upon clichéd reductions transmitted by an oral tradition, for their philosophic notions. The absence of an accessible philosophical literature creates deleterious and unnecessary scarcity. Those who are not disciples of a philosophic school have no access to systematic inquiry or logic. Cicero's histories provide some of the first accessible sources on the philosophical schools of classical antiquity; set amid dialogues, they retain the diversity of views about each philosophy as well.

Socrates' scorn of rhetoric is depicted as the origin of the "reprehensible severance of tongue and brain" that has afflicted the entire culture with two sets of teachers, "one to teach us to think, and another to teach us to speak."[12] The philosophers, it is claimed, fail to teach "thought" not only because they are removed from "the common life," but also because they will not use language that can communicate, being caught up in dialectical eristics, and because they propound the probable in a dogmatic fashion. Cicero renders the third of these ancient commonplaces concerning philosophy in a deft Gorgianic paradox: "Thus, the decision of the wise man that nothing can be perceived, is perceived."[13] Socrates' attacks on the Sophists and the Megarian relativists as depicted in Plato's dialogues find numerous parallels among Cicero's interlocutors' attacks on the Skeptics and on Socrates himself. In both cases there are accusations of eristic dialectics and hairsplitting over nuances in words. Partly as a result of the philosophers' scorn for rhetoric, the rhetoricians are deemed "half educated," and those they train for public life equally so: "But nowadays we are deluged not only with the notions of the vulgar but with the opinions of the half educated, who find it easier to deal with matters that they cannot grasp in their entirety if they split them up and take them piecemeal, and who separate words from thoughts as one might sever body from mind."[14]

The historical sections of *De Oratore, Brutus*, and *Orator* single out elements in earlier rhetorics which should be eliminated or reshaped. In this enterprise Cicero functions not merely as a translator but as a restorer and reformer as well. Like Plato and Isocrates before him, he reunites rhetoric and philosophy, strips away the overly technical elements in each, and removes rhetoric from the status it had been given in the Stoic classification as a subdivision of dialectic. The views he develops concur with both Aristotle and Plato. Rhetoric is seen as aligned with ethics; philosophy and ethics must be united to overcome "the severance of tongue and brain." A reunited philosophy and rhetoric forming the basis of education can both direct and generate liberal studies, which in turn will allow the production of improved, systematic, and *recorded* history, law, and philosophy. These in turn will improve the polis, *civitas*, the common life.

Cicero's recommendations offer a solution to the ethical dilemmas created for the rhetor by an "ignorant" audience, and to the resulting temptation of sophistic argumentation. Many in his era continued to see rhetoric as a practical *techne* and to determine its merit solely by its persuasive success. Cicero does not deny to rhetoric its practical and technical elements, but he makes extensive reading in history, philosophy, religion, and literature prerequisite to the study of these elements. It is easy to overlook a subtlety in this requirement. The written materials which could provide this prerequisite curriculum did not exist in Latin in the first century B.C. One of Cicero's purposes, then, is to simultaneously argue for and exemplify the production of the liberal arts texts necessary for the training of the new, improved orator–citizen. Once produced, compendia of "the history, life, and thoughts of man" will ensure an ongoing body of knowledge serving as a repository of cultural wisdom and as an instrument of education. The "genuine orator," a concept evocative of Plato's "true rhetoric," is glimpsed more often than achieved but nonetheless should serve as a goal and virtue. "Eloquence is one of the supreme virtues . . . [which], after compassing a knowledge of facts, gives verbal expression to the thoughts and purposes of the mind in such a manner as to have the power of driving the hearers forward in any direction in which it has applied its weight; and the stronger this faculty is, the more necessary it is for it to be combined with integrity and supreme wisdom, and if we bestow fluency of speech on persons devoid of those virtues, we shall not have made orators of them, but shall have put weapons into the hands of madmen."[15]

Like Plato's Gorgias and like Aristotle, Cicero locates ethical responsibility for the abuse of rhetoric in the individual's morality and integrity. However, by making eloquence itself a virtue, that is, a function of morality and moral training, and by requiring encyclopedic training prior to training in rhetorical technique, Cicero builds in safeguards which are not provided for in Aristotle's partitioned system. Because Cicero has so often been examined from the perspective of his continuity with Aristotelian tradition, I emphasize the explicitness of his discontinuities with that tradition. His equally legitimate forebears are the Plato of *Phaedrus*, and Isocrates, who stressed the union of philosophy and rhetoric. The main thrusts of Cicero's dual approach, to restore and reform, can be summarized in the form of an argument:

1. Technical rhetoric has become an inadequate instrument for training the orator because it fails to impart the wide knowledge, experience, and systematic thought on which eloquence depends.
2. Philosophy in its current forms has exceeded the limits of pluralism. It has abandoned any responsibility to the language arts or their learning. Academic skepticism has the best potential for resuscitation, but it must abandon its dogmatic probabilism.
3. Philosophy and rhetoric should be reunited and reconfigured as interdependent vehicles of thought and language. They should be studied only after substantive, extensive reading and study of a deliberately exemplary, comprehensive, and comprehensible literature and history.

Examined as a vast and repeated articulation of this argument, Cicero's work can be viewed as more innovative than it seems when examined retrospectively through the lenses of the medieval Aristotelian tradition and the Renaissance construction of Ciceronian humanism.

Cicero's literary innovativeness deserves special emphasis. In addition to providing a revisionist history of rhetoric, each of Cicero's works also exemplifies the reformation in rhetoric that he propounds. Though there are plentiful Greek antecedents, the genres he uses and the subjects he arranges are not drawn from a fixed storehouse of Latin literary conventions, as subsequent literary criticism sometimes suggests. Rather, they are inventive recombinations explicitly defined in each work, and in some cases, he indicates they are neologistic. His "literary" dialogues and letter follow the formula of his revisionist system of rhetoric; his technical rhetorics are expository and dialogical treatments of extant rhetorical models. Recent analyses of oral and literate discourse patterns demonstrate the infinite number of possible combinations of these patterns, and replace any simple distinctions between "oral" and "literate" with the model of mixtures, of a continuum of oral and literate patterns and resources.[16] In terms of today's understandings of literacy, Cicero's goal for his culture and its education may be re-viewed and redefined as the production of texts which impart, establish, and exemplify literacy as irreducibly and necessarily both literate and oral, a dual characterization that is manifest at many points among his definitions of eloquence.

Cicero's work reminds us that the Latin metalinguistic and metacognitive lexicon was in its infancy. Despite plentiful Greek texts and discourses, Latin expositions of the forms of thought and modes of articulation, and the emergence of a Latin literature in all fields, were new enough to be provisional in style, lexicon, and genre boundaries. In this context Cicero's *artes liberales* and *eloquentia* represent an unprecedented and encyclopedic reconceptualization of Greek knowledge, literature, and education not simply through translation into Latin but also through cultural transformation that Cicero explicitly identified as a goal. Of necessity, Cicero reshaped existing genres, extended their scope, and effected a renewed synthesis among disciplines. Simultaneously, he produced the first Latin literature written according to the rules of *eloquentia* as he redefined it, building on criteria defined in several schools of Greek rhetoric. His critique and reformulation of rhetoric impose prerequisites to the study of rhetoric, and are also prerequisite to the establishment of a liberal education, as he defines it. Only when some extant rhetorical modes are eliminated and other improved, he argues, can the textual materials needed for liberal education be produced. His dialogues on rhetoric and philosophy may be dubbed self-creating artifacts intended to disseminate both the form and the content of the liberal arts, which when assimilated would restructure the entire culture through practitioners of *eloquentia*.[17] Cicero performed a multitude of roles as transmitter, transformer, historian, and instigator of many patterns of thought and discourse that are still regarded as central concomitants of humanism and literacy. His treatment of rhetoric looked forward to and indeed instigated a literate Latin literary culture which developed through the fifth century, when the number of circulating manuscripts had returned to the fractional percentage estimated for the second century B.C.[18] Paradoxically, it was by looking back at the consequences of a residually literate oral *paideia* during the first sophistic and lasting until the beginning of his own century, that Cicero looked forward as he formulated the concept and value of literacy as *eloquentia* embedded in fully textualized discourse.

Hermes and Janus

The Egyptian Thoth and the Greek Hermes, messenger gods and inventors of writing, are also associated with cunning; as the patrons not only of writers but also of merchants, money changers, alchemists, and fortune tellers, they preside over domains in which technique manipulates varying combinations of material objects, belief, and occult powers. An awareness of the potency of language in such manipulation is intimated by the association of both gods with messages and writing, for what are messages and writing if not highly managed modes of language? Peitho, daughter of Aphrodite, is the goddess of Persuasion; the god of Rhetoric is Hermes, whose messenger role and cunning made him master of the unclear, the undecided, the probable, the future. As in earlier periods, rhetoric in Cicero's era was widely accepted, and widely rebuked, as the *techne* which operated in these areas. Cicero played Hermes and restored the god to rhetoric in several senses. In transmitting rhetoric from Greek to Latin language and culture, Cicero constructed a message about rhetoric which altered its direction, and further cemented its already well-established partnership with reading and writing. Playing the role of Hermes, Cicero transmitted rhetoric, an already ancient craft of message making, into Roman culture; his message about rhetoric relocated it within a formal, written literary milieu of his own making. Cicero's alchemy was cunning magic indeed, for it invested literacy in a rhetorical milieu and rhetoric within a literary milieu that would henceforward be associated with a literary liberal arts tradition.

Quick, efficient, clever, and cunning, Hermes lives uneasily with another god in Cicero's pantheon of roles: the more indigenous, sober, and circumspect Janus. The god of beginnings, Janus sees both inside and outside from his post at the gate. His ceremonial door — *janua foris* — is both an opener and a fastener, a portal and a barrier. In the frame of time Janus is *bifrons*, looking forward and backward, and thus is also wise, but with a wisdom that Cicero makes dependent on knowledge of history represented in texts. "To be ignorant of what occurred before you were born is to remain always a child. For what is the worth of human life, unless it is woven into the life of our ancestors by the records of history?"[19] Though he amply applauds his contemporaries, the annalists Varro and Atticus, it is Cicero who provides the history "in Latin literary style" that would become a standard and measure of subsequent Latin prose.[20] To open the door to history is simultaneously to create the vista which lies beyond it, and thereby to transform the past. Like Janus', Cicero's portal is also a barrier; he proposes that the study of history and philosophy be mandatory for the orator, and that they precede rhetoric in the curriculum. He defends their study as a barrier against "hearsay," an objection that may be understood as a critique of the then burgeoning pluralism of largely oral pedagogical and philosophical traditions. Within Cicero's mandate for the inscription of history, the demeaning use of hearsay prefigures the ways in which knowledge purchased, and created, by a canonical, standardized, and accessible literature would come to consign all versions of the past save the written to the half-true, the unauthorized, or the ceremonial.[21] "But that these men were accounted orators, or that at that time eloquence held out any prize to be coveted, *I cannot recall ever having read*; I am only led by conjecture to suspect that it was so."[22]

The privileging of the textual and the conflation of education with literacy are perhaps among Cicero's most decisive contributions to rhetoric and, more broadly, to the value assigned to formal written discourse in the West. From his era on, the educated are "well read"; their uses of language are marked and expected to be marked by the modes and patterns of what they have read. Even their speech increasingly resembles *litteratura*, that is, "the written."[23]

In the role of Janus, Cicero is *bifrons*: able to look forward only because he has already looked back, to transcend and transform extant models of rhetorical arrangement because he has internalized and scrutinized those models. Many of his works begin by inscribing the past within an extended *narratio*, the frame of a larger discourse that exemplies *eloquentia* and its tasks: to define the past, decide the present, and predict the future; to engage hearts and minds, to move in order to teach, instruct, judge, admonish, persuade, and bring about decision or change. His conception of revived, interdependent *artes liberales* markedly extends extant definitions of the relationships among literacy, rhetoric, and literature even further. Echoing Socrates' debate with Gorgias, Crassus in *De Oratore* proposes that if the idea of oratory is restricted to nothing but speaking in an orderly, graceful, and copious manner, the goal could not be attained, for it would be separated from the conception of knowledge. "Excellence in speaking cannot be made manifest unless the speaker fully comprehends the matter he speaks about. . . . If the underlying subject matter be not comprehended and mastered by the speaker [style] must inevitably be of no account or even become the sport of universal derision."[24] Aristotle's rhetoric, he intimates, does little to buttress the authority of his own views. Where Aristotle provides taxonomies of stylistic figures and devices in the *Poetics* and *Rhetoric*, Cicero both redefines and exemplifies style as a common ground linking philosophy, history, rhetoric, and poetry: "No one should be numbered with the orators who is not accomplished in all those arts that befit the well-bred."[25] But the orator, unlike the poet, "must be accomplished in every kind of discourse and in every department of culture."[26] The orator's learning must be more vast, his ability more adaptable, and his judgment more consistently sound. The literature produced by the poets may continue to serve as stylistic *exempla* in the orator's training, but his reading must embrace history, law, and philosophy as well. Within this *paideia*, the *artes liberales* not only reintegrate philosophy and rhetoric but supplement them with extensive additions of "content" as well. Thus defined, *eloquentia* is a reformulation not only of rhetoric, but also of literacy and, implicitly, of texts as well.

One virtue of eloquence, as Cicero defines it, is its heuristic capability. Grounded in texts and history, it looks both forward and back into its own past. It parallels modern portraits of high humanistic literacy and resembles several Greek conceptions of rhetoric.[27] Greek rhetoric comprised varying mixtures of poetic art, probabilistic logic, and persuasive techniques that continued to be questioned or scorned. Modern conceptualizations of literacy are often articulated in loftier ways, and include the ability to think in analytical, "systematic," logical patterns, the ability to synthesize and form generalizations and judgments, the mastery of an abstract and metalinguistic vocabulary and of subordinative discourse patterns which utilize that vocabulary, and the ability to be stylistically self-conscious. Increasing evidence supports the contention that these abilities can be imparted by wide reading and discussion of literature, history, art, philosophy, mathematics, and science. From the perspective of these contemporary understandings of literacy, Cicero can be seen not only as a proponent of literacy, but perhaps even as its most influential classical instigator. The extensions he proposes in the literacy of his own generation provide ample, revealing allusions to the existence and uses of texts in his era, as he develops some of the first detailed accounts of reading and writing as instruments of formal, institutionalized, and culturally sanctioned learning. His prolegomenon replaces technical rhetoric and craft literacy with an interpenetration of literacy and *educare* functioning as a lifelong source of *eloquentia*, a "virtue" dependent on assimilation of knowledge organized, transmitted, and standardized through writing. Unlike many Greek rhetorical models and practices, and unlike his own rhetorical training, Cicero's concept of *eloquentia* relies explicitly on the sophisticated editing skills inculcated by full and continuing literacy.[28] "For if an extempore and casual speech is easily beaten by one prepared and thought out, this latter in turn will assuredly be surpassed by what has been written with care and diligence."[29] The procedure Cicero describes here edges *memoria* further away from its close ties with extempore oral invention and toward a method for memorizing verbatim a speech which has been composed and revised in writing. Plato's prophecy—that writing will cause a conflation of memory with recollection—is here once again fulfilled.

Though his promotion of wide reading is a major innovation, Cicero's reintegration of character training with the acquisition of knowledge and skill parallels the Old Education celebrated in Aristophanes' *The Clouds*. "For in the old days at all events the same system of instruction seems to have imparted education both in right conduct and in good speech; nor were the professors in two separate groups, but the same masters gave instruction both in ethics and in rhetoric."[30] In one of his allusions to Homer, Cicero likens the training he propounds with that given by Phoenix to Achilles, yet he Romanizes as he goes, naturalizing what his contemporaries viewed as the neutral *technai* of Greek rhetoric and logic by combining them with conceptions of prerequisite virtue that should be required of the man of action, the statesman, the high-minded Roman citizen. He opposes those philosophers who, like Socrates, were "themselves copiously furnished with learning and with talent, but yet shrinking on deliberate principle from politics and affairs, scouted and scorned this practice of oratory."[31] The invectives against the philosophers and their retreat from the world of affairs are repeated as a refrain by Cicero's interlocutors, presumably an appeal to the Roman sensibility that regarded as frivolous any training in philosophy outside the sequence of an education leading to active public life. Rhetorical techniques, in the proposed curriculum, come last, following the training of character and the acquisition of knowledge through having "investigated and heard and read and discussed and handled and debated the whole of the contents of the life of mankind."[32] The literary exempla of the rhetorical schools are extended in the proposed curriculum to include not only the traditional epic and poetic canon but history, law, and philosophy as well. This constitutes a redefinition of literature that places reading squarely at the center of education and may suggest that, for the majority even of the educated, reading had been little more than a drill and a mnemonic, used much as we still use written versions of multiplication tables or verb conjugations.

Cicero's conceptualization of a written, canonical body of knowledge transforms reading into a lifelong habit sustaining and adding to both learning and ability.

Cicero attends to the ways in which oral style is transmitted by exposure and emulation as much as or more than by formal training. To correct or improve language style, use, or structure, the entire linguistic environment must be altered in order ultimately to structure the language patterns learned by young children. "Correct Latin style," Crassus asserts in *De Oratore*, is imparted by childhood education, and "fostered by a more intensive and systematic study of literature, or else by the daily habit of conversation in the family circle, and confirmed by books and by reading the old orators and poets."[33] Eloquence should be fostered in youth by exposure to spoken and written eloquence as well as by the practice of writing. That he commends the "naturalness" of his mother-in-law's speech for admirable qualities sharply contradicts the image of Cicero as a proponent solely of public eloquence shaped by formal education or decoration. "The actual sound of her voice is so unaffected and natural that she seems to introduce no trace of display or affection; and I consequently infer that this was how her father and her ancestors used to speak — not harshly . . . but neatly and evenly and smoothly."[34] Alongside listening and reading, writing improves not only style but thought as well. "The pen is the best and most eminent author and teacher of eloquence, and rightly so."[35] These delineations of the relationships among language, literacy, style, and thought are preliminaries to Cicero's definition of the curriculum in *eloquentia* for the orator. Much of the extant rhetorical curriculum is relegated to remedial status. "It is not our task to teach oratory to a person who does not know the language, nor to hope that one who cannot speak correct Latin should speak ornately, nor yet that one who does not say something that we can understand can possibly say something that we shall admire."[36]

Behind and before the genre boundaries that subsequently came to distinguish different kinds of literature, and to govern the literature of different subjects, Cicero's work rests as a paradigm at their inception. The absence of any widely established Latin textual conventions, coupled with the protean tendencies of both philosophy and rhetoric in a culture which was both oral and semiliterate, presented a setting of extreme fluidity. As in Plato's generation, the lines between oral and written discourse were drawn with difficulty, witnessed by the humorous alternations between praise and blame for writing a speech before it was to be delivered that recur in the commonplaces concerning rhetorical speeches in Cicero's dialogues. The philosopher's oral style, Cicero reports, is called *sermo*, "conversation," to denote its simple and spare qualities, more suited to the detachment with which an academic pursues questions. Yet philosophical discourse is also renowned for technical terms and dialectical procedures. Renounce dialectic, Antonius proposes in *De Oratore*, for the Stoic teaches not how to discover proofs but how to dissect them.[37] In the *Orator*, the "gentle, academic" style is deemed far from unaffected, but rather artificial and ineffective. The philosopher's style manifested by Plato and Isocrates is commonly distinguished from oratory, whose "equipment of words and phrases" can "catch the popular fancy." Cicero's juxtaposition of these popular views suggests his consciousness of many genre and style boundaries that are ultimately impossible to sustain. "All speech is oratory, yet it is the speech of the orator alone which is marked by this special name."[38] In the *Academica*, Varro's defense of the academics charges that the Epicureans "discuss matters that lie open to the view in ordinary language, without employing any technicality and entirely dispensing with definition and division and neat syllogistic proof."[39] He reports the Epicurean belief that no science of rhetoric or logic exists, an early version perhaps of natural language philosophy that Cicero condemns as a *docta ignoranta* propaedeutic to intellectual shallowness and ultimately to degeneracy. "How subtly, how profoundly even, we shall have to argue against the Stoics!" proposes Varro, a view in concord with the reconstruction of Antiochus' criticism of Carneades' probabilism and attack on sense perception as unreliable, "the decision of the wise man that nothing can be perceived" that is perceived.[40] Cicero's interlocutors discuss these divergent views with persistent attention to the thesis that philosophy has styles which are inseparable from substance and thereby definitive of it.

By the same token, this analysis repeatedly proposes, rhetoric has a philosophy. In any of several conceptualizations, rhetoric implies, even if it does not state, views of language, of the possibility of knowledge of the world, and of human nature. Theodor Adorno defines these relationships in terms which parallel Cicero's. "The persecutors of the rhetorical element that saved expression for thought did just as much for the technification of thought, for its potential abolition, as did those who cultivated rhetoric and ignored the subject."[41] Cicero's report of popular views of the philosophers of several different schools portrays Mandarin philosophers who stand apart from society and attack rhetoric as vulgar pandering. His depiction accords with the notion of persecutors of what Adorno terms "the rhetorical element that saved expression for thought," the true rhetoric Plato attempted to preserve under the designation of dialogue and that Cicero defends as *eloquentia*. Cicero's examination of the discordant views among the philosophers and rhetoricians of his time provides the framework for solutions. The philosopher's "need style," as it were, in two senses. They have adopted styles which they will not acknowledge as styles; they need to become conscious of style as inevitable. Because of their indifference to style, they are robbed of a vehicle of communication and thus fail to transmit knowledge.[42] They lack "the rhetorical element, that saves expression for thought," and are thereby blind to the self-contradiction in which they involve themselves when they mount lengthy arguments carefully following the rules of logic. Their ostensible demonstrations of the illusoriness of truth or meaning are expressed in language that is incomprehensible. To whom do they demonstrate illusoriness? To be consistent with the view being propounded when they say, "Nothing is perceived," they address dogmatic utterances to an implicitly insentient audience. Cicero's rendering reveals them as much responsible for what Adorno terms the "technification of thought" and for its "potential abolition" as the technical rhetoricians—"those who cultivated rhetoric and ignored the object." The rhetoricians who think that rhetoric is pure technique or style, and that no knowledge is necessary to its mastery, undermine knowledge in concert with the philosophers who disdain any attention to the communicability of knowledge, or who spend their lives establishing that there is no knowledge. Cicero steps into this abyss and establishes literature, in the widest sense, as a common ground and mandatory clearing house for the extant modes of thought and communication.

Cicero propounds a necessary identity between a written record and knowledge, and defines the value of wide reading knowledge and of texts, particularly written history, as paradigms for style and thought and as repositories of culture and literacy. The worth of an individual's life is bound up with that of others *through the records of history*.[43] Without that record, he asserts, individuals remain ignorant and puerile. Reversing earlier associations of writing with weak-mindedness and primary school, Cicero promotes the placement of written texts, the "record," at the center of both individual education and cultural cohesiveness.[44] Yet this record is far from monolithic or monovocal in Cicero's exposition. The history of rhetoric which he provides, an example of the history he propounds, is scattered among diverse treatises, letters, and dialogues. It is far from "mere" chronicle; it is neither linear nor expository; there are inconsistencies among the different accounts. In the Loeb translation of *De Natura Deorum*, Rackham comments that Cicero "took some recent handbook of one or other of the leading schools of philosophy and reproduced it in Latin; but he set passages of continuous exposition in a frame of dialogue, and added illustrations from Roman history and poetry."[45] This somewhat underrates Cicero's achievement, for it fails to note that in this "reproduction" of Greek handbooks Cicero was thereby effecting a double translation. He translated from Greek into Latin, often coining new words; but much more significantly, he expanded and restored lists, handbooks, and other sources, some oral, into a finished dialogue in exemplary but also accessible Latin literary style.

Among Cicero's dialogues there is a broad range of styles and arrangements. Allusions to the artificial and spare "conversational" manner of the Stoics, Epicureans, and Academics of his day support the interpretation that Cicero wished to retain the substantiveness and structure of dialogical philosophical discourse, but wanted to supplement its dry and technical lexicon by utilizing the more colorful and accessible language of everyday conversation.[46] Repeatedly, the concern is with reunifying philosophy and rhetoric, improving discourse styles and structures, and developing Latin culture by making literature a resource available and requisite. "Scholars and philosophers," he laments, "lack the vigor and sting necessary for oratorical efforts in public life." For this reason their style "is called conversation [*sermo*] rather than oratory."[47] Hesiod drew on the language and syntax of the epic oral tradition as a vehicle for a nonepic history; many philosophical and literary writers of the first century B.C. emulated or built their "classical" predecessors in an entirely different manner.[48] In the *Brutus*, Cicero assails the "Attici" contention that they emulate "ancient greats" — the spare Attic style of the fourth century B.C. — by proposing that this style is founded on a spurious, because undocumented, oral tradition.[49] Cicero, Brutus, and the other classical purists are attacked for hearkening back to Attic spareness — an illusory because undocumented style, Cicero alleges, whose practitioners received no recorded acclaim.[50] "Everyone knew" that the topics originated with Aristotle; but there is no firm evidence that Aristotle's *Topics* or *Rhetoric* was widely available as a text in the Hellenistic schools of Cicero's period.[51] Outline-form compendia of an entire philosophical tradition within rhetoric may have been the only widely used or accessible textual instruments of transmission, functioning as a kind of mnemonic outline for those few initiates who had learned the extended version of the tradition during a long apprenticeship and the conversations of the schools.[52] Very much as Plato had, Cicero assails the reductive-list approaches to teaching rhetoric and constructs his work as a counterexample, a catalyst in changing these patterns of teaching, language use, and transmission. Cicero's reformulations of the roles played by history, the written record, the resources of the orator, and the "art" of memory establish their intricate interdependence.

From *Diegesis* to *Narratio*: Rhetoric and History

After the first sophistic, epideictic oratory came to be held in particularly low regard, as symptomatic of the worst elements in sophistic rhetoric. Cicero records that "this class of speeches were composed by Sophists as show pieces and little else; . . . [they] comprised eulogies, descriptions, histories, and exhortations."[53] The inclusion of history in this list is lamented in the Loeb annotation. "History was regularly regarded in antiquity as a branch of rhetoric, much to the disadvantage of history." The persisting disdain toward rhetoric exemplified by modern attitudes like these stands as evidence of anachronistic understandings of early rhetorical and literary subgenres, including history. Heraclitus chides Pythagoras for conducting research (*historia*) and for compiling from abstracts of his own treatises "a wisdom of his own . . . a harmful craft." Solon is recorded as having been hostile to drama, and as having himself written *historia* of a confessional and reflective bent.[54] Both in his own voice and through the interlocutors in his dialogues, Cicero chides extant histories for being mere annals, or for leaving out huge areas of culture such as religion, science, and philosophy. Cicero's histories, as well as his historiography, reveal the mixed parentage of history in antiquity. His accounts suggest the extent to which history as a literary genre may well have taken its initial cues from the rhetorical models of the portion of a speech immediately following the exordium—a hypothesis that could explain why Cicero not only considers the Greek classifications which defined *historia* to be a class of epideictic oratory, but relates them to *diegesis*: "story" and "digest" as segments within individual speeches. Both *diegesis*, or "statement of facts," and *historia* are defined in Aristotle's discussion of the example (*paradeigma*), which, with the enthymeme, he defines as one of the two major kinds of rhetorical proof. Aristotle distinguishes two kinds of examples: (1) telling of things that have happened—*digest*, and (2) inventing a fictional account, hence, *history* and *fable*. These classifications place *historia* squarely within the discipline of rhetoric and locate it as a fiction. Narration (*diegesis*), the "statement of the case," is also placed in the sequential description of the parts of a speech just following the exordium, *and* is defined as a device which may be used within the proofs which follow the initial statement of the case.[55] Aristotle cites Theodorus as the originator of an emphasis on *diegesis*. An alternate tradition, he recounts, had emphasized proof—*tekmeria* and *pistis*. Hence, perhaps, Aristotle attempts a workable conflation of the two. Placed beside Aristotle's definitions, Cicero's account helps explain why history has come to be classified as a kind of epideictic oratory in later Greek rhetorics. It was regarded as fabulation. In direct descent from Greek rhetoric, *historia* continued to appear as one of three kinds of *narratio*, the Latin term adopted for the part of a speech that immediately follows the exordium. *De Inventione* exemplifies these inherited identifications and illustrates the confusion caused by erratic translations of *historia* and *diegesis* into Latin as *narratio* and *historia*. Cicero's definition and subsequent subdivisions of these modes and parts of a speech contributed additional alternations among *historia* as a kind of entertaining oratory or literature, *narratio* as digest or iteration of the facts of a case, narrative history as fabulation, and *narratio* as a carefully selected forensic statement of the case or opening argument.

De Inventione parallels Aristotle's definition. Cicero presents narrative as "an exposition of events that have occurred or are supposed to have occurred," and isolates three distinct kinds of narrative:

1. One stating just the case and the whole reason for the dispute.
2. Digression beyond the strict limits of the case for the purpose of attacking somebody or of making a comparison, or of amusing the audience in a way not incongruous with the business at hand, or for amplification.
3. One wholly unconnected with public issues, recited or written solely for amusement, practice, or training:
   a. concerned with events: *fabula, historia, argumentum.*
   b. concerned with persons: rules for probability and verisimilitude.[56]

In sharp contrast, Crassus in *De Oratore* develops a definition of history as knowledge of the past, preserved and accessible through memory and invention, the traditional resources of the rhetorician. "Further, the complete history of the past and a store of precedents must be retained in the memory, nor may a knowledge of statute law and our national law in general be omitted. . . . What need to speak of that universal treasure house of the memory?"[57] Antonius provides a brief history of history by way of demonstrating the paucity of histories and of rules for its composition. He goes on to ask pointedly, "Do you see how great a responsibility the orator has in historical writing?"[58] Today that might seem a ludicrous question. Its articulation by Antonius, both skeptic and traditionalist, only emphasizes the absence, in Cicero's era, of history beyond the epic and folkloric, and history's role as a part of rhetoric.

Antonius' lament emphasizes the absence of any systematic rules for history writing, and proposes that it is one of the unrealized offices of the orator to provide those rules.

The nature of the subject needs chronological arrangement and geographical representation: and since, in reading of important affairs worth recording, the plans of campaign, the executive actions and the results are successively looked for, it calls also, as regards such plans, for some intimation of what the writer approves, and, in the narrative of achievement, not only for a statement of what was done or said, but also of the manner of doing or saying it; and, in the estimate of consequences, for an exposition of all contributory causes, whether originating in accident, discretion or foolhardiness; and as for the individual actors, besides an account of their exploits, it demands particulars of the lives and characters of such as are outstanding in renown and dignity.[59]

Antonius here adapts and synthesizes the rules for composing an entire speech that are elsewhere described in *De Oratore* and *Orator*.[60] Cicero's dialogue treatises concerning rhetoric not only exemplify these rules of style, composition, and purpose, but also provide the histories of rhetoric, learning, and culture that have been deemed lacking in existing Latin education.

The opening *narratio* in *De Oratore* consists of a debate between Scaevola and Crassus concerning the origin and nature of rhetoric and rhetoricians in the past, a history that Scaevola asserts is conjectural at best.[61] Addressing Brutus in the *Orator*, Cicero applauds Varro and his contemporary, Atticus, for providing precisely the written record which is needed for the training of the orator. With no little irony, Cicero's accolade intimates the incompleteness of the extant record. "Our task has been lightened by the labour of our friend Atticus, who has comprised in one book the record of seven hundred years, keeping the chronology definite and omitting no important event."[62] Just as in a court of law there are matters of conjecture about which no facts exist, because there are neither witnesses nor written records, Cicero suggests, much Latin history until his own era may be relegated to the status of repositories of conjecture, because it was not written. This refrain emphasizes that there has been until his own generation no extant history written in Latin with the precision and depth he proposes is needed in a substantive, reflective record. History has been regarded as a mode of "mere" epideictic oratory, as by Timaeus, a follower of Isocrates. Cicero's resuscitation of epideictic oratory proposes that "display" speeches can also be produced as valuable exercises and as sources of a needed written record, that is, as literature broadly defined. Only records of depth and precision can train the new, improved orator. Reciprocally, such records should employ some of the extant rules of rhetoric in making the realities they record orderly and comprehensible, forging a reunion of accessible style with the multiple tasks of history.

These purposes contribute to reviewing Cicero's dialogues as deliberately polyvalent literary exercises, as instructive treatises, and as enactments of precisely the forms of literacy, literature, rhetoric, and history which they propound. In a multiplicity of purposes, subjects, and effects, they also exemplify the reapportioned, reconceived functions (*officia*) which Cicero assigns to eloquence: *delectare, instructare, movere*.[63] Within each dialogue and treatise the substantive historical role of the *narratio* confirms the view that this trinity of rhetorical objectives is not a translation or adaptation of earlier depictions of rhetoric, but rather an attempt to transform both the substance and the function of rhetoric. In a discussion criticizing the empty and mechanical lists of commonplaces, Antonius proposes that they be dispensed with. "Three things alone can carry conviction; I mean the winning over [*concilientur animi*], the instructing [*doceantur*], and the stirring [*moveantur*] of men's minds."[64] Most of all, Cicero emphasizes knowledge as the sine qua non of the consummate orator. Wide reading, extensive study, and knowledge of various religious, philosophical, and rhetorical traditions made Cicero particularly well suited to record, shape, and disseminate vaguely—because not widely—known philosophical traditions, rules on poetics, debates about the status of rhetoric, and beliefs about the gods. Though he credits Varro as a historian, he chides him for omitting any history of philosophy in his Latin chronicle on the assumption that anyone interested in philosophy would read it in Greek. Yet even Varro, by Cicero's report, notes that some doctrines are being lost; "for these doctrines could not be obtained from the Greeks, nor from the Latins either since the demise of our countryman Lucius Aelius."[65] Despite Varro's omission of philosophy, Cicero nonetheless acclaims his encyclopedic treatment of Roman life, language, and culture: "Your books led us . . . right home, and enabled us at last to realize who and where we were. You have revealed the age of our native city, the chronology of its history, the laws of its religion and its priesthood, its civil and its military institutions, the topography of its districts and its cities, the terminology, classification and moral and rational basis of all our religious and secular institutions, and you have likewise shed a flood of light upon our poets and generally on Latin literature and the Latin language."[66] Yet alongside this praise must be placed Cicero's bold assertions that Latin culture and language have as yet no rules for writing history,[67] no suitably engaging and therefore instructive philosophical vocabulary,[68] and no honorable tradition of rhetorical teaching. "Why then has it always been honourable to teach civil law, . . . while a man would be severely criticized if he trained young men for oratory?"[69]

The diverse accounts of Roman culture Cicero provides within his works on rhetoric are revealing for several reasons, but most of all, perhaps, because they so readily correct modern anachronisms in the treatment of rhetoric, literature, and literacy within this period. Because of the paucity of writings in Latin, the culture of Cicero's era, excepting the small fraction of those who read Greek, was not, even among the educated, a reading culture. Educated Romans had aversions to Greek literature, philosophy, and rhetoric and tended to associate these with a dilletantish literary culture and "Greek" eristics. At the same time, Cicero's interlocutors portray educated Romans as cautiously, somewhat provisionally, interested in the first generation of Latin writers. The anachronism which pervades modern histories of this period is understandable. It is difficult to apprehend what we now regard as literature, or history, as products of a culture that was still preponderately oral, a culture whose uses of literacy and rhetoric remained directed primarily at education and civic virtue, not at producing a large number of circulating manuscripts. Nor was there a wide readership sophisticated enough to linger over literary texts for purposes other than stylistic practice or information gathering.[70] It was in this context that Cicero set about creating the kinds of manuscripts that would encourage more uses of written materials in the classroom and in the culture at large. Cicero edited his speeches for publication, and wrote letters which were conceived as instruments for disseminating his views and a Latin literary style as much as they were actual epistles. In the four years prior to his assassination, he produced what he explicitly characterizes as an encyclopedia of rhetoric, philosophy, history, and religion, all for the first time in "Latin literary form."[71] Excepting his speeches and letters, many of his works are written in the form of dialogues; even his letters make heavy use of dialogical questions and direct address—"you will say . . . "—to provide the view of the subject held by the addressee. Like Plato's, Cicero's dialogues are carefully crafted, intended as exemplary preserved communication; they model the kind of discourse and thought that they propound.

Cicero talks about and enacts the need for change in virtually all the discourse conventions of his day, both spoken and written. Along the way, he provides witty renditions of the anti-Greek sentiments of his contemporaries. The case he mounts against technical rhetoric, and his condemnation of excessively probabilistic philosophical logic, provide ample if ironically articulated evidence of the scorn Romans felt toward Greek traditions and culture, particularly in rhetoric and philosophy. Yet Cicero's analysis of the classrooms of his day provides much more than a record of pedagogical xenophobia. In defining the flaws of technical rhetoric on the one hand, and a logic divorced from the everyday uses of language on the other, Cicero assesses problems that have persisted in the teaching and practice of literate discourse. Woven throughout, caricatures of Roman distaste for Greek dilletantism mount a subtle praise-by-blame argument directed perhaps at encouraging Roman transformation and assimilation of the scorned practices.

The Case Against Technical Rhetoric

Written in the same year as *De Partitione Oratoria*, the dialogue handbook Cicero composed for his son, the *Orator* is directed at Brutus' response to the *Brutus*, and extends Cicero's attack on classical nostalgia for spare "Attic" rhetorical training. Though critical of "the philosophers" on many points, Cicero opposes with equal force any teaching of rhetoric as style that is severed from the study of philosophy. "Whatever ability I have comes not from the workshops of the rhetoricians but from the spacious grounds of the Academy. . . . The eloquence of the courts, scorned and rejected by the philosophers, lost much valuable assistance; nevertheless with a veneer of verbiage and maxims it vaunted itself before the populace, and did not fear the unfavorable criticism of the few. As a result the learned lacked an eloquence which appealed to the people, and the fluent speakers lacked the refinement of sound learning."[72] Those trained in technical rhetoric can speak well of nothing;

the learned philosophers have no voice. Through the deft antithesis that had long been a commonplace concerning rhetoric, Cicero reiterates to Brutus and the Attici that grave harm has been done to rhetoric, philosophy, and culture by the severance and discord between the two disciplines.

Balancing the attack on philosophy, Cicero proposes that the criticism of rhetoric by philosophers, beginning with Socrates, has both enriched and deprived rhetoric. Those who have heeded the criticisms of the philosophers have improved their study and practice of rhetoric and have concomitantly improved rhetoric by refusing to restrict it to mere skill or technique, but these few are outnumbered by the many who have constituted philosophy and rhetoric as parts of a severed body. "We are deluged," Crassus complains, not only with "the notions of the vulgar but also with the opinions of the half educated, who find it easier to deal with matters that they cannot grasp in their entirety if they split them up and take them piecemeal, and who separate words from thoughts as one might sever body from mind."[73] Even the professors of rhetoric "neither teach nor understand" many of the topics.[74] These objections are directed not only at the allegedly piecemeal, reductive, and disorganized state of Roman education but also at its results. The vast majority of the orators don't know logic, semantics, or history. The common topics they are taught and employ have become mechanical and predictable vestiges of argument, residual logics so familiar that they are arguments in name only.

The *Orator* and *De Partitione Oratoria* seem contradictory — one an attack on, and the other a serious treatment of, technical rhetoric.[75] However, it is the critique of technical rhetoric provided in the *Orator*, supported by many sections in Cicero's other works, which allows us to see *De Partitione Oratoria* as distinctively different from the kind of technical rhetoric Cicero opposes. Written in dialogue form, it treats substantive questions about the whys and wherefores of the elements of rhetoric and assumes an extensive knowledge of literature, history, and law in its audience. Its existence suggests that forty years after *De Inventione*, and ten years after *De Oratore*, the workshops of the rhetoricians continued to eschew anything but the pragmatic, spare, technical approach to which *De Partitione Oratoria* stands in sharp contrast. In an emphatic rejection of his own training, Cicero opens *De Oratore* with a retraction of the technical rhetoric that his youthful *De Inventione* would transmit to subsequent centuries.[76] Cicero announces to his brother that he will not "recall from the cradle of our boyish learning of days gone by, a long string of precepts, but I shall repeat the things I heard of as once handled in a discussion between men who were the most eloquent of our nation. . . . You will forgive me if I prefer to Greek instruction the authoritative judgment of those to whom the highest honors in eloquence have been awarded by our own fellow countrymen."[77] *De Oratore* defines and develops Cicero's opposition to rhetoric as a *technologia*, the term the Stoics, following Aristotle, had come to assign to it.[78] His interlocutors display urbane and stolid Roman scorn for the Greeks' relativistic ethics and "gross habit of plunging into subtle dialectic,"[79] a scorn that Cicero intimates paradoxically accelerated the technification of rhetoric. In the vacuum created by the antipathy toward Greek eristics, skepticism, and probabilism, various tutors of rhetoric, many of them Greek, continued to teach adaptions of Stoic and Academic rhetoric which were as diverse as they were reductive.[80] Cicero's attack on technical rhetoric, then, functions as a backhanded attack on Roman negligence and willful ignorance.

The discussion of why and how orators should be trained in philosophy leads to a debate which takes up a good part of the *Orator*. *De Oratore* begins with a historical review that asks why, though rhetorical training is everywhere available, there are so few great orators. The rhetorical training that has been virtually coextensive with education for nearly two hundred years hasn't worked. The "veneer of verbiage" continues to sway the populace even while it is scorned by "the few" (philosophers) and distrusted by that same populace. Cicero alludes to his own training and to his earlier writing on the subject, recalls childhood drills and maxims, and expresses hopes that "our children . . . can form a true understanding of the greatness of their task, and not believe that they can gain their coveted object by reliance on the rules of teachers or methods of practice employed by everybody."[81] The rejection of the "rules of teachers," the "long string of precepts" learned in boyhood, and "Greek instruction" define the radical oppositeness of *De Oratore* and *De Inventione*: rules, precepts, and the Greek teachers who dispense them are placed at the center of Cicero's criticism of technical rhetoric in *De Oratore*. A corollary objection, less direct, is aimed at the Roman customs, tastes, and institutions which continue to permit the teaching of such a debased technical rhetoric. Cicero's exposition and analysis of the flaws in the lists and precepts reveal his awareness that the same questions had been defined at least as early as the debate Plato records in the *Gorgias*; some of the issues he addresses had long been set pieces for debate in the schools that trained teachers of rhetoric, a rhetoric about rhetoric that was transmitted by moots. Is rhetoric a "mere" technique to be mastered in drill at lower levels of the curriculum, or is it part and parcel of philosophy, knowledge, literary sophistication, and civic experience? Does it prepare one for life as a citizen, or is it something that continually grows out of and draws on that life?

The civic and cultural contexts with which Cicero surrounds these questions are far broader than many subsequent characterizations of this debate between philosophers and rhetoricians suggest. Recovery of these contexts will continue to aid and prompt reappraisals of that debate. The stock responses of philosopher and rhetorician to each other are distinguished, in Cicero's depictions, from their separate and joint responses to the culture which they should serve. Through his interlocutors, who themselves are statesmen, teachers, and philosophers, Cicero repeatedly addresses both groups, and provides insights into the causes and consequences of poorly educated citizens and statesmen. His contemporaries, he alleges, are being taught corrupt and reductive versions of rhetoric and virtually no philosophy. They cannot think carefully, and what is worse, they do not know what to do with their thinking when they do it, because philosophy has defined questions unrelated to the pragmatics of ethical and political choices. These shortcomings are defined with eloquent pragmatism, and with a sense of urgency. "If there were these false notions or notions imprinted on the mind by appearances of a kind that could not be distinguished from false ones, how pray could we act upon them? How moreover could we see what is consistent with any given fact and what inconsistent? At all events no place at all is left for memory, the one principal foundation not only of philosophy but also of the conduct of life and all the sciences."[82] Memory, here as in so many other passages, is treated in a way that emphasizes its centrality to cognition, ethics, and the discourse of all disciplines. It is not "merely" one of the parts of rhetoric; here, as in the appraisal that concludes the

Phaedrus, memory is tied to fundamental questions of perception and knowledge. With ample allusion to the philosophical views of his contemporaries, Cicero similarly extends the long-standing debate between Plato and Aristotle concerning the division of the sciences of knowledge from the arts of language.

The pragmatic, conventionalist view of rhetoric represented by Aristotle sustained the view that there already are rhetoric manuals, teachers of rhetoric, students of rhetoric, and practitioners who can and do pander, sell, cheat, defend, persuade, exhort, articulate, argue, delight, refute, and in countless other ways approximate careful thought and ingenuous communication. In this world of cleverness and "the probable," clever, trained wordsmiths prevail. It is on precisely this note that Aristotle begins his proposals for a "higher," more systematic rhetoric as itself a subject area and the counterpart of dialectic. In *De Oratore* Scaevola is given this line of argument, and is cast to play the practical Roman in a debate with Crassus, who proposes the loftier goal that is earlier articulated by Plato and Isocrates, a reunification of philosophy and rhetoric: "Who is going to grant you that in shutting themselves up in walled cities, human beings who had been scattered originally over mountain and forest were not so much convinced by the reasoning of the wise as snared by the speeches of the eloquent . . . ? . . . I could cite more instances of damage done than of aid given to the cause of the State by men of first-rate eloquence."[83] The reasoning here may seem badly managed.[84] Why have Scaevola articulate the Aristotelian defense of rhetoric, only to have him then reject rhetoric out of hand from an implicitly philosophical if not outright Platonic position: that it has been bad for the state to have rhetoricians controlling things? Perhaps precisely because the "bad logic" emblematizes Cicero's point. Scaevola is given the character of a Roman educated within the canons of practicality who is clearly limited in his powers of reasoning. The implication is that he would be improved by formal training in philosophy. But that the philosophers, too, need change is kept at the forefront of the issue: who believes any more that the wise are more powerful than the clever?

Cicero illustrates the paucity of wisdom that is inculcated by a reductive technical rhetoric by recounting his days in the senate. During his tenure as praetor, he met no other candidate whose "studies had embraced philosophy, the mother of excellence in deeds and in words; no one who had mastered thoroughly the civil law, . . . no one who knew thoroughly Roman history, from which as occasion demanded he could summon as from the dead most unimpeachable witnesses."[85] With strategically ambiguous import, he laments the fact that none of his peers "read more widely than the average man." His contention, though, is clear enough. The resources of the orator need to be refurbished. The teachers need to be retaught. Only a literature which is much more than lists of common topics and excerpts of quotations can provide the integrated, comprehensive, and edifying discourses necessary to the orator's training. The central object of Cicero's attack on technical rhetoric, then, is an epistemologically and thereby ethically corrupt and reductive curriculum that is defended as practical. What he in some places construes as a joint legacy of Plato and Aristotle, a philosophical rhetoric founded on knowledge, has been reduced to a pile of bones so fragmentary and disorganized that it is incapable even of sophistry.

The resuscitation and rearrangement of the parts of rhetoric, one aim of Cicero's dialogues on rhetoric, are laced with as many appraisals of the philosophers of his day as of the rhetoricians. He admires the philosophers' analytical precision, chides them for their eristics, and charges them with a serious because culturally harmful shirking of public responsibility. Yet he unambiguously applauds the virtues of a proper philosophical education. The scorn of the philosophers toward rhetoric is emphasized as a serious fault, because it leaves those trained in rhetoric with a meager "veneer of verbiage and maxims."[86] It is with the cumulative effect of salvaging some elements of Greek philosophy and rhetoric that he repeats with sharp wit the proverbial Roman anti-Greek invective that had accumulated among those Romans tutored almost exclusively by Greek teachers through Cicero's era. Thus he records that Crassus, himself a storehouse of Greek philosophy and literature, and a great proponent of a refurbished, reintegrated, and fully literate curriculum, "wanted to be known as looking down on [Greek] learning and as placing the wisdom of our fellow countrymen above that of the Greeks."[87] The same could be said of Cicero himself.

In several different settings, Cicero alludes to the story of Simonides' *memoria technica* to convey the inanity proverbially attributed to lists of *technai* and *topoi*, and to rote or technical memorization more generally: "Themistocles was endowed with wisdom and genius on a scale quite surpassing belief; a certain learned and highly accomplished person went to him and offered to impart to him the science of mnemonics. . . . The professor said that it would enable him to remember everything. Themistocles replied that he would rather be doing him a greater kindness if he taught him to forget what he wanted than if he taught him to remember."[88] A serious issue is raised in this delectable joke. If one knows a great deal, the problem is not remembering what is known, but arranging, adapting, integrating, and using it. With a related purpose, Cicero provides another version of the *memoria* anecdote in the *Academica*: "[Lucullus] had a memory for facts that was positively inspired, although Hortensius had a better memory for words, but Lucullus's memory was the more valuable, inasmuch as in the conduct of business facts are of more assistance than words; and this form of memory is recorded as having been present in a remarkable degree in Themistocles, of whom the story is told that when somebody offered to impart to him the *memoria technica* that was then first coming into vogue, he replied that he would sooner learn to forget."[89] Cicero here distinguishes memory of facts and words not only to differentiate the purposes of the statesman from those of the philosopher, but also to imply the dependence of facts on words, words on facts, and statesman on philosopher and rhetor. He who can memorize speeches but knows nothing is as powerless as he who can recall court cases but has no powers of organization and articulation.

Scores of anecdotes like these clarify Cicero's objective of instituting wide reading and knowledge as prerequisites to the techniques of arrangement and textual memorization which will supersede the older *memoria technica*. Conceived as a replacement for the topographical mnemonics described in *De Inventione* and the *Ad Herennium*, memory fed by wide reading knowledge is no longer simply heuristics for invention. Cicero restores the dual sense of memory defined by Plato: a memory which is virtually coextensive with knowledge, as distinct from memorization understood as the technical ability to replicate a written list or text. While Cicero objects to the memorization of simpleminded commonplaces which are then filled in with whatever specifics come to mind, he does advocate, very unlike Plato, the memorization of carefully composed, written, and edited manuscripts whose delivery can be controlled to give the appearance of spontaneity. Here is fulfilled the promise articulated in the opening of Book III of Aristotle's *Rhetoric*: once delivery is studied and fully understood, the identity between the rhetor and actor (*hupokritike*) will be appreciated. The memorization and delivery of written text are quite different from the inscription of a previously oral one. Regardless, Cicero deserves credit for being among the first to recognize and examine the cognitive–cultural changes effected by such interpenetrations of rhetorical paradigms, philosophical logic, and written texts.

Cicero elaborates the distinction between memory of facts and memory of words as part of a history of Lucullus, a revered Roman leader and orator. His account intimates that the great Roman orator leaders had for some time been closet students of philosophy, but, given Roman prejudice against philosophy, Cicero expresses his approval indirectly. He has the historian Varro say, "My friends who wish to study philosophy I send to Greece,"[90] as part of an indirect proposal to end the practice of sending Romans to Athens, culminating in the assertion that new Latin words must be coined to end Greek control of both the teaching and the language of philosophy. He concludes with a perfectly crafted irony: "The only precaution that need be observed by us whom the Roman nation has placed in this rank is to prevent our private studies from encroaching at all upon our public interest."[91]

The history of rhetoric that begins the *Brutus* remains one of the most detailed classical accounts of the evolution of the division of rhetoric from philosophy and of its recurrent decline. As in many of Cicero's works, this *narratio* is guided not so much by the criteria of comprehensive, factual accuracy as by a selective accounting that will guide understanding and judgment concerning the matter at hand: the nature and optimum future of rhetorical training and practice. The account provided in the *Brutus* joins the appraisals of technical rhetoric in *De Oratore, Orator*, and *Academia* in calling for vast reforms within rhetorical education and for its reunification with other subjects. The *Brutus* records that, as early as the fifth century B.C., Corax and Tisias were defining rhetoric as an art of persuasion, as a logic of probabilities, and as a prescriptive discourse model in three parts adapted to litigation: proem or introduction, central arguments and refutations, and conclusion or recapitulation. As early as Tisias and Corax, the legal–probabilistic and stylistic elements in rhetoric were tied closely to the innovations introduced by the philosophers of physical and natural science, as evidenced by Aristotle's famous identification of Empedocles as the "father of rhetoricians." Hence, also, the introduction into rhetorical theory of the language of probability and scientific inquiry: the apparent, the probable qualities (*poiotetes*) and their predication, the languages of comparison and causation. The logical types and methods compassed by Cicero's account are quite different from the lists of figures of speech and the tables of common topics and outlines for arrangement to which technical rhetoric had become reduced. The lists of schemes, tropes, and arguments had become extended far beyond the Gorgianic figures and were known to the Romans of Cicero's era as Hellenistic, decorative, or grand style. The Attici whom he addresses in the *Brutus* oppose this style and favor an exclusively simple, spare style.

Though never systematically expounded in Aristotle's work, the five parts or "offices" of rhetoric had become a commonplace of the rhetorical teaching of Cicero's era: invention, arrangement, style, memory, delivery. In *De Oratore* Crassus applauds Antonius' proposal that those outworn functions be entirely supplanted by the concept of a triad of objectives or ways of understanding and teaching rhetoric: to instruct (*instructare*), to delight (*delectare*), and to move (*movere*).[92] They agree that the parts of a speech, as well as the common topics with variations in subdivisions and terminology, had become mechanical and reductive. Cicero's criticism of the topics, functions, and models for parts of a speech effects major changes in both invention and arrangement. Had these changes rather than *De Inventione* survived, they would have made significant changes in subsequent rhetorics.

The treatises in which Cicero launches his reforms — *De Oratore, Brutus, Orator* — are often defined as "idealistic" or "philosophical" views of rhetoric and are commonly juxtaposed with *De Inventione* and *De Partitione Oratoria*, his more practical and realistic technical manuals.[93] Reappraisal of these dialogues suggests that they are far from "idealistic"; instead, they represent a coordinated definition that with some urgency as well as practicality identifies substantive faults with the schemes, tropes, and topics as they were taught and practiced in Cicero's day, faults that have persisted with striking tenacity. Cicero's treatment of Plato's concept of the *idea* substantiates the claim that his treatment of rhetoric is anything but idealistic in the pejorative sense of that term. Cicero asserts that the "ideal orator" he describes is not one who has already lived, or one who could be looked back to as the Attici attempted to do; rather, he exists in anyone in whom excellence can be observed. "So with our minds we conceive the ideal of perfect eloquence, but with our ears we catch only the copy. These patterns of things are called *ideai* or ideas by Plato."[94] Cicero contends that this fixed and very real idea of oratorical excellence can and should be observed, further studied, and known through precisely the exempla which he provides in the form and substance of his works. Otherwise, *eloquentia* will continue to be confused with either a static, nostalgic classicism which denies to eloquence a present reality and thereby a capacity for change, or will be dismissed as an unattainable ideal, utilizing a view of the *idea* which does, indeed, conflate it with an unreachable ideal impossibility. The former confusion he attacks in the Attici; the latter he attributes to the Academic abandonment of the search for a criterion of truth, a rejection which he traces back to Aristotle, "the first to undermine the Forms."[95]

In *De Oratore* Cicero has Crassus describe the practice of less substantively trained orators who apply rhetorical precepts in mechanical and barren ways so as to create a surface polish of eloquence, thereby undermining both the capacities of the art and the reputation of its practitioners. "For what so effectively proclaims the madman as the hollow thundering of words — be they never so choice and resplendent — which have no thought or knowledge behind them?"[96] This criticism of stylistic formulae as ends in themselves is complemented and extended by analysis of the topics and by proposals for their reform through more abstracted goals. Stoic logic is deemed defective as a practical model because it does little to help discover arguments, construct proofs, or compose a public address. "Let us therefore renounce entirely that art which has too little to say when proofs are being thought out, and too much when they are being assessed"[97] — a critique emphasizing that the philosophers' proofs and arguments are increasingly used for analytic and not generative purposes. The rhetoricians' topics and commonplaces have become simplistic corruptions of reasoning, the consequence of too little formal logical training. "Among these very topics there are points in abundance which the so-called professors of rhetoric neither teach nor understand."[98] Further impoverishing available resources, the Epicureans, he alleges, eschew method entirely. They "discuss matters that lie open to the view in ordinary language, without employing any technicality and entirely dispensing with definition, division, and neat syllogistic proof, and . . . in fact believe that no science of rhetoric or logic exists."[99] The Epicurean essays on various set themes, themselves topical—as for instance "On Beauty"—had in Cicero's view compounded the destructive pluralism riddling both the philosophical and rhetorical schools, because they were mere compendia of popular views. Somewhat like today's popular magazine media, at least according to Cicero's scornful depiction, the Epicurean treatises functioned more than anything else like set pieces which could be introduced with distressing predictability and little profit in most rhetorical situations. They were commonplace in the worst sense of that term. Though claiming to be "natural language," they represented reductive uses of the common topics.

"Commonplaces" (*loci*), Crassus tells Antonius in his rejection of the long-standing backbone of rhetorical invention and arrangement, "are for all that really rather easy and widely current in maxims [*praecepta*]."[100] Antonius responds by defining a distinction between the ready-made proofs (*argumenta*) given by the professors to students for every kind of case, and "sundry commonplaces" (*certos locos*) which can "open up the sources [*capita*] from which the whole argument [*disputatio*] for every case [*causa*] and speech [*orationem*] is derived."[101] These can "present themselves for setting forth the case, as the letters do for writing the word." But only to "a speaker who is a man of affairs, qualified by experience, . . . practice, listening, reading, and written composition."[102] If the commonplaces are given to someone not so qualified, Antonius asserts, "those commonplaces from which proofs are derived will avail him but little." In defending long study and reading as prerequisite to the study of rhetoric, Crassus joins Antonius in objecting to the lists of specific proofs given to very young students for memorization, case by case. There is no fundamental disagreement between their views; their discussion illuminates the distinctions then drawn between topics and arguments, both in use and in pedagogical presentation.

In these discussions, the presentation of the somewhat confusing proliferation of topics and arguments, arguments and proofs, arrangements and arguments, common topic as "general" and common topic as "colloquial," is compounded by a triple translation conundrum. Cicero and his successors were simultaneously adapting and translating Greek terms into Latin rhetoric and philosophy. Among the more notable accounts concerns the origin of "Form" for Plato's *Idea*. "This thing they called the *Idea*, a name already given it by Plato; we can correctly term it form [*speciem*]."[103] Subsequent eras have produced similarly complicated adaptations and translations, leading to an incremental confusion of cognates which persists in modern English translations. "Under this head was imparted their whole doctrine of Dialectic, that is, speech cast in the form of a logical argument; to this as a 'counterpart' [*antistrophe*] was added the faculty of Rhetoric, which sets out a continuous speech adapted to the purpose of persuasion."[104] In some technical rhetorics "arguments," like their modern mathematical counterparts, seem to have been represented by abbreviated symbols for longer stretches of discourse. In logic, however, the argument might denote a semantic unit which was a representation of, a sign for, a generally true statement. Neither of these uses is compatible with modern rhetorical notions of arguments as fully articulated and suasive segments of prose discourse.

The Greek *topoi* were themselves already diversified in Aristotle's representations; they denoted general subjects, approaches to those subjects, and arguments which would be chosen on the basis of the nature of the subject. Arguments (*logoi*) also denoted logical and rhetorical structures that were prefabricated to a certain degree. Cicero's accounts and the Loeb notes to scores of passages illustrate the equivocal meanings these terms had acquired. The summary of the "Academic philosophy" tells us that "the third part of philosophy, consisting in reason [*ratione*] and in discussion [*disserendo*]," was treated by both Academics and Stoics. The Loeb gloss on this definition explains "reason and discussion" as "a dual rendering of *logike*, or perhaps of *dialektike*."[105] In explaining the logic of the Old Academy, Cicero says that they used etymological "derivations as 'tokens' [*argumentis quibusdam*] or so to say marks of things [*quasi rerum notis*], as guides for arriving at proofs [*probandum*] or conclusions [*concludendum*] as to anything of which they desired an explanation." Apologizing for using the Latin word *qualitates* to translate the Greek *poiotetes*, Cicero explains that even the Greeks realized this was no ordinary usage. The Loeb annotation to this passage exemplifies the confusion created in part by modern disciplinary divergences and concomitant latitude in translation: "*Quasi* marks *notis* as an explanation of *argumentis* used to translate *sumbola*." As Latin culture makes philosophy and all the sciences its own, Cicero remarks, "either new names have to be coined for new things, or names taken from other things have to be used metaphorically."[106] Yet *poiotetes*, "qualities," as they are used as early as Aristotle, had come to denote actual as distinct from nominal or "merely" attributed characteristics, an ambiguity which occupied generations of subsequent logicians. Cicero is explicit on this point, noting that the Latin *qualitas* is a neologism translating a neologism, and that this process the Greeks had called *sumbola*. It was perhaps in rhetoric that the original sense of *poiotetes* survived most clearly, as a series of questions which the rhetor was taught to use heuristically for discovering in each case the most effective proofs. Cicero records both the simple and the more complex versions of these questions, and recommends the simpler set: "Is it?" "What is it?" "Of what sort is it?"[107] He tells us that inquiry into such properties and classes of things, the "general topics," is called *thesis* by Aristotle, and that it is distinguished from "Topics [*locos*], . . . a kind of sign or indication of the arguments from which a whole speech can be formed on either side of the question." Cicero adds, "The decisive arguments are not always to be found [in the same categories]."[108]

It is clear that the vast array of topics have come to be used in different ways, are presented in different ways, and comprise at least three distinct kinds: lists of shorthand "notes," mnemonics for remembering the kinds of questions to be asked; topics in sentence form which can be developed in expository and argumentative exercise, that is, heuristic theses; and an unstated understanding or knowledge of the "seats" or "headings" (*sedes argumentorum, capita*) of arguments. Cicero's widely distributed objections to technical rhetoricians' theory and practice parallel modern objections to skills-oriented conceptions and teaching of "basic" literacy. Contemporary Jeremiads about whether technical rhetoric should be taught before or after or along with "content" are similarly divided between those that locate the problem in the students' inability to write and those that locate the problem in simpleminded or mechanistic writing courses and teaching. In either case, the parallel to Cicero's critique is striking. Many intervening eras have seen similarly relentless drives toward technical, substanceless formalism, a rhetorical curriculum that is not much more than "a skeleton with tickets stuck all over it," the illusion of technique.[109]

Those Contentious Greeklings and Their Probabilities

> But of all the countless forms assumed by want of tact, I rather think that the grossest is the Greeks' habit, in any place and any company they like, of plunging into the most subtle dialectic concerning subjects that present extreme difficulty.
>
> *De Oratore* II, 18

> A purely negative dialectic which refrains from pronouncing any positive judgment. This, after being originated by Socrates, revived by Arcesilas, and reinforced by Carneades, has flourished right down to our own period. . . . But this I ascribe not to the fault of the academy but to the dullness of mankind.
>
> *De Natura Deorum* I, 11

> They hold . . . that something is "probable," or as it were resembling the truth, and that this provides them with a canon of judgement both in the conduct of life and in philosophical investigation and discussion. What is this canon of truth and falsehood, if we have no notion of truth and falsehood, for the reason that they are indistinguishable?
>
> *Academica* II, 32–33

Cicero chides Varro for omitting any treatment of philosophy in his histories on the grounds that this only perpetuates Roman xenophobia and, therefore, misunderstanding of philosophy. His intimation that Crassus' anti-Greek views are pretense[110] is evidence that Romans who were learned, especially in Greek philosophy, avoided showing it for fear they would be thought disdainful toward Romans. Cicero's interlocutors associate many aspects and affectations of "the philosophers" with Greek habits of mind, language, and behavior; contentiousness, tactlessness, pointless word play, logic chopping, and absurdities. The "Greeklings" are said to be "fonder of argument than of truth"[111]; many of their philosophies are said to propound either no criteria of truth and reliable perception or contingent criteria. A dual purpose linking the *Academica* and *De Natura Deorum* is the promotion and reform of Academic philosophy. Cicero must defend his preferred candidate for a naturalized Roman philosophy against charges of negativism, skepticism, "withholding assent," and programmatic atheism that the interlocutors in his dialogues level more generally at a variety of philosophies and philosophizing.[112] The reform of Academic philosophy that Cicero advocates entails a return to some elements of the Old Academy, "the famous old system of philosophy that took its rise from Socrates."[113] He has Varro argue that Aristotle and Speusippus, Plato's successor, taught "really one system." Both framed a definitely formulated rule of doctrine, "whereas they abandoned the famous Socratic custom of discussing everything in a doubting manner and without the admission of any positive statement. Thus was produced something that Socrates had been in the habit of reprobating entirely, a definite science of philosophy, with a regular arrangement of subjects and a formulated system of doctrine."[114]

As with his histories of rhetoric, Cicero's retellings of the history of philosophy are notably polyvalent. At times the account links Aristotle and Socrates as arch relativists and negative dialecticians who eschew positive philosophizing and undermine the Forms or *ideai*. At other times he links Aristotle with Plato through the similarity of their enterprises of founding an integrated liberal sciences curriculum. Despite Cicero's equivocation on the individuals, the issues he portrays are clear. Educated Romans are hostile toward the dogmatism of some philosophers and the skepticism and relativisms of others. Their ambivalence about the "rhetoricians' workshops" is manifest in their resistance to reincorporating an explicitly Greek philosophical rhetoric. In propounding his own list of commonplaces, Antonius acknowledges that he knows Aristotle set down a list of commonplaces, but he deems it best not to cite a Greek.[115] The "gross habit" of dialectic is singled out again and again as a Greek trait which the Romans want to avoid if not eradicate entirely.[116] This habit in turn is linked to eristics and to the Greek fondness for probabilistic logic. "In fact controversy about a word has long tormented Greeklings, fonder as they are of argument than of truth."[117] Stoic logic is frequently caricatured by Cicero's interlocutors as empty wordplay, a dillentantish Greek contentiousness. Cicero argues that the technical rhetoricians need some philosophy, because what they are producing is by any standard an impartial and errant logic. As a corrective, and conversely, Cicero proposes that the philosophers need some rhetorical training of the right kind so that their increasingly negative dialectics can be salvaged and put to positive use. He presents the possibility of forging an enlightened probabilism which can yield sound judgments and serve as the basis for action. "Thus the wise man will make use of whatever apparently probable presentation he encounters, if nothing presents itself that is contrary to that probability, and his whole plan of life will be charted out in this manner. [Even the Stoic] follows many things probable, that he has not grasped nor perceived nor assented to but that possess verisimilitude; and if he were not to approve them, life would be done away with."[118] An indigenous Latin hybrid can here be seen at the point of coalescing, one which Cicero takes great pains to exemplify and propound. He presents Cato the younger as a counterexample to the rule that Stoic oratory is "poor and unresourceful." In him, "though a Stoic through and through, I feel no craving for more perfect eloquence."[119] What were the Stoic qualities which Cato had so admirably overcome? What kinds of probabilistic logic and dialectic did Cicero approve, and for what reasons?

The notion of probability is a central object of criticism, and is repeatedly linked with procedures of definition, doctrines of causality, and methods of forming arguments. As in the case with the topics in his treatment of technical rhetoric, his examination of the probabilistic logic rejected in various degrees by the Stoics and advanced by members of the New Academy is shown to intersect or parallel rhetorical terminology and models of argumentation at several points. Reviewed from the perspective of the systematic probabilistic logic that continued to influence semantic and logical theory through Augustine's time, the links that Cicero's appraisals establish between the linguistic contingencies shared by probabilistic models in rhetorical and logical conceptions of argument and proof are insightful examinations of the transmission off formal language models in Greek and Latin culture. Cicero accepts practical and modified versions of probabilistic logic, but only those that are grounded in representational verisimilitude, a doctrine which assumes a practical criterion by which probabilistic approximations of truth may be measured. Cicero's insistent qualification on this point places important limits on the relativisms ad infinitum so favored by the Cynics and Skeptics.

The "famous old system of philosophy" that Cicero selects as his cornerstone is that of Plato's Academy, not the partitioned curriculum he attacks in Aristotle's Lyceum and the Stoic system, or the Epicurean avoidance of method entirely. Instead of emphasizing differences among physics, logic, ethics, and their subdivisions, Cicero's proposals focus relentlessly on their interdependence. The "qualities" — primary and derivative, homogeneous and simple, varied and multiform — are simultaneously described as discoveries of the Greek physicists and as terministic innovations difficult to translate into Latin. He notes that the dialecticians' vocabulary is "none of it the popular language, . . . indeed this is a quality shared by all of the sciences: either new names have to be coined for new things, or names taken from other things have to be used metaphorically [*transferenda*]." He chides Varro: "I think you will actually be doing a service to your fellow countrymen if you not only enlarge their store of facts, as you have done, but of words also."[120] This persistent attention to the tandem evolution of words and facts in Latin philosophy and literature alike — the "record" of philosophical history that he both advocates and produces — belies his objections to esoteric philosophical language and draws attention to the interdependence of words and facts, a relationship that he builds on in his account of the establishment of Old Academic philosophy in its three parts. According to his history, from the primary simple qualities were derived the "first principles, and (to translate from the Greek) elements [*stoicheia*]."[121] His running commentary on the evolution of philosophical terms traces these terms throughout the curriculum they define, from logic into physics, from physics into a summary of metaphysics, including views of Necessity, "'a fated and unchangeable concatenation of everlasting order'; although they sometimes also term it Fortune, because many of its operations are unforeseen and unexpected by us on account of

their obscurity and our ignorance of causes."[122] The emphasis on
the cognitive ability to comprehend — "our ignorance of causes" — is
interdependent, in his presentation, with the foundations of both
metaphysics and physics, and immediately precedes a discussion of
a third part of philosophy, "consisting in both reason and discussion," variously called logic and dialectic but which finally, in his
account, comprises "the whole doctrine of Dialectic, that is, speech
cast in the form of logical argument; to this as a 'counterpart' was
added the faculty of Rhetoric, which sets out a continuous speech
adapted to the purpose of persuasion."[123]

His account of the origin of logic and dialectic begins with Old
Academic epistemology, and carefully sustains its integration with
Aristotelian faculty psychology, Plato's notion of the *idea*, and the
Stoic search for a "criterion of truth." The criterion of truth, he tells
us, "arose indeed from the senses, yet was not in the senses: the
judge of things was, they held, the mind — they thought that it alone
deserves credence, because it alone perceives that which is eternally
simple and uniform and true to its own quality. This thing they
called the *Idea*." Because the senses were deemed to be dull and
sluggish, and all things in continual ebb and flow, "all this portion
of things they called the object of opinion." "Knowledge . . . they
deemed to exist nowhere except in the . . . mind, and consequently
they approved the method of defining *things*, and applied this 'real
definition' to all the subjects that they discussed."[124] Cicero's earlier
accounts of Old Academic physics are by this construction rendered
products of definition, a rendering underlined by his initial attention to the interpenetration of words and facts, and by his related
characterization of Aristotle as "the first to undermine the Forms
[*ideai*]."[125] The relationship between "the criteria of truth" and
things perceived (*visium*) or grasped (*katalepton*) by the senses becomes, through Cicero's attention to translation and definition, an
important explanation of the origins of probabilistic dialectic. His
account spans from Aristotle to the New Academy of Arcesilas, and
its focus rests on the emergence of a doctrine that nothing can be
known: a doctrine whose sources Cicero finds in Socrates, and
which resembles those expounded by Gorgias in "On Being." "Nor
is there anything that can be perceived or understood, and for these
reasons, . . . no one must make any positive statement or affirmation or give the approval of his assent to any proposition, . . . as it

would be glaring rashness to give assent either to a falsehood or to something not certainly known, and nothing is more disgraceful than for assent and approval to outstrip knowledge and perception. . . . When equally weighty reasons were found on opposite sides on the same subject, it was easier to dissent from either side. They call this school the New Academy."[126]

Examined collaterally, Cicero's diverse and yet carefully coordinated accounts of the evolution of philosophy and rhetoric map out the fault lines along which erratically aligned disciplines had repeatedly fragmented, and remains an accurate predictor of that fragmentation. Philosophy has recurrently abdicated its role as regent of ideas or truth, has in different eras turned instead to what Cicero terms a "wholly negative dialectic," and has assumed the role of instrument more for analyzing than for producing or constructing proofs. These moments find their modern equivalents in analytic philosophy and in postmodern dismantlings of rationality. Rhetoric has waxed and waned as a discipline with the academy with varying liaisons to literary stylistics, skills literacy, and theories of language and culture. As divergent as Scaevola and Brutus, today's partisans alternate among definitions of rhetoric within revivals of literary–philosophical classicism, adaptations of cognitive psychology and philosophy to the tasks of critical thinking manifest in expository prose writing, and a no-nonsense skills approach to rhetoric that is now associated with basic literacy.

Cicero's anatomy of these recurrent cycles received its first confirmation in the three centuries between his and Augustine's era. He propounded an integrated liberal arts curriculum whose most important product was not knowledge per se but *eloquentia*, defined as the virtuous application and enactment of the knowledge, wisdom, and principles learned in the schoolroom. Quintilian's educational prolegomena distilled and codified Cicero's proposals regarding rhetoric; he stands in a relationship to Cicero that resembles Aristotle's to Plato. The parallelism of these relationships further demonstrates Cicero's historical observations that taxonomy and curricular exposition tend relentlessly toward reductive formulae, toward ever more reductive, metamethodological taxonomies of taxonomies and accounts of accounts. By the fourth century, when Augustine studied and taught in the rhetorical schools of North Africa, rhetoric displayed again many of the hairline fractures observed by Cicero. It consisted of long lists of ornamental schemes and tropes, taxonomies of arguments and formulae for logical analysis, and grammatical precepts used in the study of syntax and predication. Practice and drill, dialectical refutation, memorization and declamation, and literary games in which "deception, not truth delights us," were the standard methods of the classrooms which Augustine finally abandoned.[127] Augustine's "release from the profession of rhetoric"[128] was the culmination of many experiences that parallel those first described, and criticized, by Cicero. It can be said that it is Cicero—whom he claims as a stylistic and pedagogical exemplar—and not rhetoric that Augustine found hardest to leave.

5

When the Rhetor *Lies: Augustine's Critique of Mendacity*

> Unto them that are without, all these things are done in parables: that seeing they may see, and not perceive; and hearing, they may hear and not understand.
>
> *Mark* 4: 11–12

> The Scriptures seemed quite unworthy of comparison with the stately prose of Cicero, because I had too much conceit to accept their simplicity and not enough insight to penetrate their depths. It is surely true that as the child grows these books grow with him. But I was too proud to call myself a child.
>
> AUGUSTINE, *Confessions* III, 5

> How is the truth of a statement diminished if an error is made in number or case, in preposition, particle, or conjunction?
>
> ARNOBIUS, *Adversus Nationes* I, 59

> Hence the Scripture does not say "the multitude of the eloquent," but "the multitude of the wise" is the welfare of the whole world.
>
> AUGUSTINE, *De Doctrina Christiana* IV

A persistent theme in Augustine's work is the critique of mendacity, a habitual deceitfulness that he proposes is imparted by formal training in rhetoric. He recounts as common classroom practice teaching students that successful dissembling, "deception, not truth,"[1] is one hallmark of the educated sophisticate. In the *Confessions* he depicts a classroom experience that had the effect of wedging apart ethical and rhetorical norms. "I was expected to model myself after men who were disconcerted by the rebukes they received if they used outlandish words or strange idioms to tell of some quite harmless thing they might have done but revelled in the applause they earned for the fine flow of well ordered and nicely balanced phrases with which they described their own acts of indecency."[2] Though Augustine is hardly unique in the era in his reprobation of secular rhetorical and literary teaching, the range, depth, and influence of his views marks a decentering of many classical views, and an installation of alternate views that effected gradual but radical alterations in the practice and teaching of all the language arts, literature, and hermeneutics.[3]

Augustine's portraits of the rhetoric classroom of his day constitute a provocative analysis not only of rhetoric but of literacy as well. He provides numerous instances of rhetorical teaching that perpetuated or prompted unethical uses of language: intentional deception, dissembling as sport and art, and deliberate distortions of known truth, and attributes these products of rhetorical training to inadequacies in rhetoric as a theory of language. If the abuses of language encouraged by rhetorical teaching are to be eliminated, he contends, the theory of language implicit in rhetorical models must be altered. Elements in his critique resemble and extend the reformist and reintegrative positions of Cicero on rhetoric, ethics, and an integrated liberal arts tradition. Augustine greatly admired Cicero's views as well as his prose, yet he constantly reminds himself and his readers not to let the beguiling pleasure of eloquent speech serve as a distraction. "I think that there is hardly a single eloquent man who can both speak well and think of the rules of eloquence while he is speaking. And we should beware lest what should be said escape us while we are thinking of the artistry of the discourse."[4]

Disjunctions of this kind set the stage for the many transformations Augustine introduces into extant rhetorical and linguistic theory, a series of syntheses and reintegrations of ethical and spiritual values with linguistic practices and beliefs. In a deft *antiphrasis*, Augustine convicts rhetorical assumptions concerning intention of promoting contingent canons of truth. "If we do not consider the things spoken of, but only the intentions of the one speaking, he is the better man who unknowingly speaks falsely, because he judges his statement to be true, than the one who unknowingly speaks the truth while in his heart he is attempting to deceive."[5] Rhetorical intentionality is reunited with epistemology and ethics in this distinction between the truth of the things spoken of and the intentions of the speaker, a reintegration that permits the isolation of intentional deception and dissembling as linguistic sins. There are many situations in which individuals say untrue things out of ignorance, or construct obviously fictive literary artifices. Careful delineations of these and other ethical shadings provide substance for bolder assertions that rhetoric comprises interrelated sanctions for intentional dissembling and deception; the ethical problems introduced by rhetorical intention permeate its models of semiotic, semantic, poetic, and stylistic aspects of language. The analysis of these models, culminating in a reconstruction of rhetoric, structures the sequence of books which make up *De Doctrina Christiana*.

In reappraising the semantics and the rhetorical efficacy of figurative language, Augustine addresses the aesthetics and semantics of secular literature, and particularly its claim to represent reality through imitation. Examining the commonplace that the poets lie, he conjures a dialogue between himself and Reason. She says, "You know that literary studies include fables and obvious falsehoods." He replies: "Yes. But the study of literature is not possible *for* the falsehoods. It demonstrates their nature. A fable is a falsehood composed for use and pleasure; while literary study is the art which guards and controls composition. These things are false not through any will or desire of their own, but from the necessity of following the will of their authors. On the stage Roscius wants to be a false Hecuba, but by nature he is a true man. By so wanting he is also a true tragedian, so far as he fulfills the part."[6] This solution to the problem of fiction and lying reconciles Plato's objection to any dissembling imitation of truth with Cicero's defense of a liberal arts curriculum and practice that will sustain an integration of ethics and eloquence.

The synthesis of literary and rhetorical themes and models with ethical concerns is further extended, in numerous treatments of the generation of meaning in language, by examinations of the role played by intent in determining the ethical acceptability of a given work, and by assessments of the beholder's share — the audience's responsibility for what it chooses to view and how it chooses to understand it.

> Every spectator admits that he wants to reach truth. Hence he takes care not to be deceived, and vaunts himself if he shows more acuteness and vivacity than others in watching and learning and judging. Men carefully and closely watch a juggler who professes nothing but deceit. If his tricks elude discovery they are delighted with the cleverness of the man who hoodwinks them. If he did not know how to hoodwink those who were looking on, or was believed not to know, no one would applaud. If many see through the trick the juggler is not praised, nonetheless, those who do not see it are laughed at.[7]

A comparison of this portrayal with Aristotle's advice to the public speaker reveals a striking shift in both the form and the object of address. Augustine's formulation directs attention away from a concern with "if you want to effect X, do Y," and toward an understanding of the reciprocal interactions built into the rhetorical situation. The audience is addressed as much as the speaker, as if to say, "Listeners, can you not see what you permit and encourage when the trickster does this?"

As is true of many passages throughout Augustine's work, this passage functions as a thematic microcosm, and expresses concerns that shape Augustine's transformation of rhetorical models into a hermeneutic system able to prescribe the construction of meanings not only to speakers, but first and perhaps even more importantly, to the receivers of texts — a concern that is particularly apparent in *De Doctrina*, where homilists are addressed first as readers and then as homilists, the oral transmitters of Scripture. The speaking they do will be interpretive, exhortative, and didactic, but it must shun tricks and deceptions and juggling games with an audience. They will not only have to have tools for using language and for understanding the language they must interpret; they will also have to retrain audiences whose understanding of listening has been shaped by the practices of secular rhetorical literary performance. The differences between extant rhetorical theory and the requirements of teaching homilists to compose spoken interpretations of an authoritative but sometimes ambiguous and polysemous written text were of urgent concern to Augustine during and after his conversion "from rhetoric to Christianity."[8] He recounts that he had to completely alter his own linguistic assumptions and his taste for the "stately prose of Cicero," in order to accommodate the seemingly vulgar, childlike language of Scripture.[9] Are these not, he asks himself, simply "literary" fables like the "immoral stories" he and his fellow churchmen object to in pagan literature? "Sacred" Scripture depicts adulterous kings, sons deceiving their fathers for a patrimony, fathers giving daughters as concubines to dinner guests. Every sin imaginable is portrayed, and in language that Augustine long found embarrassingly simpleminded, as if these were "stories for children."

Grappling with the language of Scripture, addressing the question of its similarity to secular fable and folklore, and defining objections to secular literature and to rhetorical teaching, merge in the project undertaken in *De Doctrina Christiana*. He extends and alters extant notions of the referential status of words (book 1), and supplements conventionalist doctrines of the meanings of words (book 2). Books I and II provide an account of dual signification and dual meanings by combining and extending several extant models of reference and semantics. The treatment of figurative language provided in Book III lays the groundwork for subsequent Christian hermeneutics, as well as for subsequent literary theories of typology, allegory, and symbol, in its appraisals of the function and interpretation of ambiguous or figurative words and language. Book IV begins, "this is not a treatise on rhetoric," only to provide the homilist with exempla of styles and arguments taken from classical rhetoric, redevising the canons of eloquence which Augustine had learned and taught during his career as a teacher of rhetoric. Taken as a whole, *De Doctrina* can be viewed as a watershed of evolving objections to secular rhetorical teaching, logic, and literature — objections that had begun even before Augustine's conversion and that he shared with many others. At the same time it is directed at conservative movements within the Church. Emblematic of the growing rigidity of those movements was a ruling passed at the Council of Carthage in 398, the same year Augustine began composing *De Doctrina*, forbidding even bishops to read *libros*

gentilum — secular literature — unless it was demonstrably necessary.[10] The wording of the ruling, and its primary object — the bishops — also reflects the extent to which literacy, if defined as wide
reading of available manuscripts, was being altered in the wake of
Christianity.

De Doctrina is a pragmatic, carefully wrought restatement and
transformation of classical rhetorical, literary, and logical theory
that preserves many elements in each of these traditions. Its significance is illuminated further by aligning it with the critical points in
Augustine's spiritual journey recounted in the *Confessions*. Diverse
corruptions that he believed were eroding the social contexts of
value, meaning, and reliable communication were of crucial concern to Augustine, yet he objected to the dogmatic Christian orthodoxies that were attempting to impose order by force. Their efforts
at absolute rule were increasingly buttressed by priestly control over
texts and their interpretation, by promotions of doggedly literalist
conceptions of reading, and by the *docta ignoranta* — a programmatic anti-intellectualism. Augustine's invectives against rhetorical
dissembling, literary lies, and depravity in rhetorical teachers, students, speakers, and audiences are themselves profoundly rhetorical. By seeming to align himself with Christian purists in several
camps, Augustine is better able to promote preservation through
transformation rather than elimination of classical texts and learning. By cleansing literature and rhetoric of their associations with
pretty lies and deceits, he extends literary and rhetorical theories of
allegory, figure, and trope, and integrates them with the concept of
levels of meaning; all become prominent features in his scriptural
hermeneutics. Literary irony and rhetorical indirection alike, reconceived as edifying enigma, are retained as powerful and strategic,
but are irrevocably changed by the relocation of all authorship in
God.

Anatomy of a Conversion: Rhetorician, Manichean, Academic, Platonist, Catechumen, Bishop

Augustine would arguably have attempted a synthesis of extant
grammar, rhetoric, and literary training with normative ethics and a
truth-seeking hermeneutics even if he had not experienced an

epiphanic conversion in a Milan garden. *De Dialectica, Contra Academicos*, and *De Magistro*, all written near the time of the Milan "conversion," assail extant logical–grammatical theory and pedagogy on secular ethical and epistemological grounds.[11] His study of several different philosophical systems underwrites a treatment of the then extant language models that, far from being simplistic or merely Christian polemic, reflects the fluent familiarity of a teacher with often taught materials.[12] The *Contra Academicos* is explicitly framed as a reply to Cicero's *Academica*, and approaches it as a misguided defense of Academic philosophy and teaching methods. Observing the technification of the general school training in grammar and the predominantly eristic and epideictic practice of rhetoric throughout the early Christian centuries, some scholars have depicted Augustine as a conservative opponent of any and all secular rhetorical and literary education.[13] However, this view ignores Augustine's substantial differences from extreme conservatives within the Church who did seek a suppression of secular learning and culture by fiat. Augustine's diatribes against secular learning may be understood, at least in part, as rhetorically strategic attempts at conciliating his more conservative colleagues. Though the conservative Church climate at the time Augustine wrote the *Confessions* and *De Doctrina Christiana* was an important stimulus to both works, it is the secular issues that had contributed to his hesitation before conversion that are given explicit exposition. The *Confessions* expresses the formidable reservation that he could never reject the life of the mind for a faith that adopted an attitude toward thought and language which was as contingent and skeptical, in its own way, as that of the philosophers. The creed attributed to Tertullian, *credo quia absurdum*, "I believe because it is impossible," pointedly and polemically employs the language of secular logic. In Cicero's accounts the philosophers are depicted as fond of demonstrating that "nothing is possible"; or, in a converse sophistry, that "nothing is anything more than possible." In Augustine's time the logical riddling persisted, continued to be regarded with either delight or scorn, and was met with *docta ignoranta* whose spiritual import was anything but frivolous.

Though he does not firmly reject secular philosophy, literature, or rhetoric outright, Augustine weaves into all his works forthright denunciations of their flaws along with accounts of the evolution of these criticisms.[14] First as a student, then as a teacher, Augustine becomes irritated with the categories and classifications of both grammar and logic. He observes a low ratio of correspondence to ordinary language, ethics, and conceptions of truth. He objects to Aristotle's *Categories* on grounds independent of religious belief; they were to him epistemologically unwieldy and logically overcomplicated.[15] What interests him instead is expressed in an agile shift to religious concerns: the "main categories of sin."[16] Augustine remembers from his early childhood and youth perceptions of the disproportionate and ethically neutral emphasis given rules, form, and correctness over and above what was being taught and said. "A man who has learnt the traditional rules of pronunciation, or teaches them to others, gives greater scandal if he breaks your rules and hates another human being, his fellow man."[17] *De Doctrina Christiana*, in seeming contrast, defends the study of grammar and rhetoric, but only by those who have assimilated the proper ratio of correctness to ethics. Not all need to study grammar and eloquence. In an ideal world, none would need to. In an account similar to Cicero's descriptions of the models spontaneously emulated by children, Augustine admonishes the readers of *De Doctrina* that "boys do not need the art of grammar which teaches correct speech if they have the opportunity to grow up and live among men who speak correctly. Without knowing any of the names of the errors they criticize and avoid anything erroneous."[18] This provisional acceptance of the explicit teaching of formal grammar is a succinct appraisal of natural learning and would no doubt have been appealing to the anti-intellectuals who sought a Christian orthodoxy of beliefs and behavior that would need no teaching because they would be universally practiced. Any teaching, Augustine posits, must be vigilant, if it is to avoid confusing its methods with its ultimate goals. Correctness, an ability to read, or knowledge of literature are for Augustine but means to other ends: understanding and communication — understanding and communicating God's presence and wisdom in all things: the book of Scripture, the world, and human beings. In the *Confessions* the vehicle he chooses to exemplify this understanding is a narrative of his early schooling and career as a teacher of rhetoric that focuses in ample measure on ways of understanding and teaching language. His detailed treatment of an array of extant language theories allows us to observe how markedly that range resembles today's linguistic pluralism and skepticism. Of equal value is his criticism of extant theories and of their pedagogical applications.

The outright immorality of the literary models given to students provokes special censure. "This traditional education taught me that Jupiter punishes the wicked with his thunderbolts and yet commits adultery himself. The two roles are quite incompatible. . . . And yet human children are pitched into this hellish torrent, together with the fees which are paid to have them taught lessons like these. . . . This is the school where men are made masters of words. This is where they learn the art of persuasion, so necessary in business and debate."[19] Augustine's concern is not "merely" pedagogical; it reflects an awareness of the interpenetration of pedagogical models, ethical values and cultural coherence, while reminding us that literature was then first taught in primary school as a set of stylistic exempla within rhetoric. The "great" literature, the *Iliad* and *Aeneid*, was also held to be a repository of cultural traditions and beliefs and was taught as representing ostensibly admirable, or familiar, behavior. It was the latter function that Augustine and others objected to more than the former; many such exempla are replaced by scriptural passages in *De Doctrina*.

Augustine's dissatisfactions with taxonomical and formalistic grammar, rhetoric, and logic continued as he completed his schooling and became ready to begin teaching rhetoric himself. "By now I was at the top of the school of rhetoric. I was pleased with my superior status and swollen with conceit."[20] By 371, at the age of sixteen, he had completed his education in law. "I behaved far more quietly than the 'Wreckers,' a title of ferocious deviltry which the fashionable set chose for themselves. . . . Without provocation they would set upon some timid newcomer, gratuitously offending his sense of decency for their own amusement and using it as fodder for their spiteful jests."[21] In 373, at the age of nineteen, while reading Cicero's *Hortensius*, he was attracted to Academic philosophy, in which he discovered a more substantive version of the vestigially theorized techniques he had been learning and teaching, and illuminating appraisals of the relationships among wisdom and knowledge, virtue, character, and truth. With Academic philosophy in hand, as a beacon which had "inflamed" him with a new notion of wisdom, he returned temporarily to the reading of Scripture. Unfortunately, he found that the wisdom defined so eloquently in the

Hortensius and the truth lurking somewhere in Scripture were uncomfortably incompatible. "It was enfolded in mysteries. . . . To me they [the scriptures] seemed unworthy of comparison with the stately prose of Cicero."[22]

During the next nine years Augustine was employed as a teacher of rhetoric, first at Carthage and then in his home town of Tagaste. He became a follower of Manicheism, "fell in with a bad lot," derided Scripture and churchmen alike, "was led astray and led others astray in my turn. We were alike deceivers and deceived in all our different aims and ambitions, both publicly when we expounded our so-called liberal ideas, and in private through our service to what we called religion." The sycophantic community of professional sophisticates and teachers, and the Manicheism to which he had turned, converged in what he presents as a corrupt spirituality and a morality driven by an intentionally dialectical pursuit of extremes. He and his friends "would hunt for worthless popular distinctions, the applause of an audience, prizes for poetry, . . . loved the idle pastimes of the stage and in self-indulgence . . . were unrestrained. On the other hand we aspired to be purged of these lowly pleasures by taking food to the holy elect, as they were called, so that in their paunches it might pass through the process of being made into angels and gods who would set us free."[23] Neither the empty victories and cash prizes nor the spiritual dialectics of repentance for such indulgences provided by Manichean rituals of self-abnegation were satisfying. Enacting the Manichean struggle of opposites in eternal cycles of deliberate depravity and cathartic cleansing was as incomplete and unfulfilling as teaching, where he felt he had constantly to justify to himself making a living by selling the tricks of debate. He expresses a growing discomfort with the commonplace defense that the uses to which rhetoric is put are not the responsibility of its teacher. "I preferred to have honest pupils, . . . and I had not evil intent when I taught the tricks of pleading, for I never meant them to be used to get the innocent condemned, but, if the occasion arose, to save the lives of the guilty. . . . For though, as I schooled my pupils, I was merely abetting their futile designs and their schemes of duplicity, nevertheless I did my best to teach them honestly."[24]

The fashionable, hypocritical dialectic of arrogant rhetorical display and Manichean penitence coexisted with these and other pedagogical soul searchings for some years, until the death of a good friend brought a sudden desolation and finally an abject realization that the god of the Manichees "was my own delusion."[25] Augustine had been to his friend "as Orestes to Pylades," who were "ready to die together for each other's sake, because each would rather die than live without the other." His great comfort became other friends who shared his love of this "huge fable, . . . the long drawn lie" of friendship. Both his Manichean god and the "fable of friendship" are presented in these accounts as chimeras—a god who is a self-delusion in Augustine's mind, an "adulterous" love of a friend with whom he engages in the idolatrous worship of a fable of friendship. These "false gods" are presented as faint contours of something else; in the criteria that define their illusoriness Augustine finds prefigured something which is neither false nor falsifiable—a love for the principle of friendship known and embraced in the mind, independent of fables, individual friends, and the ephemeral "signs" of friendship. Very gradually, he comes to experience this purified love as itself a distant echo of omnipresent divine love.

The metaphor with which Augustine begins his description of these hierarchical correspondences is that of the sign. He describes the "heartfelt tokens of affection" exchanged between friends as "signs to be read on the face and in the eyes, spoken by the tongue, and displayed in countless acts of kindness."[26] The reality and force of these signs is precisely what makes the death of a loved friend painful; with the friend's death these physical signs die, too. Augustine proposes that the inordinate love of these signs perceived by the senses is like an "insidious glue" binding persons to things which recurrently die and are lost.[27] What is lost when a friend dies? The friend, but also, in Augustine's rendering, the physical signs of the friendship which *as signs* are as corporeal and as transient as all other physical things. The similarity of Augustine's analysis of the illusoriness of physical signs to modern conceptions of the myth of presence cannot go unremarked, for both accounts express a deeply spiritual sense of loss, grief, and yearning, as well as the feeling that love, presence, and permanence have been looked for in all the wrong places. The endless cycles of coming into being and passing away, generation and decay, the Manichean opposites which had been Augustine's religion for a good many years, are superseded at this point in the narrative by a long-hoped-for apprehension of and belief in a larger whole. In a now lost work, *Beauty and Proportion*, Augustine further developed this quasi-Platonist hierarchy of signification that provided him with the path out of the Manichean maze.

Augustine's recurrent analogies to physical signs, speech, and hearing are not merely derivative Platonism, however; they extend and revive classroom grammars and rhetorics that would have been familiar to many of his readers, and are integrated with a novel cognitive faculty psychology. He adopts the analogy of speech sounds and syntax to illustrate the transformation of transient and constantly changing parts into a larger, less ephemeral whole. "For a sentence is not complete unless each word, once its syllables have been pronounced, gives way to make room for the next."[28] He then scolds his soul for enjoying the transient beauty of the physically perceived word, heard or read. "It delights you, but it is only a part and you have no knowledge of the whole. . . . If you could comprehend the whole, you would wish that whatever exists in the present would pass on, so that you might gain greater pleasure from the whole. It is one of these same bodily senses that enables you to hear the words I speak, but you do not want the syllables to sound forever in my mouth: you want them to fly from my tongue and give place to others."[29] Although his mind still ranged only "amongst material forms," Augustine discerned two classes of beautiful things, "those which please the eye because they are beautiful in themselves, and those which do so because they are a ratio of something else."[30] When in recounting his discovery of Aristotle's categories, he emphasizes that he found it a frustrating propaedeutic for *reducing* things to categories, he provides a precedent for his subsequent questioning of all of his received classifications and ratios of material things. A Christian Manichean bishop, Faustus, arrived in North Africa at the point of Augustine's greatest doubt, but disappointed his hope that the bishop's erudition in both Christian and Manichean religion could resolve his complex spiritual and philosophical questions. Faustus could not answer his questions and was not ashamed to admit this, a candor which impressed Augustine. "Modesty and candor are finer equipment for the mind than scientific knowledge of the kind that I wished to possess." The bishop nonetheless provided relief. "A deadly snare" to non-Christians, because he was a mediator between Manichean and Christian doctrine, Faustus "now began to release me from the trap in which I had been caught."[31]

It was with renewed interest in Christianity, and upon hearing that students in Rome were less contentious than those of Carthage, that Augustine decided to leave Carthage and the sycophantic Wreckers. In 383 he departed for Rome and what he hoped would be a more productive, less troubled career as a teacher of rhetoric and literature. He retained an interest in Manicheism, and continued to pursue Academic philosophy as "wiser than the rest, because they held that everything was a matter of doubt and asserted that man can know nothing for certain."[32] Because of his "materialism" he was drawn to the Manichean explanation of evil as a substance pitted against a good God, also conceived as a substance.

> And because such little piety as I had compelled me to believe that God, who is good, could not have created an evil nature, I imagined that there were two antagonist masses. . . . My theories forced me to admit that you were finite in one point only, in so far as the mass of evil was able to oppose you. . . . I thought of evil not simply as some vague substance but as an actual bodily substance, and this was because I could not conceive of mind except as a rarefied body somehow diffused in space. I also thought of our Savior, your only Son, as somehow extended or projected for our salvation from the mass of your transplendent body.[33]

Here is exemplified the residual force of the dialectics propounded by Manicheism, influencing an attempt to explain evil that is closely tied to a conceptualization of the nature of God, and an expression of the need for that explanation. Both stem from the skepticism propounded by the Academics he continues to find so attractive. Yet it is the materialism in Manicheism and Academic skepticism alike that impels him toward a desperately needed resolution of the problem of knowledge: What is the mind? How does it know what it knows? How is its substance akin to or related to the ambiguous corporeality of the relationships between good and evil, God and his son?

Augustine's reasoning becomes increasingly synthesizing and integrative at this point, illuminating parallels and hierarchies within the larger whole he is discovering—or constructing. The analytic categories dividing parts of speech, parts of arguments, and arguments from logical proofs are dissolving. Manichean opposites no

longer provide adequate explanations. If what they imply about
God is extended to the mind, then both mind and God are bodies
somehow diffused in space, somehow related to each other and
struggling with an evil whose relationship to either God or mind is
also a matter of vague bodies. "It was principally the idea of the two
masses of good and evil that held me fast and stifled me, for I was
unable to conceive of any but material realities. Under the weight of
these two masses I gasped for the pure clear air of your truth, but I
could draw no breath of it."[34] His growing obsession with the problem of knowledge coincided with the unhappy discovery that the
students in Rome were indeed more polite than those of North
Africa, but only because their polished urbanity concealed unscru-
pulousness. They transferred from one teacher to another in con-
spiratorial strategies to avoid paying fees. To these students, "justice
meant nothing compared with the love of money."[35]

Disappointed in Rome, and increasingly unsatisfied by attempts
at reconciling Manicheism with Christianity, Augustine accepted a
post in Milan, where a new teacher of rhetoric was needed. Ambrose, the bishop, was a proponent of the view that in Platonism
"God and his Word are constantly implied."[36] Augustine found himself impressed by Ambrose's goodness and also by his eloquence,
though "while I paid the closest attention to the words he used, I
was quite uninterested in the subject matter and was even contemptuous of it. . . . Nevertheless his meaning, which I tried to ignore,
found its way into my mind together with his words, which I admired so much. I could not keep the two apart."[37] Ambrose's figurative explication of passages from the Old Testament provided
Augustine with the long-sought instrument of refuting Manichean
derisions of Scripture as mere fable. The surface of the deceptively
simple stories, in Ambrose's explications, was shown to hold a
deeper truth. The conceptualization of plural but not contradictory
meanings, and of a simultaneity among levels of meaning, moved
Augustine one step further toward a solution to the problem of
knowledge he had posed for himself. Even with this advance, however, the Christian positions remained "unbeaten but still not victo-
rious."[38] The lack of positive proof left him still in the Academic
camp. Though finally able to abandon the Manichees' dialectical
materialism at this point, he still found the Academic philosophers
attractive in their resolutely cautious skepticism. "Nevertheless, I

utterly refused to entrust the healing of the maladies of my soul to these philosophers."[39] He became a catechumen, a formal novice student, in the Catholic church.

The "moment" of his conversion—which the *Confessions* presents as the culmination of a quite gradual progression—occurred in a garden while he was fitfully reading with a friend, Alypius. He is tormented with thoughts that his body with its great desires controls him. His mind should control his mind, not his body his mind, an especially urgent concern after his rejection of Manichean materialism and the alternating, cyclical dualism of mind and body it permitted. Sexual continence has been his self-imposed test of this rule, and he has failed the test in his mind, where desires continue to torment him. He hears children in a nearby house chanting in what seems to be a game, *Tolle lege, Tolle lege*, "Take it and read, take it and read." But Augustine cannot remember any such game. "This could only be a divine command to open my book of Scripture and read the first passage on which my eyes should fall." He returns to his Gospel and it falls open at Paul's letter to the Romans: "spend no more thought on nature and nature's appetites. Find room among you for a man of over-delicate conscience."[40] Surrendering his will, first to divine command and then to the words to which it leads him, he masters his will. In the paradox which releases him, he has "submitted to the divine master."

After Augustine's conversion from skepticism to belief, a second kind of conversion occurred. "The day came when my release from the profession of rhetoric was to become a reality. . . . You rescued my tongue as you had already rescued my heart." While reading the *Psalms* aloud he is set on fire with a desire to echo them to all the world, to communicate Scripture and not teach or compose rhetoric, a distinction he exemplifies by an account of his desire to pronounce the words of the psalms to the Manichees. "How I wish that they could have heard me speak these words! And how I wish that I might have been unaware that they could hear, so that they need have no cause to think that my own words, which escaped from me as I recited the Psalm, were uttered for their benefit alone! And it is true enough that I would not have uttered them, or if I had, I should not have uttered them in the same way, if I had known that they were watching and listening. And if I had uttered them, the Manichees would not have understood them in the way that I spoke them."[41] Augustine deftly describes a cruel paradox which implicates the conventions of rhetoric and its practice among the sycophants of his day. If the listeners he wishes for—his Manichean friends—were to hear him speak these words as he now speaks them, they would have to hear him while remaining unobserved by him. He conjectures that if they knew he knew they were listening, they would think he regarded them as an audience, that he was speaking "for their benefit alone." If this were the case, he could not utter the words, or at least not in the same way as at this moment. Assuming he regarded them as an audience, they would also assume that he had designs on them, that he was performing. In this characterization he describes how rhetorical teaching and the habits it imparts promote strategy-oriented assumptions about verbal exchanges, rob words of their literal meaning, and speakers of any direct and ingenuous relationship to that meaning. Furthermore, "all spectators," as Augustine often calls audiences, have through rhetorical training and conventions come to assume that delivery is contrived, tailored, or strategic. Thus the Manichees whom he conjures here cannot "hear" what he is saying aloud. If he were to say to the Manichees exactly what he says aloud in this act of audienceless communication, the meaning of the utterance would be altered, lost, tangled in the web of assumptions about why someone is saying something to someone. How can he speak and not be perceived as persuading, arguing, or performing?

Augustine's reflection on his thoughts while reading the Psalms recounts how he came to an awareness of a different sort of tangle as well. He shifts his attention from the assumptions auditors make about what is said to them to the meaning of the words themselves, particularly when those words are regarded as already true and perfectly crafted, as exemplum and teacher. "What is true of the whole psalm is also true of all its parts and of each syllable. It is true of any longer action in which I may be engaged and of which the recitation of the psalm may only be a small part. It is true of a man's whole life, of which all his actions are parts. It is true of the whole history of mankind, of which each man's life is a part."[42] The hermeneutic defined here asserts an interpenetration of past and present, of Old Testament and New Testament words, of surface signification and underlying meaning, of reading, recitation, and all other actions. In this account of analogies, parallels, and hierarchies can be seen, in miniature, the theory of signs, language, hermeneutics, and homiletics developed in the four books of *De Doctrina Christiana*.

Recounted as a spiritual journey which *per exemplum* will lead others along the same path, the *Confessions* provides numerous depictions of conventions and of assumptions which directly alter meaning. Augustine's account of why he cannot "say" the psalm he recites *to* the Manichees addresses interpretive assumptions which alter "textual" meaning and understanding simultaneously.[43] Once a psalm is regarded as a vehicle of truth, as exemplary and as a teacher, it is seen, experienced, and understood in terms of multiple correspondences and applications to past and present, to the individual and to all humankind. The act of its recitation is a microcosm of all other acts. With only slight changes the same analysis can be extended to an appraisal of the understanding of any text, the focus Augustine adopts in *De Doctrina*. The narrative specificity of *Confessions*, far from being a limitation, provides a highly detailed investigation into the power of any written texts held to be authoritative, an inquiry into conceptions of meaning, language, and textuality that have by no means been exhausted in modern appraisals of literacy, literary discourse, and rhetoric. The specific changes that the more theoretical *De Doctrina Christiana* makes in extant theories of hermeneutics and rhetoric adapt existing theories to serve truth-conveying and truth-telling modes of language. There is observable continuity with the themes recorded in the *Confessions*: the relationships among words as material signs, sentences which mean, and truth; the need for imposing ethical standards on verbal intention; the problem of good and evil and their representation in Scripture and literature; and the need for retraining communicators and audiences alike to seek truth in themselves and through each other.

Of Signs, Signification, Literary Lies, and Rhetorical Fables

The apparent directness and simplicity of the *Confessions* belie the fact that it was composed late in Augustine's career in the midst of intense doctrinal controversy, and that it was directed with strong rhetorical force at several of the involved factions. *De Doctrina*

Christiana and the *Confessions* were both begun in 396–398, when
Augustine had returned to North Africa, and had reluctantly agreed
to be ordained assistant bishop. In 398 the Council of Carthage
took up several questions of doctrine and heresy that were stirring
up controversy in the North African church. The Donatists had set
up an independent sect in 311 and continued to refuse the authority
of the orthodox bishops of North Africa. Among their party were
writers on grammar and scriptural interpretation who quoted Scripture in support of the position that neither grammar nor rhetoric
should be taught at all, on the grounds that plain speech expressing
sincere belief is the only language needed by the believer.[44] Cyprian
and Tertullian strongly opposed most study of pagan philosophy,
rhetoric, and literature. The more moderate Clement of Alexandria
wanted Christianity to use pagan philosophy which was compatible
with its teachings, but objected nonetheless to the study of much
pagan literature and secular eloquence.[45] Origen, and Makrina and
Gregory of Nyssa contributed to the development of a Christian
Platonism which Augustine encountered only indirectly, through
Ambrose and through Victorinus' Latin translations of Plotinus.[46]

Basil, Ambrose, and Jerome—all educated, as Augustine had
been, in secular schools of literary eloquence, rhetoric, and philosophy—articulate ambivalent feelings about the proper mixture of pagan with Christian teaching. Educated Christians were struggling with
the same ethical and scriptural aesthetic problems Augustine had
wrestled with, and found themselves repeatedly in disputes pitting
the arguments and eloquence of the secular world against scriptural
truth, precepts, and style. In response to the ban on reading any and
all secular literature, Jerome and Augustine shared an ambivalence,
and alternated for a time between agreeing with and objecting to it
as an imprudent restriction. The *Confessions* animates the intensity
of these contradictory views, and dramatizes them as long-standing
and evolving inner dialogues and struggles within Augustine's
mind. In *De Doctrina* Augustine adapts and expands on Ambrose's
figural hermeneutic, and forges a systematic integration of secular
and scriptural conceptions of truth. Both works are carefully
crafted and reveal less than they might of the polemical urgency
Augustine must have felt while writing them. Yet their doctrinal
context explains the detailed attention Augustine gives in both
books to countless small details of grammar, rhetoric, semantics,

literature, and their teaching. The two books can be productively apprehended as of a piece, as articulations not only of Augustine's growing understanding of his own faith, but also of defenses of secular literature, learning, and eloquence against the more conservative churchmen who wanted to legislate their abolition.

In neither work is Augustine an opponent, purely or simply, of the teaching and secular learning of his day. Yet he evolves definitions of word, sentence, intent, meaning, truth, and understanding which go beyond the models he learned and taught. In the *Confessions* he examines distinctions between literary education and literacy which have renewed interest and urgency today.

> For these elementary lessons were far more valuable than those which followed, because the subjects were practical. They gave me the power, which I still have, of reading whatever is set before me and writing whatever I wish to write. But in the later lessons I was forced to memorize the wanderings of a hero named Aeneas, while in the meantime I failed to remember my own erratic ways.
>
> . . . I would rather forget the wanderings of Aeneas and all that goes with them, than how to read and write. . . . For if I put to them the question whether it is true, as the poet says, that Aeneas once came to Carthage, the less learned will plead ignorance and the better informed will admit that it is not true. But if I ask how the name of Aeneas is spelt, anyone who has learnt to read will give me the right answer, based on the agreed convention which fixes the alphabet for all of us. If I next ask them whether a man would lose more by forgetting how to read and write or by forgetting the fancies dreamed up by the poets, surely everyone who is not out of his wits can see the answer they would give.[47]

Touching on parallel points, Augustine begins *De Doctrina Christiana* with a direct address to three groups of anticipated adversaries: those who will condemn his "precepts" because they do not understand them, those who believe in approaching Scripture with no precepts or methods other than their own faith, and those who believe biblical stories are fictions. In each case the defense he provides is a microcosm of themes developed throughout the work as he transforms extant notions of language, textual meaning and truth, and understanding. In an indirect allusion to the depiction of parables in Mark he argues that if his readers do not understand what he says, he is not to blame any more than if he pointed a finger at a star they were unable to see. To those who oppose the use of any precepts in understanding Scripture, and who regard Scripture as complete, to be approached on the literal level, and as the only needed text, he proposes that even as they rejoice in this, God's gift, they should remember that they have learned at least the alphabet by which they read from a human teacher. Thus, he intimates, human wisdom is perhaps not to be entirely ignored. To those who join the Manichees in charging that biblical stories are mere fictions and fables, he offers no defense. His silence on this point clears a field for the hermeneutics based on indirect and figural meanings developed in Book III of *De Doctrina*, an interpretation theory that supplants the simpler mimetic concept of representation underlying the Manichees' charge that Scripture is mere fable. The *Confessions* emphasizes the difficulty Augustine had weaning himself from, and finally relinquishing, the representational materialism embedded in extant secular concepts of language and reference, including the notion that stories are fictions and even clever deceptions simply because what they refer to did not really happen. In *De Doctrina*, he converts this concern into an invitation to those Christians who already rejoice in knowing Scripture but wish to understand it more completely. Those things that can be learned from other human beings, he concludes, should be learned "without pride," and those who teach should "communicate what they have received" in humility. He addresses listeners — congregations, students — and homilists/teachers jointly, altering definitions of the secular classroom to fit the tasks of Christian teaching, learning, and understanding. "He who reads to others pronounces the words he recognizes; he who teaches reading does so that others may also read; but both make known what they receive. In the same way, he who explains to listeners what he understands in the Scriptures is like a reader who pronounces the words he knows, but he who teaches how the Scriptures are to be understood is like a teacher who advises how the words are to be read."[48] Throughout Book I of *De Doctrina* Augustine addresses the relationships between secular and Christian learning, and particularly the doctrines of signs and signification that distinguish Christian from secular modes of understanding. In examining their differences, he draws a distinction between things which are to be used and things which are to be enjoyed. Just as those who teach reading teach so that others may read, both teacher and student learn in order to make known what they have received.

Reading, alphabet letters, grammatical rules, and secular literature alike are things to be used, not things to be enjoyed in and of themselves.

By redefining the hierarchies of semiotic and semantic relationships that he has learned and taught, Augustine establishes a system in which signs may be used to construct, or apprehend, both physical and conceptual entities which are themselves in his reconfiguration signs of an ineffable and sometimes inexpressible truth. It is this truth which alone is to be enjoyed. The lines which Augustine reads in the Milan garden emblematize the task of weaning away from misplaced pleasure in surfaces and appearances. "Spend no more thought on nature and nature's appetites." Augustine's account of his reading of these words parallels other injunctions to seek that which alone can satisfy: truth and understanding. To enjoy signs, or the physical representations which are made with them, he asserts, is a fleeting pleasure and a kind of idolatry as well.[49] "They love the words of the artificer more than the artificer or his art, and are punished by falling into the error of expecting to find the artificer and his art in his works, and when they cannot do so they think that the works are both the art and the artificer. . . . They wish to scrutinize the creation contrary to the commandment of God and enjoy *it* rather than God's law and truth."[50] For Augustine neither the pursuit of knowledge nor the reading of literature is its own reward. The value of study is an increase in understanding and wisdom that allows one to communicate understanding to others. In Augustine's scheme of things, that which is meant to be used as a vehicle of truth or understanding cannot be enjoyed in itself; any effort to seek satisfaction in the possession of surfaces will always be disappointed.

Is this not an instrumentalist conception of language as a tool which one uses to do things? Yes, but with the very important difference that the aim Augustine defines for every use of signs is heuristic: "to discover those things which are to be understood, and a way of teaching what we have learned."[51] In contrast to Aristotle's focus on the discovery of available means of persuasion and of *topoi* appropriate to subjects, Augustine's characterization resuscitates the broader question of the relationship of teaching and persuasion. Rhetoric teaches how to persuade; teaching is sometimes persuasive, but the goal of teaching as Augustine defines it is not persuasive in the secular senses that he attributes to that procedure. Like Plato in the *Phaedrus* and *Gorgias*, he contends that the mind grasps or understands truth and meaning in a manner unrelated to the coaxing, seduction, or force entailed in many rhetorical conceptions of persuasion and argument. Extending Cicero's notions of *eloquentia*, he develops explicit distinctions between the truth of the rules of eloquence and the uses of those rules "to make false-hoods."[52] He turns the sciences of dialectic and valid inference in which antecedents allow certain consequents from analytic to hermeneutic uses. Antecedent/consequent relationships, he points out, may be found in Scripture; like division and partition, they have been "discovered" by human beings because they are "in the order of things" given to us to be used.[53] It is not necessary to accept the theological bases of Augustine's precepts in order to recognize the pedagogical wisdom implicit in his formulation. A mastery of reading or learning or knowledge is bound to be unsatisfying or at the very least unclear in its objectives, if there are no clear definitions of its larger value and purposes.

Augustine was the first Latin author to call words "signs."[54] Cicero and Varro, for example, use the term *signum* to denote neutral pointers, and not words. "All doctrine [i.e., teaching] concerns either things or signs, but things are learned by signs."[55] In Augustine's usage "things" are, strictly speaking, those things which do not signify something else: wool, stone, cattle. But, he points out, that wood which Moses cast into bitter waters to remove bitterness is a thing which is also a sign of other things. Still other kinds of signs, words, "have as their sole purpose" signifying. The kind of signifying Augustine seems to have in mind goes well beyond the "pointer" functions denoted by most extant Latin uses of "sign" and even "word." For Augustine all signification is inextricably bound up with the intent to mean, or signify. It is telling that his use of *intentio* — literally, "pointing to" — denotes the will to signify more than it emphasizes the correspondence between sign and referent.[56]

Collateral comparison of Augustine's usage with the Stoic and Academic terminology of his time reveals even more precisely the extent of his innovations. In the Stoic schema recorded by Sextus Empiricus, three things are linked together: that which is signified (*to te semainomenon*), that which signifies (*to semainon*), and the object (*to tungkanon*). That which signifies through this combination is speech (*phone*). Even at the level of single terms, Augustine sustains his integrative, multiple-level approach to extant language models and their relationships to values. For example, in the case of "Dion": "the thing itself which is revealed by it and which we apprehend as subsisting in our thought but [which] the barbarians do not understand." This understanding-in-thought is termed the *lekton*, which alone is true or false.[57] In Aristotle's system written words (*grammata*) are signs of spoken words (*phonai*), which are signs of affections or movements in the mind (*en te psuche pathemata*) which are representations or likenesses (*homoiomata*) of things (*pragmata*). Boethius' Latin translation of this Aristotelian model gives *litterae* as signs of (*notae*) *uoces*, and *uoces* as signs of *in anima passionarum*, which are likenesses (*similitudines*) of things (*res*). Augustine develops several rearrangements of this representational, referential model and employs alternate terms. Written words (*litterae*) are signs (*signa*) of spoken words (*uoces, uerba*), which make known (*demonstrare*) thoughts or mental movements (*motus animi*). What about the reference to reality, to which in the other schema thoughts stand as likenesses or representations? In Augustine's model, *res* becomes a vehicle of signifying thoughts which are themselves not defined solely as representations of external reality:

litterae ⟶ *uoces, uerba* ⟶ *motus animi*
     (*signa*)   (*demonstrare*)
                               ↙
                         (*signa*) *res*

Augustine does not say that words are signs of thoughts, those movements in the mind that Aristotle had called *en te psuche pathemata*. He distinguishes natural signs from conventional signs as those which "without any desire or intention of signifying, *make us aware of something beyond themselves*, like smoke which signifies fire."[58] Conventional signs are used by "living creatures . . . for the purpose of conveying, in so far as they are able, the motion of their spirits or something which they have sensed *or understood*. Nor is there any other reason for signifying, or for giving signs, except for bringing forth and transferring to another mind the action of the mind in the person who makes the sign."[59] Aristotle had limited his analysis to the relationship and correspondence between sign and referent: the single thought and the single word. Augustine extends this narrowly referential definition in order to account for words which mean what they mean not just because of what they represent, but also because they are intended to signify *to*, for a reason. Not only the "content" but the entire process of understanding must be transferred from one person to another. There are other innovations in Augustine's usage, some arguably developed from Stoic rather than Academic or Aristotelian sources. Instead of the Aristotelian *pragmata* (thing, referent) or the Stoic *tungkanon* (thing, matter, body), Augustine uses *res*, and with a breadth of application which conflates it in some uses with the Stoic *lekton*: that which alone is true or false, is in conformity with rational presentation, can be conveyed by discourse. Bearing some resemblance to the pre-Aristotelian *logos*, the *lekton* is a thought–statement–sentence autonomous in authority and conveying meaning. The Augustinian *res* is a sign of or a vehicle for what Augustine terms the *dicibile*, that which is understood in a word and conceived in the mind. Like the *lekton*, the *dicibile* is made known by signs and is about things/referents but is a distinct and separate unit, a sentence-saying-something-about-and-conveying-to-another. "Just as *lekton* is drawn from *legein*, so *dictum*, and Augustine's *dicibile* and *dictio* seem to be drawn from *dicere*."[60] The extensive technical analysis of grammar and syntax that was widely available in Augustine's time explains perhaps his corrective emphasis on intent, will, communication, and understanding as elements which must accompany any treatment of language, even single words.[61]

The primary objectives of *De Doctrina* are to construct a hermeneutic directed at a canonical manuscript that was being read in divergent ways, and to devise a teachable means of disseminating that hermeneutic. Augustine breaks with the precedent of isolated, analytic, technical accounts of words and meanings, and builds strong warnings into his text which forbid the student to separate elements and topics from each other. The transition from the nature of things in Book I of *De Doctrina* to the nature of signs in Book II exemplifies his rigorous avoidance of analytic dissection. "Just as I began, when I was writing about things, by warning that no one should consider them except as they are, without reference to what they signify beyond themselves, now when I am discussing signs I wish it understood that no one should consider them for what they are but rather for their value as signs which signify something else. A sign is a thing which causes us to think of something beyond the impression the thing itself makes upon the senses."[62] After dealing with such signs as the means by which people express their meanings to one another, Augustine turns to a discussion of ambiguous and figurative signs in which he propounds a rationale for the study of language. A lack of understanding, he posits, is caused by either unknown or ambiguous words. Aristotle's and subsequent classical rhetorics emphasize equivocal and ambiguous terms from the perspectives of logical precision, semantic integrity, and rhetorical suasiveness. Augustine shifts the emphasis from use to interpretation, from the construction of statements to their comprehension. If words are ambiguous because they are unknown, he argues, then the study of different languages is needed. The student of the Old Testament, he notes, comes to understand the meanings of the original Hebrew words only by means of their translations.

Augustine extends this example into a defense of the need for formal study. If signs are ambiguous because the things of which they speak are unknown or unfamiliar, study of those things is needed before any attempt at interpretation is attempted. "An ignorance of things makes figurative expressions obscure when we are ignorant of the natures of animals, or stones, or plants, or other things which are often used in the construction of similitudes." But this is the least difficult kind of ambiguity. What of Varro's history, or the classics of Latin literature? "We should not think that we ought not to learn literature because Mercury is said to be its inventor, nor that because the pagans dedicated temples to Justice and Virtue . . . we should therefore avoid justice and virtue. Rather, every good and true Christian should understand that wherever he may find truth, it is his Lord's."[63] By reauthorizing all truth as God's, Augustine allows for the utilization of any and all secular learning that develops, anticipates, or represents — in whatever way — truths that are found in Scripture. The Egyptian gold passages of *De Doctrina* provide a biblical pretext for permitting secular learning, including literature, to be used in the enterprise of understanding God's truth and disseminating God's word. "Just as the Egyptians had not only idols and grave burdens which the people of Israel detested and avoided, so also they had vases and ornaments of gold and silver and clothing which the Israelites took with them

secretly when they fled, as if to put them to a better use. . . .
In the same way the teachings of the pagans contain not only simu-
lated and superstitious imaginings . . . but also liberal disciplines
more suited to the uses of truth, and some most useful precepts
concerning morals. . . . These are, as it were, their gold and silver;
which they did not institute themselves but dug up from certain
mines of divine Providence, which is everywhere infused."[64] The
same notion, that there is a fully authorized integral truth to be
found, also facilitates Augustine's realignment of earlier conceptions of figurative language.

Book III of *De Doctrina* forges the difficult link between ambiguous signs in general and the peculiarities of the ambiguous
constructions found in Scripture, a transition from a descriptive
account of language, signs, and signification to hermeneutic applications of that account. "The principles I have described for the
treatment of ambiguous pointing serve also for ambiguous constructions."[65] Lest the model lapse into analytic or sequential components, Augustine sustains the integration of simultaneous meanings within a hierarchy of individual signs, phrases, things which
ambiguously signify, and stories whose meaning is not that of the
literal story. "We must beware not to take figurative or transferred
expressions as though they were literal; a further warning must be
added lest we wish to take literal expressions as though they were
figurative."[66] The guide for this must be the love of one's neighbor
and of God. "Therefore whatever is read in the Scriptures concerning bitterness or anger in the words or deeds of the person of God
or of his saints is of value for the destruction of the reign of cupidi-
ty."[67] Scriptural depictions of evil and sin deeply troubled Augustine, and frustrated his efforts at addressing church conservatives
who objected to secular literature on precisely the grounds that it
represented sinful behavior with playful lightheartedness or ambiguous moral import. Equally problematic were the Manichees, who
recognized no distinction between biblical and secular tales of evil
and wrongdoing.

Augustine's solutions to this problem define a hermeneutics for
the moral teaching embodied in scriptural depictions of evil, a conceptualization that would contribute to the definition of the tropological level of meaning as a function of stories that cause the soul
or conscience to turn toward moral truths. In discussing the biblical

story of Jacob, who puts on hairy skins to deceive his blind father and receive his brother's patrimony, Augustine develops this tropology in a distinction between the mendacious and the fallacious which allows him to accept literary fables, including biblical stories whose truth is allegorical, and yet reject any and all deliberate deceptions, first and foremost those rhetorical tricks of persuasion which he had taught so long and so uncomfortably. "Jacob did not tell a lie; rather, it was great mystery that he deceived his father. If we call this lying then we must call all parables and figures upon every kind of thing that has shown a sign, . . . to be taken not literally but as prompting the understanding of one thing by means of another. We must refuse to call them lies, for whoever thinks them so can make the same charge against figures of speech and numerous other forms of discourse."[68] The point, theme, and moral truth of this story for Augustine is that Jacob deliberately and despicably deceived his father. The intent to deceive is the sin represented and emphasized in this story, not the putting on of hairy skins per se. One could put on hairy skins for any of a number of reasons; veiling and disguise are not inherently sin. If putting on hairy skins were always morally deceitful, Augustine argues, then any kind of veiled truth would also be deceitful, an untenable position insofar as Scripture contains numerous veiled truths and enigmas. If these are dismissed as empty of meaning, the scriptural literalists and the opponents of secular literature alike would win in their efforts to denounce any and all figural signification. Conversely, he proposes, what is wrong with rhetorical dissembling and deception is not that it uses untruths, fables, and partial accounts, but that it uses these *in order to deceive*. Once again it is clear that intention, as both a semantic and an ethical phenomenon, is of preeminent concern.

Augustine emphasizes that the intent of a speaker or author is only part of an entire process of understanding. The beholder's share, and intention, are equally central to determining the meaning and truth imputed to a given work, whether scientific, literary, or historical. "What is true of the whole psalm is also true of all its parts and of each syllable . . . ; it is true of the whole history of mankind, of which each man's life is a part."[69] Just as it is an author's responsibility not to use language in order to deceive, it is a beholder's responsibility not to enjoy deceit, and to instead seek within stories of deceit and acts of deception truth about the erosion caused by deceit rather than looking to these stories for evidence of the inevitability of depravity and delusion. Implicit in this injunction is a retort to the Manichees. The surface similarity of biblical and other stories cannot be used as the sole determinant, and debunker, of the moral authority of Christianity's biblical base. Moreover, Augustine asserts, the truths of Christianity expressed in Scripture are expressed elsewhere: in the natural world, in the thoughts and stories of other people, in history itself. This is not simply a statement about content type; it also redirects habits of apprehending and interpreting so that the dilemma so poignantly described in the *Confessions* can be transcended: "And if I had uttered them, the Manichees would not have understood them in the way that I spoke them."[70] Veiled truth, figurative language, styled language of all kinds are not inherently debased verbal toys most at home in fables and epideictic oratory. These are also, Augustine proposes, among the valid instruments of moral teaching in both divine and human communication. Rejecting them outright as vehicles of truth, Augustine intimates, places the reactionary church literalists and the Manichean sycophants in the same camp.

To Use Language to Lie Is a Sin

Augustine's ethical objections to intentional deceit of any kind are not difficult to understand. However, his articulation of why deceit and dissembling are specifically linguistic sins does not rest solely with the answer that they are violations of interpersonal trust. Deceit and dissembling are also depicted as corrosive, diabolical lies; as deliberate subversions of the canons of truth which undergird language as a healthy, working medium of both thought and communication.[71] "A man who lies says the opposite of what is in his heart, with the deliberate attempt to deceive. Now clearly, language, in its proper function, was developed not as a means whereby men could deceive one another, but as a medium through which a man could communicate his thought to others. Wherefore to use language in order to deceive, and not as it was designed to be used, is a sin."[72] Saying untrue things and saying untrue things in order to deceive are both wrong, but they are wrong in different ways. Augustine's analysis of this point parallels the examination of the simple imitation of truth versus the consciously dissembling imitation of truth that Plato develops in the *Sophist*. An untrue statement may be simply an error, and thereby wrong only in the sense of incorrect. But if an untrue thing is said knowingly, and with the intent to deceive, it is wrong not only because the trust of another human being has been violated. Deliberate deceit is also a betrayal of language, an appropriation and subversion of a part of creation, a violation of what Augustine holds to be the order of things. To define how it is that deceit undermines the very vehicle that is used to construct it, Augustine separates the truth of things spoken of from the intentions of the one speaking. "If we do not consider the things spoken of, but only the intentions of the one speaking, he is the better man who unknowingly speaks falsely, because he judges his statement to be true, than the one who unknowingly speaks the truth while in his heart he is intending to deceive."[73] As in the distinction Plato draws in the *Sophist* between unknowing versus deliberate imitations of truth, Augustine emphasizes that the interior knowledge and intent which exists in an individual's mind is the definitive criterion of deceit. Literary fabulation and allegorical or historical narratives of dubious literal truth lie outside this attack, because they are "obviously" and transparently not true in any referential or representational sense. They are treated as "lies" which convey truth, and as therefore outside the domain of intentional deceit.[74]

Augustine's most emphatic objection to secular rhetorical study, including some of the literary aesthetics it comprises, is that these can promulgate intellectual and moral corruption by cultivating a taste for deception, dissembling, eristic quibbles over words, and confidence games. "Men carefully and closely watch a [word] juggler who professes nothing but deceit." If the speaker is believed not to know how to do such juggling, or if many immediately see through his trick, "no one would applaud, . . . nonetheless, those who do not see it are laughed at." He attacks the taste for such games in which "deception, not truth, delight us," because "by our own judgment and out of our own mouths we are sentenced because we approve one thing by reason and approve another in our vanity." The intelligentsia say they seek truth—"every spectator admits that he wants to reach truth"—in philosophizing and through debate; yet their taste for deception belies this claim. They *enjoy* deception more than truth.[75] This particular critique of rhetorical jousting and the pleasures of literary irony begins with "every spectator." In a psychologically astute analysis of the values implicit in the audience's appreciation of successful dissembling, Augustine shifts from the traditional rhetorical focus on the speaker to an emphasis on the audience's tastes and values that are implicit in their behavior. The Aristotelian model of a gullible audience vulnerable to the rhetorical skillfulness of a trained speaker is in this shift superseded by a portrait of educated and clever audiences that have become quite familiar with rhetorical strategies. The rhetorical strategies whose use Augustine describes are no longer utilitarian. The educated and uneducated alike swarm to public performances of confidence games that have become fine art and good fun, one-upsmanship contests in which the stakes—the detection of deceit—have gotten higher and higher. As these games have become more common—the verbal equivalents of public gladiatorial displays and staged battles between lions and bears—attention to what the words of a speaker really meant has been supplanted, and incrementally eroded, Augustine charges, by appreciation of verbal cleverness in and of itself. The beholder's share has become self-victimization.[76] Augustine does not attack the speaker's manipulation of an audience's gullibility as singularly as Plato does in the *Phaedrus, Gorgias*, and *Sophist*. Instead, he charges the audience with willful allegiance to a self-contradictory set of critical standards, with tastes that demean self and other alike. Audiences titillate themselves; they enjoy seeing if they can be deceived. If they are, they praise the cleverness of the deceiving speaker who has eluded detection. As a subtext, Augustine questions the cultural consequences of such innocent sports. What kind of legislators and governments do such people make? What kinds of parents, teachers, and public servants? Within ten years of the writing of *De Doctrina*, Rome was overtaken by Alaric, and in another fifteen, Hippo by the Vandals. In retrospect Augustine's analysis seems prophetic.

Though uninviting to many modern readers, Augustine's severely moralistic tone reflects the urgency he must have felt as he beheld a breakdown of language use and meaning brought about by the burgeoning pluralism among secular language models and schools of biblical interpretation. There had resulted a need for a shared method of interpretation which would activate both readers and hearers and make them responsible for seeking and communicating truth. Understanding the impending chaos within and outside the Church, and appreciating the subtleties in his theories of truth, language, and signification, may foster some sympathy for his ardent desire to quell any and all admiration for clever deception. His tolerance for secular learning is manifestly resolute, as evidenced by his recommendations of various styles of eloquent speaking and logical modes of reasoning in Book IV of *De Doctrina*. Both of these, he emphasizes, are to be found in Scripture itself. But deception and lies named, known, and enjoyed as such have crossed the line dividing wrongdoing and evil from enigma, ambiguity, figurative and plural meanings, and obscurity. Yet Augustine's omnipresent concern with lying and deception is given exposition alongside tolerant depictions of irony and antiphrasis as tropes, and generous allowances for latitude and even contradictory readings of different passages of Scripture. Irony appears comfortably alongside *antiphrasis, allegoria, aenigma*, and *parabola* in the list of tropes covered in Book III of *De Doctrina*. These and other tropes, Augustine proclaims, are "to be found in reading the sacred books [and] also the names of some of them, like allegoria, aenigma, parabola." "Lettered men should know, moreover, that all those modes of expression which the grammarians designate with the Greek word tropes were used by some of our authors, and more abundantly and copiously than those who do not know them and have learned about such expressions elsewhere are able to suppose or believe."[77] The criticism intimated here addresses the views of those literalists who would forbid any and all secular learning, including grammar and rhetoric. Augustine implicitly instructs this group in the presence and subtlety of tropes and figures in Scripture, and adopts the same attitude toward tropes that he holds toward inference: these are facts of language and thought, a part of linguistic "creation"; by whatever name they are known, they are in his view *discovered* rather than "learned" in any usual sense of that term. Ironically, his analysis reveals, the literalists and the secular Manichees held similar views of figural language: that it is decorative and without semantic substance, suspect and prone to multiple interpretations. Unless the aim is to hoodwink the audience through a strategic use of what the rhetoric manuals termed ambiguous and equivocal terms, such language is either decoratively ornate or unclear.

Seven centuries later Thomas Aquinas, out of a concern for excessively figurative and latitudinarian readings of Scripture in a time of heresies and philosophical wars that was very much like Augustine's, revived the literalist caveat restricting figural meanings. "Many different senses in one text produce confusion and deception and destroy all *force of argument*. Hence no *argument*, but only *fallacies*, can be deduced from a multiplicity of propositions. But Holy Scripture ought to be able to state the truth without any fallacy. . . . The multiplicity of these senses does not produce equivocation or any other kind of multiplicity, seeing that these senses are not multiplied because one word signifies several things; but because the things signified by the words can themselves be types of other things."[78] The tactic Abelard adopted in *Sic et Non* for resolving the problem of plural and figural meanings in the face of an insurgence of Aristotelian logic was to reconcile the different senses of Scripture in a final moral or spiritual level immune to, because outside, the domain of logical attack. Aquinas, in contrast, places the primacy of meaning at the literal level and argues that the multiplicity of meanings in Scripture comes from the fact that *things* can be types of, that is, understood as analogous to, other *things*. But analogy is a logical matrix that avoids the figural, plural, and ultimately metaphysical semantics implicit in Augustinian hermeneutics. Aquinas provides a method for examining the propositional as the "literal" meaning of scriptural sentences by applying the rules of Aristotelian predicate logic; the drawing of analogies among things is left to the theologians. In this provision Aquinas can be viewed as constructing a semantic logic that could be shared by philosophers and theologians, if they could agree that discursive meaning and its statement in propositions are to be given primacy, and that such meaning resides in what had in the four-fold hermeneutic levels been termed the "literal" level. One effect of this reconstruction was to relegate symbolic and allegorical language once again to the domain of meaningless structure and ornamental surface: to constitute metaphor a mistake.[79] Contemporary structural linguistics in much the same fashion has posited the arbitrary nature of the linguistic sign and the concomitant need for structural rules in accounting for purely conventional meaning. The renunciation of the symbol in Saussure's linguistics is expressed with doctrinal insistence. "The word symbol has been used to designate the linguistic sign, or more specifically, what is here called the signifier. Principle I [the arbitrary nature of the sign] in particular weighs against the use of this term. One characteristic of the symbol is that it is not arbitrary; it is not empty for there is the rudiment of a natural bond between the signifier and the signified."[80] Within such conventionalist conceptualizations of language and meaning, irony, along with other tropes, becomes virtually impossible because prior, assumed, or intentional meaning has been abolished by desiccated notions of the conventional and the arbitrary. There is no "what is" or "what is meant" to play off against "what appears to be" or "what is said." When all meaning is designated as arbitrary, truth and falsehood as well as semantic intentions are disbanded.

Augustine's emphasis on the presence of tropes and figures in Scripture is framed to refute not only the Christian literalists, but a second group of opponents as well, the secular Manichees and others among the educated who through their rhetorical and literary understandings of tropological and figurative language thought of these mainly as devices and ornaments, much as structural and descriptive linguists do today. In refuting the Manichean sycophants, cynically dismissive of any difference between Scripture and other fables as being alike tales for children, Augustine defines two aspects of figuration. Most of the deeds depicted in the Old Testament, he asserts, "are to be taken figuratively as well as literally," because "many things were done in the course of duty in those times which now cannot be done without libidinousness. If he reads of the sins of great men, even though he can see and verify in them figures of future things, he may put the nature of the things done to this use, that he will never hear himself boast of his own virtuous deeds and condemn others from the vantage of his righteousness when he sees in such men the tempests that are to be shunned and the shipwrecks that are to be lamented."[81] The emphasis here is clearly on changing habits of reading, interpreting, and understanding — changes that he is at great pains to formulate, precisely so that some of the objections raised by the Manichees and others can be addressed, or at the very least circumvented. Lest plural and contradictory meanings open the door to interpretive license or abuse, he provides a rule that comes quite close to describing what Cicero identifies as one form of irony: *aenigma*, and what Aristotle presents as a form of sophistic reasoning and strategic mistake: deliberate use of equivocal or ambiguous terms. "When, however, from a single passage in the Scripture not one but two or more meanings are elicited, even if what he who wrote the passage intended remains hidden, there is no danger if any of the meanings may be seen to be congruous with the truth taught in other passages of the Holy Scriptures. For he who examines the divine eloquence, desiring to discover the intention of the author through whom the Holy Spirit created the Scripture, whether he attains this end or finds another meaning in the words not contrary to right faith, is free from blame if he has evidence from some other place in the divine books."[82]

The emphasis on desiring to know the intention of the author and on researching that intention through careful study directs the acts of reading, interpretation, and understanding toward a goal much less simple than the recognition of tropes familiar from secular learning. Augustine's message to the secular learned is that "tropes were used by our authors" and that through them something else is being said. A hint of discomfort with irony may lurk in Augustine's avoidance of providing scriptural examples for either irony or antiphrasis. "Now irony indicates by inflection what it wishes to be understood, as when we say to a man who is doing evil, 'You are doing well.' Antiphrasis, however does not rely on inflection that it may signify the contrary, but either uses it own words whose origin is from the contrary, like *lucas*, 'grove,' so called *quod minime lucedat*, 'because it has very little light'; or it indicates that a thing is so when it wishes to imply the contrary, as when we seek to obtain what is not there and we are told, 'There is plenty.'"[83] Augustine deems an awareness of such tropes essential for the proper solution of the many scriptural ambiguities and opacities through whose understanding "many hidden things are discovered." Sensitivity to the epistemological as well as ethical problems presented by figural and tropological language perhaps led Augustine to forbid the use and construction of any new figurative language to the homilist and teacher. The homilist is advised to construct his discourses literally and not figuratively "as is permitted to the prophets."[84] Nonetheless, a certain kind of rhetorical ornament, that of the levels of style, is permitted the homilist and teacher as appropriate to the

subject matter, as long as Cicero's "to teach, to delight, and to persuade" are combined with the added objectives "to pray and strive
that he be heard intelligently, willingly, and obediently."[85]

Discerning the intended meaning of the authors of Scripture,
along with defining the proper intentions of the homilist and teacher, keep Augustine's concern with intentionality and ethics consistently prominent in *De Doctrina*. His replacement of secular literary examples with scriptural examples for tropes and figures
continued throughout the Middle Ages, alongside his treatment of
tropes as vehicles for the biblical authors' intentions. For our edifi-
cation, according to Augustine's and subsequent views, these tropes
were employed to present a veiled or enigmatic truth or, alternately,
to compose passages that might have several interpretations. Bede's
De Schematibus et Tropis (702 A.D.) completes one of the tasks
begun by Augustine's *De Doctrina*, that is, to provide scriptural
examples for each rhetorical figure and trope. Bede's work is the
first medieval listing of tropological exempla that does not include a
pagan author.[86] He carries over from Donatus his definitions of
irony, enigma, parable, and other tropes, which he defines in a
quasi-Aristotelian fashion as figures in which "a word, either from
need or for the purpose of embellishment, is shifted from its proper
meaning to one similar but not proper to it."[87] The distinction
between irony and antiphrasis that he provides hearkens back to
Augustine's delicate recasting of irony as didactic indirection. While
emphasizing intent, as any definition of irony must, both Augustine
and Bede are gingerly commenting on their Author's intention.
"Irony is a trope by means of which one thing is said while its opposite is intended. . . . Without the aid of impressive delivery the
speaker will seem to be admitting what he really intends to deny.
Antiphrasis is irony expressed in one word. . . . Irony, from the
manner of delivery alone, indicates what it wishes to be understood; antiphrasis does not express a contrary thought through the
vocal intonation, but merely through words used with a meaning
contrary to their true, original meaning."[88] On one level this is a
standard definition of tropes as "of words" rather than "of meanings"; tropes are words and phrases whose meaning has shifted
from their "proper" or usual meaning to one that is proximate. In
the case of irony, however, intention is an unavoidable concomitant,
for it is "from the manner of delivery alone" and "through intona-

tion" that irony, and the ironist, conceal and reveal themselves. For this reason it is no surprise that, beginning with Augustine's *De Doctrina*, irony in the Christian rhetorical tradition settles in among the tropes of edifying and didactic indirection: allegory, parable, enigma, and antiphrasis — tropes that are permitted only to Scripture's authors. These become interpreters' rather than composers' concerns until the resurgence of secular literary composition in the late Middle Ages and Renaissance. The question of a speaker's or originator's intent is submerged in the proviso that ironic passages be understood as edifying, as leading toward revelation and understanding. The irony of manner that, as early as Aristotle's praise of Plato's Gorgias and Socrates, is associated with understatement and reserve, Cicero styles urbanity. By Augustine's time this educated manner of speaking is regularly contrasted to country speech. "City dwellers, even if they are illiterate, criticize the speech of rustics."[89] An urbane manner acquires a designation separate from irony in the medieval rhetorics following Augustine: *asteismos* or urbanity "is a trope of great and inestimable power. Every expression which is free of rustic simplicity and has the polish of urbane elegance is considered an instance of *Asteismos*."[90]

Although the juggler delighting an audience with deceit resembles several modern kinds of irony, the secular literary or rhetorical ironist is not linked with irony by Augustine. Instead, Augustine's anecdote of the word "juggler" exemplifies deceit pure and simple and advances the argument that human cleverness is not to be enjoyed except insofar as it teaches and leads toward understanding. The emphasis on the complicity and responsibility of the listener's habits and understanding, coupled with the axiom that God is the sole author, shifts the definition of irony from clever human dissembling to edifying scriptural enigma. Instructions to reader and homilist in *De Doctrina* allow for apparently contradictory readings of the same passage, for enigma, for what would now be termed plagiarism, for the avoidance or restatement of difficult passages for "popular" audiences, and for adding endings or transitions to scriptural passages that seem "incomplete."[91] Are not some if not all of these things a kind of deception or lying? Plagiarism would certainly seem to qualify. Augustine's injunction to borrow, if need be, the best expression of a truth or understanding is directed at the teacher, student, and homilist. He encourages the use of whatever means are available to communicate forcefully, effectively, and clearly. For Augustine, no one owns the truth; it has already been given and is to be found and articulated. The words of anyone who happens to have found it or a part of it, even a pagan, can and should be used by the less eloquent homilist, if those words will convey the truth of Scripture he is trying to communicate. Plagiarism in this framework is impossible. Similarly, Augustine posits that the same passage can have different meanings to different readers, since all meanings convey part of the truth and help in the common enterprise of understanding. A diversity of readings is not confusingly contradictory but is rather a gift of divine plenitude. "For what could God have more generously and abundantly provided in the divine writings than that the same words might be understood in different ways which other no less divine witnesses approve?"[92] In all these examples it is clear that intent is once again an important determinant of crimes against language. Though many of the practices Augustine describes would be considered plagiarism or even lying today, they are rendered benign by the common enterprise he defines and propounds, the hermeneutic and edifying motive which links teachers, homilists, students, and congregations alike.

Augustine's attack on deception, and on the taste for deception, is markedly relentless in its focus on the audience's responsibility for what it enjoys and for what it allows to be done to itself. The interpersonal distances and manipulable meanings on which such sportive deceptions depend are collapsed by Augustine's explicitly ethical linguistic doctrines and by a theory of language which forges interdependent hierarchies among rhetoric, semantics, and hermeneutics. Abstract thought and knowledge had already come to be grounded upon a firm separation of philosophical logic and language from all other modes of discourse; formal logic functioned as a pristine technical instrument and repository of whatever truth such knowledge was deemed capable of. The model of knowledge as content preserved by technique in hermetically sealed forms of language, whether spoken or written, is precisely what Augustine rejects as vanity, as unsatisfying, and ultimately as evil if not used to further and communicate understanding. Saussure's insistence on the arbitrary nature of the linguistic sign is a latter-day expression of the doctrine to which Augustine objects, the conventionalist view of names and nouns advanced in Parmenides' Way of Opinion, recounted in Plato's *Cratylus*, and dominant in Aristotle's *Categories*. Saussure's is among the most emphatic recent articulations of the view that language speaks us. "The individual does not have the power to change a sign in any way once it has become established in the linguistic community; . . . it is unmotivated, i.e. arbitrary in that it actually has no natural connection with the signified."[93] Unmotivated names and nouns—like the interpersonal distances created by rhetorical depictions of the rhetor–spectator roles, and like the neutral, manipulable opinions which orators push around like discs on a shuffleboard—the pursuit of knowledge as content collected, hoarded, and owned: these are for Augustine unethical and corrupting idolatries of language.

The views and theories that coalesce in Augustine's work had long-lasting influence. It was not until the twelfth century that secular literature and classical rhetorical theory began to assert their independence from the cleric-controlled teaching of medieval rhetoric and from the hermeneutic commentaries that were the most common applications of formal learning. It is tempting to make Augustine seem more original or singularly influential than he was. What was accomplished by the Augustinian synthesis, however, and by its extensions in subsequent traditions, was nonetheless a distillation and definition of a complex set of theories, moral concerns, and theological doctrines which had needed integration and articulation for some time prior to Augustine. Among Augustine's more provocative legacies is his portrayal of secular rhetoric as a culturally sanctioned curriculum in linguistic contingency and lying. Rhetoric in Western culture has for the most part been conceptualized, taught, and practiced as a means of describing and utilizing extant linguistic conventions. Insofar as it has adopted a neutral position toward the conventions of form and content that it describes, most rhetorical training has encouraged the view that meaning, as distinct from formal logical validity, is nothing more than a matter of convention. Augustine proposes that this marriage of analytic descriptiveness with moral neutrality facilitates the manipulation of meanings through standardized definitions of kinds of discourse. Learned consciousness of discourse modes, according to this view, promotes an ability to exert control over frame—to set the tone of a conversation, for example, in such a way that it is clear from the onset that nothing being said is to be taken seriously. This is only one among the many practices promoted, according to Augustine, by the semiotics, arbitrary and conventionalist semantics, and instrumentalism implicit in the language model codified in classical rhetorics.

There are alternate possibilities created by a self-consciousness of linguistic forms and by the existence of a metalanguage for those forms and their uses, among them Plato's vision of "true rhetoric" as perpetual dialogue among earnest individuals possessing good will and candor. Augustine extends an earnest truth-seeking language model in the doctrine that language should always be used to say what is in the speaker's heart—the *verbum cordis*—the word which expresses a truth that has been found by the reflecting mind seeking truth through contemplative thought. Though with very different purposes, Augustine parallels Plato in many of his objections to the standardized secular rhetoric practiced in his day. He deems the semiotic epistemology on which it is based to be reductive, materialist, mechanistic, a propaedeutic for the conscious manipulation of set phrases, familiar anecdotal or causal plots and narratives, and logical formulae. To study such a rhetoric, he emphasizes, entails a careful study of audience types and audience responses structured so that what works adversarially can be, indeed will be, systematically chosen. The objective of discourse thus taught becomes to make the case, to make the point, to win.

Fictions, fallacious arguments, and rhetorical discourse can all be lies. Successful rhetoricians persuade audiences that things are the way they say they are, when the way they say they are is often not so or only plausibly or possibly so. Plato and Augustine concur in the view that, although referential error in itself is not necessarily a lie, stating a known referential error because it is strategically expedient or plausible is the quintessential rhetorical lie. The classical taxonomies that divorced reference error from deceit also advanced the classification of many fictions and of much rhetorical discourse as benign or even entertaining lies: an instructive fable, an epideictic testimonial, a "white" lie that saves face or avoids giving pain.[94] The self-expressive misrepresentation fostered by some versions of the rhetorical conception of *ethos* had become less than benign in Augustine's time. Habitually repeated ethopoieia can be insidiously erosive, as exemplified in the clever conceit that begins one of Shakespeare's sonnets. "When my love swears that she is made of truth,/I do believe her though I know she lies."[95] Self-deception and other deception alike toy dangerously with deeply held beliefs and shared assumptions.

6

Inscriptions of Self and the Erasure of Truth

The Other is in Me: I am an . . . Other. This humanity lives in, and on, separation. Analysis is apprenticeship in separation as both alienation and loss. Analytic experience reveals that the discourse of the father, king, prince or intellectual is your discourse. It is a logic that is within you, which you can domesticate but never dominate.

JULIA KRISTEVA, *In the Beginning Was Love: Psychoanalysis and Faith*

Modern man does not proclaim, he speaks. That is, he speaks with reservations. . . . The speaking subjects of high proclamatory genres — of priests, prophets, preachers, judges, leaders, patriarchal fathers, and so forth — have departed this life. They have been replaced by the writer, simply the writer, who has fallen prey to their styles. He either parodies them or stylizes them.

MIKHAIL BAKHTIN, *Speech Genres*

A priestess refused to allow her son to speak in public; "for if," said she, "you say what is just, men will hate you; if you say what is unjust, the gods will." On the other hand, "you should speak in public; for if you say what is just, the gods will love you, if you say what is unjust, men will." . . . Men do not praise the same things in public and in secret; but in public chiefly praise what is just and beautiful, and in secret rather wish for what is expedient.

ARISTOTLE, *Rhetoric*

In *The Point of View* Kierkegaard asserts that he speaks without authority, and that there can be no single or final point of view; his aim, he says, is to call attention to, to increase awareness of, and to affect.[1] Those who already know a great deal, he proposes, have no need of having more knowledge conveyed to them. Rather, they perhaps more than others are most in need of learning to be "personally affected," to be restored to their connectedness with other people, to be reunited with the meanings and values of the inner spirit that can be sustained only within the web of relationships.[2] In expressing this therapeutic and restorative aim, Kierkegaard extends the characterization of irony developed in his thesis, *The Concept of Irony, with Constant Reference to Socrates*, wherein he proposes that Socrates' "destruction of what is distorted and one-sided does not occur in order that the truth may appear, but merely to begin again with something equally distorted and one-sided." Instead of building a pathway to truth, Socrates is an exponent of radical negation. "This master is none other than the total irony which, when all the minor skirmishes have been fought and all the ramparts leveled, gazes out upon the total desolation and becomes conscious that nothing remains, or rather, that what remains is nothingness."[3] Yet Kierkegaard's catalogue of irony from Socrates through Hegel's absolute infinite negative subjectivity does not conclude with a renunciation of any and all irony. "As philosophers claim that no true philosophy is possible without doubt, so by the same token no authentic human life is possible without irony."[4] Proposing therapeutic uses for irony in the ethical, affective, and interpersonal domains, Kierkegaard calls for irony to be tamed, for restraints on absolute infinite negative subjectivity—"the wild infinity wherein it storms consumingly forth. There is in every personal life so much that must be sheared away. Here again Irony is an excellent surgeon. For when irony has been mastered . . . its function is then of the utmost importance in order for the personal life to acquire health and truth."[5]

Kierkegaard's vision of a benign and therapeutic irony lingers amid lesser and less noble deployments of irony that have prospered, and have continued to be used and abused among the literate educated. In her novel *Cat's Eye*, Margaret Atwood depicts the speech of nine-year-old Cordelia and her older sisters. Cordelia is a wealthy, would-be upper-class schoolmate of Elaine, the protagonist of the novel, whose parents are erratically employed academicians during the late 1940s. "'After you eat the egg,' Cordelia tells us, 'you have to put a hole in the bottom of the shell.' 'Why?' we say. 'So the witches can't put out to sea.' She says this lightly but scornfully, as if only a fool would need to ask. But there's the possibility she's joking, or teasing. Her two older sisters have this habit also. It's hard to tell when they mean to be taken seriously. They have an extravagant, mocking way of talking, which seems like an imitation of something, only it's unclear what they're imitating."[6] The ironic, urbane manner enshrined in the aesthetic canon by Aristotle and recommended by Cicero as a token of gentlemen's speech is also the vehicle of the delight in teasing deception so roundly denounced by Augustine. Both of these aspects of detached dissimulation—the slight hypocrisies characteristic of educated speech—find their latter-day manifestations in Atwood's representation. An urbane upper class ironic manner persists among those who value education not for any particular erudition, wisdom, or knowledge but rather for the manner of speaking that it imparts, a manner that can be imitated or emulated by any pretender to class, status, or power. Elaine, a child of academicians, is mocked by the intellectually indolent whose arch manner of speaking finds its antecedents in British upper-class and educated speech that leads directly back to classical canons of ironic wit. Cordelia and her sisters have little interest in knowledge or wisdom. They are depicted as caring much more about manicures and sweater sets than about books, school, or the issues of the day; but they have mastered the dry mock, the urbane ambiguities of seeming to imitate something, "only it's unclear what they're imitating," and the ethical *frisson* of the interpersonal tease with which this manner confronts the uninitiated. Like incompletely trained ventriloquists, the three sisters know just enough about an ironic manner of speech to replicate its tones, and use it to tease and intimidate. Just as the illiterate city dwellers of Augustine's time laughed at the speech of rustics, Atwood's nine-year-olds know enough about the manner of educated speech to use it, even when they do not fully understand its meanings or the import of its intonations. Their way of speaking exemplifies the fine line that distinguishes education from the imitation of speech genres devoid of knowledge; the same line links rhetoric and irony, and is pursued in Socrates' interrogation of Gorgias. Augustine's and Kierkegaard's denunciations of ironic pretense seek its dissolution; Cordelia and her sisters have mastered it. For others who, like their friend Elaine, are tone deaf to irony, the experiences of socialization and education are fraught with an alienation brought about by the demands of emulating unfamiliar speech, language, and discourse paradigms.

In an account of his education in bilingual southern California, Richard Rodriguez provides a telling description of the alienation he felt as he learned school English. "Once I learned public language, it would never again be easy for me to hear intimate family voices. . . . The day I raised my hand in class and spoke loudly to an entire roomful of faces, my childhood started to end."[7] For some, learning "public," schooled, educated language is painful, as witnessed by Rodriguez and other minorities and by the experience of many women as well. Marguerite Duras describes the feelings of darkness and muteness that circumscribe many women's initial efforts at speaking in the public voices demanded by the classroom and by writing. "Women have been in darkness for centuries. They don't know themselves. Or only poorly. And when women write, they translate this darkness. Men don't translate. They begin from a theoretical platform that is already in place, already elaborated. The writing of women is really translated from the unknown, like a new way of communicating, rather than an already formed language."[8] The recursive relationship between becoming educated and replicating the speech of the educated and of the schools forms a distinctive increment within the history of rhetoric. Quintilian schematized processes of imitation that Cicero and Aristotle had treated more briefly under style and ethos; the rhetorics of the centuries that followed spawned numerous subdivisions of imitation: prosopopoieia, eidolopoieia, ethopoieia—habits and understandings of imitation that continue to shape concepts of self and voice, school language and public language, the ongoing evolution of writing conventions, and the practice of literary interpretation. Elaine's perception of Cordelia and her sisters illustrates the degree to which many today perceive, and are being taught to understand, formal language and writing as "already written," that is, as inevitably an imitation. Lacan's notion of the insistence of the letter in the unconscious extends this view to the self as well, an extension that is continued in Derrida's critique of the notion of presence and by

Foucault's dismantling of the knowing subject — *le sujet, l'homme du désir* — and of the author.[9]

The habit of teasing duplicity inculcated by the emulation of a dissimulating manner manifests an additional legacy of classical imitation, the promotion of delight in deception. I have emphasized that taking pleasure in a text or utterance known to be unreliable or illusory is a taste that has been a central element in Western literary aesthetics and educated speech almost from their beginnings. It is vividly embodied in the fourth-century concept of ethopoieia, the imitation of character in which character itself, already defined as successfully projecting a contrived appearance (*phainesthai*) within the canon of Aristotelian *ethos*, comes to be conceived of as a well-wrought image; identity becomes an aesthetic artifact. Kierke-gaard's "Diary of the Seducer" captures the infinite possibilities of the aestheticization of self in his portrait of Johannes, who styles himself splendidly practiced in the arts of deception and manipula-tion. Johannes goes to his last meeting with his fiancée Cordelia in anticipation not of the meeting itself but of its aftermath. "Every-thing is symbol; I myself am a myth about myself." He congratu-lates himself on his success in "poetizing" himself out of a girl and in making her so arrogant and ironic that she imagines it is she who tired of the relationship.[10] A letter from Cordelia to Johannes re-veals her complicity in and knowledge of her "betrayal," an abjec-tion that is rendered even more stirring — and perhaps therapeutical-ly confessional — with the discovery that "Cordelia's" letter was written by Kierkegaard's former fiancée, Regina Olsen.[11]

Kierkegaard defends irony as an excellent surgeon. That which shears away can brutally hurt, but can also heal. Having submitted to the negative dialectics of learning that language speaks us, can we now reclaim and remake the language we speak? Can our under-standings of others' speaking and writing be guided by something other than the wastes of shame that are expended in excessive her-meneutics of suspicion? Companion to the concepts of irony and rhetoric as deceptive, Heidegger's notion that Being talk — the West-ern philosophical *logos* — deceives can propel us forward, fore-warned, in search of truth and understanding — else why such talk's express concern with deceit?[12] Reviewing our many histories within rhetoric, within literacy, within the cultures thus constituted, create understandings of truth and meaning, self and voice that can restore what Kierkegaard calls "health and truth" to our conceptions of education and culture. When the many voices are heard again, when we have learned to listen to different voices, a culture can be more fully and richly one with the many lives that it shapes and is shaped by. To that end, the following sections address rhetoric and irony, literacy and lies from the restorative and therapeutic perspective of the future perfect, as they may come to have been. In developing these views of the "what will have been," I extend some of their long-standing ties with deception, illusion, fiction, and lies into recent theoretical problematics of language, self, and knowledge. When the hammering of wholly negative dialectics dies away, knowing, knower, and known can shape one another anew, and perhaps create the networks within which the abilities to be affected, and connected, can be restored.[13]

Being Talk Deceives

Those who challenge the hegemony of bankrupt Being talk remain within that talk to the extent that they continue to manufacture hypostasized terms and propositions. "As it reveals itself in beings, Being withdraws. . . . By illuminating them, Being sets beings adrift in errancy. . . . Error is the space in which history unfolds."[14] Though propounding semantic and hermeneutic indeterminacy, postmodern philosophy nonetheless propounds, and produces postulates about, terms and categories that have remained constants since the earliest philosophical traditions. Like Havelock's, Heidegger's appraisals of the range of "to be" terms among the Preplatonics address their odd conflations of statements asserting an underlying Being unifying the cosmos, defining a grammatical Being that authorizes their statements about the cosmos, and announcing attributes of the cosmos and of statements that always are. Talk about the "justness" of trees mingles with assertions of the underlying law of the universe that authorizes *logos* statements. Yet even in problematizing such talk and demonstrating how it creates a space for error, the post-Nietzschean critical tradition lingers within the bounds of that space, a world where a single rational, knowing, and speaking subject remains identical with the subject of history. *L'homme du désir* remains a definitively male subject, alienated in his autonomy but still a would-be master and superior — even in the fulfilled death drive of self-erasure. The contemporary German poet Heinrich Müller asserts, "It is good to be a woman, and no victor."[15] The knowing subject who stands apart from nature, apart from self, and apart from previous philosophy, even when problematized, remains the protagonist in Western philosophy and aesthetics.

Underlying this *agonia* is a hero and war cult that — still, even in its renunciations — memorializes lost and dead ancestors and continues to privilege absence, loss, and death. The anxiety of influence represented in the tales of Zeus and Kronos lingers on in the banishment of Being talk and idealism, in celebrations of all reading as misreading, and in the cognate view that all selves are false selves. The early Greek tribes produced no great pyramids; instead, their first written history is dated by the Olympiads, the years of the funeral games re-enacting the exploits of heroes,[16] just as later the dramatic and rhetorical *agon* and the rhetorical *epitaphia* would represent and recount valor in struggle, sacrifice, and death. Psychoanalytic models drawn from Freud, despite their claims of ahistoricism,[17] further entrench the early Greek necrophilia that was, and persists in, a strange love of absence, a pursuit of the errors and spaces within which history, discourse, and self continue to be shaped. In explicit violation of Father Parmenides' proscription of the pursuit of not-being, the Elean Stranger in Plato's *Sophist*, and Gorgias' "On Being" both inaugurate a long line of proofs that Being talk deceives. The reign of the Father, Freud teaches, is also a desire for his death, a love of separation, absence, and removal that is epitomized in many Western conceptualizations of individualism, of the self knowing that it is always failing to know itself. *Tragos* is a story of "great" characters in struggle, an aesthetic focused on known-to-be-false gods that from the genre's first definitions was intended to inspire pity and awe — dread-full emotions that mark and measure the centrality of *agon* to Western aesthetics, philosophy, and rhetoric.[18] These have often functioned as systems of categorization and control, advocating certain views about the subject matter of each genre, about their different constructions of reality, and yet have, if anything, enabled further removal from reality by promoting ways of warding it off, distorting it, protecting against it. The contemporary German novelist Christa Wolf annotates her novel *Cassandra* with three essays appraising the persistence of these cognate patterns within Western aesthetics and intellectual paradigms. "'Know Thyself,' the maxim of the Delphic oracle, with which we identify, is one of Apollo's slogans. . . . This god . . . of noble intellectual freedom who by definition does not come into contact with the earth, is unable to achieve the self-knowledge he strives for. The thin regions whither he and his disciples retreat, fearing to be touched — thinking, yes, and writing — are cold. They need cunning little devices to avoid dying of the cold."[19] *Either/Or* provides a similar image of necrophilia in Western intellectual traditions, a report on the annual meetings of the *Symparanecromenoi*, a scholarly society whose name — Kierkegaard's invention — means "those who like to be close to/beside/in sympathy with the dead."

Being talk deceives in several ways; yet is not any talk of the inevitability of deceit at once an instance of Being talk and its heir? The notion of Being, and particularly its hypostatization in the lineage of concepts and predicational syntax postmoderns now trace from Parmenides through Plato and Christian Platonism into German idealism, is deemed deceptive because, whether positing "is" of ideas or renouncing them, Being talk speaks through ideas and uses them to philosophize, often with a hammer. Megarian paradoxes persist. Being talk can be truly deceptive to the same degree that it can be posited with finality that statements asserting its deceptiveness are themselves illusory. The form of this philosophical assertion belies a continuity between the idealist and positivist traditions, and the postmodern philosophies that seek to disarm them: being and not-being have been locked in a dance of death since Parmenides first named them as a binary opposition rather than as harmonic complementaries. An alternate understanding of Heidegger's claim that Being talk deceives could align it with Havelock's work on the copula to focus on the propositional and logical machinery that becomes so thoroughly detached from phenomenological reality, interlocution, and rhetorical discourse in the machinery set up in Aristotle's *Analytics, Categories,* and *On Interpretation*. "As it reveals itself in beings, Being withdraws." The One suppresses the many; there can be only one true proposition among the contending propositions tested by dialectic. Heidegger's assertion emphasizes that the reverse is also true. If plural truths and beings are acknowledged, hypostatic Truth and Being dissolve back into the multiplicity of particulars.

The notion that the only "coherent" stories are "held together by war and murder and . . .the heroic deeds which accrue to them" is not the only measure of coherence. In a letter to "A" — Aristotle — proposing alternatives to linear, heroic, crisis-centered poetics, Christa Wolf asks:

> What kind of memory does the prose of Virginia Woolf require and endorse? Why should the brain be able to "retain" a linear narrative better than a narrative network, given that the brain itself is often compared with a network? What other way is there for an author to tackle the custom (which no longer meets the needs of our time) of remembering history as the story of heroes? The heroes are exchangeable, the model remains. Aesthetics developed on this model.[20]

The linear function of the individualizing propositional "is" links the coherence of epic history, which is purchased by inordinate selectivity and given its aesthetics in Aristotle's *muthos*, with the deceptively comprehensive *logos* statements of systematic philosophy and its statements of pure reason. Aristotle's *Poetics* shuns ambiguity and discourages metaphor even as it defines them, in sharp contrast to a poetics that would promote what Wolf terms "precise indefiniteness, the clearest ambiguity." "In the thinking of Aristotle, even about poetic discourse, things are this way and no other way, it says; and at the same time (this cannot be thought logically) things are that way, a different way. You are I, I am he, it cannot be explained. The grammar of manifold simultaneous relations."[21] Otherness is not incomprehensible, not a strange dark continent, except in a poetics, epistemology, and psychology preoccupied with order, coherence, and form defined in narrowly binarist and linear exclusivities. A "one-track-minded route is the one that has been followed by Western thought: the route of segregation, of the renunciation of the manifoldness of phenomena, in favor of dualism and monism, in favor of closed systems and pictures of the world; of the renunciation of subjectivity in favor of a sealed objectivity."[22] Being talk deceives when it places itself in opposition to, outside of, and superior to the manifoldness and simultaneities of phenomena and thought alike. The belligerent opposition of Being talkers to lesser mortals, thought, and discourse begins with the polemic of the Preplatonics.

Yet another understanding of the claim that Being talk deceives could place the pair Being–beings under scrutiny and ask whether there is not too much Being talk in this binarism. The renunciation of idealism in favor of a return to Dionysian narcissism (Nietzsche) or programmatic fragmentarianism (Heidegger and Derrida) relies heavily upon binary dialectics that are themselves legacies of Being talk. It is all too easy to embolden a renunciation of rationality with a reckless irrationalism buttressed by idealizations of prerational stages in human history of pre-Oedipal stages in individual psychological development.[23] The age of reason was father to the reign of terror.[24] A weak point in Western culture, Christa Wolf charges, is manifest in its recurrent equation of revolution — in both art and politics — with regression and narcissism, with the willful adolescent's failure to grow up: the worst are full of passionate intensity.[25] Many now seek new models of voice and thought, authenticities that can be forged outside of borrowed or imposed forms of art and rationality without wholly renouncing either art or rationality simply because most of them have been produced by men, or whites, or the West. Insofar as they have shaped as well as depended upon varying conceptions of both art and rationality, rhetoric and literacy should be reappraised historically from the perspective of authorized Western deployments of lying, deceit, fiction, and dissimulation that persist in literature and poetics. Observing the roles played by logic and other concepts of rationality that have defined these deceits, can aid in this enterprise, particularly if it is approached from a perspective that views literacy and rhetoric simultaneously. There are many ways of telling the intertwined stories of rhetoric and irony, literacy and lies, as they have evolved, as they may one day come to be understood. "They evolved," is an instance of Being talk; the story as I tell it in what follows alternates between that form of talk — convenient, habitual, familiar, but not for that reason wholly avoided — and a more resolute and express conjecture that hovers somewhere between self-proclaimed fiction and a Kierkegaardian invitation to explore, to be affected by, to recognize.

Literary Fiction, Rhetorical Lie, and Logic as Illusion

The story of how rhetoric, irony, and literacy itself continued to be associated with lying and to shape Western canons of literacy must be extended well beyond Augustine; it is a story of intricate refractions and recursions. The Middle Ages and the Renaissance adapted rhetoric and irony for uses they had not served before. Homiletics and exegesis extended Augustine's reforms in the conceptualization of voice and self that had held in classical rhetorical theory and practice. The notions of author and speaking subject, as they are known today, went through a multitude of transformations, each one affecting the ratios of speaker and hearer, knower and known.[26] Augustine's poetics renounced overt audience-deceiving irony and rhetoric as aestheticizations of lying but permitted several literary and logical cousins to classical rhetorical and Socratic irony. The aspect of irony that depends on giving the appearance of saying one thing while actually saying another influenced conceptualizations of allegory, enigma, and parable, and finds a parallel in the Augustinian hermeneutic concept that the manifold layers of meaning could be simultaneous and noncontradictory. In this development a binarist conception of truth and meaning, that a statement is either true or not true, was reshaped to permit both semantic and hermeneutic heterogeneity.[27] Homiletics continued to adapt this heterogeneity to the preacher's task of speaking to different audiences with different purposes, and of selecting from the multitude of meanings in biblical passages those that with a specific audience at a specific time will convey the intended message and bring about the desired change or action. That aspect of irony that resides in contrariety or double meanings fed literary and logical concepts listed in the increasingly complex rhetorics of the Middle Ages under figures and schemes. Figures of speech, "in the words only," parallel and draw on the concept of the literal level of meaning that was evolving during the same period. Sometimes called tropes, these figures of speech acquired ample literary exempla from Scripture and were given more by literary rhetoricians in the twelfth-century revival of a Ciceronian liberal arts tradition. Schemes or figures of thought emphasized logical *topoi* and the juxtaposition of ideas: the familiar patterns of contrast, comparison, opposition, similarity. Residing within ever more complex rhetorical taxonomies, irony shaped and came to be shaped by burgeoning conceptualizations of allegory, enigma, paradox, and other figural tropes, because of the discrepancy between its surface and its substance, and its related conceptual resemblance to those schemes of thought that stressed oppositeness, contradiction, surface–content disjunction, and the opposition or contrariety of ideas.

Scholarship in the history of rhetoric now traces the diverging rhetorical taxonomies that transmitted conceptualizations of voice, self, audience, and discourse itself into the postclassical schools. During the Middle Ages the Ciceronian notion of a storehouse of readings and exempla, though these latter were increasingly taken from Scripture, remained the basis of school and university curricula. That the resurgence of liberal arts curricula and secular vernacular literatures during the thirteenth through sixteenth centuries resuscitated some of the darker sides of irony and rhetoric as well, is evident in works such as the *Roman de la Rose, The Book of the Courtier, The Canterbury Tales, The Divine Comedy, The Decameron, Gargantua and Pantagruel, The Prince*, and *In Praise of Folly*, works composed amid state and church hierarchies whose greed and hypocrisy had become corruptions of the darkest kind. A living instance of *inversio* was manifest in the masterful exercise of the darker sides of rhetorical manipulation and ironic dissimulation among churchmen and princes that can only have prompted literary and artistic responses to that corruption that began to call themselves humanism. Much of the literature of the late Middle Ages and the Renaissance, rich in paradox and conceit, could be said to expound the view that it is better to be an honest *eiron* than a saintly hypocrite. The new philosophy that emerged from the demise of scholasticism influenced reformulations of rhetoric within secular humanism. The doubt of perception and thought expressed in the opening lines of the *Roman de la Rose* frames the poem as a dream within which there are dreams and visions, all illusions. Like Occam's razor, such literary images of mind and thought were shaped by rhetorical poetics, tropes that propounded but also jousted with the view that excessive reliance on individual thought and perception leads to delusion. When Donne laments, "the new philosophie casts all in doubt," he delineates precursors of the systematic doubt of Descartes that had emerged in Baconian conceptualizations of science as true induction.[28] Ramus' conflation of dialectic with rhetoric, a reunification aimed at utility, coincided with a secularization of humanism within the universities that can be viewed as one point of origin of the modern university tradition of the humanities.[29]

Because they made a practical rhetorical education available to a nonclerical and nonacademic mercantile class, Ramist rhetorics expedited the rise of an educated merchant class and contributed to what would become, by the eighteenth and nineteenth centuries, the elocutionist and bellettristic traditions refurbished in the schools, drawing increasingly on vernacular literary models and shaping a bourgeois gentility. The notion of education as a smattering of familiarity with great cultural artifacts and an ability to manage language in a graceful and pragmatic but not particularly profound manner has been deemed a modern legacy of Ramist reductions and disjunctions. Echoing Cicero's practical-minded contemporaries, Ramus asks, "Is it not far easier for a boy to learn and memorize an art from a few precepts than to make excruciating efforts to pursue it as it lies scattered and diffused in a great many books?"[30] The scholar, as in earlier eras of sophistic, was upstaged by the lawyer, the merchant, and the shrewd government bureaucrat in the repertoire of cultural types. These in turn were supplanted by gentrification, aestheticization, and, as in earlier eras, the *letteraturizzazione* of rhetoric. The Scottish and English bellettristic, epistemological, and elocutionist rhetorical treatises of the eighteenth and nineteenth centuries merged taxonomical and preceptorial rhetoric with a philosophical, moral, and cultural conception that shaped nineteenth-century implementations of democratized education. Though it emphasized style in some of the ways that Ramism had eschewed, the elocutionist movement promoted literary and popular prose essay genres as implements of an edifying exemplary culture. Being well read in ancient and modern literature and being well spoken were interdependent objectives.

One among many traces of the shifts in uses and understandings of rhetoric, irony, and literacy is embodied in the alterations in the representation of the allegorical figure of Rhetoric herself. In the twelfth-century liberal arts tradition of the Chartres school, Rhetoric is one of the fourteen Virtues. "In her right hand she bears a trumpet, and in her left a bugle on which to sound a battle call. She wears a robe of the greatest beauty, whose brilliant colors shimmer in ever-changing beauty." Lingering in this characterization are some of the earliest associations between rhetoric and the "ever changing hues" of the worlds of opinion and appearance. The beauty of Rhetoric's many-hued robe is emphasized, a beauty that becomes "even more beautiful because of the power of the artist." Rhetoric teaches "how the introduction moves the mind, appeals to the ear, excites the audience, prepares the judge for the decision,

. . . renders the hearer more attentive and amenable, wins sympathy and makes the audience more receptive to the argument; . . . the narration in a few words sets the scene, explains the truth, and exposes falsehoods masquerading as truth."[31] The powers of Rhetoric's beauty are celebrated with intensives and hyperbole reminiscent of Gorgias' praise of the powers of speech in the *Helen*. "The beauties of Rhetoric are also present and her colorful flowers of speech which add brilliance to her starlike words. . . . In her bounty, Rhetoric scatters a power of language, a beauty, a majestic sweep of words; she touches the tongue of the youth, giving to his words the seal of her colorful variety; . . . when his speech changes to flow too freely in a flood of loquacity, then she takes care that more meaning flows forth as well, an abundance of fruits from a forest of leaves."[32] The beneficent richness of rhetoric in this allegory is continued in later Renaissance representations of Lady Rhetoric with a sword and with a mirror. As late as the seventeenth century, representations of rhetoric as a benign handmaiden among the seven sister liberal arts persisted in the schools. In *La Respuesta*, Sor Juana Inez de la Cruz asserts, "How, without Logic, could I be apprised of the general and specific way in which the Holy Scripture is written? How, without Rhetoric, could I understand its figures, its tropes, its locutions?"[33]

The more sinister characterizations and understandings of rhetoric that emerged during the Renaissance are given ample expression by Shakespeare, More, Erasmus, Castiglione, and Machiavelli. Erasmus' *In Praise of Folly* deploys the then current convention of depicting any intellectual discourse spoken by a woman as a joke. Folly is actually a fool and a whore; it is only through an ironic pretense that she presents herself, lewdly and leeringly, as the exponent of serious views. The noble and beautiful Lady Rhetoric of the twelfth and thirteenth centuries has become a whore, a mother of harlots and lies. Drawing on familiar images of women's wiles and guiles, Erasmus' characterization of Folly emphasizes aspects of her language that can be pretended, an emphasis that revives classical rhetorical *topoi* depicting seriousness, innocence, and authenticity as rhetorical contrivances. Shakespeare's numerous allusions to rhetoric, to pale clerics, and to lawyers' rhetorical tricks provide ample expressions of the mixed feelings about the wider dissemination of rhetorical and logical training in this period. Hamlet's pale cast of thought personifies and caricatures the scholarly intensity then associated with scholasticism; he is a living image of why the scholarly life demanded of generations of university students was being renounced as unsuited for statecraft. He is sickly and pale, and indecisive as well. Yet in moments of resolve he is himself able to reject the overly subtle. "I know not 'seems.' . . . But I have that within that passeth show./These but the trappings and the suits of woe."[34]

The emergence of a literary poetics independent of rhetoric in the Renaissance and the seventeenth century, particularly in Britain, incorporated along the lines of Aristotle's *Poetics* stylistic segments of medieval rhetorics and directed them to the task of instructing vernacular literary writers in the uses of tropes and figures.[35] At the same time, Ramist rhetorics excised some of the more elaborate listings of tropes and figures, and, as they converged with Baconian canons of true induction and scientific clarity, discouraged figurative language in political, legal, and scientific discourse. The independence of Renaissance and seventeenth-century poetics from rhetoric has been somewhat overemphasized, obscuring the continuity of themes and personae that link Renaissance Ciceronianism and early neoclassicism with the dissembling emphasized in many classical models of irony and rhetoric. These sustained continuities resuscitated or perhaps were reinvigorated by dissimulative conceptions of political discourse and *ethos*, while the doubling of meanings and intentions fostered by aesthetic canons of ironic discourse came to be deployed in a number of ways. Expanding canons of literary character and voice permitted the creation of speaking personae in poetry and the novel that were understood as fictions, as literary extensions of rhetorical *ethos*. These were often cleverly ironic; the Metaphysical conceit deployed ironies of philosophical paradox, honed to crystalline precision, whose logic is reminiscent of Heraclitus' bombastic aphorisms and Gorgias' spare, teasing ambiguities. The epidemic paradoxy of the Metaphysical poets' self-consuming artifacts was drier and sparer than the dry mock favored by the Augustans, but both drew on and extended earlier concepts and practices of irony.[36]

Augustan satire, rich as it is in the dry mock, was in many of its manifestations too stable and recognizable a mannerism to sustain the deeper philosophical and ethical conundra that irony and rhetorical dissembling had raised for Plato and Augustine. The evolution of neoclassical literary culture prompted critical attempts to define the nuances in genre and style, among them paradox, irony, and satire, culminating in the literary histories and criticism of the eighteenth century. The marriage of Ramism and Puritanism is an important segment in the history of rhetoric that pointedly addresses these conundra.[37] Augustinian elements in Puritanism are evident in the return to the project of constructing a hermeneutic that could draw on rhetorical models while at the same time promoting literacy for all believers within the distinctively Protestant initiatives of individual study, reflection, and diligent meditative understanding of the tropes and figures of Scripture. The Epistle preceding Milton's tract *Concerning Christian Doctrine* enjoins all believers to read, reflect, and understand Scripture by discovering therein the devices and categories of rhetoric. Baconian and Ramist proscriptions on figurative language merged with Puritan aversions to the construction of new literary figuration, culminating in the promotion of plain style and expository logic for newly constructed discourses. The tension between approving of the study of tropes and figures as necessary to scriptural interpretation and forbidding the creation of any new figurative or poetic discourse among the early Protestants, and particularly among the Puritans, is manifest in the literary work of George Herbert and John Donne. Herbert's work balances precariously on the line dividing literary from religious discourse.[38] Donne's career as both cleric and literary figure appears to have been less anguished on this point, but the literary eloquence of his sermons provoked censure as calling too much attention to his art, an issue that is addressed within several of the sermons.

The preeminent concern of Protestantism with the individual's responsibility to study and interpret Scripture has had a profound impact on the understanding and uses of rhetoric and literacy alike, a preoccupation with the interpreter's share that continues to be central to and definitive of literacy. Protestant promotion of study and education led to a much wider dissemination of literacy, education, and reading materials; educated readership was both motivated by, and an important motivation for, the printing press.[39] Latin as well as vernacular Bibles, and Ramist rhetorics were among the most widely printed and circulated texts during the first two centuries of the printing press, though the rhetorics, and the basic curriculum in which they were taught, remained preponderantly Latin well into the eighteenth century. As they had been during classical period, rhetoric and literacy were virtually coextensive during the centuries that inaugurated modern literacy in the West. The uses of literacy and rhetoric, however, once the basic curriculum had been completed, diversified rapidly. The literary and philosophical cultures of the eighteenth and nineteenth centuries flourished as much outside academia as within. Literary histories and criticism drew on developments in philosophy, sometimes merging with philosophical movements, sometimes taking an antagonistic and corrective role in relationship to philosophy, as was the case with German and English Romanticism. High-minded moral exemplarity, an underlying conception of the elocutionist movement, was sometimes at odds with Romantic literary aesthetics — particularly with conceptualizations of voice and persona and experimentation with genre during the nineteenth century. The bourgeois proprieties inculcated by elocutionist education began to draw derisive rejoinders from many literary writers and critics, even as the rise of literary histories and criticism helped promote the production and reading of vernacular and classical literature.

Critical objections to naive and sentimental literature, as well as literary depictions of naive and sentimental readers, ushered in an era of bombastic prose writers whose experimentations with voice revived some of the deepest epistemological and ethical manifestations of Socratic irony. Shaftesbury's *On the Characteristics of Men, Manners, Morals, Opinions, and Times* was admired by Friedrich Schlegel for its insights into voice, style, authenticity, selfmasking, and the shaping of individual character and culture alike by the voices, the "masks," represented in literary and philosophical work. Shaftesbury's voice draws on the kind of philosophical parodic irony that is later evident in Pope's *Dunciad*, but Shaftesbury's work presents itself as a literary and cultural history, a shift in genre that — much in the manner of Sterne in *Tristram Shandy* — he alludes to as he writes. Friedrich Schlegel in the *Dialogue on Poetry and Literary Aphorisms* similarly experiments with voice and genre simultaneously, referring explicitly to both as he writes. Schleiermacher's translations of Plato's dialogues into German inform the dialogical model he presents in *Hermeneutik*, which resusciatates the questions of knowing and understanding between author and reader, speaker and audience.

A subjective identification that would today be defined in some quarters as projection characterizes many Romantic views of author and meaning. To know the mind of the author better than he knew himself became a hallmark of German Romantic hermeneutics, and of an era in which genius author and poet *vates* were elevated to the status of divinities.[40] Schiller praises Goethe for overthrowing the "old, inferior nature that had previously been imposed upon your imagination." "Now it was your task . . . to correct it in the light of the superior model which your creative genius was fashioning."[41] Fichte and Solger conceptualize the ego as objectifying itself through "intellectual perception," an ability to "raise oneself above oneself" in deliberate acts of detachment. For Solger this ability becomes a definitive characteristic of the artist. "The spirit of the artist must concentrate all tendencies into one all-comprehensive gaze, and this gaze, superior to everything and destroying everything, is called irony."[42] Schlegel mingles a concept of irony as a characteristic of the genius artist's detached and all-comprehending gaze with irony as a characteristic of genre. "Philosophy," he says, "is the true home of irony, which might be defined as logical beauty. For wherever men are philosophizing in spoken or written dialogues, and providing they are not entirely systematical irony ought to be produced and postulated."[43] The ability of an author to "distribute" himself among the persons in a novel, in a virtually algebraic sense, is one of the qualities that Schlegel praises in Goethe. He parallels this distributive ability to two other kinds of "duplicity," conceptual and formal, but retains a separate definition for "rhetorical irony," that "manner of speaking" in which one says one thing but clearly intends another. "If sparingly used," he says, it "performs a very excellent function, especially in polemics, but compared to the lofty urbanity of the Socratic muse, rhetorical irony is like the splendor of the most brilliant oratory compared to ancient high tragedy."[44]

Complex interconnections link German Romantic notions of the author, ironic detachment and duplicity, intention and control, fiction and falsity, and a diabolical sublime. Schlegel asks, since "God the Father, and, even more often, the devil himself, appears at times in the place of fate in the modern tragedy, why is it that this has not induced any scholar to develop a theory of diabolical genre?"[45] The dark Faustian side of the Romantic critique of pure reason is given vivid expression by Schlegel's rendition of Ludovico's concluding remarks in the "Dialogue on Poetry." "Ludovico, who, with his revolutionary philosophy pursued annihilation on a grand scale, began to talk of a *system of false poetry* that he wanted to present, which raged and still rages to some extent in this age, especially with the English and the French. The deep, basic connection of all those false trends harmonizing so beautifully, complementing each other, and meeting each other half way in a friendly fashion, he thought as peculiar and instructive as it was amusing and grotesque."[46] Schlegel's *Lucinde* realizes the goal of diabolical genre, a sinister seduction novel, parodied in Kierkegaard's "Diary of the Seducer." Both works invert and subvert the *Bildungsroman* genre as well. A young woman submits to her lover's Pygmalion-like efforts to dismantle her naive and sentimental sensibility, a project that inverts earlier works depicting the education of women, such as Rousseau's *Emile*, in which Sophie's proposed education is resoundingly conventional; she is to be taught to be modest and compliant, to sustain precisely the kind of sentimental sensibility that Faustian Romantics seek to corrupt.

Solger, Schlegel, and Kierkegaard find cousins among the voices of England and America during the mid-nineteenth century. Carlyle and Melville storm consumingly forth while the slender sentences of Jane Austen convey an arch and lyrical edifying irony. The self that sees itself in what it represents, that can lose itself in what it represents — an aestheticized self that can distribute itself among the voices and fictions of its own making endlessly — is itself a realization of diabolical genre, a conceptualization that promotes and finally comes to regard as inevitable the illusion of technique.[47] Postmodern conceptions of both the author — or of what Foucault terms the "author function" — and of texts have been indelibly shaped by these Romantic conceptualizations. With the Romantics' notion of philosophy in need of poetry to give it back a voice and a character came a revival of notions of philosophy as fiction, as illusion, as voiceless, and the notion that poetry — literature in the broad senses given it by the Romantics — would assume the mantle not only of diabolical genre but of philosophy and religion as well. It is ironic that the notion of edifying literature grounded in realistic depictions of the human condition—the realism practiced by nine-teenth-century authors such as George Eliot and Charles Dickens—has come under the purview of a contemporary literary theory that sometimes fails to recognize it as deeply "postmodern" in its questioning of class and power relations. Always a two-edged sword, the idea that logic is an illusion, a fiction with its own poetics, is no more unfamiliar to these authors—and to many of their characters, disenfranchised as they so often are by law and education alike—than it was to the Sophists who challenged the first Being talkers' claim to universal authority and truth.

Reinscribing the Self

Cicero noted that the audible voice and the palpable self that says "nothing can be perceived" dogmatically contrast starkly with the meaning of the pronouncement. "Logic is an illusion" and "Being talk deceives" are, after all, neither more nor less than baldly logical propositions, self-consuming artifacts. Not only what is said but also who makes such statements have long been at issue for proponents of literacy and reformers of rhetoric alike, as they have repeatedly appraised the ways in which teaching how to write and how to read is teaching voice and self as well. A phenomenology of self and voice that can reconcile contemporary cultural, critical, and disciplinary divergences is badly needed to bridge the curricular gaps that continue to disenfranchise traditionally marginal groups. Contemporary studies of rhetoric and literacy, particularly when combined as fields of study, have already begun to uncover points of potential reconciliation, for they have scrutinized with increased attention the paradigms of language and of self that are shaped with subtle and often only implicit directive force by linguistic practice, literary and curricular content, and schooling.[48] Understanding the disparities between continental reappraisals of the subject and American reappraisals of conceptualizations of self and identity provide further avenues for exploring possible reintegrations and opportunities for constructing a shared phenomenology of self and knowledge. Observing the tandem development of European and American reappraisals reveals parallels in the midst of what may initially appear to be only divisions among feminist, minority,

and cultural theorists, positivist psychologists and social construc-
tivists, literary deconstructionists, poststructuralists, and new his-
toricists, neoclassical humanists and neo-Marxist postmodernists.[49]
Charges that traditional Western conceptualizations of self, knowledge, and discourse are in need of revision or even abandonment
have increased an awareness that epistemology, self, and the value
placed on knowledge are cultural constructs that vary widely from
culture to culture, and among subcultures within America. At the
same time, caution is urged by those who resist wholesale rejection
of existing models. The claims of personal experience and authority
that are foregrounded by women and minorities as they build new
intellectual cultures, literatures, and voices need not entail a wholesale rejection of the notions of rationality and objectivity, "the
waste of reinventing the wheel that occurs when nonpersonal authority is rejected."[50] Christa Wolf defends traditional modes of
rationality against feminist and postmodern promoters of what she
deems to be regressive returns to the discourses of revolution or to a
Dionysian irrationality.

> Why do I feel uneasy when I read so many publications — even in the
> field of archaeology, ancient history — which go under the title of "wom-
> en's literature"? Not just because I know by experience the dead end into
> which sectarian thinking — thinking that rules out any points of view not
> sanctioned by one's own group — invariably leads. Above all, it is be-
> cause I feel a genuine horror at that critique of rationalism which itself
> ends up in reckless irrationalism. It is not merely a dreadful, shameful,
> and scandalous fact for women that women were allowed to contribute
> virtually nothing to the culture we live in, officially and directly, for
> thousands of years. No, it is, strictly speaking, the weak point of cul-
> ture, which leads to its becoming self-destructive — namely, its inability
> to grow up. But it does not make it any easier to achieve maturity if a
> masculinity mania is replaced by a femininity mania, and if women
> throw over the achievements of rational thought simply because men
> produced them, in order to substitute an idealization of prerational
> stages in human history. The tribe, the clan, blood-and-soil — these are
> not values to which men and women of today can adhere. We Germans,
> of all people, should know that these catchwords can supply pretexts for
> hideous regressions.[51]

Defining the nature and defending the value of rationality within
contemporary culture, and directing this redefinition to the renewed
promotion of reading, writing, and mass-media literacy, may be one

of the most important impending tasks of literacy scholarship. It is
a task that can be happily wed to cross-cultural studies of language
acquisition and socialization, analyses of cognitive and metacognitive development, studies of identity and ego formation and their
ties to patterns of moral reasoning and decision making, and reappraisals of literary canon and genre. Literature is now being re-
viewed as not simply an archival storehouse of cultural artifacts but
as a living museum of actual voices, possible selves, and models for
seeing and participating in both knowledge and experience, and for
interacting with others.[52] Jerome Bruner remarks, "One of the most
powerful ways of controlling and shaping participants in a society is
through canonical images of selfhood."[53] Among these canonical
images is the rational metacognitive self that has been highly prized
and promoted in the West. "Metacognitive activity is unevenly distributed, and varies according to cultural background, and . . . can
be taught successfully as a skill. An *Anlage* of metacognition is
present as early as the eighteenth month of life. How much and
in what form it develops will . . . depend upon the demands of
the culture in which one lives—represented by particular others
one encounters and by some notion of generalized other that one
forms."[54] Augustine's *Confessions* recounts the assimilation of one
such generalized Other, and at the same time embodies the expression of a self and voice that is fully conscious of itself as an interpreting subject.

The emphasis on separation, autonomy, and egocentrism characteristic of many canonical Western concepts of self, identity, and
mind is undergoing reappraisal from several perspectives. Freud's
and Piaget's notion of egocentrism and their equation of maturity
with separation and programmatically independent thought are being challenged by new studies of early childhood identity formation
and altruistic behavior that show egocentrism to be just as often
maladaptive, as much the exception as the rule. Bruner proposes
that when children can grasp a situation they are in by sharing the
perspective or emulating the behavior of another, they will do so. It
is primarily when this seeing through another's eyes, or modeling, is
unavailable or frustrated that they display the classical patterns of
egocentrism.[55] Reappraisals of this kind suggest that what Kenneth
Burke terms identification with, an altruism based on reciprocity,
may be found to be more adaptive, or "natural," by way of enlight-

ened self-interest if nothing else, than the egocentrism and narcissism propounded in Freudian models. The notion of a private, egocentric self can now be viewed as itself an instance of a canonical generalized Other that shapes and models the formation of identity and voice. Bruner proposes: "The notion of the 'private' Self free of cultural definition is part of the stance inherent in our Western conception of Self. . . . The divide between 'private' and 'public' meanings prescribed by a given culture makes a great difference in the way people in that culture view such meanings. In our culture, for example, a good deal of heavy emotional weather is made out of the distinction, and there is (at least among the educated) a push to get the private into the public domain—whether through confession or psychoanalysis."[56]

Post-Freudian reintroductions of the private into the public domain have conjured an inner self that is isolated, suspect, and suspicious, and caught up with concealing and revealing hidden things. Though anticipated in confessional and epistolary literature, the very narrow and overspecialized conception of self that has emerged from recent psychoanalytic and literary theory has become a programmatically impoverished and neurotic self. As with the Augustinian self that understands itself as interpreting and that is held responsible for the nature and values of its interpretation—the individual reader prototypical of Protestantism and literary study alike—the Western concept of the self and of thought more generally has promoted and privileged individual rather than collaborative learning, thinking, and interpretation. Adversarial debate and the imposition of abstract rules and laws have structured classroom and public discourse alike, rather than modes of discourse, interpretation, and decision making that are mutually contracted and collectively pursued. A classroom discussion need not be a debate between individuals' already completed interpretations or propositions that are defended and proved by example; it can also be styled as "a conversation in which teacher and student collaborate in constructing a new interpretation."[57] The analysis Carol Gilligan provides of the identity development and moral reasoning of women in our culture parallels studies of men as well as women in non-Western cultures. "Women stay with, build on, and develop in a context of attachment and affiliation with others; women's sense of self becomes organized around being able to make, and then to maintain, affiliations and relationships. . . . Affiliation is valued as highly as, or more highly than, self-enhancement."[58] So deep is many women's commitment to affiliation and attachment that any threat or loss is perceived not simply as the loss of a relationship but as a loss of identity as well. Gilligan proposes that there is more of a gap between the perceived experiences of women and men in our culture than existing studies of identity and development reflect. "Men and women speak different languages that they assume are the same, using similar words to encode disparate experiences of self and social relationships."[59]

Attachment and separation — key stages in identity as defined by Western psychology, and paradigmatic of rationalism and thought in Western philosophy — are experienced differently and have different value for men and women in our culture, Gilligan proposes. She has been joined by Belenky and her colleagues in proposing that neither the psychological literature nor the philosophical and literary canon has represented or delineated the experiences of adult women in their own terms and from their own perspectives. A more comprehensive, inclusive psychology of adulthood, Gilligan posits, would depict development, identity, and thought in ways that do not "displace the value of ongoing attachment and the continuing importance of care in relationships."[60] The concept of identity should be expanded "to include the experience of interconnection. The moral domain is similarly enlarged by the inclusion of responsibility and care in relationships; . . . the underlying epistemology shifts from the Greek ideal of knowledge as correspondence between mind and form to the Biblical conception of knowing as a process of human relationship."[61] Masculine, Western modes of authority have long been rooted in what Patricia Meyers Spacks calls a "universal systematic methodology," a parallel to the "logic of justice" that Gilligan contrasts with an "ethic of care." Women can, and have, Spacks proposes, learned to mimic this mode of authority, "but can also construct a different kind of authority based on personal experience and acknowledging the uncertainties implicit in an approach which values the personal."[62] Gilligan shows how the models of Freud and Piaget, drawn preponderantly from male experience, have been used to mismeasure women's psychological and moral development. The underlying cultural associations that link rationality, abstract rule systems, control, mastery and dominance, and masculinity may account for why it is that "men move quickly to impose their own conceptual schemes on the experience of women. These schemes do not help women make sense of their experience; they extinguish the experience."[63]

In *Truth and Method*, Gadamer asks: is the experience of dominance, mastery, and control the quintessentially Western experience? Is rationality destined to expend itself repeatedly in the horrible excesses of reigns of terror? That question is being answered affirmatively by some postmodernists today, as it was by Sade, in nineteenth-century literary depictions of the excesses of industrial magnates and colonial Europeans, and by the *entre deux guerres* surrealists who propounded fragmentation, parody, and deliberately distorted vision as more honest and more consciousness-raising than avowal and affirmation of limp images and slogans, the failed rhetoric of democracy. Concluding *Heart of Darkness*, Conrad's depiction of Kurtz's dementia as the derailed rationality of a former idealist is a chilling vision of this inevitability. "He seemed to stare at me out of the glassy panel — stare with that wide and immense stare embracing, condemning, loathing all the universe. I seemed to hear the whispered cry, 'The horror! The horror!'" Marlow remembers Kurtz's earlier dreams and visions of his time in Africa, the vision of the civilizing colonist expressed in language that now seems "broken phrases, . . . ominous" in their simplicity. And what has Kurtz become? Hoarder of a cache of ivory that he claims the company did not pay for. "I want no more than justice."[64] Creon's justice — that is, the justice of the new order, the bureaucratic order, the landholder's order, the owner's and master's order. The voices in which the masters speak are imperious; what they say cleverly conceals infinite manipulability; what they avow is as changeable as their laws. Phaedra's rebuke in the *Hippolytus* joins Antigone's resolute challenge to Creon's self-made laws.

> This is the deadly thing which devastates
> well-ordered cities and the homes of men —
> that's it, this art of oversubtle words.
> It's not the words ringing delight in the ear
> that one should speak, but those that have the power
> to save their hearer's honorable name.[65]

Contemporary cross-cultural studies of cognition, knowledge, and identity provide welcome perspective and reassurance that, although some Western and masculine uses of reason have been monstrously arrogant, a domesticated rationality is not only possible but desirable, since non-Western and nonliterate ways with words and ways of knowing have limitations as well. Bruner notes that in many nonliterate cultures and subcultures the commonest mode of approaching knowledge is to "take it from authority in contrast to a more Western European version of generating it oneself, autonomously, once one has acquired the constituents of reckoning from the society. . . . A mode of schooling in which one 'figures out things for oneself' changes one's conception of oneself and one's role, and also undermines the role of authority that exists generally within the culture, even to the point of being marked by modes of address reserved for those in authority."[66] Bakhtin asserts a total departure of the old authority. His proclamation is at the very least an accurate depiction of a group of attitudes and beliefs that are now routinely imparted by schooling. "The speaking subjects of high proclamatory genres — of priests, prophets, preachers, judges, leaders, patriarchal fathers, and so forth, have departed this life. They have been replaced by the writer, simply the writer, who has fallen prey to their styles. He either stylizes them or parodies them."[67]

Like the procedural learners described by Belenky and her colleagues, and the correctness-centered Roadville culture described by Shirley Brice Heath in *Ways With Words*, the knowers Jerome Bruner characterizes as taking knowledge unidirectionally from authority figures are limited to, and by, a one-way mode of learning and developing: everything is taken from authority, is rule-governed, and is not questioned. The autonomy requisite to "Western European" — that is, literate, educated, rhetorically contoured — knowing creates ambiguities and requires skepticism as it sharpens identity and ego boundaries. Knowing, knower, and known shape one another. *"How* one *talks* comes eventually to be how one *represents* what one talks about."[68] Language is in this sense "two-faced," Bruner proposes. Janus-like, it is both a mode of communication and a way of representing, constructing, and bringing into being the reality about which it then communicates. The stances adopted toward talking and toward what is talked about then in turn become features of the world, a part of the reality toward which stances are taken. The same holds true for the self once that self comes to be understood as inscribed, as a text that is created through our reading of ourselves. Says Augustine: "What is true of the whole psalm is also true of all its parts and of each syllable. It is true of any longer action in which I may be engaged and of which the recitation of the psalm may only be a small part. It is true of a man's whole life, of which all his actions are parts. It is true of the whole history of mankind, of which each man's life is a part."[69] This self-enriching and self-creating hermeneutic imparts habits of reading and knowing that, despite the reflective and intending consciousness they rely on, differ from the reflective intervention in knowledge that has long been defended as a quintessential hallmark of Western secular rationality.[70] Schooled in a skepticism he has come to regard as sycophantic, Augustine with no little difficulty adopts a mode of taking knowledge from authority. In his account of reading a psalm, he represents to himself a way of knowing that takes Scripture as paradigmatic and exemplary, as the one true teacher and guide, but with the crucially important addition of the extensive responsibility he places on the interpreter's share in knowing and in sustaining the meanings he encounters.

The mode of knowing, understanding, and reading from perspectives defined by authority today remains far more common than the skeptical modes of thought and styles of self promoted by "high" Western educated culture, literature, and literacy. Few achieve or seek to achieve the self-conscious, self-creating, and world-constructing sensibility that Bruner defends as a crucial goal of Western education. "If he fails to develop any sense of . . . reflective intervention in the knowledge he encounters, the young person will be operating continually from the outside in — knowledge will control and guide him. If he succeeds in developing such a sense, he will control and select knowledge as needed. If he develops a sense of self that is premised on his ability *to penetrate knowledge for his own uses*, and if he can share and negotiate the result of his penetrations, then he becomes a member of a culture-creating community."[71] The mastery-control language Bruner employs here, and the model of penetrating knowledge for "his own uses," bear traces of the hyperindividualist and egocentric bias that has at times manifested itself as a dark Faustian side of Western concepts of self and thought, a problem that Schiller captures deftly. "In man as a being who explores and dominates nature lies the possibility of achieving the highest freedom and self-determination, but also the deepest slavery and self-estrangement. The more man dominates nature and shapes his world, the more dependent he is upon his creation."[72] The notion of an ongoing recursion of self creating and yet being shaped by culture, mastering and being mastered by language, nature, or culture, is also, perhaps, too much the legacy of Western dialectics, as is the corollary masculine–Western–rationalist preoccupation with control as distinct from collaboration and cocreation, alternate modes that Bruner employs in the second half of his depiction: the self he profiles must not only be able to penetrate knowledge and put it to his own uses, she must also be able to "share and negotiate" the results.

Bruner reminisces that Vygotsky, the Russian cognitive psychologist and colleague of Alexander Luria, was sent into Afghanistan with the expressly political purpose of imparting literacy in order to "modernize" the Afghan mind. Yet in a way that may have protected him from Marxism's — and psychology's — dogmatic preference for historical determinism, Vygotsky came under the shelter of Pavlov's Second Signal System, whose Principle of Spontaneity was an attempt to account for generativity and creativeness that could not be explained in terms of historical antecedents.[73] It is this protection, Bruner suggests, that shielded Vygotsky from Soviet intellectual dogmatism and may explain the liberalism in his views of dialogue and inner speech. He came to depict conceptual learning as an analogue to language acquisition, as a "collaborative enterprise involving an adult who enters into dialogue with a child in a fashion that provides the child with hints and props that allow him to begin a new climb . . . 'a loan of consciousness' that gets the child through the zone of proximal development. The model is Socrates guiding the slave boy through geometry in the *Meno*."[74]

Though a Socratic *paideia* has non-Western parallels, the agonistic paradigms of conceptually articulated formal discourse — as long taught under the auspices of rhetoric in the West: argument, thesis, contention, and proof — are at odds with the discourse paradigms and ways of knowing of many nonmainstream Western cultures and non-Western cultures alike.[75] Studies in basic literacy spawned by the exigencies of open admissions and declining literacy rates during the 1970s and early 1980s have converged quite significantly with feminist and minority studies' appraisals of the concepts of self, voice, and knowledge that nonmainstream students bring to the classroom at all levels.[76] There is renewed pedagogical interest in collaborative and cooperative modes of learning, thinking, knowing, and writing born of the realization that some hierarchical models of pedagogy, learning, and authority do not work well with traditionally disenfranchised groups beyond a certain point. The banking metaphor of schooling and learning, and classrooms that place students in the passive role of movie watchers, have not been successfully overcome even in some progressive institutions where an ostensible freedom from traditional structures has nonetheless replicated the worst elements in the old models at the expense of the best in the new. One of the women studied by Belenky and her colleagues reported that "my experience with free-form classes has been the professor free-forming it. He does all the talking. . . . It's almost impossible to flunk out. . . . There are no social guidelines. Some very basic expectations should be set up so that people have an obligation to their peers and to the faculty and to the administration."[77] This student's complaint comes ironically from within a group of economically and educationally marginalized lower-class women who want very much to move into the mainstream academic tradition but find little exposition or modeling of its value and who, during the transitional period of acculturation to academia that Belenky terms "procedural learning," define a need for "taking from authority" structures that will facilitate, finally, their individualism and confidence, but within an ongoing network of shared social guidelines and defined obligations—the needed merger of connected knowing and knowledge that Gilligan and Belenky and her colleagues define.[78]

American feminist scholarship on the psychology and language of moral development, and on the formation of self and voice that is essential to this development, has contributed much to an understanding of how perceived gender differences influence patterns of thought, knowing, and speaking. The generic use of "women" is now generally conceded to be reductive, and methods used for studying difference are undergoing revision within feminist theory to address the problems of monolithic gender or class categories and to facilitate better understandings of significant differences among groups of women, as well as to create methodologies that can study sameness and difference simultaneously—a double stroke that Gilligan achieves in the conclusion to *In a Different Voice*.[79]

With this proviso, that "women" is now acknowledged as an overly broad category, it can still be said that there has been an important revision of both psychological and moral theory advanced by recent American feminist scholarship on the psychology and language of moral development, and on the formation of self and voice that is essential to this development.[80] Perceived gender differences in patterns of thinking, knowing, and speaking are recounted by the subjects of these studies themselves as important to their sense of identity, their understandings and uses of language, and their choices in acquiring and using knowledge in their lives. In our culture, men identify with contest, struggle, and violence more often than women do. It is arguable that a woman might not have selected the primal horde or the Oedipus story as a paradigm of psychological identity and development.[81] Women more often than men, according to recent gender studies in psychology, take strength, a sense of self, and knowledge from empowering others and sharing knowledge rather than from controlling others and hoarding knowledge. They regard listening not as passive but as active participation in knowing, a dialogical model that can readily be seen as consonant with Vygotsky's, Luria's, and Bakhtin's notions of incremental zones of proximal learning, dialogue and inner speech, and polyvocality.

Belenky and her colleagues draw explicitly on Vygotsky's models of inner speech and dialogue, and establish ties between these models and literate paradigms as well.

> Literacy does not automatically lead to reflective abstract thought. In order for reflection to occur, oral and written forms must pass back and forth between persons who both speak and listen or read and write, sharing, expanding, and reflecting on each other's experiences. . . . Each of the women had the gifts of intelligence and of all their senses, yet they felt "deaf" because they could not learn from the words of others, "dumb" because they felt so voiceless. . . . Words were perceived as weapons. Words were used to separate and diminish people, not to connect and empower them. The silent women worried that they would be punished just for using words — any words. . . . There were no words that suggested an awareness of mental acts, consciousness, or introspection. . . . [Cindy] did not comprehend words that suggest an interior voice that could give herself mental directions and exhortations. . . . Growing up without opportunities for play and dialogue poses the

gravest danger for the growing child. Lev Vygotsky and his colleagues suggest that exterior dialogues are a necessary precursor to inner speech and an awareness of one's own thought process. They argue that play itself is a precursor to symbolization and meaning-making.[82]

Though the family contexts for this group of women were unusually deprived and negative, the patterns they imparted often function as extreme, exaggerated versions of larger patterns in the socialization of women and other disenfranchised groups in our culture. At least one of the parents routinely used violence rather than words for controlling others' behavior. Often the other parent as well as other family members remained silent, passive, and victimized in the face of the violence. One woman said, "I was brought up to believe that you kept your troubles to yourself, you didn't talk about them. I never let anyone know what was going on, what was troubling you. You just didn't do it."[83] Belenky and her colleagues conclude that such individuals come to see themselves as deaf and dumb only after a long period of profound psychic isolation under demeaning circumstances. Lacking even the communal, shared oral culture of nonliterate societies and subcultures, they have the worst of both worlds, oral and literate alike. There is in their environment no representation of preserved speech, no speech models or genres, and no communal or interlocutory paradigms for voice. Without such models, neither voice nor self can develop. The settings in which such modeling can be emulated, practiced, responded to, and rewarded are of equal importance.

Classical paradigms provide ample evidence of the creation of such settings in antiquity and of the exclusion of women from the training they provided. Despite some of the negative aspects of the *dissoi logoi* and other classical moots, they, like Aeschylus' addition of a second actor, provided a model of enacted rather than narrated interlocution, a give-and-take of themes and arguments concerning ideas and events that remains an aim of educated discourse today. If participation in such a discourse is not permitted, or if this form of discourse is denigrated, ignored, or simply overpowered by abusive speech or violence, it quickly atrophies. For many women and minorities, for all those who feel deaf and dumb because they are regularly relegated to the peripheral vision of classroom and society, the absence of a port of entry to such modeling and training is a crucial barrier. Social and culturally transmitted attitudes can function as such a barrier, as has been the case with the views that women are incapable of, uninterested in, or made hysterical by education and intellectual activity. Aristotle's exposition of the view that women's minds, like their bodies, are imperfect, incomplete, and misbegotten males has had a powerful influence, and until this century has been used forcefully and recurrently to support arguments against the education or public political presence of women. Turned on their heads, Aristotle's arguments can be seen as a logical alchemy deployed in defense of the cultural and social superiority of males on the grounds that gender differences are rooted in essential natures. In the *Politics* he asserts, "the slave has absolutely no deliberative faculty; the woman has, but its authority is imperfect; so has the child, but in this case it is immature."[84] He appears to argue that women are defective in their authority because of innate cognitive or deliberative incapacity. Judith Hughes proposes that the argument is the reverse: women observably lack authority, therefore they must lack some moral or cognitive capacity. "Aristotle's women are not autonomous, not because they lack abilities or capacities but because they lack authority; that is, their right to make decisions, to speak for themselves is not acknowledged. This acknowledgment is absolutely essential, for without it no mental act which they perform, however well, will count as a decision at all."[85] If and when a speaker is ignored, silenced, or rebuked simply for speaking, or for speaking in a certain place or setting—as is the case with Antigone and Phaedra—attention to what is being said is shifted toward the fact that they are speaking at all. They are rendered dumb even as they speak.

Sociolinguistic research demonstrates that in childhood games and adult speech many women avoid adversarial, confrontational discourse, particularly in mixed-gender and public settings. One reason for this avoidance is undoubtedly socialization. Another, yet to be sufficiently investigated, could align the moral values and ethical reasoning patterns that women in Western culture, at least as profiled by Gilligan and by Belenky and her colleagues, share with those of men and women in non-Western cultures. Such study could include the treatment of non-Western moral philosophies. Like Rousseau's Sophie, women, children, and the underclasses in the

West have been socialized to be obedient, deferential, agreeable, and pleasant. Though Atwood's Cordelia and her sisters may mimic an ironic manner, they are not expected to practice it among adults, particularly with prospective husbands. Rather tellingly, the girls use it primarily to mock and scorn Elaine, the underling within their own group. Democritus' rebuke echoes from the fifth century B.C., still very much a part of the folklore of perceived gender roles and expectations but true as well for other Others: "A woman must not practice argument: this is dreadful. To be ruled by a woman is the ultimate outrage for a man."[86] When the women studied by Gilligan and by Belenky and her colleagues define their own reasons for avoiding confrontational and adversarial discourse, they identify the ethical value of avoiding giving harm to another person, and ethical discomfort with competitive situations in which one person wins at the expense of another—a direct corollary to the cross-culturally prominent ethical rule of avoiding harm.

Historically women have rarely seen or heard other women admired for contending or arguing; in public and formal settings, many of them represented in literary depictions, the strong-speaking woman is censured as insolent, shrewish, strident, mannish, out of place, out of line, or simply difficult.[87] Studies of mixed-gender conversations reveal that women are interrupted by men far more frequently than men by women, that their topic-changing initiatives are accepted significantly less frequently—by men and by women—than men's are, and that they hold the floor individually and collectively for a fraction of the time that men do. The same paradigm holds in most classrooms, even when the teacher is female. An inference that can be drawn from the contrast between social censure of strong women's speech and linguistic reality is that *any* speech, and particularly "bold" or argumentative speech, is responded to as out of line. Belenky's subjects express the internalization of this view in its most extreme form when they say they fear they will be punished simply for using words, "any words." In Alice Walker's *The Color Purple*, Celie is punished in this way when, after years of silence, she finds the voice to rebuke her husband. "He laugh. Who you think you is? he say. You can't curse nobody. Look at you. You black, you pore, you ugly, you a woman. Goddam, he say, you nothing at all."[88]

Hidden Truth and Hidden Meaning

One of the legacies of the hermeneutics of suspicion has been to sustain, even as it deconstructs, notions of self and subject as entities that can be found, discovered, uncovered, and, like truth — *aletheia* — become unconcealed. The double movement in such hermeneutics forms a dialectic and, if viewed from the perspectives I have attempted to develop, a dialogue. Within Freud's work can be found traces of this double movement, for Freud at times presents the psychoanalyst's task as uncovering and discovering that which has been suppressed, cathected, elided — a truth of self or past that, once found, can liberate the mind from pathological preoccupations and energies misspent on the tasks of hiding, covering, running from unwanted truth. Yet Freud also depicts the psychoanalyst's task as parallel to that point in literary interpretation understood as making rather than discovering meaning. Within this movement psychoanalyst and analysand are, like text and reader — or like author and reader, depending on your metaphysics — cocreators of meaning, of a self, a new cover story, an official paradigmatic narrative within which, to invoke Kierkegaard's way of putting it, health and truth can be restored to the personal life. Long before Aristotle distilled Pythagorean oppositions into a dialectical table of opposites, Pythagorean doctrines of *harmonia* depicted harmonic interdependencies between pairs. Empedocles and Heraclitus bear traces of a conceptualization of complementarities that later came to be thought of disjunctively. Disjunctive thinking pits complementarity against dialectical opposition and plagues conceptualizations of self, subject, truth, and meaning. Dialectical reasoning continues to manifest itself in the binarist contours of Western thought about thought. Yet the binarism of this dialectic also sustains an awareness that lies, fictions, and illusions imply their opposites: truth, reality, the *viseo beatifica* of understanding.

In many feminist reappraisals of psychoanalytic models of self, identity, knowing, and thinking, the metaphor of voice rather than of sight predominates. The speaking subject so central to oral culture, to interlocution, and to dialogue, rather than an interiorized mental speculum, is the self through which women name themselves in many of these studies, an intimation perhaps of the legacy of women's exclusion from acknowledged speech, speaking, being heard, having a voice, and particularly from the political and public voices of rhetoric, argument, and philosophy. Similarly, the ways of knowing described by women and other Others in cross-cultural studies are collaborative, and bespeak a sense of cocreation rather than the long-standing models of *disputatio* and originality, the generation of new views and new knowledge through a process of ongoing critique of former views and knowledge, with incrementally separate knower and known, knower and knower. The plural self, a plural sense of identity, discourses, and knowledge, need not be construed as fragmented or split. Rather—along the lines exemplified by Plato's depictions of discourse as weaving and blending, and by Augustinian and subsequent hermeneutics that permit multiple, simultaneous meanings—such plurality can be orchestrated as plentiful, participatory, self-creating, and knowledge-creating in and through others: *dialogos*. The study of orality has brought much to an understanding of the presence and life of the spoken word and the Western modes of oral interlocution that have been shaped by rhetorical and philosophical paradigms. The atrophy of interlocutionary modes of discourse within the media milieu of contemporary secondary orality should be of crucial concern to educators and parents as a modern decay of dialogue, a third sophistic.[89] Latter-day Ramists abound in writing pedagogies whose methods provide outlines without rationale and pay little attention to the contexts that students come from and will move into. This failure to define and connect is further compounded by literary theorists working at such a remove from literature and from what it represents that they are increasingly unable to talk about literature or language in a way that is accessible to most students or to the culture at large. Just as troubling, however, is the fact that teachers and parents with the best of intentions are constrained by the demands of legislators and state boards of education, and by the media saturation that is one of the privileges of life in developed countries; they find less than five minutes each day in the average classroom and seven minutes each day in the average home to spend in conversation with their children on matters other than settling disputes or deciding schedules for the following day.[90]

A willing avowal of participatory cocreation lingers in religious as well as classroom rituals that require antiphonal interlocutionary and collective speech. Whether refusing to participate hypocritically in such rituals — the position taken and propounded on ethical and philosophical grounds in Western skeptical traditions — or engaging in hypocritical participation, "the conscious minds of humans become divorced from those deep and hidden portions of themselves to which ritual participation reintroduced and bound them. The self becomes fragmented and some of the fragments may be lost. The consciousness that remains is likely to remain trapped in its radical separation. For those not deluded there is alienation."[91] Contemporary theory focused on dismantling the author and textual meaning is an Occamite routing of illusion meaningful only to those privileged enough to countenance delusion. "Dispersed authorship mirrors this dispersed self, this inconstant subject, just as the incompleteness of the text mirrors the dissolution of the author."[92] Alternative antidotes subsist in nonhypocritical, consenting, meaning-making participation, the web of relationship, the pattern that connects.

Whether in a liturgy, a conversation, or a debate, willing participation is a requirement if not a constituent of meaning, self, and discourse. Movement away from the voices of the Others, first and foremost perhaps from the voice of the Mother, has been promoted with virile intensity in Western tradition, and for that reason may have come to be experienced as reflexive or even innate by many Westerners so shaped. Post-Freudian models of psychological development that have emphasized the centrality of separation from the Mother and from the Other are now being corrected to include the patterns of sustained connection and identification through which many women, non-Westerners, and Western minorities define themselves. Kierkegaard's work defined a similar supplement in the philosophical and ethical domain with its goal "to affect" and to reconnect the hyperseparated aestheticized self, to restore to the personal life health and truth. An intuition that the separated, oppositional way of experiencing identity and of using language is only one among many provinces of culture and identity is perhaps the source of resistance on the part of those not yet fully acculturated. Given further articulation, this resistance has begun to provide alternate voices and ways of knowing, a renewed acceptance of meaningful rituals of collaboration within education and cultural practices of language.[93] In *Caring*, Nel Nodding proposes, "It is time for the voice of the Mother to be heard in education."[94] Henry Louis Gates applauds the view that "it is the heritage of the *mother* that the African–American male must regain as an aspect of his own personhood—the power of 'yes' to the 'female' within. . . . For us as scholar critics, learning to speak in the voice of the black mother is perhaps the ultimate challenge of producing a discourse of the Other."[95]

In a harmonic conception of negative dialectics, rhetoric and irony—understood as the lies that literacy sustains—become dialogue, ethical resonance, the value of shared history, and the understanding that history, literature, and culture are one—or many— depending on the ways of knowing brought to them. Ways of knowing imparted and imprinted by ways of speaking, including what is read, constitute truth if we permit it to, through mutually constructed discourse, communally supported and valued, alive only for as long as it has participants, even if that sustaining participant is the solitary reader. For what is the worth of human life, asks Cicero, if it is not woven together with the lives of others through the records of history? History, as Cicero redefined and transformed it, can now be seen as coextensive with evolving modern understandings of literature and culture, with storytelling, dialogue, oral history, family narratives, autobiographies, the mother's first song—all the *loci*, the true homes of truth and meaning, and of the voices that speak into being the worth of human life.

It is only when there are, at a minimum, two parties involved in an exchange, at least one of whom assumes that both are telling the truth and that truth can be told, that deceit can exist. Otherwise all is error, mistake, miscommunication, misreading, or misunderstanding. Yet is there not in the notion of misunderstanding, as in the notion of misreading, a *via negativa* that leads perilously close to truth? The erosion of interpersonal trust, social coherence, and cultural values is as responsible for the demise of truth as any longstanding caveats within philosophical traditions, yet these erosions are by no means unrelated to the philosophical, rhetorical, and literary traditions that shape education and public and private discourse. Renewed attention to rhetoric and to literary aesthetics as models and vehicles of the ethics of language use can restore health and depth to the understandings of literacy that guide and train our uses of language, our sense of the value and meaning of language, and, by means of language, our connection through understanding with others. The intricate hierarchy of lies that is imparted by our literate literary tradition finds one of its most chilling exempla in the lie told by Marlow to Kurtz's intended, concluding *Heart of Darkness*.

> "The last word he pronounced was — your name."
> I heard a light sigh and then my heart stood still, stopped dead short by an exulting and terrible cry, by the cry of unconceivable triumph and of unspeakable pain. "I knew it — I was sure!" . . . She knew. She was sure. I heard her weeping; she had hidden her face in her hands. It seemed to me that the heavens should fall upon my head. But nothing happened. The heavens do not fall for such a trifle. Would they have fallen, I wonder, if I had rendered Kurtz that justice which was his due? Hadn't he said he wanted only justice? But I couldn't. I could not tell her. It would have been too dark — too dark altogether.[96]

The heavens were silent; the next lie, ostensibly protective again perhaps, will come more easily, and will be more readily justified as protecting her, protecting a view of history that is quite other than what it really was. "She knew. She was sure." Relying on Marlow's reliability, she is deceived, a reliance intertwined with paternalism in ways that parallel the roles between teacher and student, parent and child, greater and lesser, other and Other, the West and the rest. Yet without such reliance — on which any communication and decision depend — there can be ultimately no communication, no value, no decision. It is here that the story of rhetoric rejoins the evolving discourses and practices of philosophy and ethics. Marlow's lie to the intended illuminates the delicate webwork intertwining intention and ethics as both choice and value, assumptions about audience, presumptions about interlocutors, and uses of language. The intended is both affianced and audience. Her love for Kurtz, Marlow knows — assumes — will lead her to believe the lie, to embrace the deception. In his action he exploits her love in order to protect — deceive — her, and in so doing undermines the canons of trust and truth in much the same way that he has observed Kurtz corrupted.

Adrienne Rich's *On Lies, Secrets, and Silence* defines a related conundrum for teachers and, more broadly, for the academy. "How can we connect the process of learning to write well with the student's own reality, and not simply teach her/him how to write acceptable lies in standard English?"[97] Exemplifying the failure to connect that Rich defines, Faith, a college student who participated in Belenky and her colleagues' study of college women, reported that she could not remember the views of the moral philosophers she had studied only a semester before. "I couldn't tell you right now the philosophies of most of the people we studied, but I can tell you how you would set about criticizing their arguments and what types of things you should look for. . . . It does not matter . . . whether you decide to have your baby or abort it. It matters only that you think the decision through carefully."[98] It doesn't matter. "But nothing happened. The heavens do not fall for such a trifle." The next lie will be easier. Whose next decision will be more easily rationalized by the notion of the lie of language, a notion that displaces and can lead to an abandonment of ethical responsibility as chosen, shared, and mutually sustained?

These are the darker possibilities, and realities, of rhetoric and literacy, of irony and Western lies — those slight hypocrisies on which our civilization seems to depend. I have exaggerated them, but with a chiaroscuro intended to illuminate their dangers and their local cultural origins. In an era that has come to demand renewed attention to ethics and cultural values as played out within the academy and amid the intercultural tensions that the academy professes to address, these dangers surely warrant reflection; simple slogans cannot remedy, nor simpleminded relativism avoid, the choices that confront pedagogue and pundit alike. The reappraisal of Plato's dialogues as dramatic art and interlocutory logic, and not simply as tangled argument, harmonizes with the appraisals of moral reasoning and of orality that have been advanced within the past decade. Women analyzing women find that their thinking is not indecisive, wavering, or incoherent, even though they themselves may initially describe it in those terms. Re-viewed, they are shown to deploy multivariable modes of choice and decision that as often as not are more complex than the linear logic of justice. Their thought is not muddled or equivocating; rather, it is now being appraised as the product of complex alignments of moral axioms — the logic of justice — with contexts and consequences involving many individuals: an ethic of care. Similarly, ways of knowing practiced in traditional oral societies are now being explored and shared by ethnographers and anthropologists newly sensitive to the possibility that these ways are rich in epistemological and linguistic subtleties long invisible to Western eyes, and inaudible to ears that have searched for knowledge and language use only in the well-marked packages we have employed for so long. Collective knowing and speaking, much more than alienated separated thinking and discourse, remain central media of thought and language for many in the Western and non-Western worlds alike. These ways with words and ways of knowing are gradually being redefined as far from passive or herd behavior. Even postmoderns have begun to summon voices reminiscent of Antigone: "The Voice sings from a time before the law, before the Symbolic took one's breath away and reapportioned it into language under its authority of separation. The deepest, the oldest, the loveliest Visitation."[99]

Epi Dia Logos

Sperma semnas mega matros
Great seed of our holy mother[1]

A conversation begins
with a lie. And each

speaker of the so-called common language feels
the ice-flow split, the drift apart

as if powerless, as if up against
a force of nature.[2]

> In man as a being who explores and
> dominates nature lies the possibility
> of achieving the highest freedom and
> self-determination, but also the deep-
> est slavery and self-estrangement.
> The more man dominates nature and
> shapes his world, the more dependent
> he is upon his creation.[3]

The technology of silence
The rituals, etiquette

The blurring of terms
silence not absence

of word or music or even
raw sounds

Silence can be a plan
rigorously executed

the blueprint to a life

It is a presence
it has a history a form

Do not confuse it
with any kind of absence

> No anonymous author can more cun-
> ningly conceal himself, no practition-
> er of the maieutic art can more care-
> fully withdraw himself from the
> direct relationship, than God. He is
> in the creation, and present every-
> where in it, but directly He is not
> there; . . . like an elusive author who
> nowhere sets down his result in large
> type, or gives it to the reader before-
> hand in a preface.[4]

No. Let me have this dust,
these pale clouds dourly lingering, these words

moving with ferocious accuracy
like the blind child's fingers

or the newborn infant's mouth
violent with hunger.

> Who you think you is? he say. You
> can't curse nobody. Look at you. You
> black, you pore, you ugly, you a
> woman. Goddam, he say, "you noth-
> ing at all.
>   . . . All I'm telling you ain't com-
> ing just from me. Look like when I
> open my mouth the air rush in and

shape words. . . . A voice say to everything listening, But I'm here.[5]

If from time to time I envy
the pure annunciations to the eye.

the *viseo beatifica*
if from time to time I long to turn

like the Eleusinian hierophant
holding up a simple ear of grain

for return to the concrete and everlasting world
what in fact I keep choosing

are these words, these whispers, conversations
from which time after time the truth breaks moist and green.

Notes

Introduction

1. Cicero, *De Oratore* II, 299. Here and at several other points Cicero uses this example with ambiguous irony, perhaps to repeat a well-known joke and call into question the reasoning behind it, and perhaps to emphasize the technification of thought embodied in formulaic memorization.

2. Secondary orality denotes the evolution of a preponderantly oral culture following a period of textual literacy. In extending Marshall McLuhan's examination of the effects of different media on the evolution of consciousness, Walter Ong formulated the concept to define the differences between primary or pristine orality in cultures that have never encountered literacy, and orality that coexists with or supersedes literacy (*Orality and Literacy*, 136; *Rhetoric, Romance, and Technology*, 284–303; *Interfaces of the Word*, 16–49, 305–41). Eric Havelock coined the compatible but different concept of "craft literacy" to denote an incomplete, "mere skills," or temporary use of literacy in which the individual never achieves fluent reflexive literacy in reading and writing (*The Muse Learns to Write*, 45–50; *Preface to Plato*, 39–60). On the ontological as well as methodological problems of positing the "evolution of consciousness," see Ong, *Orality and Literacy*, 178–79, and Havelock, *The Muse Learns to Write*, 117–26.

3. The history, psychology, and cultural impact of literacy are being widely studied in a number of fields, prompted in no small part by allegations of decline in contemporary literacy. Walter Ong's and Eric Havelock's work, as well as Robert Pattison's *On Literacy* and Paul Corcoran's *Political Language and Rhetoric*, have contributed to the study of this decline by showing how it may be understood in ways other than simply a loss or failure: it may also be understood as the emergence of secondary orality accompanied by a resurgence of craft literacy. Shirley Brice Heath's *Ways With Words* applies ethnographic methods in a longitudinal study of literacy acquisition, uses, and teaching among rural Appalachian Piedmont black and white communities. Deborah Tannen's work applies and more recently questions the literate-oral dichotomy as defined and used within descriptive linguistics. Of particular value is her comparison of modes of interpretive analysis imparted by Western schooling with those used by indigenous modern Greeks, using a Greek-American group as a control for cultural values. Her findings were that Western-

schooled literates interpreted a film using analytic, formalist, and topicalized criteria — "bad choice of characters; nonconclusive ending" — while the indigenous Greeks interpreted the film as narrative and parable conveying a moral lesson. Through this comparison and others Tannen has come to question the simple dichtomoy dividing literate from oral cultures, modes of thought, or forms of language ("The Oral–Literate Continuum in Discourse," in *Spoken and Written Language*, 1–16; "The Myth of Orality and Literacy"). Similarly, Sylvia Scribner's and Michael Cole's *The Psychology of Literacy* appraises an African culture, the Vai, which evolved an indigenous writing system used exclusively by males for letter-writing purposes, and is a culture that has not, in contrast to the Afghan subjects of Luria's study, come into contact with Western literate schooling. Study of the literate but unschooled combination among the Vai led Scribner and Cole to dispute the view that any and all literacy automatically imparts changes in cognition or language. Instead, they propose, the particular tasks and language forms evolved in Western schooling have shaped specifically Western uses of literacy, and not the reverse. It is schooling, and not literacy per se, according to this view, that has shaped the Western literate mind. In contrast, Eric Havelock's work, beginning with *Preface to Plato* and continuing through *The Muse Learns to Write*, and Walter Ong's *Orality and Literacy*, and Jack Goody's *The Domestication of the Savage Mind* and *Interfaces Between the Written and the Oral* develop the hypothesis that there are general contours shared by "oral" and "literate" modes of thought and language. The view that there are recognizable shared patterns in literate versus oral discourse continues to be investigated, with growing recognition that defining the general contours of each mode of thought is a heuristic process rather than an empirical generalization based on statistical evidence. It is foolhardy to deny textual evidence of formulas shared by the "oral literature" of widely divergent cultures. It is equally foolhardy to claim that the formulas and genres sought and found by ethnographers and philologists are independent, natural occurrences rather than phenomena shaped in part by the conceptual constructs of the investigator. Jay Robinson provides a useful five-point working definition of literacy that comprises many of these questions: "(1) The ability to crack a code: to make sense of marks on paper; (2) the ability to derive information from that code; (3) the ability to derive personal, social, and cognitive meaning from the information derived; (4) the ability to act on such meanings; (5) the ability to make inferential and other cognitive structures from the meanings acquired in order to find new meanings" (in Bailey and Fosheim, eds., *Literacy for Life*, 16). More recently, Rosalind Thomas' *Oral Tradition and Written Record in Classical Athens*, Tony Lentz's *Orality and Literacy in Hellenic Greece*, and Jan Vansina's *Oral Tradition as History* have contributed to the definition of orality in Greek antiquity.

4. Two separate issues converge on these points: the evolution of the propositional and predicative statement, *logos*, whose essence was an independent copula; and the evolution of a theory of the truth of such statements that eventually came to restrict truth to statements thus constructed. The second of these developments — paradoxically, at least in the West — seems to have introduced an irreversible relativism into formal language uses and theories. Among the Preplatonic Greek philosophers, taxonomical, hierarchical, and metalinguistic conceptualizations of statements and kinds of statements (*logoi*) were linked, early on, with considerations of "truth value," that is, with the formalization of rules for constructed statements of truth.

Pace Gadamer's ironic "truth and method," I contend that formalizing truth proce-dures, or formulating truth as the product of a procedure, far from protecting truth, has continually instigated debates about which statements or arguments were true, and equivocations about which of several meanings of "truth" should be normative. Cicero alludes to this problem in the history of philosophical schools he provides in the *Academica*, when he talks about the abandonment of the search for a criterion of truth, a process he asserts began with Aristotle's "undermining the Forms."

Aristotle was the first among many to ponder the illogic of metaphor. That meta-phor, first and foremost among poetic devices, has long been a stumbling block for logicians, Walker Percy sums up in "Metaphor as Mistake." W. B. Sanford's *Am-biguity in Greek Literature* and Thomas Rosenmeyer's "Gorgias, Aeschylus, and *Apate*" provide meticulous surveys of uses and understandings of metaphoric and ambiguous language between the sixth and first centuries B.C. Only by the logical standards that converged in Aristotle's work, however, were metaphor and symbol puzzling but somehow powerful mistakes, "tropes" that turned and twisted away from "normal" language. Though the unease about metaphor and symbol was subse-quently muted within scriptural hermeneutics, with its highly developed conceptual-ization of allegorical, historical, moral, and spiritual meanings, the logical and analytical modern philosophical tradition has worried the problem once again. I. A. Richards ruminates over the meanings and power of metaphoric and more general symbolic uses of language in *The Philosophy of Rhetoric*, an examination that joins Peirce's and Saussure's opposing views of the symbolic within modern linguistic "science." Yet in modern times poetic language and "oral literature" have been viewed not as crafted "arts," *technai*, or tropes but instead as "primitive," as natural, as quintessentially unself-conscious. The modern hypostatization of "poetic language and linguistic indeterminacy" within anthropology and ethnography is worked out and exemplified by Paul Friedrich in *The Language Parallax*. Jerome Bruner's *Actual Minds, Possible Worlds* provides a similarly thoughtful and balanced view of the locus and ontology of "two fundamental modes" of thought: narrative and argument.

A growing literature on the precise chronology and deployment of the "to be" verb within the Preplatonic *logos*, in Plato, and in Aristotle brings textual evidence to bear on these otherwise speculative questions about the origin of Western concep-tions of truth, logic, propositions, and abstractions. Jacques Derrida's "The Supple-ment of the Copula: Philosophy Before Linguistics," Eric Havelock's "The Linguis-tic Task of the Presocratics," Charles Kahn's "The Greek Verb 'To Be' and the Concept of Being," Richard Robinson's *Plato's Earlier Dialectic*, G. E. L. Owen's "Plato and Parmenides on the Timeless Present" and "Plato on Not-Being," and J. L. Ackrill's "Plato and the Copula" provide a wide range of views of these complicated interrelations. Among the major subtopics in this debate are the meaning of predi-cation in the *Categories* versus earlier classical treatments, the validity of imposing a copular syntax not in the Greek on Preplatonic discourse on the grounds that the copula is "implicit," and the emergence of conscious named distinctions between existential and predicative senses of the verb "to be."

On the subject of *poiesis* as craft and as lying, Tom Rosenmeyer's "Gorgias, Aeschylus, and *Apate*" works out some of the possible connections between the assumption that something is made or crafted, and the belief that it is false. In particular, he proposes that *pseudos*, the false, and *apate*, intentional deceit, shift in meaning alongside *logos* during the fifth and fourth centuries, settling into a novel equilibrium in which *apate* comes to be associated with successful artifice, and *pseudos* with something that is rather neutrally "wrong," false, a mistake. To this etymological chronology I add "irony," utilizing an analysis that has grown out of the approaches developed by D. C. Muecke, G. G. Sedgwick, and J. A. K. Thomson. Of particular value has been the meticulous and probing treatment of *pseudos* and *eironikos* in Stanley Rosen's reading of Plato's *Sophist*.

5. Aristotle, *Rhetoric*, 1403. All references to Loeb translation unless otherwise indicated.

6. Aristotle, *Nichomachean Ethics*, 1124.

7. Cross-cultural studies as well as gender studies are directing attention to the details of these differences, which entail psychological as well as cultural patterns of language, thought, and behavior. In *The Muse Learns to Write*, Havelock proposes that the very concepts of self and identity that Westerners—or at least educated Westerners—have long held to be universal "may be an invention of the Socratic vocabulary" (114). A true statement must have a judge; knowledge, a knower. Jerome Bruner reflects on these matters from the standpoint of developmental psychology and particularly from the perspective of transactional models of the notion of self. Are we not taught very carefully, he asks, throughout our schooling, to figure things out for ourselves, to reflect on the acquisition of knowledge, to question and test perception and received information, to select, manipulate, and generate knowledge? Autonomy and knowledge gained through questioning and testing are placed at a premium in our conceptions of learning (*Actual Minds, Possible Worlds*, 131–32). In contrast, Jack Goody's *The Domestication of the Savage Mind*, Scribner and Cole's *The Psychology of Literacy*, and other cross-cultural studies find strongly hierarchical sources of knowledge and truth in most non-Western cultures; elders and religion most commonly enforce homogeneity, punish nonconformity, and reinforce collaborative modes of knowing, discoursing, and decision making. Cross-cultural studies of educated, literate cultures that have developed philosophical "systems" and philosophies of language, as in India, China, and Japan, will enhance an understanding of these complex relationships among cultural belief systems, formal philosophy and education, and practice.

8. H. M. Hubbell's translation and commentary in Loeb edition: *Orator*, xi, 36.

9. Walter Ong develops the apt phrase "residual logic" in *Ramus, Method, and the Decay of Dialogue*, and with it denotes an ongoing recursive reductiveness. A similar sequence is defined as "inherited knowledge" by Hegel in the preface to the *Phenomenology of Mind* (89–90):

> What was formerly an objective fact [*die Sache selbst*] is now only a single trace. . . . What in former days occupied the energies of men of mature mental abilities sinks to the level of information, exercises, and even pastimes, for children; and in this educational progress we can see the history of the world's culture delineated in faint outline. . . . Culture means nothing else than that this substance [the mind] gives itself its own self-consciousness, brings about its own inherent process and its own reflection into self.

10. A growing number of histories of this modern curriculum trace the separation of "skills" literacy training from literary study, a progression that Susan Jarratt has

termed the "third sophistic." See Arthur Appleby, *Tradition and Reform in the Teaching of English*, and James Berlin, *Rhetoric and Reality: Writing Instruction in American Colleges, 1900-1985*, for extended examinations of modern classroom rhetorics.

11. Parmenides, fragment 8. Translations of the Preplatonics are Kathleen Freeman's, in *Ancilla to the Pre-Socratic Philosophers*, which follows the numbering in Diels, *Fragmente der Vorsokratiker*, 5th ed. Occasional use of alternate translations from Kirk and Raven's *The Presocratic Philosophers*, is cited in the note in each case.

12. Heraclitus, fragments 93, 28.

13. I base these conjectures on two points and on a synthesis. First, Thomas Rosenmeyer's "Gorgias, Aeschylus, and *Apate*" puts some flesh on the bones of Havelock's observation that the prephilosophic Greeks seem completely without guile, or at least without specifically contrived, premeditated verbal guile. Rosenmeyer provides a chronology of changes in the meanings of *pseudos* and *apate* as associated with linguistic usage: poetry, rhetoric, philosophic discourse, epic, history. Though he doesn't focus pointedly on rhetoric, Rosenmeyer's analysis lays some groundwork for Havelock's observation that the Sophists were trying to adapt and perpetuate the audience psychology of the epic poetic performance, and that this was doomed to failure, since the Sophists' oratory could never cast the "total spell" required (*Preface to Plato*, 161, n. 25). Gorgias, Rosenmeyer notes, explicitly links such "word wizardry" with successful *apate*, perhaps for the first time naming one paradox that became a keystone of subsequent Western aesthetics—that a verbal or visual work of art is successful to the extent that it successfully imitates reality. In doing so perfectly the work of art, i.e., the "fabrication," is indistinguishable from reality, hence, in Western tradition, is a perfectly executed lie.

Second, I contend that rhetoric quickly came to be associated with lying because it was so obviously crafted, strategically planned, because it manipulated interchangeable parts as well as calculated audience responses for optimum effects. Given this dual history, rhetoric from its beginnings has had two seemingly opposite guises— that of the cunning, crafty, lying politician, and that of the beautiful, admirably crafted work of art in which both the speaker's persona and the language spoken are spellbindingly attractive. Kennedy's *Classical Rhetoric and Its Christian and Secular Tradition from Ancient to Modern Times* documents a cyclical pattern of "literaturization" of rhetoric that recurs in several classical periods. His analysis of this process is a valuable complement to Rosenmeyer's, which concentrates on the dramatists. Brian Vickers' recent *In Defence of Rhetoric* addresses the charges brought against rhetoric as being mere skills and lying, and defends rhetoric in traditional anti-Platonist terms. He does not link his otherwise excellent history of rhetoric to orality or literacy.

14. Aristotle, *On Interpretation*, 17a.

Chapter 1

1. Havelock, "The Linguistic Task of the Presocratics," 11; *Preface to Plato*, 308, n. 38. Also see Nussbaum, *The Fragility of Goodness*, for a more recent appraisal of the fluid boundaries dividing poetry, epic, rhetoric, and philosophy during this

period, and for an illuminating appraisal of Plato's uses of writing and the dialogue genre, in Interlude I and in chs. 6 and 7. Nussbaum provides an informative updating of the controversy surrounding Ryle's contention (in *Plato's Progress*) that the Platonic dialogues were "read aloud," and adds, "but some form of public performance may have taken place" (455, n. 23).

2. Havelock, "The Linguistic Task," 11; *The Literate Revolution*, 18–19.

3. Parmenides, fragment 1. On the frame narrative in Parmenides' fragment there is an encouraging breakdown in an earlier consensus that it is a literary allegorical convention. Havelock argues it is Homeric, provided to lend familiarity ("Parmenides and Odysseus"). Harrison conjectures more literal truth to it, and places Parmenides in a priestly tradition (*Themis*, 507). Kirk and Raven follow the philological view that this "goddess" and other figures such as Plato's Diotima are allegorical, (265–68): "as Diels suggested, the allegorical form is borrowed from oracle-and-mystery-literature" (268). Waithe's *A History of Women Philosophers*, vol. 1, provides a review of the literature during the past two centuries, summarizing the confident nineteenth-century view that Diotima, Aspasia, and other women were allegorical figures, and citing more recent scholarship disputing that view (83–116).

4. Fragments 116, 117, 118.

5. Havelock, *Preface to Plato*, 288.

6. Hymn to Hermes, in Hesiod, *Homeric Hymns and Homerica*, 363–406, ll. 533–59.

7. Parmenides, fragment 6.

8. Havelock, *Preface to Plato*, 243–46. Also see Stephen Tyler's "The Vision Quest in the West" for an illuminating exegesis of Western sight-knowledge metaphors (*The Unspeakable*, 149–70).

9. In his *Lives and Opinions of Eminent Philosophers*, Diogenes Laertius records that after Aristotle was impeached at the age of seventy for impiety, he was exiled and committed suicide by draught of aconite. Also see I. F. Stone, *The Trial of Socrates*, for a reinterpretation of Socrates' trial as the expulsion of a reactionary antidemocratic elitist.

10. For example, Olson, "Mind and Media"; Goody, *The Domestication of the Savage Mind*; Ong, *Orality and Literacy*; Havelock, *The Muse Learns to Write* and "The Linguistic Task of the Presocratics"; Heath, *Ways With Words*; and Tannen, "The Myth of Orality and Literacy."

11. Havelock, "The Linguistic Task," 9–12. Havelock extends this milieu through Socrates, hence his adoption of "Preplatonic" to denote figures who did not write to be read.

12. A position taken by I. F. Stone in *The Trial of Socrates* and W. Robert Connor, *Thucydides*, among recent scholars. Havelock's treatment of Antiphon in *The Liberal Temper* further illustrates the range of political and moral sensibilities even among the Sophists. The different portraits of Socrates in classical histories and literary works are receiving renewed attention by historians and philosophers. Thomas C. Brickhouse and Nicholas D. Smith's recent *Socrates on Trial* follows I. F. Stone's *The Trial of Socrates*, for a reinterpretation of Socrates' trial as the expulsion of a reactionary antidemocratic elitist.

13. Havelock, *Preface to Plato*, ch. 15, and Gadamer, *Truth and Method*, characterize the evolution of philosophy and rhetoric along with different deployments of

writing, as a struggle for the control of education and, through education, of Athenian youth. Gadamer expresses the relation between grammar and culture in this period as an increment of detachments. "For only a grammar that is based on logic will distinguish between the real and the metaphorical meaning of a word. What originally constituted the basis of the life of language and made up its logical productivity, the spontaneous and inventive seeking out of similarities by means of which it is possible to order things, is now pushed to the side and instrumentalised into a rhetorical figure called metaphor. The struggle between philosophy and rhetoric for the training of Greek youth, which was decided with the victory of Attic philosophy, has also this side to it, namely that the thinking about language becomes the object of a grammar and rhetoric that have already recognised the ideal of scientific concept formation. Thus the sphere of linguistic meanings begins to become detached from the sphere of things encountered in linguistic form" (392).

14. Parmenides, fragment 5.

15. T. S. Eliot, "Burnt Norton" l. 62, in *The Four Quartets*, (New York: Harcourt, Brace, 1976). Heraclitus, fragments 1, 2, 31, 44, 45, 50, 72, 87, 114, and 115 further illustrate the multiple senses of *logos* as law, unity, harmony, and hidden order in the *kosmos*.

16. For different views of the implicit and explicit "is" among the Preplatonics see Havelock, "The Linguistic Task"; Kahn, "The Greek Verb 'To Be' and the Concept of Being"; and Kirk and Raven's *The Presocratic Philosophers*, distinguishing predicative and existential senses of the "to be" verb (269).

17. Parmenides, fragments 7, 8.

18. Heraclitus, fragment 32.

19. Parmenides, fragments 7, 8; Heraclitus, fragment 54.

20. Parmenides, fragment 6.

21. Anaxagoras, fragment 17.

22. Parmenides, fragment 19.

23. Heraclitus, fragment 32.

24. Xenophanes, fragments 24–27.

25. Parmenides, fragment 3.

26. Fragments 7, 8.

27. Fragment 8.

28. Fragments 7, 8.

29. Fragment 19.

30. Heraclitus, fragment 30.

31. Parmenides, fragment 6.

32. Heraclitus, fragments 43, 41.

33. Heraclitus, fragments 1, 2.

34. Plato, *Symposium*, 209e–212c.

35. Heraclitus, fragment 1.

36. Fragment 36.

37. Fragment 37.

38. *The Lives and Opinions of Eminent Philosophers*, 9, 378–79.

39. Heraclitus, fragment 12.

40. Fragment 93.

41. Fragments 54, 55.

42. Parmenides, fragment 1.

43. *Gorgias*, 524b.

44. Kirk and Raven, fragment 8.

45. Heidegger, *Early Greek Thinking*, 23–25.

46. Havelock, *Preface to Plato*, 197–233.

47. Havelock, *The Muse Learns to Write*, 94–97, and Rosen, *Plato's Sophist*, 31–48, provide needed retranslations that convey the oddity of the literal Greek without interpolated copular verbs and pronoun subjects.

48. The literature on the early Greek copula now spans several fields. Of particular value in disentangling Preplatonic from subsequent uses, in addition to Kirk and Raven's analysis of the Parmenidean *esti*, are Derrida, "The Supplement of the Copula: Philosophy Before Linguistics"; Kahn, "The Greek Verb 'To Be' and the Concept of Being"; Moravcsik, "Being and Meaning in the Sophist"; and Ackrill, "Plato and the Copula."

49. Rosenmeyer, "Gorgias, Aeschylus, and *Apate*," 234.

50. Havelock, *Preface to Plato*, 260–305; *The Muse Learns to Write*, 94–97.

51. Ong, *Orality and Literacy*, 33–57. Also see David Olson, "Mind and Media."

52. Parmenides, fragment 8, Kirk and Raven translation.

53. Heraclitus, fragments 28, 40, 42.

54. Xenophanes, fragments 12, 1.

55. Rosenmeyer, in "Gorgias, Aeschylus and *Apate*," argues the plausibility of the view that Homeric "religion" was itself quite new, especially in the form given it in Athenian drama, and that both Homeric and dramatic myths were produced and consumed more in literary than cultic religious terms. Aeschylus, he emphasizes, has been depicted as an agnostic, and perhaps uses Zeus as he does because, as a new "literary" god, he was safe. "Aeschylus avails himself of Zeus to avoid a religious commitment" (252). De Kerckhove's work on dialogue in Greek tragedy supplements these views with the contention that drama was additionally transitional, mediatory, in preparing the Attic consciousness for linearity, causality, and sequence of the kinds that literacy requires for reading ("A Theory of Greek Tragedy").

56. Rosenmeyer notes for example that Solon reputedly practiced *historia*, which was then conceived of as an "autobiographical and confessional" mode, and regarded as lesser than the *muthos* of drama. Connor's *Thucydides* provides a similarly revisionist analysis of Thucydides' historiography as the vehicle for an antidemocratic "polemic." On several counts these distinctions present a stark contrast to nineteenth- and twentieth-century genre boundaries and values that promote the conception of literary discourse as more expressive and poetic, and historical discourse as flatly factual. The early Greek view of history seems to link flat factuality with "subjectivity," personal polemic, and rhetoric. In any of these cases, as Havelock proposes, "to call it literature in our sense is a misnomer" (*Preface to Plato*, 39).

57. Havelock, *The Literate Revolution*, 26. I. J. Gelb defines a similar calligraphic sensibility in *A Study of Writing*.

58. Havelock, *The Literate Revolution*, 27.

59. Ibid., 97.

60. Ong, *Orality and Literacy*, 130.

61. Ibid., 96. Also see Belenky et al., *Women's Ways of Knowing*, for a cogent appraisal of how ways of knowing are shaped, and hobbled, by access to available written and spoken discourse modes.

62. Havelock, *The Literate Revolution*, 331–36; *Preface to Plato*, 55–56, n. 16; Kennedy, "The Earliest Rhetorical Handbooks," 169–78.

63. Havelock, *The Literate Revolution*, 25, for all quotations in this paragraph.

64. *Rhetoric*, 1402a.

65. *Phaedrus*, 267a.

66. *Rhetoric*, 1402a.

67. See Kennedy, *Classical Rhetoric and Its Christian and Secular Tradition from Ancient to Modern Times* and *The Art of Persuasion in Ancient Greece*, for comprehensive accounts of what is known of rhetoricians in the fifth century. His accounts of Antiphon, Gorgias, and Isocrates are especially helpful summaries of technical developments during this era, as are Havelock's in *The Liberal Temper*. "Exactly what went on in the schools of the sophists is not well known, but a central activity was certainly listening to the sophist speak or reading versions of his speeches, followed by the memorization or imitation of these works as models" (*Classical Rhetoric*, 26). Along with Havelock's analyses of fifth-century Greek schools and literacy, and the "writing class" vase of 480 B.C. (*Preface to Plato*, 36–60; *The Literate Revolution*, 185–207), Kennedy's remarks contribute a welcome cautiousness to any characterizations of rhetorical, literary, or literacy training during this period.

68. In addition to Kennedy's and Havelock's histories of rhetorical and literacy training, even a partial survey of histories of Greek education reveals diverse interpretations of equally diverse records. See for example Davidson, *The Education of the Greek People*; Drever, *Greek Education, Its Practice and Principles*; Kenneth Freeman, *Schools of Hellas*; Guthrie, *The Sophists*; Jaeger, *Paideia*; Lynch, *Aristotle's School*; and Marrou, *A History of Education in Antiquity*.

69. Summary, sec. 10, in Kathleen Freeman, *Ancilla*. Also see de Romilly, *Magic and Rhetoric in Ancient Greece*, for further documentation of the sophistry-magic-rhetoric associations in this period.

70. Gorgias, "Encomium" summary, 11.

71. "On Being," in Freeman, *Ancilla*.

72. Parmenides, fragments 7, 8.

73. Gorgias, "Encomium" summary, 11. See Enos, "The Epistemology of Gorgia's Rhetoric," for a defense of the philosophical substantiveness of Gorgias' thought.

74. Parmenides, fragments 7, 8.

75. An alternate middle position is defined by Thucydides, *Peloponnesian War*, II, 40: "The great impediment to action is not discussion, but the want of that knowledge which is gained by discussion preparatory to action. For we have a peculiar power of thinking before we act and of acting too, whereas other men are courageous from ignorance, but hesitate upon reflection" Jowett trans. in *The Greek Historians*, ed. Francis R. B. Godolphin, Vol. 1, New York: Random House, 1942. Havelock notes a similar implicit ambivalence toward intellectuals and intellectualizing reflected in Pericles' funeral speech, where he detects a slight note of apology in the line "We Athenians can intellectualise without sacrifice of manliness" (*Preface to Plato*, 286).

76. I borrow this deft phrase from Enos, "The Epistemology of Gorgias's Rhetoric," 41.

77. Empedocles, fragment 17.

78. Gorgias, "On Being," in Freeman, *Ancilla*.

79. Parmenides, fragments 7, 8. Kirk-Raven translation.

80. Empedocles, fragment 123. Also see Havelock, *The Muse Learns to Write*, 79–82, and *Preface to Plato*, 104–14, for cognate explications of the Muses in Hesiod and earlier tradition.

81. Though there are Homeric uses of *rhetor* and *rhetorike* to denote a powerful speaker or powerful speech, a case can be made that there is not as yet a sense of an art of rhetoric. Havelock provides additional chronologies for Hellenic words about words. In *The Literate Revolution*, 32, n. 5, he cites post-Homeric beginnings for *phthegma* and *rhema* along with the Homeric *epos, muthos, logos, phatis*, and *rhesis*. All these words for word, speech, or utterances, coexisted without any one being designated as a word for a single word until, at the very earliest, Plato. Even in Plato, Havelock contends, it is unclear whether the referent is a single word.

82. For a clarifying account of the *Categories* as Aristotle's list of words for words, and for analysis of the ambiguities in his usage — some categories are ontological while others seem to be predicative — see Ackrill's "Commentary" to *Aristotle's Categories and On Interpretation*, 71–81.

Chapter 2

1. I refer to "Plato" rather than "Socrates" for the most part because my focus is on the incremental critical positions which Plato evolves throughout the dialogues. A part of this pattern is his characterization of Socrates. For a concise review of ontological, dramatic, and predicationalist approaches to Plato, see Rosen, *Plato's Sophist*, 1–48. Rosen defends "dramatic phenomenology" as the most profitable approach to the dialogues, and argues that it allows us, among other things, to disregard obvious differences between the Socrates of one dialogue and another, and between the Socrates of the dialogues and the Socrates of other classical biographers. The one disadvantage of this approach is that it doesn't get us any further along in our knowledge of Socrates.

2. Havelock, "The Linguistic Task of the Presocratics," both summarizes this debate and ties it to the argument that the Preplatonics and their audiences were far from fully literate.

3. *Eikos* (apparent truth or an argument of probability), *phainesthai* (to appear to be, to give the appearance), *dokeo* (to give a false impression, to misrepresent oneself), *doxa* (belief and opinion, as opposed to truth or knowledge), *eidolon* (semblance, idol, unreal image) — these new terms, and new uses of old terms, identify what Plato believed was resulting from rhetoric and literacy as inculcators of metalinguistic self-consciousness.

4. Havelock, *Preface to Plato*, 281–84; 306–7, n. 8.

5. Plato, *Sophist* (Loeb), 268b.

6. I have adapted the term "instrumentalist" from Gadamer, *Truth and Method*, who uses the term to define an incorrect, because incomplete, model of language and its use: "An instrumentalist theory of signs that sees words and concepts as *handy tools* has missed the point of the hermeneutic phenomenon" (364). "There is a development from the complete unconsciousness of language that we find in classical Greece to the instrumentalist devaluation of language that we find in modern times" (365). "It can be stated as a fundamental principle that wherever words assume a

mere sign function, the original connection between speaking and thinking, with which we are concerned, is changed into an instrumental relationship" (392).

7. Havelock, *Preface to Plato*, 158.

8. Plato, *Phaedrus*, 275d, 278d.

9. Plato, *Letter VII*, 344c-d.

10. Ibid., 344a-d.

11. Ibid., 341a-b.

12. Havelock, *Preface to Plato*, 162-63, nn. 27, 28; 306, n. 8.

13. See Arrowsmith's commentary on the Old and New Education following his translation of *The Clouds*, 135-58.

14. Plato, *Phaedrus*, 274c-276c, *Letter VII*, 341a-345b; *Laws*, 809b-812b.

15. See Barrett, *The Illusion of Technique*, 1-25; Gadamer on *techne*, passim; and Ong on method (*Ramus*) and on technologizing the word (*Orality and Literacy*).

16. Havelock, *The Literate Revolution in Greece and Its Cultural Consequences*, 3-38, 185-207; "The Linguistic Task of the Presocratics," 1-6.

17. Havelock, *Preface to Plato*, 39, nn. 3-4.

18. Havelock, *Preface to Plato*, 55, n. 16. Also see Kennedy, "The Earliest Rhetorical Handbooks," 169-78.

19. Havelock, *Preface to Plato*, 39; 54, n. 10.

20. Havelock, *Literate Revolution*, 201-5. For an older interpretation of this image, exemplifying the assumption of early full literacy to which Havelock objects, see Freeman, *Schools of Hellas*, 50-54.

21. Havelock, *Literate Revolution*, 203.

22. Havelock, *Preface to Plato*, 55, n. 16.

23. See, Ryle, *Plato's Progress*, 115-17.

24. *Phaedrus*, 257a.

25. Havelock, *Literate Revolution*, 202-5.

26. Plato, *Phaedrus*, 275a.

27. Havelock, *Literate Revolution*, 185-207; Smith, *The Art of Rhetoric in Alexandria*, 124-25; Havelock, *Preface to Plato*, 52-60, nn. 6-24; 117, 127; Diringer, *The Book Before Printing*, 228-242; Kenyon, *Books and Readers in Ancient Greece and Rome*, 25. Thomas, *Oral and Written Record in Classical Athens*, provides an ample extension of these earlier sources.

28. Havelock, *Preface to Plato*, 54, nn. 14-16. Gadamer's *Philosophical Hermeneutics*, and Havelock in personal correspondence, defend *Letter VII* as an account, if not of Plato's views directly, then of positions consonant with his views in the dialogues. *Letter VII* may express views developed within Plato's school after his death. Gadamer reviews the literature on both sides of the *Letter VII* controversy.

29. Havelock, *Preface to Plato*, 127.

30. Two literary examples illustrate resistance to priestly and hierarchical authority. The priest Calchas figures prominently in the *Iliad*, the *Agamemnon*, and *Iphigenia at Aulis*, where his interpretations of oracular statements and sacrificial auguries are roundly questioned and he is charged with word-cleverness. Likewise, Oedipus' problematic status as a stranger and rescuer, but also as a man who places his own wits above traditional authorities and religion, provides a classic case of the tension created in any culture when "intelligence" supplants "tradition" at the center of political power.

31. Smith, *The Art of Rhetoric in Alexandria*, 41-42.

32. Derrida, "The Filial Inscription," *Dissemination*, 75–94; Goody, *The Domestication of the Savage Mind*, 43–51; Havelock, *Preface to Plato*, 56, n. 17.

33. See Goody, *The Domestication of the Savage Mind*, 50.

34. Havelock, *Preface to Plato*, 115–33.

35. See Kennedy, *Classical Rhetoric and Its Christian and Secular Tradition from Ancient to Modern Times*, 10–15, and "The Earliest Rhetorical Handbooks," 33–35, for a defense of "rhetoric," albeit unconscious or tacit, in the Homeric era, and a summary of ancient and modern discussions of its existence.

36. Havelock, "The Linguistic Task of the Presocratics," 1–20; *Preface to Plato*, 115–33; 161, n. 25; 178–82.

37. See Benardete in Plato, *The Being of the Beautiful*, 86–87; and Booth, *The Rhetoric of Fiction*, 3. Rosen's *Plato's Sophist* and Nussbaum's *The Fragility of Goodness* also provide ample commentary on the use of the dialogue form by Plato.

38. Plato, *Phaedrus*, 272d.

39. Plato, *Gorgias*, 459b–c.

40. Ibid., 463d. Cf. Aristotle, *Rhetoric*, 1356a: "Rhetoric is as it were an offshoot of Dialectic and of the science of Ethics, which may reasonably be called Politics." For attention to the "counterpart" (*antistrophe*) definition of rhetoric that also figures prominently in Aristotle's schematization, also see Price, "Some Antistrophes to the Rhetoric."

41. Plato, *Sophist*, 268a.

42. Havelock, *Preface to Plato*, 251.

43. Ong, *Interfaces of the Word*, 44–47, defines this apt contribution to modern terms for the interpenetration of thought and language.

44. See the discussion of Plato's and other negative views of mimesis in Havelock, *Preface to Plato*, 20–35; 57, n. 22; 159, 249.

45. Plato, *Phaedrus*, 266d–267a.

46. Ibid. Cf. Aristotle, *Rhetoric*, 1402a, where these probabilistic proofs are attributed to Protagoras.

47. Plato, *Phaedrus*, 267d–e.

48. Aristophanes, *The Clouds*, 91; Plato, *Apology*, 18b–c. Aristotle disclaims this use of the Protagoran *eikos* at *Rhetoric*, 1402a.

49. Plato, *Phaedrus*, 265d–e. See Gadamer, "Language as Horizon of a Hermeneutic Ontology," *Truth and Method*, 397–431. He elaborates on the root *horizomenos*, and its transformation in Plato's treatment.

50. Plato, *Phaedrus*, 265d–e.

51. Ibid., 266c.

52. See Rosen, *Plato's Sophist*, 42–57, 256–314, and Robinson, *Plato's Earlier Dialectic*, 69–92, for extended accounts of the different depictions of dialectic among the dialogues, and of their import. Stokes, *Plato's Socratic Conversations*, takes up the argument that Plato's dialogue form may be more and not less complex than subsequent logic.

53. Aristotle, *Rhetoric*, 1357b, where Aristotle notes the appropriateness of the term: "for in the old language *tekmar* and *peras* have the same meaning."

54. Ryle, *Plato's Progress*, 10–117. Robinson, *Plato's Earlier Dialectic*, 88–92 gives a brief history of the origin of dialectic and proposes that Socrates is the first to define the "what is X?" paradigm. Also see Havelock's appraisal of Aristotle's account of the Megarians in "The Linguistic Task of the Presocratics."

55. Plato, *Gorgias*, 458d–459a. See du Bois, *Sowing the Body*, on Derrida concerning the public and private contexts of Plato's philosopher and philosophizing.

56. See Muecke, *Irony*; Sedgewick, *Of Irony: Especially in Drama*; and Thomson, *A Study of Irony in Drama*, for extensive etymological summaries and analysis of the occurrence of the term in the classical and subsequent periods.

57. See Havelock, *Language and Thought in Early Greek Philosophy*, 7–15; Ricoeur, *Interpretation Theory: Discourse and the Surplus of Meaning*, 32 and passim; Ong, *Interfaces of the Word*, 78–116, 277–302, for lucid and provocative comments on textuality, distanciation, alienation, concomitant reflection, and their relationship to the evolution of abstract thought.

58. Saussure, *General Course in Linguistics*, 69.

59. Aristotle, *Rhetoric*, 1355b.

60. I have adapted this characterization from Rosen, *Plato's Sophist*, 322.

61. See Ricoeur, *Interpretation Theory: Discourse and the Surplus of Meaning*, 32 and passim for a useful history and analysis of the notion of semantic autonomy. Olson, "Mind and Media," appraises the range of assumptions about text, content, and meaning that are inaugurated by Plato's and subsequent analyses of writing and cognition. Also relevant is Hirsch, *Validity in Interpretation*, and *per contra*, Derrida, *Of Grammatology*, 67–87.

62. Aristotle, *On Interpretation*, 17a.

63. Plato, *Sophist*, 268a.

64. Ibid., 260a–b.

65. Ibid., 258b and ff.

66. Ibid., 260b–c.

67. Ibid., 264d; my emphasis.

68. Ibid., 259d–e.

69. Ibid., 253e.

70. Ibid., 254a, 268a.

71. Plato, *Theaetetus*, 143b–c. Benardete's translation and commentary on the *Theaetetus* in *The Being of the Beautiful* provides a painstaking analysis of the subleties in this frame (86–88): "As a Megarian, Euclides recognizes nothing but speech; . . . in a dialogue about knowledge, the body in its manifestations of what the soul harbors seems to be suppressed along with the silent thinking of the mind. . . . Only the explicit and utterable are admitted by Euclides or acknowledged by Theaetetus and Theodorus." Benardete also provides a good overall summary of the diversity of narrative methods used among the dialogues, from Socrates' prominence in the *Protagoras* to his virtual elimination here. "In eliminating Socrates Euclides also eliminates himself."

72. In "The Sophists and Relativism" Bett provides a fastidiously documented defense of the contention that the conventionalist views promoted by some of the Sophists such as Cratylus, and criticized by Plato and others, cannot with any precision be termed "relativism," and states that to do so is a misleading anachronism. Friedrich's *The Language Parallax* provides a lucid counterpoint to this position by illustrating cross-cultural, psychopoetic "paleolithic" expressions of "linguistic indeterminacy," examined jointly from the perspectives of poetics and anthropology.

73. See Benardete in Plato, *The Being of the Beautiful*, 143–48; Rosen, *Plato's Sophist*, 61–69, 212–25, 314; and Havelock, *Preface to Plato*, 258–75, for comple-

mentary illustrations of these replacements. Tyler's "The Vision Quest in the West" (in *The Unspeakable* 149-70) appraises the centrality of visual metaphors for knowledge to Western conceptualizations of epistemology. Ong and Havelock provide complementary accounts of "the eye" and "the ear" in relation to the impact of literacy on the visual apprehension of words.

74. *Sophist*, 260a and passim. There is a growing recent literature on Plato's treatment of predication, the meanings of his technical grammatical and logical terms, and the implicit linguistic theory which lay behind his and his contemporaries' treatments of discourse. It is unfortunate that much scholarship has imposed predicationalist and analytic logical categories on Plato and the Preplatonics and found them lacking. The nature and sources of this bias, and of the inquiry into the restrictive characteristics of the Aristotelian tradition, are examined in Cherniss, *Aristotle's Criticism of PreSocratic Philosophy*, and *Aristotle's Criticism of Plato and the Academy*; Mates, *Stoic Logic*, 1-10; Robinson, *Plato's Earlier Dialectic*, 1-92; Vlastos, *Plato I: Metaphysics and Epistemology*; Bluck, *Plato's Sophist*; Derrida, "The Supplement of the Copula"; Rosen, *Plato's Sophist*, 29-57, 229-68; and Havelock, "The Linguistic Task of the Presocratics," 40-82. The Bluck and Rosen studies provide evidence for the extremely fluid and neologistic status of Plato's terms. Two points in particular are noteworthy. There is growing agreement that an explicit concept and definition of predication, essential to a grammar based on parts of speech, does not antedate Aristotle. And Bluck and Rosen agree that the *einai* and variant "to be" or "being" terms, even as used by Plato, do not function as a fully independent copula. Havelock maintains that the copula is explicit and independent after Parmenides. Robinson posits that Socrates originated the "What is an X?" question, but notes that the verb "distinguish" or "determine" occurs as much as "define" (*horizomeno*) in stating this question. None of these terms, it should be noted, is a "to be" verb. Thus Robinson's analysis complements Bluck's and Rosen's, rather than contradicting them. The controversial claims on both sides of this issue are addressed with very different purposes by Rosen, *Plato's Sophist*, 29-48, and Havelock, *Preface to Plato*, 258-61.

75. However, see du Bois, *Sowing the Body*, 169-83, for an analysis of an insidious appropriation of metaphors for reproduction that can be taken as evidence of Plato's misogyny. The debates concerning Plato's feminism are reviewed with cogency and detail by Vlastos in "Was Plato a Feminist?"; he provides a short bibliography of works on both sides of this debate.

76. Plato, *Sophist*, 260b, 262d, 264a.

77. Ibid., 261d.

78. Ibid., 259e.

79. Ryle, *Plato's Progress*, 271. Rosen, *Plato's Sophist*, 29-48, also notes that the ambiguity of formal grammatical terms in Plato, a function of their novelty and lack of standardization, remains a problem in translation, e.g., Plato, *Sophist*, 252a-b, and 261e, n. 1.

80. Plato, *Theaetetus*, 149a.

81. Ibid., 151b-c.

82. E.g., *Phaedrus*, 277a. However, see du Bois, *Sowing the Body*, ch. 2, sec. 3 for a discussion of the "field" and "planting" metaphors as usurpations of female activities, traits, and thought. Per contra, in *Therapeutic Discourse and Socratic Dia-*

logue, Maranhão explicates a benign and curative function of Socrates' theory and practice of dialogue that can instruct and enlighten contemporary, reductive therapeutic discourses.

83. Plato, *Phaedrus*, 278a.

84. Ibid., 275d.

85. Ibid., 277a.

86. Ibid., 277d.

87. *Letter VII*, 344d.

88. Ibid., 341c.

89. Ibid., 344a.

90. Ibid., 340d.

91. *Sophist*, 237a.

92. Kierkegaard, *The Concept of Irony*, 202–3.

93. Plato, *Sophist*, 268c–d.

94. Kierkegaard, *The Concept of Irony*, 338. Cf. Ricoeur, *Interpretation Theory*, 32, who defends distanciation and alienation in a parallel and apt characterization of the same relationship: "Hermeneutics begins where dialogue ends."

95. "Notes Toward a Supreme Fiction," in *The Collected Poems of Wallace Stevens* (New York: Knopf, 1975), 387.

Chapter 3

1. On the links between convention, belief, and behavior, and particularly on the point of their conscious versus unconscious learning, see Gadamer, *Truth and Method*, 377; Bateson, *Mind in the Waters*, 162; Rappaport, "The Sacred in Human Evolution," 32.

2. Heath, *Ways With Words*, 113–48, and passim; Piaget, *Genetic Epistemology*; Scribner and Cole, *The Psychology of Literacy*; Olson and Astington, "Children's Acquisition of Metalinguistic and Metacognitive Verbs"; Rosch and Lloyd, eds., *Cognition and Categorization*; and Tannen, "The Myth of Orality and Literacy," all provide differing expositions of the still widely debated question of linguistic universals that is so central to the study of language acquisition and to questions of linguistic relativism.

3. *Rhetoric*, 1356a, 1355a–b.

4. *On Interpretation*, 16a.

5. Ibid., 17a.

6. The effects of this incremental distanciation from immediate experience and immersion in a shared but unreflected-upon consciousness have been appraised with renewed attention at least since the Kant–Hegel debate concerning the *ding an sich* — the thing-in-itself. Kierkegaard's appraisal of Socrates' dialectical vacuum pump is simultaneously a critique of Hegel's promotion of distanciation in the name of reflection, of consciousness, and of controlled mediation. Sartre's *en soi* and *pour soi* are lineal descendants of this debate as well, and bear further attention as one of the models of consciousness and self that is grounded in reflective distanciation.

Ultimately, analytic separation from the Other can effect alienation from self as well. The relativizing, as distinct from idealizing, effects of such consciousness and analytic distance are addressed in Kant's *Fundamental Principles of the Metaphysics of Morals*. He argues that the comparative study of morals as an empirical, "anthropological" inquiry will introduce a fatal relativism into morality, moral reasoning, and moral principles. In a manner very like Aristotle's he establishes a "twofold metaphysic": a metaphysic of nature and a metaphysic of morals. Just as each science will have an empirical and a rational part, ethics will have an empirical part, practical anthropology, and a rational part, morality (4). He then asks "whether it is not of the utmost necessity to construct a pure moral philosophy, perfectly cleared of everything which is only empirical, and which belongs to anthropology. . . . Yet in as far as it rests even in the least degree on an empirical basis, perhaps only as to a motive, such a precept, while it may be a practical rule, can never called a moral law" (5). This segment of the argument concludes with an assertion that directly parallels subsequent distinctions based on *an sich* and *en soi*: "For in order that an action should be morally good, it is not enough that it *conform* to the moral law, but it must also be done *for the sake of the law*" (7). In this view of morality an ethics as products of pure thought and will, and not as derivations of empirical investigation and knowledge — anthropology, psychology — there is undeniable absolutism. Nonetheless, Kant's insistent separation of moral thought from empirical investigation and analytics provides a counterpoint to Aristotle's position. Aristotle argues for the derivation of moral laws from empirical "anthropological" investigation, not anticipating the problem of pluralism and the absence of a criterion of judgment that this kind of analytic tends toward, a pattern that may have some bearing as well on Cicero's report that Aristotle was allegedly among the first to undermine the Forms.

7. Bateson, "Observations of a Cetacean Community," 162.

8. In *The Concept of Mind*, Ryle distinguishes "knowing that" and "knowing how" — a similar difference but not quite to the same point (25–61). See also Yaden and Templeton, eds., *Metalinguistic Awareness and Beginning Literacy*, for ample empirical evidence of the influence of beliefs and attitudes upon linguistic behavior. Bateson's concept of "deutero learning" — learning how to learn — also parallels these distinctions.

9. *On Interpretation*, 16a.

10. Havelock, *The Literate Revolution in Greece and Its Cultural Consequences*, 48, 64.

11. *Rhetoric*, 1355b, defending rhetoric as a neutral *techne*, and 1402a, denouncing the Protagoran *eikos*, are two of many instances of this antiphonal relationship.

12. *Cratylus*, 440c.

13. Antiphon, fragment 44, from "Truth," trans. Havelock, in *The Liberal Temper in Greek Politics*.

14. A subject addressed in Havelock's chapter on Antiphon in *The Liberal Temper*, and in the concluding chapter to *Preface to Plato*.

15. *On Interpretation*, 16b; my emphasis.

16. Ibid., 16a.

17. Ibid.

18. *On Interpretation*, 21a.

19. Ibid.

20. Aristotle, *Categories*, 1a–b. Aristotle's attempt to avoid Plato's unity of notional "essence" and ontological "existence" is partially successful, but is equally noteworthy as just that, an avoidance of Plato's theory of the autonomous existence of ideas as fundamental essences. There is an extensive literature on this, to which I cannot do justice in a note. The *Posterior Analytics*, 99b–100b, provides a useful collateral account of universal ideas (*katholou*) and first principles (*archai*). These are said to be apprehended by faculties in the mind which are neither innate—*pace* Plato's reminiscence—nor derived from any higher plane of knowledge deductively. They arise, says Aristotle, from sense perception—*aisthesis*—which builds up from individual percepts universals that finally begin to be present in the mind and subsequently in direct perception. "Because although it is the particular we perceive, the act of perception involves the universal, e.g. 'man,' not 'a man, Callias.'" According to Aristotle, this incremental process finally yields "the indivisible genera or universals [*ta amere ste ai ta katholou*]." *Metaphysics* 980b and 1014b provide parallel definitions, the latter with an explicit allusion to the *Categories*. Cherniss, "Diaeresis, Definition, and Demonstration," provides a valuable account of the differences between Plato and Aristotle on these matters, albeit one which emphasizes Aristotle's inconsistencies and failures on this issue. Aristotle boldly "denies the identification of existence and essence" (2), then goes on to conflate common (*koine*) predicables with universals (45), to posit "that ideas arise out of the mind and are then abstracted as intelligible forms" (78), and to imply a separate autonomy of ideas when he says that *diaersis* cannot demonstrate them, because they are givens and thereby undemonstrable (81).

Evans, *Aristotle's Concept of Dialectic*, takes as its subject the ontological–logical aspects of Aristotle's dialectic. While I do not agree entirely with this characterization, Evans' commentary is a valuable corrective to the analytic philosophers' adoption—indeed, distortion—of Aristotle as their man for all seasons, the formalist par excellence. Rosen, *Plato's Sophist*, takes great care to correct the errors of "those translators who render these allusions in the formal mode and thereby make Aristotle concerned exclusively with the words of the definition, rather than with the things which those definitions represent. . . . He has some substantive points to make about things; and *considerations of language are invoked to this end*" (114–15; my emphasis).

Ackrill, *Aristotle's Categories and On Interpretation*, treats most of Aristotle's comments in the *Categories* as statements about things rather than words, whether consciously or unconsciously, and refers the treatment in the *Categories* to the *Topics* and *Metaphysics* where, he remarks, "the discussion of substance goes a good bit deeper than this discussion in the *Categories*" (81). While referring the ontology of the *Categories* to the *Metaphysics* helps us understand the flaws or "superficiality" of the *Categories*' metaphysics, it does not greatly illuminate Aristotle's efforts to construct a grammar based on the separation of logic from ontology. However unsuccessful that effort may be in modern philosophical terms, it has been enormously influential in grammar and rhetorical logic.

21. I compromise here among three interpretations of these relationships, exemplified by Cooke's Introduction to Aristotle's *Categories* and *On Interpretation*, 1–4; Ackrill, *Aristotle's Categories and On Interpretation*, 71, 115; and Cherniss, *Aristotle's Criticism of Plato and the Academy*, 2, 7.

22. I cannot attempt a comprehensive summary of the extensive history and technical literature on this term, its meaning, its centrality to Aristotelian and subsequent logic, and the metaphysical problems it generates. For useful analyses, see Evans, *Aristotle's Concept of Dialectic*, 9–16, 105–13; and Ackrill, *Aristotle's Categories and On Interpretation*. Evans' discussion is particularly useful on the problem of translating *ousia* as "isness," "essence," "substance," or "being." It alternates contextually among these meanings; Evans suggests that Aristotle's usage is not entirely consistent.

23. Aristotle, *Categories*, 1b; Augustine, *Confessions IV*, 16.

24. Cf. *Metaphysics*, 194b–195b; *On Coming to Be and Passing Away*, 335a–b.

25. *Rhetoric*, 1392a–1393a, 1397a–1400b. See Ackrill's commentary to the Loeb edition, *Aristotle's Categories and On Interpretation*. In a brief allusion to the parallels between the lists in the *Categories* and the *Topics*, Ackrill remarks, "the whole chapter [i] of the *Topics* deserves study" (80). To this comparison, the *Rhetoric* should surely be added.

26. *Topics*, 100a–101b.

27. Ibid., 103b.

28. Ibid.

29. Ibid., 104a.

30. Ibid.

31. Debate continues about whether the *Topics* is an early version of the remaining logical treatises and the *Rhetoric*. See Stump, *Boethius's De Topicis Differentiis*, 159; Ackrill, *Aristotle's Categories and On Interpretation*, 79; Solmsen, "Dialectic Without the Forms," in *Aristotle on Dialectic: The Topics*, 55; and Owen, ed., *Aristotle on Dialectic: The Topics*, 105.

32. Rosen, *Plato's Sophist*, 29–47, 229–44, though treating Plato's *Sophist*, nicely defines this paradox of anachronism, and the problems it creates in constructing an internally derived interpretation of terms in this era.

33. Only recently has Stoic logic been freshly examined as something other than a corrupt and inadequate Aristotelian system. See Mates, *Stoic Logic*, 1–26; Rist, *Stoic Philosophy* and *The Stoics*; Annas and Barnes, *The Modes of Scepticism*.

34. Ong, *Ramus, Method, and the Decay of Dialogue*, 7, discusses the effects of "residual logic" in Ramist taxonomies. I use his very useful phrase and definition here.

35. Hegel, *The Phenomenology of Mind*, 89–90, 110, 112.

36. See Lynch, *Aristotle's School: A Study of a Greek Educational Institution*.

37. *Gorgias*, 453d.

38. *Rhetoric*, 1404a.

39. *Rhetoric*, 1355a, Roberts translation.

40. Ibid., 1404a.

41. *Rhetoric*, 1404b, Freese translation. Also see the discussions of proper style for writings at 1407b, 1413b.

42. In advancing this thesis I extend Eric Havelock's still debated profile of the emergence of Attic literacy to the case of Aristotle's *Rhetoric*. See Havelock, *Language and Thought in Early Greek Philosophy*, 12–15, 65–82; and *The Literate Revolution in Greece and Its Cultural Consequences*, 25–31, 48, 221–23. Havelock,

Literate Revolution, 48, notes Aristotle's practice of using *gramma* interchangeably with *phone*.

43. An apt characterization developed and defended by Kennedy, *Classical Rhetoric and Its Christian and Secular Tradition from Ancient to Modern Times*, 5–17, 108–19.

44. de Romilly, *Magic and Rhetoric in Ancient Greece*, provides an extensive study of Gorgias' notion of the magic of words, and of the discomfort with and distrust of this view that Aristotle is among the first to articulate. Plain stylists of later eras would revive this distrust, as witnessed by Thomist, Ramist, and Puritan caveats.

45. *Rhetoric*, 1404a.

46. *Rhetoric*, 1404b, Roberts translation.

47. Grimaldi, "Studies in the Philosophy of Aristotle's Rhetoric," 17, n. 27, notes the problematic absence of a treatment of the misuses of *ethos* or *pathos*, though substantial attention is given to the misuses of *logos*.

48. *Rhetoric*, 1404a, 1413b, Roberts translation.

49. Ibid., 1378a.

50. *Rhetoric*, 1413b.

51. Ibid., 1404a.

52. Aristotle's treatment of rhetoric is examined within a number of contemporary disciplines, each with a different conception of rhetoric and different methods for its study. This further complicates the longstanding Plato-versus-Aristotle and/or philosophical-rhetoric-versus-technical-rhetoric approaches to Aristotle's *Rhetoric*. An additional conundrum is created by the habitual omission of the *Rhetoric* from studies of Aristotle's logical system and from most collections of classical philosophy. The text itself has not been held to be interesting or significant, and rhetoric as its subject has been of little interest in classics or philosophy, with a few notable exceptions.

"Aristotle the cynical, shrewd calculator marketing a scheme for manipulating the mob" has been the view of Platonists for the most part, who like neither the *Rhetoric* nor the logical treatises. Correcting Aristotle's treatment of Plato, and his reading of Plato in terms of his own logical system, is a valid and productively developed purpose of these studies; not all deal with the *Rhetoric*. To the best of my knowledge, the lineage of this approach within the last century begins with the Cambridge Platonists, and is exemplified by Cornford, Cherniss, Owen, Robinson, Allen, and Rosen, to give a very abbreviated list.

Ackrill's comment on the importance of Aristotle's *Rhetoric* illustrates the milder opprobrium expressed by those who find Aristotle's logic and metaphysics sound if not brilliant, but see no particular relation between the *Rhetoric* and the other works: "the *Rhetoric* is not of great philosophical importance, though it contains some interesting material" (*Aristotle the Philosopher*, 158). This simple omission, which pervades studies in philosophy and classics, deserves correction. Havelock's treatment of Plato's development of an abstract lexicon and formula for "thought," for example, does address his treatment of the poets and his poetics, but excludes any extensive discussion of Plato's treatment of rhetoric as similarly a system of thought. Most studies of Aristotle's logical treatises, even those focused on the *Topics*, as for instance Owen, ed., *Aristotle on Dialectic: The Topics*, include only brief, if any, mention of the *Rhetoric*.

These omissions have delayed an understanding of the *Rhetoric* collaterally with the logical treatises. Grimaldi addresses the paucity of this approach. However, Grimaldi, like many philosopher–historians of rhetoric, tends toward a conflation of the *Rhetoric* with the logical treatises and rejects depictions of it as a "rhetoric of persuasion with the understanding of 'persuasion at any cost'" (Grimaldi, "Studies in the Philosophy of Aristotle's Rhetoric," 4). His treatments of the centrality of the enthymeme and his treatment of probablistic logic are scrupulously detailed, but skirt the prominence of "giving an appearance," "appearing to be," and the strongly adversarial characterizations Aristotle uses in both the *Rhetoric* and the *Topics*. For example, the concluding section of book 8 of the *Topics* is expressly directed at instructing the arguer in how to break down an *opponent's* arguments in whatever way. Grimaldi, however, maintains that throughout Aristotle's treatment "rhetoric functions as a method of communication, spoken or written, between people as they seek to determine truth or fallacy in real situations" (18). While this is an admirable attempt at correcting the "Aristotle the shrewd manipulator" view, it errs in the other direction by presenting his views as compatible with Plato's, and as incompatible with concepts of rhetoric as manipulative.

Grimaldi's philosophizing of the *Rhetoric* is presented as a recovery of rhetoric from the hands of "an academic tradition" which has seen it as a "facile manipulation of language" (1). This tradition he exemplifies with E. P. J. Corbett's statement, "Advertising . . . is perhaps the best example of an activity which practices what Aristotle preached" (1). And he rejects any equation of the *paideusis* of Aristotle with "public relations, advertising, or even college textbooks on English composition" (1). Dismissing these disciplines as inferior and themselves specious, unworthy of Aristotle, is an unfortunate slur, and a futile attempt at obscuring the clearly practical, pedagogical aims of the *Rhetoric* which are perhaps most prominent in Book III. Grimaldi's study is nonetheless valuable; despite his philosophical bias, his account provides an excellent history and analysis of the divergent treatments of the *Rhetoric* (1–17).

Within Speech and English departments, historical and theoretical approaches to rhetoric per se have erred just as often in Grimaldi's direction as in the other. The sound studies of Baldwin, Howell, Clark, McKeon, Murphy, and Kennedy tend as often toward philosophizing the *Rhetoric* as toward demeaning it or applauding its shrewdness. In "Rhetoric in the Middle Ages," McKeon gives a detailed history of rearrangements and recombinations of (mostly Aristotelian) rhetoric, grammar, poetics, and dialectic through the thirteenth century that is complemented by Greenfield. Kennedy, *Classical Rhetoric and Its Christian and Secular Tradition from Ancient to Modern Times*, provides a valuable summary of the incremental development of four distinct approaches to rhetoric in the classical period: sophistic, philosophical, technical, and literary.

All these studies imply, if they do not state, what Grimaldi articulates with precision: "Thus, the meaning of 'rhetoric' is very largely dependent upon the epistemology, psychology, and metaphysics of the philosophical system in which it occurs" ("Studies in the Philosophy of Aristotle's Rhetoric," 20). But both the meaning and the practice of rhetoric within different periods is affected not only by the philosophical system of its originator but also by factors beyond any individual's control. "Rhetoric" must be analyzed, albeit problematically, as a body of practices directed by cultural beliefs and assumptions as much as by the textual meaning of the author(s) of an individual rhetoric such as Aristotle's, which is now believed to be a compilation of students' reports — an authorship that places it in yet another juxtaposition with Plato's representations of Socrates. The incremental interdependence of rhetoric as a body of textual descriptions and theory, and as a set of practices guided by such texts, is precisely what makes rhetoric both problematic and challenging as an object of study.

53. *Nichomachean Ethics*, 1124b.

54. Ibid., 1108a.

55. *Rhetoric*, 1393a.

56. *Poetics*, 1451b, Bywater translation.

57. Diogenes Laertius, *Lives and Opinions of Eminent Philosophers* V, 11. *Rhetoric* 1399a.

58. *Rhetoric*, 1419b, Roberts translation.

59. Ibid., 1420a.

60. Sedgewick, *Of Irony*, 11-13.

61. Ibid., "Aristotle not only suggested to a far later time the equating of irony and litotes, but he also fixed the general sense of Socratic irony for all time."

62. *Poetics*, 1449a, Bywater translation.

63. Ibid., 1452b.

64. The *Oxford English Dictionary* confirms this date, noted as well by Sedgewick and Thomson.

65. See Kennedy, "The Conceptualization of Rhetoric," *Classical Rhetoric*, 15ff., for a companionable appraisal of many of these issues. Bateson, in "Toward a Theory of Schizophrenia," 254, gives the following description of the "double-bind" and its parallels.

> The Zen Master attempts to bring about enlightenment in his pupil in various ways. One of the things he does is hold a stick over the pupil's head and say fiercely, "If you say this stick is real, I will strike you with it. If you don't say anything, I will strike you with it." We feel that the schizophrenic finds himself continually in the same situation as the pupil, but he achieves something like disorientation rather than enlightenment. The Zen pupil might reach up and take the stick away from the Master — who might accept this response, but the schizophrenic has no such choice since with him there is no not caring about the relationship, and his mother's aims and awareness are not like the Master's.
>
> We hypothesize that there will be a breakdown in any individual's ability to discriminate between Logical Types whenever a double-bind situation occurs. The general characteristics of the situation are the following:
>
> (1) When the individual is involved in an intense relationship; that is, a relationship in which he feels it is vitally important that he discriminate accurately what sort of message is being communicated so that he might respond appropriately.
>
> (2) And, the individual is caught in a situation in which the other person

in the relationship is expressing two orders of message, and one of these denies the other.

(3) And, the individual is unable to comment on the messages being expressed to correct his discrimination of what order of message to respond to, i.e., he cannot make a metacommunicative statement.

Bateson's characterization emphasizes the importance of the relationship between listener and speaker in order for destructive uses of double messages, or double meanings, to be effective. Moreover, he gives the psychological cognate for specifically ironic statements when he says of the double-bind message that one level of it must deny the other. Finally, in (3) he characterizes the difference between the interpreter and the victim of double-bind messages — for my purposes, rhetorical or ironic statements: the *victim* is unable to comment "metacommunicatively" on the statement to himself or to the speaker, while the *interpreter* can make such comments, if not to the speaker, at least to himself.

Chapter 4

1. In the introduction to the Loeb translation, Rackham cites Cicero's description of *De Oratore*, "scripsi igitur Aristotelio more" (*Ad Fam*. i. 9. 230) and notes, "its method is very different from that of the dialogues of Plato. . . . In Cicero's dialogues . . . doctrines are expounded as dogmatic truths, the dialogue form being adopted as a vivid method of exhibiting the many-sided nature of the subject and the departments into which a systematic treatment of it falls" (xi). Despite the apparent authority of Cicero, Rackham's distinction seems exaggerated; Plato's dialogues often represent "dogmatic" views as well. Lynch gives a precisely detailed outline of the diverse meanings of "Aristotelian" and "peripatetic" in the first century B.C. (*Aristotle's School: A Study of a Greek Educational Institution*, 135–40).

A second point of general similarity between Plato's and Cicero's dialogues is an avoidance of final conclusions which tie up, answer, or resolve the issue. The views are left in suspended relation to one another, for the reflection of the reader. Cicero explicitly announces that *De Oratore* will be an emulation of the *Phaedrus* (I, 28). Kennedy provides these additional assessments of *De Oratore*: that the form of the dialogue may reasonably be called Aristotelian, owing to the well-developed viewpoints of all participants, but that Cicero's avoidance of producing a manual by definition and rule is in the spirit of the Platonic dialogue, an interpretation which is supported by Cicero's explicit allusion to the setting of the *Phaedrus* as an inspiration for the dialogue (*The Art of Rhetoric in the Roman World*, 209). Clark, *Rhetoric in Graeco-Roman Education*, 145, notes that Cicero's dialogues are themselves the only surviving exemplars of the Aristotelian dialogue. In his preface to the *Brutus*, Hendrickson cites the modern recovery of an Aristotelian dialogue by the Peripatetic Satyrus, the only surviving dialogue from Aristotle's era written "in the Aristotelian manner" alluded to by Cicero. Satyrus' text, compared with Cicero's several dialogues, permits the characterization of the Aristotelian dialogue as a "modified Socratic form, . . . assigning to a leading speaker a larger and more continuous role, lightened by interludes, interruptions, and transitions, shared by other speakers. Through this device the dialogue was made serviceable, not only for dialectical inquiry, but also for continuous presentation of almost any subject matter" (*Brutus*, trans. G. L. Hendrickson, 9). Baldwin defines *De Oratore*'s form as "obviously the Platonic dialogue" (*Ancient Rhetoric and Poetic*, 40). It is clear that both the form and the function of Platonic and Aristotelian dialogues remain the subject of disagreement, and invite further investigation.

2. The *Academica* continues to provide one of the soundest interpretive histories of ancient and classical philosophy. Diogenes Laertius draws from it as well as from the histories in Cicero's other works. Cicero's eclecticism and lack of dogmatism have also rendered his histories valuable measures of the degree of bias in other historians, most notably Sextus Empiricus' anti-Stoicism, which obscured the substantiveness of Stoic logic well into this century. See Bochenski, *Ancient Formal Logic*; Jackson, *De Dialectica*, 112-24; Mates, *Stoic Logic*, 1-26; Kirk, *Heraclitus, the Cosmic Fragments*, 1-30; and Annas and Barnes, *The Modes of Scepticism*, 1-30, for excellent analyses of these historiographical labyrinths. Kirk's summary is particularly valuable for Cicero's era, since it traces the now lost doxographical collection of the first century b.c., which was the only channel through which any written account of the Greek philosophers reached Roman and subsequent historians. Kirk's comparisons of Cicero's and Diogenes Laertius' histories point out the absence of linear chronological structure in Cicero's and illuminate how and why he located the histories in a much broader context of concerns and issues.

3. *De Oratore* II, 30.

4. *De Oratore* III, 60; *Academica* I, 17.

5. *De Oratore* III, 69-77, 125; *Academica* I, 3-24.

6. *Academica* I, 33.

7. *De Oratore* I, 61-64, and III, 58-60; *Academica* 25, 33; *Orator*, 12, 15.

8. *De Oratore* II, 61.

9. *Orator*, 13.

10. *De Oratore* III, 61.

11. *Academica* I, 16, 43.

12. *De Oratore* III, 59-61.

13. *Academica* II, 109.

14. *De Oratore* III, 24.

15. Ibid. III, 55.

16. See Finnegan, "Literacy vs. Non-Literacy: the Great Divide?" in Horton and Finnegan, eds. *Modes of Thought*; and Tannen, "The Oral-Literate Continuum in Discourse," in Tannen, ed., *Spoken and Written Language*.

17. I have reversed Stanley Fish's well known title, *Self-Consuming Artifacts*. Seventeenth-century poetry and poetics, the subject of that study, could be productively studied alongside some of the "so called *paradoxa* of the Stoics [which] belong to Socrates" (*Academica* II, 136). Walter Ong and Rosalie Colie have commented on the preoccupation with form and content, and with their reality, which increased during the seventeenth century. "Self-consuming" riddles and conceits, very like the Stoic paradoxes, can reflect deep uncertainty and a sense of decay. Ong characterizes the period 1550-1650 as a time of method gone berserk, leading to a "decay of dialogue." Cicero can be seen as attempting to reverse similar patterns in his immedi-

ate precursors, and as reinventing dialogue as a literate mode which can contain, preserve, and transmit the substance of the liberal arts.

18. Diringer, *The Book Before Printing*, 248.

19. *Orator*, 120.

20. *Academica* I, 9–18.

21. The terms "wisdom" and "literature" are carefully chosen here, to suggest the fluidity and range of understandings of both substance and genre in Cicero's era. Janus' circumspection was equated with wisdom in part because his far-reaching access to the past allowed some knowledge of the future as well. Cicero adopts the same equation in defining the training of the orator. The more he knows precedents, laws, human experiences, the better he will be at effecting decision in the present and arguing future probabilities. His uses of the terms "wisdom" and "virtue" to describe eloquence emphasize the substantiveness of his reform of rhetoric through literature. Literature itself then denoted entertainments and literary exempla, the written samples used in drills for elementary students. Cicero's reform facilitated the extension of literature to its fullest modern sense: the "literature" of a field. It is paradoxical, to say the least, that in this century the connotation of "literature" has returned to its earlier, often trivial or pejorative, sense. Cicero's relegation of the unrecorded to the unreliable, uncertain, or half-true parallels very closely Aristotle's dismissal of "rhetoric, poetry, and prayer" from the domain of true and false statements, i.e., logic. In this sense, the authorative status Cicero assigns to texts replaces Aristotle's logic as the official locus of truth.

22. *Brutus*, 56; my emphasis.

23. See Kennedy, *Classical Rhetoric and Its Christian and Secular Tradition from Ancient to Modern Times*, for a lucid account of the *letteraturizzazione* of rhetoric during and after Cicero's era.

24. *De Oratore* I, 47–51.

25. Ibid. I, 72.

26. Ibid. I, 71.

27. See Robinson, *Plato's Earlier Dialectic*, 1–18.

28. See Ong, *Ramus, Method, and the Decay of Dialogue*, 152, and Havelock, *Preface to Plato*, 44–60, for elaborations of these interdependencies.

29. *De Oratore* I, 150.

30. Ibid. III, 57.

31. Ibid. III, 59.

32. Ibid. III, 54.

33. Ibid. III, 48.

34. Ibid. III, 45.

35. Ibid. I, 150.

36. Ibid. III, 38.

37. Ibid. II, 158–60.

38. *Orator*, 64.

39. *Academica* I, 5.

40. Ibid. I, 8; II, 109, 110.

41. Adorno, *Negative Dialectics*, 55.

42. *De Oratore* III, 143–44.

43. *Orator*, 120.

44. See Olson, "Mind and Media: The Epistemic Functions of Literacy," for an extended analysis of the "archival" functions of written texts in "high" literacy.

45. *De Natura Deorum*, introduction, xii.

46. Lynch, *Aristotle's School: A Study of a Greek Educational Institution*, 136–37; Smith, *The Art of Rhetoric in Alexandria*, 16; and n. 1 of this chapter.

47. *Orator*, 64.

48. Kennedy, *The Art of Rhetoric in the Roman World*, 115.

49. Kennedy, in *Classical Rhetoric*, 117, comments on the nostalgic classicism of the Attici.

50. *Brutus*, 56.

51. Smith, *The Art of Rhetoric in Alexandria*, 136.

52. Havelock, *The Literate Revolution in Greece and Its Cultural Consequences*, 60–76, 89–121, suggests this paradigm for fifth-century Greece.

53. *Orator*, 37. I cannot here do justice to the welcome wealth of recent work on epideictic and epitaphic oratory and on the related inquiry into the Sophists and history. That the Sophists became disparaged for rewriting history to suit the interests of those in power, and for teaching those in power how to do so, is now a commonplace of fifth-century Athenian history. The specifics of the epitaphic and epideictic rhetorical genres become more interesting in this context, for it can be seen that, once preserved and used as classroom pieces, they functioned much as sample essays do today in writing classes. Drawing attention to the relationships among topic, audience, and purpose, these compendia no doubt provided Aristotle with the raw data upon which he could build his *ethos–logos–pathos* and speaker–topic–audience models. I am indebted to the Princeton NEH Summer Institute for College Teachers, "Approaches to Language in the Greek Enlightenment: Ethics, Rhetoric, and Poetics," 1989, for discussions and bibliography on these issues. Elaine Fantham's translations of Gorgias' and Isocrates' *epitaphia* and epideictics, prepared especially for the Institute, as well as our discussions of the same, familiarized me with the extant understandings of these genres within the classics. Fellow participant Takis Poulakos' work on the *epitaphia* provides important cultural and political contexts for reappraising not only the role of the Sophists but also the range of their alignments with the ruling classes. Mary Ellen Waithe's chapter on Aspasia in *A History of Women Philosophers*, vol. 1, develops a careful and cogent appraisal of Aspasia's speech within the *Menexenos* and of her role as teacher of Socrates and Pericles. The historical work of M. I. Finley and Charles Fornara provides additional resources for understanding the complex intersections among history, fiction, and rhetoric in the fifth and fourth centuries. I here extend that inquiry into Cicero's time by way of indicating directions that further study of his era can take.

54. Heraclitus, fragment 129; Rosenmeyer, "Gorgias, Aeschylus, and *Apate*," 243; Diogenes Laertius, *Lives and Opinions of Eminent Philosophers* I, 23–24.

55. *Rhetoric*, 1414b–1418b, 1393a–1394b.

56. *De Inventione* I, 25–31.

57. *De Oratore* I, 18.

58. Ibid. II, 62, 51–61.

59. Ibid. II, 62–63.

60. Ibid. I, 137–43; *Orator*, 43–50.

61. *De Oratore* I, 36–37.

62. *Orator*, 120.

63. *De Oratore* I, 201; II, 128–29, 310–11; III, 142.

64. *De Oratore* II, 121.

65. *Academica* I, 8.

66. Ibid. I, 9.

67. *De Oratore* II, 51–64; *Orator*, 66–68.

68. *Orator* 61–70; *Academica* I, 15–42.

69. *Orator*, 142.

70. See Havelock, *Literate Revolution*, 225, for a comparable period in Greek literacy, and Diringer, *The Book Before Print* who reviews the evidence of circulating manuscripts during the first six centuries of "full" literacy.

71. *Academica* I, 3, 4–8; *De Finibus* I, 2–14.

72. *Orator*, 12–13.

73. *De Oratore* III, 24.

74. Ibid. I, 52.

75. For the divergent views of Cicero as a literary humanist or rhetorical technician see Kennedy, *Classical Rhetoric* and *The Art of Rhetoric in the Roman World*; Murphy, *Rhetoric in the Middle Ages*; Clark, *Rhetoric in Graeco-Roman Education*; Marrou, *A History of Education in Antiquity*; and Baldwin, *Ancient Rhetoric and Poetic*.

76. Kennedy, *The Art of Rhetoric in the Roman World*, 103–26, provides an excellent comparison and history of *De Inventione* and the *Ad Herennium*, as does Caplan's introduction to the Loeb *Ad Herennium*.

77. *De Oratore* I, 2.

78. *Academica* I, 113–20; *Brutus*, 118–21; Diogenes Laertius, *Lives* VII, 274–83, within the account of Stoicism that takes up much of the biograpy of Zeno.

79. *De Oratore* II, 18.

80. Caplan's introduction to the Loeb edition of the *Ad Herennium* surveys these schools and defends the view that there is no Ur-text from which both *De Inventione* and the *Ad Herennium* derive (xxviii). He also proposes that the "crude textbooks" lambasted in *De Oratore* are not represented in *De Inventione*, a view that I differ with here.

81. *De Oratore* I, 19. Brian Vickers, *In Defence of Rhetoric*, reprises and takes up the defense of rhetoric that long has argued against the philosophers that rhetoric sustains and imparts knowledge of the subjects it addresses.

82. *Academica* II, 16–35, 22.

83. *De Oratore* I, 19.

84. Kennedy, *The Art of Rhetoric in the Roman World*, and Baldwin, *Ancient Rhetoric and Poetic*, judge this argument one of Cicero's less successful efforts.

85. *Brutus*, 322.

86. *Orator*, 13.

87. *De Oratore* II, 4.

88. Ibid. II, 299.

89. *Academica* II, 2.

90. Ibid. I, 7.

91. Ibid. II, 6.

92. *De Oratore* II, 128–30.

93. Kennedy, *The Art of Rhetoric in the Roman World*, 276, asserts that Cicero "always regarded rhetoric as a practical art to be judged by its effectiveness with the audience."

94. *Orator*, 9–10.

95. *Academica* I, 33.

96. *De Oratore* I, 51.

97. Ibid. II, 160.

98. Ibid. I, 52.

99. *Academica* I, 5.

100. *De Oratore* II, 127.

101. Ibid. II, 130.

102. Ibid. II, 130–31.

103. *Academica* I, 30.

104. Ibid. I, 33.

105. Ibid. I, 30.

106. Ibid. I, 25.

107. *Orator*, 45; *De Oratore* II, 132.

108. *Orator*, 46–48.

109. For example, the Ramist rhetorics analyzed by Ong, eighteenth-century elocutionist rhetorics, and the apt characterizations by Hegel and William Barret cited here.

110. *De Oratore* II, 4.

111. Ibid. I, 47–48.

112. E.g., *De Natura Deorum* I, 101–6. But on these designations caution should be exercised lest modern conceptions of relativism be attributed to the philosophies Cicero addresses, a warning given crisp exposition by Richard Bett, "The Sophists and Relativism," albeit for an earlier period.

113. *Academica* I, 3.

114. Ibid. I, 17–18.

115. *De Oratore* II, 152–53.

116. Ibid. II, 18.

117. Ibid. I, 47–48.

118. *Academica* II, 99.

119. *Brutus*, 118.

120. *Academica* I, 26.

121. Ibid.

122. Ibid. I, 29.

123. Ibid. I, 32.

124. Ibid.

125. Ibid. I, 33

126. Ibid. I, 45–46.

127. *De Vera Religione*, 49, 94.

128. *Confessions*, 8.

Chapter 5

1. *De Vera Religione* xlix, 94.

2. *Confessions* I, 18.

3. Compare, for example, Arnobius' *Adversus Nationes* I, 59: "How is the truth of a statement diminished if an error is made in number or case, in preposition, particle, or conjunction?" And, Titian's *Oratio*, 1–3: "You have invented rhetoric for injustice and calumny. . . . You have invented poetry to sing of battles, the loves of the gods, of everything which corrupts the spirit." Menucius Felix denounces the study of how to improve such works through "poetics" in his *Octavius* xxiv. 2. 7 – "especially in the works of the poets, who have had such fatal influence in injuring the case of truth." Translations in Murphy, "Saint Augustine and the Debate About a Christian Rhetoric," 401–4.

4. *De Doctrina Christiana* IV, 3. In the text I employ the Latin title *De Doctrina Christiana* (shortened at times to *De Doctrina*), even though I am citing from D. W. Robertson's *On Christian Doctrine*, because the Latin *doctrina* denotes attention to effective teaching, apart from indoctrination, in ways that the English "doctrine" does not.

5. *Enchiridion* VI, 18.

6. *Soliloquies* xi, 19; x, 18.

7. *De Vera Religione* xlix, 94.

8. Murphy, *Rhetoric in the Middle Ages*, 51.

9. *Confessions* III, 5.

10. Murphy, "Saint Augustine and the Debate About a Christian Rhetoric," 402.

11. Jackson, introduction to Augustine, *De Dialectica*, defends the authenticity and dating of *De Dialectica* as prior to Augustine's conversion through a collateral study of its terminology with Augustine's other works.

12. Markus, ed., *Augustine: A Collection of Critical Essays*, provides diverse appraisals of Augustine's philosophical milieu and of the extent of his knowledge of Stoic, Academic, and other philosophical traditions that he draws on in shaping his doctrines of meaning and signification.

13. See Baldwin, *Ancient Rhetoric and Poetics*, 51; Murphy, "Saint Augustine and the Debate About a Christian Rhetoric," 400–401, provides a useful summary of the divergent depictions of Augustine vis-a-vis secular rhetoric. Kennedy, *Classical Rhetoric and Its Christian and Secular Tradition from Ancient to Modern Times*, 159, provides a complementary summary.

14. O'Meara, in his translator's preface to Augustine's *Against the Academics*, 18–33, defends the accuracy of the chronology in the *Confessions*. B. Darrell Jackson, "The Theory of Signs in Augustine's *De Doctrina Christiana*," 99–102, 119, 121, 125 (in Markus, ed., *Augustine*), and Bubacz, *St. Augustine's Theory of Knowledge: A Contemporary Analysis*, 8–38, provide readings which illustrate a more gradual conversion.

15. *Confessions* IV, 16.

16. Ibid. III, 8.

17. Ibid. I, 18.

18. *De Doctrina Christiana* IV, 3.

19. *Confessions* I, 16.
20. Ibid. III, 3.
21. III, 3.
22. III, 5.
23. IV, 1.
24. IV, 2.
25. IV, 7.
26. IV, 8.
27. IV, 9–10.
28. IV, 10.
29. IV, 11.
30. IV, 15.
31. V, 7.
32. V, 10.
33. V, 10.
34. V, 11.
35. V, 12.
36. VIII, 2.
37. V, 14.
38. V, 14.
39. V, 14.
40. VIII, 12.
41. IX, 4.
42. XI, 28. William Pahkla, *St. Augustine's Meter and George Herbert's Will*, provides cogent and beautifully articulated appraisals of Augustine's movement from conceptualizing harmony, beauty, and proportion into the kind of multiple simultaneous typological and hermeneutic levels exemplified here.

43. See Foucault, *The Archaeology of Knowledge and the Discourse on Language*, 5–8, 220–28, and "What Is an Author?" in Harari, ed., *Textual Strategies*; and Handelman, *The Slayers of Moses*, 83–122. Modern literary critical approaches to Augustine have often been indifferent to the novelty of his approaches to intention and to the self as interpreter. Anachronistic impositions of a clever or ironic self-presentation, particularly in the voice of the *Confessions*, fly in the face of Augustine's avowed intentions, as with attributions of Plato's cunning in slyly constructing the narrative frames of the dialogues. The aestheticization of self that has been so common as a modern assumption regarding the author is precisely the corrupting and decadent movement that Augustine with such labor reversed in himself. In "How Does One Speak to Literature?" Julia Kristeva exemplifies this common modern attitude. "The *death drive* of the writer becomes *irony* in the critic, because there is irony each time an ephemeral meaning crystallizes for a reader" (*Desire in Language*, 109). Parallels between this way of speaking to literature and the classical literary milieu out of which Augustine forged a reformed hermeneutics deserve more study, as the epistemologies of self and interpretation they share with today's postmodernist doctrines are provocatively parallel. The fictive status of Augustine's voice and persona, particularly in the *Confessions* are of continuing interest, owing to the premium he places upon the *verbum cordis* and upon authenticity.

44. E.g., Cresconius, at whom Augustine directed *Contra Cresconium et Donatistam Libri III* in 402, and the Donatist bishop of Citar, at whom Augustine directed *Contra Litteras Petiliani* also in 402. See Copelston, *A History of Philosophy*, vol. 2, part 1: *Augustine to Bonaventure*, 60–63; and Murphy, "Saint Augustine and the Debate About a Christian Rhetoric," 402–3, for additional summaries of this context.

45. Copelston, *Augustine to Bonaventure*, 40–41, emphasizes the former point, and Murphy, "Saint Augustine," the latter.

46. *Confessions* VIII, 2. Also see the chapter on Makrina of Nyssa, sister of Gregory, by Cornelia W. Wolfskeel in Waithe, *A History of Women Philosophers*, vol. 1 (139–68).

47. Ibid. I, 13.

48. *De Doctrina Christiana*, prologue, 9.

49. See Vance, "Love's Concordance: The Poetics of Desire and the Joy of the Text," for an exposition of the correspondences between Augustine's treatment of desire and that advanced within recent literary theory, drawing on Lacan and Roland Barthes.

50. *De Vera Religione* xxxvi, 68.

51. *De Doctrina Christiana* I, 1.

52. Ibid. II, 35–36.

53. Ibid. II, 31–36.

54. Jackson, "The Theory of Signs in Augustine's *De Doctrina Christiana*," 136, in Markus, ed., *Augustine*.

55. *De Doctrina Christiana* I, 2.

56. Markus, "St. Augustine on Signs," in Markus, ed., *Augustine*, 72. Pahlka, *St. Augustine's Meter and George Herbert's Will*, provides illuminating appraisals of the centrality of will to Augustine's poetics and semantics.

57. In this discussion I am indebted to Jackson, "The Theory of Signs in Augustine's *De Doctrina Christiana*," 92–137, though my purposes and conclusions are in places quite different from his.

58. Jackson, "Theory of Signs," 132, on *De Doctrina Christiana* II, 1; my emphasis.

59. *De Doctrina Christiana* II, 2; my emphasis.

60. Jackson, "Theory of Signs," 136.

61. Mates, *Stoic Logic*, provides a useful synopsis of the transmission of Stoic teachings and an account of the different sources of bias in classical reports of their doctrines. Handelman, *The Slayers of Moses*, and Jackson, "Theory of Signs," concur on Augustine's important and possibly original divergence from Aristotle's referentiality, though Stoic sources remain unclear. The directions secular humanism and language teaching take after the Renaissance warrant further comparison with the classical gulf between Stoic/intentional and Aristotelian/predicational models. Unfortunately many of the sources for Stoic teachings, such as Sextus Empiricus' accounts, are distorted by Aristotelian, Skeptic, or anti-Greek bias, and do not permit confident appraisals of their survival in Augustine's models.

62. *De Doctrina Christiana* II, 1.

63. Ibid. II, 16, 18.

64. II, 40.

65. III, 3.

66. III, 10.

67. III, 11.

68. *Liber Contra Mendacium*, translation and commentary by M. D. Chenu in *Nature, Man, and Society in the Twelfth Century*, 160.

69. *Confessions* XI, 28.

70. Ibid. IX, 4.

71. Rappaport, *Ecology, Meaning, and Religion*, 223, 242–43, and in "Word, Words, and the Problems of Language," extends and examines the concept of "diabolical lies" (*pace* De Rougemont, *La Part du Diable*) from the anthropological perspective of language as an adaptive human ecosystem, and in the contexts of the sacred, enacted in ritual, as one locus for stabilizing and sustaining canons of truth and meaning.

72. *Enchiridion*, 22.

73. Ibid., 18.

74. Booth, *A Rhetoric of Irony*, adopts a similar classification for modern literary irony when he isolates, among kinds of "intended irony," "stable-overt" irony.

75. *De Vera Religione*, 49, 94.

76. I adapt this emphatically strong term from McKee, *Literary Irony and the Literary Audience: The Victimization of the Audience in Augustan Fiction*.

77. *De Doctrina Christiana* III, 29.

78. Aquinas, *Summa Theologiae*, 1, 10, objection 1, first reply.

79. Richards, *The Philosophy of Rhetoric*, and Percy, "Metaphor as Mistake," review this question from the perspectives of contemporary philosophies of language and poetics. Also compare Verdenius, "Gorgias' Doctrine of Deception," and Rosenmeyer, "Gorgias, Aeschylus, and *Apate*," for treatments of earlier ways of working out divisions among fiction, multiple meaning, and deception. I am indebted to Louis Mackey for introducing me to the substantial literature on metaphor that is drawn on here.

80. Saussure, *Course in General Linguistics*, 68–69.

81. *De Doctrina Christiana* III, 22, 23.

82. Ibid. III, 27.

83. III, 29.

84. IV, 6–10.

85. IV, 26.

86. Bede, *De Schematibus et Tropis*, preface, 238.

87. Ibid., 244.

88. Ibid., 250.

89. *De Doctrina Christiana* IV, 3.

90. Bede, *De Schematibus et Tropis*, 251.

91. *De Doctrina Christiana* III, 10, 27–29; II, 40–43; IV, 5, 8–10, and 20, respectively.

92. Ibid. III, 27.

93. Saussssure, *Course in General Linguistics*, 69.

94. See Bok, *Lying*, 57–72, for insightful and instructive appraisals of comparable beliefs and attitudes today, particularly of the "white" lie that protects but also patronizes.

95. Sonnet 138, in *The Complete Works of William Shakespeare*, 1267.

Chapter 6

1. Kierkegaard, *The Point of View*, 155, 138. See also *Concluding Unscientific Postscript*, 241.

2. I employ Gilligan's phrase "web of relationship" (*In a Different Voice*) to emphasize the parallelism and continuity between Augustine's and Kierkegaard's therapeutic understandings of language directed ethically at restorative and connective projects, and her emphasis on the sustaining of connection and relationship as the basis for the ethic of care she finds central to many women's understandings and uses of language, knowledge, and moral reasoning.

3. Kierkegaard, *The Concept of Irony*, 143.

4. Ibid., 338.

5. Ibid.

6. Atwood, *Cat's Eye*, 76.

7. Rodriguez, *Hunger of Memory*, 28.

8. Quoted in Belenky et al., *Women's Ways of Knowing*, 203.

9. Page du Bois, in *Sowing the Body: Psychoanalysis and Ancient Representations of Women*, identifies a problematic perpetuation of phallogocentrism and logocentrism within discourses that are purportedly decentering these traditions. Her treatment has the added value of appraising the mutual dependence of postmodern philosophy and Freudian psychoanalysis not only upon each other but upon what she argues is a specious claim of ahistoricism as well.

10. *Either/Or*, vol. 1, 440.

11. Kierkegaard, *Letters and Documents*, letter 54, 102.

12. Heidegger, *Early Greek Thinking*, 24–26. See also Tyler, *The Unspeakable*, for accounts of "The Vision Quest in the West" that complement Havelock's and Heidegger's cosmogonies of Western conceptual paradigms and languages.

13. For an appraisal of how feminist and postmodern theories converge and diverge on these points, see Hawkesworth, "Knowers, Knowing, Known: Feminist Theory and Claims of Truth." In drawing on deMan's notions of the rhetoric of temporality and of the future perfect, I am indebted to the illumination of these issues by Bryan C. Short, "The Temporality of Rhetoric."

14. Heidegger, *Early Greek Thinking*, 26; the appraisal of "to be" terms extends over 13–58.

15. Müller, *Quartett*, quoted by Christa Wolf, *Cassandra*, 296. I draw on Page du Bois' critique of Foucault's *l'homme du désir* as well as on Wolf in these appraisals.

16. Wolf, *Cassandra*, 259–305, discusses the "death cult" of ancient epic and its continuation in the use of the Olympiad to date the events recorded in the earliest written Greek histories.

17. du Bois, *Sowing the Body*, 2–7.

18. In "Gorgias, Aeschylus, and *Apate*," Rosenmeyer proposes that Aeschylus' agnosticism was no secret, that he knew the Olympians as literary fictions, as "false gods." Christa Wolf extends this paradigm back to Homer.

19. Wolf, *Cassandra*, 294.

20. Ibid., 262.

21. Ibid., 276.

22. Ibid., 287.

23. In "Women's Time" Kristeva observes this as a flaw in French proponents of *l'écriture féminine*, yet her semiotic, to the extent that it is associated with pre-Oedipal and preverbal oceanic experience, would appear to commit the same error.

24. Jane Marcus suggests this alignment in "Storming the Toolshed."

25. Wolf, *Cassandra*, 260, spells out this notion of a weak point; I draw from her exposition here.

26. See Foucault, "What is An Author?"

27. Curtius in *European Literature and the Latin Middle Ages* provides an appendix on the medieval rhetorics' "Inexpressibility Topoi" that illustrates this alternation. Greenfield, *Humanist and Scholastic Poetics*, provides a helpful survey of these shifts, as does Colie, *Paradoxia Epidemica*.

28. Donne, "The First Anniversarie," 205.

29. Ong, *Ramus, Method, and the Decay of Dialogue*, provides a magisterial account of this conflation. Grafton and Jardine, *From Humanism to the Humanities*, elucidate further curricular and conceptual consequences of these shifts.

30. Quoted in Grafton and Jardine, *From Humanism to the Humanities*, 169. Ong's study of Ramus provides numerous examples of the same tendencies.

31. Alain de Lille, *Anticlaudianus* III, 2-3; VII, 6.

32. Ibid.

33. Sor Juana Inez de la Cruz, *Respuesta*, 34.

34. *Hamlet*, I. 2, in *Complete Works*, 1130.

35. Howell, *Logic and Rhetoric in England, 1500-1700*, provides a thorough account of this tradition, though one biased toward a philosophical view of rhetoric, as does Olson, *Aristotle's Poetics and English Literature*, which similarly privileges poetics and poetry over rhetoric.

36. See Colie, *Paradoxia Epidemica*, and McKee, *Literary Irony and the Literary Audience: The Victimization of the Audience in Augustan Fiction*. Also of help in appraising this period are France, *Rhetoric and Truth in France; Descartes to Diderot*, and Greenfield, *Humanist and Scholastic Poetics, 1250-1500*. The treatments of Erasmus' Folly and More's *Richard III* provided in Marius, *Thomas More*, are valuable studies in the rich and changing rhetorical assumptions and training of the period, particularly the persistent view that history was edifying rhetoric, a role very different from the reportorial objectivity and evidence that until recently were expected of history and historians.

37. Ong, *Ramus, Method and the Decay of Dialogue*, explores these ties with an erudition that is particularly attentive to curricular materials and assumptions.

38. Pahlka, *Saint Augustine's Meter and George Herbert's Will*, and Yearwood, "The Rhetoric of Form in *The Temple*," illuminate these tensions, with attention to the indelible presence of rhetoric in Herbert's and Donne's religious and poetic milieu.

39. Eisenstein, *The Printing Press as an Agent of Change*, is a welcome contribution to the study of the role played by print during this and later periods. Stock, Clanchy, Ebeling, Grafton and Jardine, Olson, Handelman, Howell, Kennedy, Ong, Maier and Tollers, and Moreau illuminate in different ways both the backdrops and

the evolution of this concern with an expanded delineation of the interpreter's duties, aims, and responsibilities, a concern directly parallel to Augustine's at several points, but greatly expanded by the availability of printed vernacular Bibles.

40. Ricoeur, *Interpretation Theory*, provides an illuminating account of the psychologizing move in Schleiermacher's *Hermeneutik* and its successors in Romantic dialogics. Mellor's *English Romantic Irony* probes these differences as well, with valuable attention to nuances distinguishing one form or use of irony from another.

41. Schiller, letter to Goethe, in *Friedrich Schiller*, 92.

42. Solger, in Gilbert and Kuhn, *A History of Aesthetics*, 456.

43. Schlegel, "Lyceum," #42, in *Dialogue on Poetry and Literary Aphorisms*, 126.

44. Ibid.

45. Schlegel, "Lyceum," #30, ibid., 123.

46. "Dialogue on Poetry," ibid., 58–59.

47. "The Illusion of Technique" is William Barrett's apt title, and the concern of Frankfurt School hermeneutics as well. Barrett's study facilitates the observation of links between German discussions of the technification of thought, instrumentalism, mastery, and control models, and the Anglo-American positivist and analytic traditions.

48. Appleby, Bailey and Fosheim, Berlin, Welch, Cressy, Schieffelin and Gilmore, Bauman and Sherzer, Yaden and Templeton, Scribner and Cole, Corcoran, Goody, Havelock, Pattison, Olson, and Heath are among the many contributors to this scrutiny. Their work should be read alongside that of neoconservatives such as Copperman and Rodriguez, who argue that the conception of literacy as a remediable crisis is flawed and misguided, that those who have achieved it have done so in an intellectual and educational free-enterprise system that rightly rewards hard work on the part of the upwardly mobile. Copperman maintains that the literacy "crisis" is a hoax perpetrated by wasteful mismeasurers of remedial successes. Edward M. White, Heath, Elbow, and Pattison, among others, define a humane middle ground that defends standardized language and learning but also promotes initiative, choice, and pluralism in curricula, teaching, and literacy styles. Havelock, Ong, Goody, and Tyler, among others, critique some of the misguided ossifications of Western literate and educated standards from the perspective of non-Western and nonliterate cultures.

49. See Hawkesworth, "Knowers, Knowing, Known," for a comprehensive and balanced overview of these debates. The critique of a reductive and monolithic caricature of rationality advanced by postmodernists is one theme at issue in recent theory wars, a turn that Bernstein addresses deftly in "The Rage Against Reason" and *Beyond Objectivism and Relativism*. The position that Western ideals of reason and rationality have effectively excluded women, or the feminine, is developed and appraised by Lloyd, *The Man of Reason*, and by Bordo, "The Cartesian Masculinization of Thought." David Olson, in "Mind and Media" also proposes that a Cartesian self remains the paradigm for Western concepts of thought, rationality, and knowledge, and that it is marked as well as sustained by metalinguistic and metacognitive language: "I believe that . . . ," "he contends that. . . . " Goody, "Alternative Paths to Knowledge in Oral and Literate Cultures" (in Tannen, ed., *Spoken and Written Language*, 201–15), defends a recuperation of nonliterate and non-schooled forms and ways of knowing, particularly "knowledge acquired through the

use of language" (202). He argues that traditional, nonliterate cultures' practices of oral recitation "are not simply incessant reduplications of the same thing, a pre-literate photo-copier" (207), and that there is observable growth and change in the knowledge thus transacted and transmitted, a change that is sometimes perceived or named by the actors as well. This reconciling defense of the cognitive and epistemo-logical workings of nonliterate ways of knowing and of using language is also being advanced in the work of Ong, Havelock, Heath, and, as I propose here, among feminist scholars in psychology and literary study who seek a both/and rather than an either/or approach to rationality, literacy, and ways of knowing. Ong's work has long addressed the ties between masculine identity and agonistic paradigms in aca-demia by way of illuminating the palpable nineteenth- and twentieth-century resis-tance to women's entrance into the academy as teachers and students. Ong's analysis of this history complements feminist appraisals of the ties between masculinity and rationality. Similarly, Ong's and Havelock's extended delineations and defenses of the workings of oral culture, knowledge, and language use can be seen to comple-ment rather than contrast with the views advanced by deconstructionist and post-modern critiques of rationalism. Ong's *Orality and Literacy*, Henry Sussman has re-cently proposed, "embodies Ong's response, after decades of research in oral com-munication and culture, to deconstruction and other current theoretical approaches. We are particularly indebted to this book for enlarging upon and fleshing out the [conceptual] position of the voice in Derrida's work to the point at which oral culture becomes an actual and substantial phenomenon. To a remarkable degree, Ong suc-cessfully extrapolates a model of orality that can stand alongside the Derridean constellation of qualities and attitudes associated with writing in its explicitness and comprehensiveness. The fundamental agreement between Derrida and Ong far out-weighs any specific divergence of opinion" (*High Resolution*, 215). The approach Sussman takes defines the complementarity rather than the disjunction between the critique of presence and voice advanced by Derrida, and the illumination and pro-motion of presence and orality by scholars working in the area of oral culture. A similar line of thought, and one that parallels Handelman's analysis of Augustine and Derrida in *Slayers of Moses*, is developed by Tyler in *The Unspeakable*. Tyler proposes that Derrida manifests an almost palpable discomfort with presence and orality, and that "in his own way, Derrida continues the dominant tradition of Western thought that has always tried to break down the relation between words and things (*verbum* and *res*) by transforming the former into the latter. . . . His desire to write by means of things (*rebus*) rather than words is a kind of latter-day positivism" (*The Unspeakable*, 38). Noting the correspondence between traditional rhetoric in the West and Ong's notion of secondary orality, Tyler comments that traditional rhetoric, "which we might think is not only oral but oral method, is actually second-ary orality—orality based on written discourse which, as the *Phaedrus* makes clear, is the analogical source of its method" (191). The overviews of Hawkesworth, Bern-stein, and Kittay and Meyers in *Women and Moral Theory*, among other recent appraisals, provide the materials for additional complementarities to be established as a way out of the binarist impasses that have been reached in recent debates.

50. Catharine Stimpson, "Women's Studies: An Overview," 17, cited in Belenky et al., *Women's Ways of Knowing*, 221. This caution parallels Christa Wolf's warnings against rejecting the rationalist tradition entirely.

51. *Cassandra*, 260.

52. David Olson's "Mind and Media" examines literacy in terms of archival notions of texts. Havelock's incrementally developed profile of the oral epic performance as modeling through preserved communication a pattern of speech, interaction, and knowing parallels Ricoeur's reminder that oral discourse and oral literature must be viewed as more than the simple inscription of previously oral discourse (*Interpretation Theory*, 28) — the "pre-literate photo-copier" model that Goody discredits. Heath's *Ways With Words* opens up similarly ample horizons with the provision of interlanguages and transitional modes of learning, reading, and knowing that can more effectively bring marginalized populations into mainstream school success without sacrificing the richness and viability of their home languages and modes of negotiating knowledge. Smitherman provides similar interlanguages for Black English speakers, and eloquently defends Black vernacular as living speech that should not be demeaned or denied to its users. Spacks contributes another detail to these distinctions with the contrast between discourse *to* and gossip *with* (*Gossip*, 24–25).

53. *Actual Minds, Possible Worlds*, 130.

54. Ibid., 67.

55. Ibid., 68.

56. Ibid.

57. Belenky et al., *Women's Ways of Knowing*, 221.

58. Gilligan, *In a Different Voice*, 169, building on Jean Baker Miller, *Toward a New Psychology of Women*.

59. Ibid., 173.

60. Ibid., 170.

61. Ibid., 173.

62. Spacks, "The Difference It Makes," 16, in Langland and Gove, eds., *A Feminist Perspective in the Academy*, 7–24.

63. Belenky et al., *Women's Ways of Knowing*, 203.

64. Conrad, *Heart of Darkness*, 74; Gadamer, *Truth and Method*, 494.

65. *Hippolytus*, 484–89.

66. Bruner, *Actual Minds, Possible Worlds*, 71, citing Scribner and Cole, *The Psychology of Literacy*.

67. Bakhtin, *Speech Genres*, 132–33.

68. Bruner, *Actual Minds, Possible Worlds*, 131.

69. *Confessions* XI, 28.

70. Bruner, *Actual Minds, Possible Worlds*, 132, in a direct parallel to Hegel's promotion of consciousness that we are the mediators of our own knowledge.

71. Ibid.; my emphasis.

72. Schiller, "Aesthetic Letters," in *Friedrich Schiller*, 29.

73. Bruner, *Actual Minds, Possible Worlds*, 75.

74. Ibid., 132.

75. See Robert T. Oliver, *Communication and Culture in Ancient China and India*, and Curtis F. Oliver, "Some Aspects of Literacy in Ancient India." Curtis Oliver's treatment provides welcome caution through a number of detailed emendations of overly facile oral–literate dichotomies, as does Tannen, "The Myth of Orality and Literacy."

76. See Rich, *On Lies, Secrets, and Silence*; Heath, *Ways With Words*; Belenky et al., *Women's Ways of Knowing*; and Richard Rodriguez, *Hunger of Memory*.

77. Belenky et al., *Women's Ways of Knowing*, 205.

78. See more recent extensions of this approach in Gilligan et al., *Mapping the Moral Domain*.

79. However, Epstein, *Deceptive Distinctions: Sex, Gender, and the Social Order*, and Kittay and Meyers, eds., *Women and Moral Theory*, challenge the both/and solution from several perspectives. Epstein argues that social science research on difference outweighs studies of shared patterns across gender or other cultural groups, and that this disproportion has the effect of perpetuating focus on and consciousness of traditional and stereotypical gender roles and self concepts. Draine, "Refusing the Wisdom of Solomon," defends a both/and approach by proposing combinations of French and American approaches and methods that, once combined, may resolve the fight "to gain custody of feminist theory" (145).

80. du Bois, *Sowing the Body*; Nussbaum, *The Fragility of Goodness*; and Griffiths and Whitford, eds., *Feminist Perspectives in Philosophy*, extend these debates further back in time by looking at classical and subsequent philosophical treatments of ethics, ethical reasoning, reasoning, and women's participation in them. Jarratt, "The First Sophists and Discourses of the 'Other,'" appraises the parallels and disjunctions between women's and other marginalized discourses in the classical period from the perspective of feminist theory.

81. This hypothesis is explored at length by du Bois in *Sowing the Body*, and within Gilligan's discussion of the Demeter–Persephone myth (*In a Different Voice*, 22–23).

82. Belenky et al., *Women's Ways of Knowing*, 23–33.

83. Ibid., 32.

84. *Politics*, 1260a.

85. Hughes, "The Philosopher's Child," in Griffiths and Whitford, eds., *Feminist Perspectives in Philosophy*, 81, 82.

86. Democritus, fragments 110, 111, in Freeman, *Ancilla*.

87. The classic, inhospitably received, study of these negative images was Lakoff, *Language and Woman's Place*, now supplemented by Poynton, *Language and Gender, Making the Difference*.

88. *The Color Purple*, 213.

89. Susan Jarratt's work has similarly defined the contemporary field of composition teaching and research as a third sophistic.

90. Shirley Brice Heath, "The Fourth Vision."

91. Rappaport, "Word, Words, and the Problems of Language," 50.

92. Tyler, *The Unspeakable*, 216.

93. E.g., Andrea Lunsford and Lisa Ede, "Rhetoric in a New Key: Women and Collaboration." Manuscript of a paper presented at the meetings of the MLA on December 27–30, 1988.

94. Cited in Belenky et al., *Women's Ways of Knowing*, 214.

95. *New York Times Book Review*, February 26, 1989, 1, 44–45.

96. Conrad, *Heart of Darkness*, 76.

97. Rich, *On Lies, Secrets, and Silence*, 239.

98. Belenky et al., *Women's Ways of Knowing*, 95.

99. Cixous and Clement, *The Newly Born Woman*, 93. They add, slightly later, "Women have not sublimated. Fortunately" (95).

Epi Dia Logos

1. Aeschylus, *Suppliants*, 141: the Danaeds' designation of themselves in refusing marriage.

2. Rich, "Cartographies of Silence," *The Dream of a Common Language*, 16–20, here and throughout on the left hand side of the dialogue.

3. Schiller, "Aesthetic Letters," in *Friedrich Schiller*, 69.

4. Kierkegaard, *Concluding Unscientific Postscript*, 218.

5. Walker, *The Color Purple*, 213.

References

Ackrill, J.L. *Aristotle the Philosopher*. New York: Oxford University Press, 1981.

_____. *Aristotle's Categories and On Interpretation*. Oxford: Clarendon Press, 1963.

_____. "Plato and the Copula: *Sophist* 251–259." In *Plato I, Metaphysics and Epistemology*, edited by Gregory Vlastos. New York: Double-day Anchor, 1971.

Adorno, Theodor. *Negative Dialectics*. Translated by E. B. Ashton. New York: Seabury, 1973.

Allen, R.E., ed. *Studies in Plato's Metaphysics*. London: Routledge and Kegan Paul, 1967.

Annas, Julia, and Jonathan Barnes. *The Modes of Scepticism*. New York: Cambridge University Press, 1985.

Appleby, Arthur N. *Tradition and Reform in the Teaching of English*. Urbana, Ill.: National Council of Teachers of English, 1974.

Aquinas, Thomas. *Summa Theologica*. Translated and edited by Anton C. Pegis. New York: Modern Library, 1948.

Aristophanes. *The Clouds*. Translated by William Arrowsmith. Ann Arbor: University of Michigan Press, 1962.

Aristotle. *Art of Rhetoric*. Translated by John H. Freese. Cambridge, Mass.: Harvard University Press, Loeb, 1959.

_____. *The Categories, On Interpretation, Prior Analytics*. Translated by H. P. Cooke (*The Categories, On Interpretation*) and H. Tredennick (*Prior Analytics*). Cambridge, Mass.: Harvard University Press, Loeb, 1962.

_____. *Nichomachean Ethics*. Translated by H. Rackham. Cambridge, Mass.: Harvard University Press, Loeb, 1962.

_____. *Poetics*. Translated by W. Hamilton Fyfe. Cambridge, Mass.: Harvard University Press, Loeb, 1960.

_____. *The Rhetoric and the Poetics of Aristotle*. Translated by W. Rhys Roberts (*Rhetoric*) and Ingram Bywater (*Poetics*). New York: Modern Library, 1954.

_____. *Rhetoric to Alexander, Problems II*. Translated by H. Rackham. Cambridge, Mass.: Harvard University Press, Loeb, 1957.

Atwood, Margaret. *Cat's Eye*. New York: Doubleday, 1989.

Augustine. *Against the Academics*. Translated by John J. O'Meara. Ancient Christian Writers 12. Westminster, Mary.: Newman Press, 1950.

_____. *Concerning the Teacher and On the Immortality of Soul*. Translated by George G. Leckie. New York: Appleton-Century-Crofts, 1938.

_____. *Confessions*. Translated by R. S. Pine-Coffin. Harmondsworth, England: Penguin, 1961.

_____. *De Dialectica*. Translated with introduction and notes by B. Darrell Jackson. Boston: D. Reidel, 1975.

_____. *De Vera Religione*. Translated by J. H. S. Burleigh. Chicago: Henry Regency, 1959.

_____. *Earlier Writings*. Translated by John H. Burleigh. Philadelphia: Westminster Press, 1953.

_____. *Enchiridion*. Translated by Albert C. Outler. Philadelphia: Westminster Press, 1940.

_____. *The Literal Meaning of Genesis*. Translated by John Hammond Taylor, S.J. Ancient Christian Writers 41. New York: Newman Press, 1982.

_____. *On Christian Doctrine*. Translated by D. W. Robertson. New York: Bobbs-Merrill, 1983.

Bailey, Richard W., and Melanie Fosheim, eds. *Literacy for Life, the Demand for Reading and Writing*. New York: Modern Language Association, 1983.

Bakhtin, M.M. *The Dialogic Imagination*. Translated by Caryl Emerson and Michael Holquist. Austin: University of Texas Press, 1981.

_____. *Problems of Doestoevsky's Poetics*. Translated by Caryl Emerson. Minneapolis: University of Minnesota Press, 1984.

_____. *Speech Genres and Other Late Essays*. Translated by Vern W. McGee. Austin: University of Texas Press, 1986.

Baldwin, Charles. *Ancient Rhetoric and Poetic*. New York: Macmillan, 1924.

Barrett, William. *The Illusion of Technique*. New York: Doubleday/Anchor, 1979.

Bateson, Gregory. "Observations of a Cetacean Community." *Mind in the Waters*. Edited by Joan McIntyre. New York: Scribners, 1974.

_____. *Steps to an Ecology of Mind*. New York: Ballantine, 1972.

_____. "Toward a Theory of Schizophrenia." *Behavioral Science* 1 (1956): 251–64.

Bauman, Richard, and Joel Sherzer, eds. *Explorations in the Ethnography of Speaking*. New York: Cambridge University Press, 1974.

Bede. *De Schematibus et Tropis*. Translated by Guissie Hecht Tanenhaus. *Quarterly Journal of Speech* 68:3 (1962): 237–53.

Belenky, Mary Field, Blythe McVicker Clinchy, Nancy Rule Goldberger, and Jill Mattuck Tarule. *Women's Ways of Knowing*. New York: Basic Books, 1986.

Berlin, James A. *Rhetoric and Reality: Writing Instruction in American Colleges, 1900–1985*. Carbondale: Southern Illinois University Press, 1987.

_____. *Writing Instruction in Nineteenth-Century American Colleges*. CCCC Studies in Writing Rhetoric Series. Carbondale: Southern Illinois University Press, 1984.

Bernstein, Richard J. *Beyond Objectivism and Relativism: Science, Hermeneutics, and Practice*. Philadelphia: University of Pennsylvania Press, 1983.

_____. "The Rage Against Reason." *Philosophy and Literature* 10:2 (October 1986): 186–210.

Bett, Richard. "The Sophists and Relativism." *Phronesis* 34:2 (1989): 139–69.

Bevan, Edwyn. *Stoics and Sceptics*. Cambridge: W. Heffner and Sons, 1959.

Bluck, Richard S. *Plato's Sophist*. Manchester: University of Manchester Press, 1975.

Booth, Wayne. *Critical Understanding*. Chicago: University of Chicago Press, 1979.

_____. "Introduction." In Mikhail Bakhtin, *Problems of Dostoevsky's Poetics*, translated by Caryl Emerson. Minneapolis: University of Minnesota Press, 1984.

_____. *The Rhetoric of Fiction*. Chicago: University of Chicago Press, 1961.

_____. *A Rhetoric of Irony*. Chicago: University of Chicago Press, 1974.

Bochenski, Joseph M. *Ancient Formal Logic*. Amsterdam: North Holland Publishing C., 1951.

Bok, Sissela. *Lying*. New York: Pantheon Books, 1978.

Bordo, Susan. "The Cartesian Masculinization of Thought." *Signs* 11:3 (1986): 439–56.

Brickhouse, Thomas C., and Nicholas D. Smith. *Socrates on Trial*. Princeton: Princeton University Press, 1990.

Brindel, June. *Ariadne*. New York: St. Martin's Press, 1981.

Bruner, Jerome S. *Actual Minds, Possible Worlds*. Cambridge, Mass.: Harvard University Press, 1987.

_____, and David R. Olson. "Symbols and Texts as the Tools of Intellect." *Interchange* 8:4 (1978): 1–15.

Bryant, Donald C. *Ancient Greek and Roman Rhetoricians*. Columbia, Mo.: Artcraft Press, 1968.

Bubacz, Bruce. *St. Augustine's Theory of Knowledge: A Contemporary Analysis*. New York: Edwin Mellen, 1982.

Burger, Ronna. *Plato's Phaedrus: A Defense of a Philosophic Art of Writing*. University, Ala.: University of Alabama Press, 1980.

Burke, Kenneth. *The Rhetoric of Religion*. Berkeley: University of California Press, 1961.

Butterworth, Charles E. *Averroes' Middle Commentaries on Aristotle's "Categories" and "On Interpretation."* Princeton: Princeton University Press, 1983.

————. *Averroes' Three Short Commentaries on Aristotle's "Topics," "Rhetoric," and "Poetics."* Albany: State University of New York Press, 1977.

Caplan, Harry. "Classical Rhetoric and Medieval Theory of Preaching." *Classical Philology* 27 (1933): 73–93.

————. "The Four Senses of Scriptural Interpretation and the Medieval Theory of Preaching." *Speculum* 4 (1929): 282–90.

Carnap, Rudolf. "Religious Language Is Meaningless." In *Logical Positivism*, edited by A. J. Ayer. Glencoe, Ill.: The Free Press, 1959.

Charlesworth, M.J. *The Problem of Religious Language.* Englewood Cliffs, N.J.: Prentice-Hall, 1974.

Chenu, M.D. *Nature, Man, and Society in the Twelfth Century.* Chicago: University of Chicago Press, 1968.

Cherniss, Harold. *Aristotle's Criticism of Plato and the Academy.* Baltimore: The Johns Hopkins University Press, 1944.

————. *Aristotle's Criticism of PreSocratic Philosophy.* Baltimore: The Johns Hopkins University Press, 1935.

Cicero. *Brutus; Orator.* Translated by G. L. Hendrickson and H. M. Hubbell respectively. Cambridge, Mass.: Harvard University Press, Loeb, 1939.

————. *De Inventione; De Optimo; Genere Oratorium; Topica.* Translated by H. M. Hubbell. Cambridge, Mass.: Harvard University Press, Loeb, 1949.

————. *De Natura Deorum; Academica.* Translated by H. Rackham. Cambridge, Mass.: Harvard University Press, Loeb, 1933.

————. *De Oratore,* Vol. 1, Books 1 and 2. Translated by E. W. Sutton. Cambridge, Mass.: Harvard University Press, Loeb, 1942.

————. *De Oratore,* Vol. 2, Book 3; *De Fato; Paradoxa Stoicorum; De Partitione Oratoria.* Translated by H. Rackham. Cambridge, Mass.: Harvard University Press, Loeb, 1944.

————. *Rhetorica ad Herennium.* Translated by Harry Caplan. Cambridge, Mass.: Harvard University Press, Loeb, 1954.

Cipolla, C.M. *Literacy and Development in the West.* Baltimore: Penguin, 1969.

Cixous, Helene, and Catherine Clement. *The Newly Born Woman.* Translated by Betsy Wing. Minneapolis: University of Minnesota Press, 1986.

Clanchy, M.T. *From Memory to Written Record in England, 1066–1307.* Cambridge, Mass.: Harvard University Press, 1979.

Clark, Donald Leman. *Rhetoric in Graeco-Roman Education.* New York: Columbia University Press, 1957.

Classen, Carl Joachim. "The Study of Language Among Socrates' Contemporaries." *Proceedings of the African Classical Association* (1959), 33–49.

Clement of Alexandria. *Christ the Educator.* Translated by Simon P. Wood, C.P. New York: Fathers of the Church, 1954.

Colie, Rosalie, *Paradoxia Epidemica*. Princeton: Princeton University Press, 1966.

Conners, Robert John. "Greek Rhetoric and the Transition from Orality." *Philosophy and Rhetoric* 19 (1986): 38–65.

Connor, W. Robert. *Thucydides*. Princeton: Princeton University Press, 1984.

Conrad, Joseph. *Heart of Darkness*. Edited by Robert Kimbrough. New York: W. W. Norton, 1987.

Cook-Gumperz, Jenny, and John Gumperz. "From Oral to Written Culture: The Transition to Literacy." In *Variation in Writing*, edited by Marcia Farr Whiteman. Hillsdale, N.J.: Lawrence Erlbaum, 1981.

Cope, E.M. *An Introduction to Aristotle's Rhetoric*. London: MacMillan and Co., 1867.

Copelston, Frederick, S.J. *A History of Philosophy*, vol. 2, part 1. *Augustine to Bonaventure*. New York: Doubleday/Image, 1962.

Copperman, Paul. *The Literacy Hoax*. New York: Morrow, 1978.

Corcoran, Paul. *Political Language and Rhetoric*. Austin: University of Texas Press, 1979.

Cornford, Francis Macdonald. *Plato and Parmenides*. London: Routledge and Kegan Paul, 1939.

Coulmas, Florian. *The Writing Systems of the World*. Oxford: Blackwell, 1989.

Covino, William. *The Art of Wondering: A Revisionist Return to the History of Rhetoric*. Portsmouth, N.H.: Boynton/Cook, Heinemann, 1988.

Cressy, David. *Literacy and the Social Order*. New York: Cambridge University Press, 1980.

Davidson, Thomas. *The Education of the Greek People*. New York: Appleton, Century, Crofts, 1912.

DeFrancis, John. *Visible Speech: The Diverse Oneness of Writing Systems*. Honolulu: University of Hawaii Press, 1989.

de Kerckhove, Derrick. "A Theory of Greek Tragedy." *Sub-Stance*, 29 (1981): 23–36.

de la Cruz, Sor Juana Inez. *La Respuesta/A Woman of Genius*. Translated by Margaret Sayers Peden. Salisbury, Conn.: Lime Rock Press, 1982.

de Lille, Alain. *Anticlaudianus, or The Good and Perfect Man*. Translated by James J. Sheridan. Toronto: Pontifical Institute of Medieval Studies, 1973.

deMan, Paul. "Semiology and Rhetoric." In *Textual Strategies*, edited by Josue Harari. Ithaca, N.Y.: Cornell University Press, 1979.

de Romilly, Jacqueline. *Magic and Rhetoric in Ancient Greece*. Cambridge, Mass.: Harvard University Press, 1975.

Derrida, Jacques. *Dissemination*. Translated by Barbara Johnson. Chicago: University of Chicago Press, 1981.

———. *Of Grammatology*. Translated by Gayatri Chakravorti Spivak. Baltimore: The Johns Hopkins University Press, 1976.

———. *Positions*. Translated by Alan Bass. Chicago: University of Chicago Press, 1981.

———. "The Supplement of Copula: Philosophy *before* Linguistics." In *Textual Strategies*, edited by Josue Harari. Ithaca, N.Y.: Cornell University Press, 1979.

———. *Writing and Difference*. Translated by Alan Bass. Chicago: University of Chicago Press, 1978.

Dimond, S.J. *The Double Brain*. Baltimore: Wilkins and Wilkins, 1972.

Diogenes Laertius. *Lives and Opinions of Eminent Philosophers*. Translated by C. D. Yonge. London: George Bell and Sons, 1901.

Diringer, David. *The Alphabet*. New York: Philosophical Library, 1948.

———. *The Book Before Printing*. New York: Dover, 1982.

———. *Writing*. New York: Praeger, 1962.

Donlan, Walter, ed. *The Classical World Bibliography of Philosophy, Religion, and Rhetoric*. New York: Garland, 1978.

Donne, John. *The Complete Poetry of John Donne*. Edited by John Shawcross. New York: New York University Press, 1968.

Draine, Betsy. "Refusing the Wisdom of Solomon." *Signs* 15:1 (Autumn 1989): 144–71.

Drever, James. *Greek Education, Its Practice and Principles*. Cambridge: Cambridge University Press, 1912.

du Bois, Page. *Sowing the Body: Psychoanalysis and Ancient Representations of Women*. Chicago: University of Chicago Press, 1988.

Ebeling, Gerhard. *Introduction to a Theological Theory of Language*. Philadelphia: Fortress Press, 1971.

Ehninger, Douglas. *Contemporary Rhetoric*. Glenview, Ill.: Scott, Foresman, and Co., 1972.

Eisenstein, Elizabeth. *The Printing Press as an Agent of Change*. Cambridge: Cambridge University Press, 1979.

Elbow, Peter. *Embracing Contraries: Explorations in Learning and Teaching*. New York: Oxford University Press, 1986.

Else, Gerald. *Aristotle's Poetics: The Argument*. Ann Arbor, University of Michigan Press, 1967.

Enos, Richard Leo. "The Epistemology of Gorgias's Rhetoric: A Re-examination." *Southern Speech Communication Journal* 42 (Fall 1976): 35–51.

Epstein, Cynthia Fuchs. *Deceptive Distinctions: Sex, Gender, and the Social Order*. New Haven: Yale University Press; New York: Russell Sage Foundation, 1988.

Euripides. *Hippolytus*. In *Greek Tragedies*, edited by David Grene and Richard Lattimore, vol. 1. Chicago: University of Chicago Press, 1968.

Evans, J.D.G. *Aristotle's Concept of Dialectic*. Cambridge: Cambridge University Press, 1977.

Findlay, J.N. *Plato: The Written and Unwritten Doctrines*. New York: Humanities Press, 1974.

Finley, M.I. *Ancient History, Evidence and Models*. New York: Viking Penguin, 1987.

_____. *The Use and Abuse of History*. Rev. ed. New York: Viking Penguin, 1987.

Fornara, Charles William. *The Nature of History in Ancient Greece and Rome*. Berkeley: University of California Press, 1983.

Foucault, Michel. *The Archaeology of Knowledge and the Discourse on Language*. Translated by A. M. Sheridan Smith. New York: Pantheon, 1972.

_____. "What Is an Author?" In *Textual Strategies*, edited by Josue Harari. Ithaca, N.Y.: Cornell University Press, 1979.

France, Peter. *Rhetoric and Truth in France, Descartes to Diderot*. Oxford: Clarendon Press, 1972.

Freeman, Kathleen. *Ancilla to the Pre-Socratic Philosophers*. Cambridge, Mass.: Harvard University Press, 1983.

Freeman, Kenneth. *Schools of Hellas*. 1907. Reprint. Port Washington, N.Y.: Kennikat Press, 1969.

Friedrich, Paul. *The Language Parallax: Linguistic Relativism and Poetic Indeterminacy*. Austin: University of Texas Press, 1986.

Frye, Northrup. *The Great Code: The Bible and Literature*. New York: Harvest/Harcourt Brace Jovanovich, 1982.

Gadamer, Hans Georg. *Dialogue and Dialectic*. Translated by P. Christopher Smith. New Haven: Yale University Press, 1980.

_____. *Truth and Method*. New York: Seabury, 1975.

Gallop, Jane. *Reading Lacan*. Ithaca, N.Y.: Cornell University Press, 1985.

Gelb, I.J. *A Study of Writing*. Chicago: University of Chicago Press, 1963.

Gilbert, K.E., and Helmut Kuhn. *A History of Esthetics*. New York: Dover, 1972.

Gilligan, Carol. *In a Different Voice*. Cambridge, Mass.: Harvard University Press, 1982.

Gilligan, Carol, Janie Victoria Ward, and Jean McLean Taylor, with Betty Bardige. *Mapping the Moral Domain: A Contribution of Women's Thinking to Psychological Theory and Education*. Cambridge, Mass.: Harvard University Press, 1989.

Goody, Jack. *The Domestication of the Savage Mind*. New York: Cambridge University Press, 1977.

_____. *The Interface Between the Written and the Oral*. New York: Cambridge University Press, 1987.

_____., ed. *Literacy in Traditional Societies*. New York: Cambridge University Press, 1968.

Graff, Harvey J. *The Legacies of Literacy: Continuities and Contradictions in Western Culture and Society*. Bloomington: University of Indiana Press, 1987.

Grafton, Anthony, and Lisa Jardine. *From Humanism to the Humanities.* Cambridge, Mass.: Harvard University Press, 1986.

Greene, W.C. "The Spoken and the Written Word." *Harvard Studies in Classical Philology* 60 (1951): 23–59.

Greenfield, Concetta. *Humanist and Scholastic Poetics, 1250–1500.* Philadelphia: Bucknell, 1981.

Grene, David, and Richard Lattimore, eds. *Greek Tragedies.* Vol. 1. Chicago: University of Chicago Press, 1960.

Griffiths, Morwena, and Margaret Whitford, eds. *Feminist Perspectives in Philosophy.* Bloomington: Indiana University Press, 1988.

Grimaldi, William M.A., S.J. "Studies in the Philosophy of Aristotle's Rhetoric." *Hermes* 25 (1972): 1–151.

Griswold, Charles L. *Self-knowledge in Plato's* Phaedrus. New Haven: Yale University Press, 1986.

Guthrie, W.K.C. *The Sophists.* New York: Cambridge University Press, 1971.

Gwynn, A.O. *Roman Education from Cicero to Quintilian.* Oxford: Oxford University Press, 1926.

Haber, R.N. "Twenty Years of Hunting Eidetic Imagery: Where's the Ghost?" *The Behavioral and Brain Sciences* 3 (1979): 583–629.

Halloran, Stephen Michael. "On the End of Rhetoric, Classical and Modern." *College English* 36 (1975): 621–31.

Handelman, Susan. *The Slayers of Moses.* Albany, N.Y.: State University of New York Press, 1983.

Harari, Josue, ed. *Textual Strategies.* Ithaca, N.Y.: Cornell University Press, 1979.

Harrison, Jane Ellen. *Themis; Epilegomena.* 1921, 1927. Reprint. New Hyde Park, N.Y.: University Books, 1962.

Havelock, Eric A. *The Liberal Temper in Greek Politics.* New Haven: Yale University Press, 1957.

———. "The Linguistic Task of the Presocratics." In *Language and Thought in Early Greek Philosophy*, edited by Kevin Robb. LaSalle, Ill.: Hegeler Institute, 1983.

———. *The Literate Revolution in Greece and Its Cultural Consequences.* Princeton: Princeton University Press, 1982.

———. *The Muse Learns to Write.* New Haven: Yale University Press, 1986.

———. "Parmenides and Odysseus." *Harvard Studies in Classical Philology* 63 (1958): 133–43.

———. *Preface to Plato.* Cambridge, Mass.: Harvard University Press, 1963.

Hawkesworth, Mary E. "Knowers, Knowing, Known: Feminist Theory and Claims of Truth." *Signs* 14:3 (Spring 1989): 533–57.

Heath, Shirley Brice. "The Fourth Vision: Literate Language at Work." In *The Right to Literacy*, edited by Andrea A. Lunsford, Helene Moglen, and James Slevin. New York: Modern Language Association, 1990.

_____. *Ways With Words*. New York: Cambridge University Press, 1983.

Hegel, G.W.F. *The Phenomenology of Mind*. Translated by J. B. Baillie. New York: Harper and Row, 1967.

Heidegger, Martin. *Early Greek Thinking*. New York: Harper and Row, 1975.

Herrnstein-Smith, Barbara. *Contingencies of Value*. Cambridge, Mass.: Harvard University Press, 1988.

Hesiod. *Homeric Hymns and Homerica*. Translated by Hugh G. Evelyn White. Cambridge, Mass.: Harvard University Press, 1936.

Hinks, D.A.G. "Tisias and Corax and the Invention of Rhetoric." *Classical Quarterly* 34 (1940): 61–67.

Hoggart, Richard. *The Uses of Literacy*. Fairlawn, N.J.: Essential Books, 1957.

Horton, Robin, and Ruth Finnegan, eds. *Modes of Thought*. London: Faber and Faber, 1973.

Howell, Wilbur Samuel. *Logic and Rhetoric in England, 1500–1700*. Princeton: Princeton University Press, 1956.

Huppé, Bernard F. *Doctrine and Poetry: Augustine's Influence on Old English Poetry*. New York: State University of New York Press, 1959.

Jaeger, Werner. *Paideia*. New York: Oxford University Press, 1979.

Jarratt, Susan C. "The First Sophists and Feminism: Discourses of the 'Other.'" *Hypatia* 5:1 (1990): 27–41.

_____. "The First Sophists and the Uses of History." *Rhetoric Review* 6 (1987): 166–78.

_____. "Toward a Sophistic Historiography." *Pre/Text* 8:1–2 (1988): 9–27.

Kahn, Charles H. *The Art and Thought of Heraclitus*. New York: Cambridge University Press, 1983.

_____. "The Greek Verb 'To Be' and the Concept of Being." *Foundations of Language* 2 (1966): 245–65.

Kant, Immanuel. *Fundamental Principles of the Metaphysics of Morals*. Translated by Thomas K. Abbot. New York: Bobbs Merrill, 1949.

Kelber, Werner. *The Oral and the Written Gospel: The Hermeneutics of Speaking and Writing in the Synoptic Tradition, Mark, Paul, and Q*. Philadelphia: Fortress Press, 1983.

Kennedy, George A. *The Art of Persuasion in Greece*. Princeton: Princeton University Press, 1963.

_____. *The Art of Rhetoric in the Roman World*. Princeton: Princeton University Press, 1972.

_____. *Classical Rhetoric and Its Christian and Secular Tradition from Ancient to Modern Times*. Chapel Hill: University of North Carolina Press, 1980.

_____. "The Earliest Rhetorical Handbooks." *American Journal of Philology* 80 (1959): 169–78.

_____. *New Testament Interpretation Through Rhetorical Criticism*. Chapel Hill, N.C.: University of North Carolina Press, 1984.

Kenyon, Frederic G. *Books and Readers in Ancient Greece and Rome*. Oxford: Oxford University Press, 1932.

Kerferd, G.B. "The First Greek Sophists." *Classical Review* 64:1 (April 1950): 8–10.

―――. "Gorgias on Nature or That Which Is Not." *Phronesis* 1 (1955): 3–25.

Kierkegaard, Søren. *The Concept of Irony, with Constant Reference to Socrates*. Translated by Lee M. Capel. New York: Harper and Row, 1966.

―――. *Concluding Unscientific Postscript*. Translated by D. F. Swensen and W. Lowrie. Princeton: Princeton University Press, 1941.

―――. *Either/Or*. 2 vols. Translated by David F. and Lillian Marvin Swenson. Garden City, N.Y.: Doubleday, 1959.

―――. *Letters and Documents*. Translated and edited by Henirk Rosenmeier. Princeton: Princeton University Press, 1978.

―――. *The Point of View*. Translated by Walter L. Lowrie. New York: Oxford University Press, 1939.

King, Charles. *Hieroglyphs to Alphabets*. London: Frederick Muller, 1977.

Kirk, G.S. *Heraclitus, the Cosmic Fragments*. New York: Cambridge University Press, 1954.

Kirk, G.S., and J. E. Raven. *The Presocratic Philosophers*. New York: Cambridge University Press, 1957.

Kittay, Eva Feder, and Diana T. Meyers, eds. *Women and Moral Theory*. Totowa, N.J.: Rowman and Littlefield, 1987.

Klein, Jacob. *Plato's Trilogy: The Theaetetus, Sophist, and Statesman*. Chicago: University of Chicago Press, 1977.

Kristeva, Julia. *Desire in Language*. Translated by Thomas Gora, Alice Jardine, and Leon S. Roudiez. New York: Columbia University Press, 1980.

―――. *In the Beginning Was Love: Psychoanalysis and Faith*. New York: Columbia University Press, 1988.

―――. "Women's Time." *Signs* 7:1 (1981): 13–35.

Kroll, Barry M., and Robert J. Vann, eds. *Exploring Speaking-Writing Relationships: Connections and Contrasts*. Urbana, Ill.: National Council of Teachers of English, 1981.

Lakoff, Robin. *Language and Woman's Place*. New York: Harper and Row, 1975.

Langland, E., and W. Gove, eds. *A Feminist Perspective in the Academy*. Chicago: University of Chicago Press, 1983.

Lefkowitz, Mary. *Women in Greek Myth*. Baltimore: The Johns Hopkins University Press, 1986.

Lentz, Tony. *Orality and Literacy in Hellenic Greece*. Carbondale, Ill.: Southern Illinois University Press, 1989.

Lloyd, Genevieve. *The Man of Reason: "Male" and "Female" in Western Philosophy*. Minneapolis: University of Minnesota Press, 1984.

Loenen, J.H.M.M. *Parmenides, Melissus, Gorgias: A Reinterpretation of Eleatic Philosophy*. Amsterdam: 1959.

Logan, Robert K. *The Alphabet Effect*. New York: William Morrow, 1986.

Lonergan, Bernard J. *Verbum: Word and Idea in Aquinas*. Notre Dame, Ind.: University of Notre Dame Press, 1967.

Lord, Albert B. "Perspectives on Recent Work in Oral Literature." In *Oral Literature*, edited by Joseph J. Duggan. New York: Barnes and Noble, 1975.

_____. *Singer of Tales*. Cambridge, Mass.: Harvard University Press, 1960.

Luriia, A.R. *Cognitive Development: Its Cultural and Social Foundations*. Translated by Martin Lopez-Morillas and Lynn Solotaroff. Cambridge, Mass.: Harvard University Press, 1976.

_____. *Language and Cognition*. Translated by Iazyk L. Soznanie. New York: Wiley, 1981.

Lynch, John Patrick. *Aristotle's School: A Study of a Greek Educational Institution*. Berkeley: University of California Press, 1972.

Mackie, Robert, ed. *Literacy and Revolution: The Pedagogy of Paolo Friere*. London: Pluto, 1980.

Maier, John, and Vincent Tollers, eds. *The Bible in Its Literacy Milieu*. Grand Rapids, Mich.: Eerdmans, 1979.

Maranhāo, Tullio. *Therapeutic Discourse and Socratic Dialogue: A Cultural Critique*. Madison: University of Wisconsin Press, 1986.

Marcus, Jane. "Storming the Toolshed." *Signs* 7:3 (1982): 622–40.

Markus, R.A., ed. *Augustine: A Collection of Critical Essays*. New York: Doubleday/Anchor, 1972.

Marrou, H.I. *A History of Education in Antiquity*. Translated by George Lamb. New York: Sheed and Ward, 1956.

Mates, Benson. *Stoic Logic*. 1953. Reprint. Berkeley: University of California Press, 1973.

McCall, Marsh H. *Ancient Rhetorical Theories of Simile and Comparison*. Cambridge, Mass.: Harvard University Press, 1969.

McKee, John. *Literary Irony and the Literary Audience: The Victimization of the Audience in Augustan Fiction*. Amsterdam: Rodopi, 1974.

McKeon, Richard. "Rhetoric in the Middle Ages." *Speculum* 52:1 (1942): 1–32.

Mellor, Anne K. *English Romantic Irony*. Cambridge, Mass.: Harvard University Press, 1980.

Milton, John. *The Complete Prose Works of John Milton*. Vol. 6 (1658–1660). New Haven: Yale University Press, 1957.

Moreau, Jules Laurence. *Language and Religious Language*. Philadelphia: Westminster Press, 1951.

Muecke, D.C. *Irony*. London: Methuen, 1970.

Murphy, James J. *Rhetoric in the Middle Ages: A History of Rhetorical Theory from Saint Augustine to the Renaissance*. Berkeley: University of California Press, 1974.

_____. "Saint Augustine and the Debate About a Christian Rhetoric." *Quarterly Journal of Speech* 46:4 (1960): 400–410.

Nadeau, Ray. "Hermogenes on 'Stock Issues' in Deliberative Speaking." *Speech Monographs* 25 (1958): 19–37, 56–66.

Nelson, John, Alan Megill, and Donald McCloskey, eds. *The Rhetoric of the Human Sciences: Language and Argument in Scholarship and Public Affairs*. Madison: University of Wisconsin Press, 1987.

Noddings, Nel. *Caring*. Berkeley: University of California Press, 1984.

Nussbaum, Martha. *The Fragility of Goodness*. New York: Cambridge University Press, 1986.

Ober, Josiah. *Mass and Elite in Democratic Athens: Rhetoric, Ideology and the Power of the People*. Princeton: Princeton University Press, 1989.

Oliver, Curtis I. "Some Aspects of Literacy in Ancient India." *Quarterly Newsletter of the Laboratory of Comparative Human Cognition* 1:4 (October 1979): 57–62.

Oliver, Robert T. *Communication and Culture in Ancient China and India*. Syracuse, N.Y.: Syracuse University Press, 1971.

Olson, David. "From Utterance to Text: The Bias of Language in Speech and Writing." *Harvard Educational Review* 47 (1977): 257–81.

_____. "The Language of Instruction and the Literate Bias of Schooling." *Schooling and the Acquisition of Knowledge*. Edited by R. C. Anderson, F. J. Siro, and W. E. Montague. Hillsdale, N.J.: Erlbaum, 1977.

_____. "Mind and Media: The Epistemic Functions of Literacy." *Journal of Communication* 38:3 (Summer 1988): 27–36.

_____. "Oral and Written Language and the Cognitive Processes of Children." *Journal of Communication* 27 (1927): 10–26.

Olson, David, and Janet Astington. "Children's Acquisition of Metalinguistic and Metacognitive Verbs." In *Language, Learning, and Concept Acquisition*, edited by W. Demopoulos and A. Marras. Norwood, N.J.: Ablex, 1986.

Olson, Elder. *Aristotle's "Poetics" and English Literature*. Chicago: University of Chicago Press, 1965.

Ong, Walter J., S.J. *Interfaces of the Word*. Ithaca, N.Y.: Cornell University Press, 1977.

_____. *Orality and Literacy*. New York: Methuen, 1982.

_____. *Ramus, Method, and the Decay of Dialogue*. Cambridge, Mass.: Harvard University Press, 1958.

_____. *Rhetoric, Romance, and Technology*. Ithaca, N.Y.: Cornell University Press, 1971.

Organ, Troy Wilson. *An Index to Aristotle*. New York: Gordian, 1966.

Owen, G.E.L. *Logic, Science, and Dialectic*. Ithaca, N.Y.: Cornell University Press, 1986.

_____, ed. *Aristotle on Dialectic: The Topics*. Oxford: Clarendon Press, 1968.

Oxenham, John. *Literacy: Writing, Reading and Social Organisation*. London: Routledge and Kegan Paul, 1980.

Pahlka, William Hale. *Saint Augustine's Meter and George Herbert's Will*. Kent, Ohio: Kent State University Press, 1987.

Patrick, Mary Mills. *The Greek Sceptics*. New York: Columbia University Press, 1929.

Pattison, Robert. *On Literacy*. New York: Oxford University Press, 1982.

Peck, A.L. "Plato and the *megista gene* of the *Sophist*: A Reinterpretation." *Classical Quarterly* 2 (1952): 32–56.

Percy, Walker. "Metaphor as Mistake." *Sewanee Review* 66 (1958): 79–99.

Peters, F.E. *Greek Philosophical Terms*. New York: New York University Press, 1967.

Phelps, Louise Wetherbee. *Composition as a Human Science*. New York: Oxford University Press, 1988.

Piaget, Jean. *Genetic Epistemology*. Translated by Eleanor Duckworth. New York: Norton, 1971.

Plato. *The Being of the Beautiful: Theaetetus, Sophist, Statesman*. Translated with commentary by Seth Benardete. Chicago: University of Chicago Press, 1984.

————. *Cratylus, Parmenides, Greater Hippias, Lesser Hippias*. Translated by H. N. Fowler. Cambridge, Mass.: Harvard University Press, Loeb, 1963.

————. *Euthyphro, Apology, Crito, Phaedo, Phaedrus*. Translated by H. N. Fowler. Cambridge, Mass.: Harvard University Press, Loeb, 1966.

————. *Gorgias*. Translated by W. C. Helmbold. New York: Bobbs-Merrill/Library of Liberal Arts, 1952.

————. *Laws*. Translated with interpretive essay by Thomas L. Pangle. New York: Basic Books, 1980.

————. *Lysis, Symposium, Gorgias*. Translated by W. R. M. Lamb. Cambridge, Mass.: Harvard University Press, Loeb, 1975.

————. *Parmenides*. Translated with analysis by R. E. Allen. Minneapolis: University of Minnesota Press, 1983.

————. *Phaedrus and Letter VII*. Translated by Walter Hamilton. Harmondsworth, England: Penguin, 1973.

————. *Protagoras*. Translated with commentary by B. A. F. Hubbard and E. S. Karnofsky. Chicago: University of Chicago Press, 1982.

————. *Theaetetus, Sophist*. Translated by H. N. Fowler. Cambridge, Mass.: Harvard University Press, Loeb, 1977.

Poulakos, Takis. "Continuities and Discontinuities in the History of Rhetoric: A Brief History of Classical Funeral Orations." *Western Journal of Speech* 54:2 (Spring 1990): 172–88.

————. "Epideictic Rhetoric as Social Hegemony: Isocrates *Helen*." In *Rhetoric and Ideology: Compositions and Criticisms of Power*, edited by Charles Kneupper. Arlington, Tex.: Rhetoric Society of America, 1989.

————. "The Historical Intervention of Gorgias' *Epitaphios*: The Genre of Funeral Oration and the Athenian Institution of Public Burials." *Pre/Text* 10:1–2 (1989): 90–99.

Poynton, Cate. *Language and Gender: Making the Difference.* New York: Oxford University Press, 1989.

Price, Robert. "Some Antistrophes to the Rhetoric." *Aristotle: The Classical Heritage of Rhetoric.* Edited by Keith Erickson. Metuchen, N.J.: Scarecrow Press, 1974.

Rappaport, Roy A. *Ecology, Meaning, and Religion.* Richmond, Calif.: North Atlantic Books, 1988.

———. "The Sacred in Human Evolution." *Annual Review of Ecology and Systematics* 2 (1971): 23–44.

———. "Word, Words, and the Problems of Language." In *The Word: Studies in the Language of Religion and the Religious Meaning of Language,* edited by C. Jan Swearingen. Tucson: University of Arizona Press, forthcoming.

Raymond, James C., ed. *Literacy as a Human Problem.* University, Ala.: University of Alabama Press, 1982.

Resnick, D.P., and L. B. Resnick. "The Nature of Literacy: An Historical Exploration." *Harvard Educational Review* 47 (1977): 370–85.

Rexine, John E. *Religion in Plato and Cicero.* New York: Philosophical Library, 1959.

Rich, Adrienne. *The Dream of a Common Language.* New York: Norton, 1978.

———. *On Lies, Secrets, and Silence.* New York: Norton, 1979.

Richards, I.A. *The Philosophy of Rhetoric.* New York: Oxford University Press, 1965.

Ricoeur, Paul. *Interpretation Theory: Discourse and the Surplus of Meaning.* Fort Worth, Tex.: Texas Christian University Press, 1976.

———. "Toward a Post-Critical Rhetoric?" *Pre/Text* 5:1 (1984): 9–18.

Rist, John M., ed. *The Stoics.* Berkeley: University of California Press, 1978.

———. *Stoic Philosophy.* London: Cambridge University Press, 1969.

Robinson, Richard. *Plato's Earlier Dialectic.* Oxford: Clarendon Press, 1953.

Rodriguez, Richard. *Hunger of Memory.* New York: Bantam, 1982.

Rosch, Eleanor, and Barbara B. Lloyd, eds. *Cognition and Categorization.* Hillsdale, N.J.: Erlbaum, 1978.

Rose, Lynn E. *Aristotle's Syllogistic.* Springfield, Ill.: Charles C. Thomas, 1968.

Rosen, Stanley. *Plato's Sophist.* New Haven: Yale University Press, 1983.

Rosenmeyer, Thomas G. *The Art of Aeschylus.* Berkeley: University of California Press, 1982.

———. "Gorgias, Aeschylus, and *Apate.*" *American Journal of Philology* 76:3 (1955): 225–60.

Ryle, Gilbert. *The Concept of Mind.* New York: Barnes and Noble, 1960.

———. *Dilemmas.* Cambridge: Cambridge University Press, 1964.

———. *Plato's Progress.* Cambridge: Cambridge University Press, 1966.

Sanford, W.B. *Ambiguity in Greek Literature.* New York: Johnson Reprint Co., 1972.

Santas, Gerasimos. *Plato and Freud: Two Theories of Love*. Oxford: Blackwell, 1988.

Sapir, Edward. "Conceptual Categories in Primitive Language." *Science* 5 (1931): 578.

Saussure, Ferdinand de. *Course General in Linguistics*. Translated by Wade Baskin. New York: McGraw-Hill, 1966.

Schieffelin, Bambi, and Parry Gilmore, eds. *The Aquisition of Literacy: Ethnographic Perspectives*. Norwood, N.J.: Ablex, 1986.

Schilb, John. "The History of Rhetoric and the Rhetoric of History." *Pre/Text* 7 (1987): 11–34.

Schiller, Friedrich. *Friedrich Schiller*. Translated and edited by Friedrich Ungar. New York: Ungar, 1959.

Schlegel, Friedrich. *Dialogue on Poetry and Literary Aphorisms*. Translated by Ernst Behler and Roman Struc. University Park: Pennsylvania State University Press, 1968.

Schmandt-Besserat, Denise. "The Earliest Precursor of Writing." *Scientific American* 238:6 (1978): 50–59.

Scribner, Sylvia, and Michael Cole. *The Psychology of Literacy*. Cambridge, Mass.: Harvard University Press, 1981.

Sedgwick, G.G. *Of Irony: Especially in Drama*. Toronto: University of Toronto Press, 1948.

Seeskin, Kenneth. "Is the *Apology* of Socrates a Parody?" *Philosophy and Literature* 6 (1982): 94–105.

Sextus Empiricus. *Against the Logicians*. Translated by R. G. Bury. Cambridge, Mass.: Harvard University Press, Loeb, 1935.

_____. *Against the Physicists, Against the Ethicists*. Translated by R. G. Bury. Cambridge, Mass.: Harvard University Press, Loeb, 1936.

_____. *Outlines of Pyrrhonism*. Translated by R. G. Bury. Cambridge, Mass.: Harvard University Press, Loeb, 1933.

Shakespeare, William. *The Complete Works of William Shakespeare*. New York: Walter J. Black, 1929.

Short, Bryan C. "The Temporality of Rhetoric." *Rhetoric Review* 7:2 (Spring 1989): 367–69.

Smith, Anthony. *The Geopolitics of Information*. New York: Oxford University Press, 1980.

Smith, Robert W. *The Art of Rhetoric in Alexandria*. The Hague: Martinus Nijhoff, 1974.

Solmsen, Friedrich. "Dialectic Without the Forms." In *Aristotle on Dialectic: The Topics*, edited by G. E. L. Owen. Oxford: Clarendon Press, 1968.

Spacks, Patricia Meyers. *Gossip*. Chicago: University of Chicago Press, 1986.

Sprague, Rosamond Kent. *Plato's Use of Fallacy*. London: Routledge and Kegan Paul, 1962.

Stock, Brian. *The Implications of Literacy: Written Language and Models of Interpretation in the Eleventh and Twelfth Centuries*. Princeton: Princeton University Press, 1983.

Stokes, Michael C. *Plato's Socratic Conversations: Drama and Dialectic in Three Dialogues*. Baltimore, Md.: Johns Hopkins University Press, 1986.

Stoltz, Benjamin, and Richard S. Shannon, eds. *Oral Literature and the Formula*. Ann Arbor, Mich.: Center for the Coordination of Ancient and Modern Studies, 1975.

Stone, I.F. *The Trial of Socrates*. Denver: Little, Brown, 1988.

Stowers, Stanley Kent. *The Diatribe and Paul's Letter to the Romans*. Chico, Calif.: Scholars Press, 1981.

Stump, Eleanor. *Boethius's De Topicis Differentiis*. Ithaca, N.Y.: Cornell University Press, 1978.

Sussman, Henry. *High Resolution: Critical Theory and the Problem of Literacy*. New York: Oxford University Press, 1989.

Sutton, Jane. "The Death of Rhetoric and Its Rebirth in Philosophy." *Rhetorica* 4 (1986): 203–26.

Talmor, Ezra. *Language and Ethics*. New York: Pergamon, 1984.

Tannen, Deborah. "The Myth of Orality and Literacy." In *Linguistics and Literacy*, edited by William Frawley. New York: Plenum, 1982.

———, ed. *Coherence in Spoken and Written Discourse*. Norwood, N.J.: Ablex, 1984.

———, ed. *Spoken and Written Language*. Norwood, N.J.: Ablex, 1982.

Thomas, Rosalind. *Oral Tradition and Written Record in Classical Athens*. Cambridge: Cambridge University Press, 1989.

Thomson, J.A.K. *The Art of the Logos*. London: Allen and Unwin, 1935.

———. *The Dry Mock: A Study of Irony in Drama*. Cambridge, Mass.: Harvard University Press, 1927.

Tyler, Stephen A. *The Unspeakable: Discourse, Dialogue, and Rhetoric in the Post-Modern World*. Madison: University of Wisconsin Press, 1987.

Vance, Eugene. "Love's Concordance: The Poetics of Desire and the Joy of the Text." *Diacritics* 5:1 (Spring 1975): 40–52.

Vansina, Jan. *Oral Tradition as History*. Madison: University of Wisconsin Press, 1985.

Verdenius, W.J. "Gorgias' Doctrine of Deception." In *The Sophists and Their Legacy*, edited by G. B. Kerferd. *Hermes* 44 (1982): 116–28.

Vickers, Brian. *In Defense of Rhetoric*. Oxford: Clarendon Press, 1988.

Vlastos, Gregory. *Plato I: Metaphysics and Epistemology*. New York: Doubleday/Anchor, 1971.

———. *Platonic Studies*. Princeton: Princeton University Press, 1973.

———. "Was Plato a Feminist?" *Times Literary Supplement*, March 17–23, 1989, pp. 276–89.

von Humboldt, Wilhelm. *Linguistic Variability and Intellectual Development*. Philadelphia: University of Pennsylvania Press, 1971.

Vygotsky, Lev S. *Thought and Language*. Translated by Eugenia Hanfmann and Gertrude Vakar. Cambridge, Mass.: MIT Press and Wiley, 1962.

Waithe, Mary Ellen, ed. *A History of Women Philosophers.* Vol. 1. *600 B.C.–500 A.D.* Boston: Martinus Nijhoff, 1987.

Welch, Kathleen. "A Critique of Classical Rhetoric: The Appropriation of Ancient Discourse." *Rhetoric Review* 6:1 (Fall 1987): 79–86.

———. "The Platonic Paradox: Plato's Rhetoric in Contemporary Rhetoric and Composition Studies." *Written Communication* 5:1 (Winter 1988): 1–21.

White, Edward M. *Teaching and Assessing Writing.* San Francisco: Jossey-Bass, 1985.

White, Hayden. *Metahistory.* Baltimore: The Johns Hopkins University Press, 1973.

———. *Tropics of Discourse.* Baltimore: The Johns Hopkins University Press, 1978.

Wickelgren, W.A. "Relations, Operators, Predicates, and the Syntax of (Verbal) Propositional and (Spatial) Operational Memory." *Bulletin of the Psychonomic Society* 6 (1975): 161–64.

Wilcox, Stanley. "The Scope of Early Rhetorical Instruction." *Harvard Studies in Classical Philology* 53 (1942): 121–55.

Wilson, Reginald. "Standardized Tests and Educational Inequality." In *Black English and the Education of Black Children and Youth,* edited by Geneva Smitherman. Detroit: Center for Black Studies, 1981.

Wolf, Christa, *Cassandra.* Translated by Jan Van Heurck. New York: Farrar Strauss Giroux, 1984.

Xenophon. *Cyropaedia.* Translated by J.S. Watson and Henry Dale. London: Bohn's Classical Library, 1895.

Yaden, David B., and Shane Templeton, eds. *Metalinguistic Awareness and Beginning Literacy.* Portsmouth, N.H.: Heinemann, 1986.

Yates, Frances A. *The Art of Memory.* Chicago: University of Chicago Press, 1966.

Yearwood, Stephenie. "The Rhetoric of Form in 'The Temple.'" *Studies in English Literature* 23 (1983): 131–44.

Zaehner, R.C., trans. *Hindu Scriptures.* London: J. M. Dent, 1966.

Index

Abstract thought and terms, 7, 15, 27–37, 63, 93, 237–42
Academic philosophy in antiquity, 138, 166, 171, 183, 187
Adorno, Theodor (*Negative Dialectics*), 146–47
Aesthetic criteria, 4, 7, 80, 125–31, 177–79, 203–4, 219, 251
Agon, agonistic debate, 38, 73, 83, 103, 213, 221, 242
  common by fifth century in moots and courts, 51, 103
Aletheia (truth, the unconcealed), 20–23, 25, 37, 248
All, "the all" (*to pan*), 29, 34
Alphabetic technology, 43–44
Ambiguity, 47–49, 76–77, 179, 199, 206
  strategic, 72
Anaxagoras, 30
Antigone, 239, 254
Antiphon, 103
Apate (lying, deception), 11, 126
Arguments, argumentation, "argument" (*logos*), 53, 165–66, 206
  seats or bases of, 167
Aristophanes, 64, 70, 144
  The Clouds, 144
Aristotle, 4, 13, 95–98, 135, 186
  criticism of and response to Plato, 123
  dialogues of, 121
  disjunctive, taxonomical style, 101, 104, 183
  division of "rhetoric, poetry, and prayer" from "true and false discourse," 14, 77, 97
  effects of *Rhetoric*, 116, 149
  emphasis upon manipulation, 117, 213

  first to undermine Plato's Forms, 172
  implicit audience of *Rhetoric*, 118–20
  neologisms, 103
  Rhetoric presented as study of persuasion, 118
  system built upon divisions, 96, 100, 102, 103
  treatises on logic, rhetoric, and poetics, 95, 104

  Analytics, 54, 104
  Categories, 41, 54, 57, 93, 97, 104, 106, 109–13, 186
  On Interpretation, 97, 104
  Organon, 104
  Poetics, 7, 122, 223
  Rhetoric, 54, 104, 109–26
  Topics, 95, 104, 111–16, 149

Attachment, concept of, in identity formation, 238
Atwood, Margaret, 216, 247
Audience, 53, 68, 73, 74, 190, 210–11
  duping of, 67, 190
  ignorance of, 137
  of Aristotle's *Rhetoric*, 118–20
  responsibility for irony and rhetoric, 127, 178, 211
  as spectators, 190, 210–12
Augustine, 4, 8, 17, 213, 217
  admiration for Cicero, 179
  analysis of classroom teaching and materials, 176
  appraisal of truth criteria of his time, 177
  concept of *logos*, 17
  conversion, 174, 189
  critique of mendacity in rhetoric as central theme, 176